THE WHO'S WHO OF

WIGAN ATHLETIC

IN THE FOOTBALL LEAGUE – 1978-2004

THE WHO'S WHO OF

WIGAN ATHLETIC

IN THE FOOTBALL LEAGUE – 1978-2004

by Dean P. Hayes

breedon **books**
PUBLISHING

First published in Great Britain in 2004 by
The Breedon Books Publishing Company Limited
Breedon House, 3 The Parker Centre,
Derby, DE21 4SZ.

ISBN 1 85983 420 6

Printed and bound by Scotprint, Gateside Commerce Park,
Haddington, East Lothian, Scotland.

Contents

Acknowledgements

The publisher would like to thank
John Fillingham, Elaine Mitchinson, Stuart Hayton
and Chris Ammonds
at Wigan Athletic FC for their cooperation and
support in the production of this book.
Thanks also to Trevor Smith at Smith's Bookshop in
Wigan
and Matt Swindells at the *Wigan Observer*.

Introduction

The *Who's Who of Wigan Athletic 1978–2004*, revisits the many contrasting experiences of the Latics through its life blood – the players. Some great, some good, some others, all with one thing in common – all have pulled on a Wigan shirt and taken to the field to represent the club in a Football League game. A total of 291 Wigan players have taken to the field during the Latics' League matches.

Competitive first-team matches are defined as those in the following competitions: Football League, FA Cup, Football League Cup and Associate Members Cup and Play-Off games.

Playing careers include games played and goals scored while with Football League clubs only and relate just to Football League appearances (i.e. no cup matches). The figures in the brackets relate to substitute appearances where the player actually took to the field. Abandoned games are not included.

The figures within the boxes relate to games played and goals scored for Wigan Athletic during each season that the player in question was at Springfield Park or the JJB Stadium. Games and goals in the Football League, FA Cup and Football League Cup are shown separately while games and goals in all other competitions mentioned are shown collectively under 'others'.

Although the *Who's Who of Wigan Athletic* is as statistically accurate as possible, inevitably errors will creep in and I offer my apologies in advance.

Dean P. Hayes
Pembrokeshire
February 2004

ADAMCZUK Darius

Full-Back/Midfield
Born: Szczecin, Poland, 21 October 1969.
Career: Pogan Szczecin. January 1996 Dundee 95 (7) 8. July 1999
Glasgow Rangers 6 (7) 0. August 2001, on loan, WIGAN ATHLETIC
3 (0) 0.

The Polish international defender began his career with his local club Pogan Szczecin before joining Dundee in January 1996. Over the next three-and-a-half seasons, Adamczuk was a regular in the Dens Park side, appearing in 121 League and Cup games as well as helping the side win the Scottish First Division Championship in 1997–98.

In the summer of 1999, he joined Glasgow Rangers on a free transfer and in 1999–2000 appeared in 10 League games as the Ibrox club won the Scottish Premier League title.

Injuries then restricted his first-team opportunities and at the start of the 2001–02 season, he joined Wigan on a three-month loan.

He made his Latics debut in the 1–1 home draw against Brentford on the opening day of the season and went on to appear in the first three League games plus the League Cup defeat at Blackpool. The versatile and experienced right-sided midfield player, who can also play in a full-back position, suffered an ankle injury in the game against Bristol City and returned to Ibrox before his loan spell had expired.

Wigan Athletic Playing Record

	League		FA Cup		FL Cup		Others		Total	
	App	Gls	App	Gls	App	Gls	App	Gls	App	Gls
2001–02	3	0	0	0	1	0	0	0	4	0
TOTAL	3	0	0	0	1	0	0	0	4	0

ADEKOLA David Adeolu

Forward
Born: Liverpool, 19 May 1968.
Career: Cannes, France. January 1993 Bury 21 (14) 12. February
1994, on loan, Exeter City 1 (2) 1. August 1994 Bournemouth.
October 1994 WIGAN ATHLETIC 1 (3) 0. Hereford United. Halifax
Town. Bath City. July 1995 Cambridge United 1 (4) 1. Bishop's
Stortford. December 1995 Preussen Munster, Cologne. October 1996
Brighton and Hove Albion 1 (0) 0. Bishop's Stortford.

Nigerian international David Adekola played his first League football for Bury where he was a very direct winger, using his pace to go past defenders.

Despite scoring 12 goals in 21 starts for the Shakers, he was loaned out to Exeter City before joining Bournemouth on a free transfer.

Unable to settle on the south coast, he joined Wigan Athletic in October 1994, making his Latics debut as a substitute for Matthew Carragher in a 1–0 defeat of Northampton Town. Adekola's only start for Wigan came in a 3–3 draw at his first club Bury, but he was substituted towards the end of the game and released without being offered a contract shortly afterwards.

After trial periods with Hereford United, Halifax Town and Bath City, he joined Cambridge United. Unable to hold down a first-team spot, he was loaned to Bishop's Stortford where he scored regularly before a surprise move to Cologne-based club Preussen Munster in December 1995. He returned to these shores for a trial period with Brighton and Hove Albion but after just one appearance for the Seagulls, he rejoined his former club, Bishop's Stortford.

Wigan Athletic Playing Record

	League		FA Cup		FL Cup		Others		Total	
	App	Gls	App	Gls	App	Gls	App	Gls	App	Gls
1994–95	1 (3)	0	0 (1)	0	0	0	0 (1)	0	1 (5)	0
TOTAL	1 (3)	0	0 (1)	0	0	0	0 (1)	0	1 (5)	0

ADKINS Nigel Howard

Goalkeeper
Born: Birkenhead, 11 March 1965.
Career: March 1983 Tranmere Rovers 86 (0) 0. August 1986
WIGAN ATHLETIC 155 (0) 0. July 1993 Bangor City.

An England schoolboy international goalkeeper, Nigel Adkins began his Football League career with his local club, Tranmere Rovers, making his first-team debut for the Wirral-based club in a 4–2 defeat at Colchester United in November 1982. It was to be another two seasons before he won a regular place between the posts for Rovers but in September 1986, after appearing in 98 League and Cup games for the Prenton Park club, he joined Wigan Athletic.

Adkins made his Latics debut as a replacement for the injured Roy Tunks at Blackpool, but didn't have the best of days as the Seasiders ran out 5–1 winners and he was deemed responsible for three of the goals. Even after Tunks had left Springfield Park, Adkins faced stiff opposition from Northern Ireland international 'keeper Phil Hughes and for the next few seasons shared the goalkeeping duties with him. It was the 1991–92 season before Adkins won a regular place in the Latics side. An ever-present, he

Nigel Adkins

kept 12 clean sheets as Wigan ended the season in 15th place in the Third Division. After one more season, he lost his place to Simon Farnworth and decided to leave the club to play for Bangor City. After his playing days were over, he joined Scunthorpe United as the club's physiotherapist.

Wigan Athletic Playing Record

	League		FA Cup		FL Cup		Others		Total	
	App	Gls	App	Gls	App	Gls	App	Gls	App	Gls
1986–87	8	0	1	0	0	0	0	0	9	0
1987–88	2	0	0	0	1	0	1	0	4	0
1988–89	30	0	1	0	0	0	3	0	34	0
1989–90	13	0	0	0	4	0	0	0	17	0
1990–91	18	0	2	0	2	0	2	0	24	0
1991–92	46	0	3	0	4	0	2	0	55	0
1992–93	38	0	2	0	4	0	5	0	49	0
TOTAL	155	0	9	0	15	0	13	0	192	0

AINSCOW Andrew Paul

Forward
Born: Orrell, 1 October 1968.
Career: October 1986 WIGAN ATHLETIC 14 (8) 4. August 1989 Rotherham United 0 (1) 0. Ashton Town.

England youth international Andy Ainscow worked his way up through the ranks to make his Wigan debut in the 1987–88 Third Division campaign against Doncaster Rovers at Springfield Park. Coming on as a substitute for the injured Chris Thompson, he scored the Latics' winner in a 2–1 defeat of the Yorkshire club. However, he couldn't find a place in the starting line-up and it took another couple of appearances in the substitute's role before he made his first start against Fulham. Midway through the season he was given an extended run in the side and netted three goals in consecutive victories over Doncaster Rovers in the return match

Andrew Ainscow

(away 4–3) and Walsall (home 3–1). Injuries restricted his first-team appearances in 1988–89 and at the end of the season he left to join Rotherham United. Unable to force his way into the Millers' side on a regular basis, he decided to move into non-League football with Ashton Town.

Wigan Athletic Playing Record

	League		FA Cup		FL Cup		Others		Total	
	App	Gls	App	Gls	App	Gls	App	Gls	App	Gls
1987–88	9 (6)	4	0	0	0 (1)	0	1	0	10 (7)	4
1988–89	5 (2)	0	0 (1)	0	0	0	1 (1)	0	6 (4)	0
TOTAL	14 (8)	4	0 (1)	0	0 (1)	0	2 (1)	0	16 (11)	4

APPLETON Stephen

Central Defender
Born: Liverpool, 27 July 1973.
Career: September 1990 WIGAN ATHLETIC 31 (17) 1.

Liverpool-born central defender Stephen Appleton was a trainee with the Latics until turning professional in the summer of 1990. He made his League debut as a substitute for Ronnie Hildersley in a 4–3 defeat at Grimsby Town in the second game of the 1990–91 season. He kept his place in the side for the League Cup first round second-leg tie against Barnsley which the Latics won 1–0 to take the tie to penalties. Unfortunately Wigan lost 4–3 but Appleton

Stephen Appleton

had helped keep a clean sheet over the 90 minutes and made his first start at League level four days later in a 2–0 win over Bournemouth.

In his first two seasons at Springfield Park, Appleton was in and out of the side, but in 1992–93 played on a much more regular basis, scoring his only goal for the club in a 2–1 home defeat at the hands of Chester City. At the end of the season, however, he was released and left to play non-League football.

Wigan Athletic Playing Record

	League		FA Cup		FL Cup		Others		Total	
	App	Gls	App	Gls	App	Gls	App	Gls	App	Gls
1990–91	3 (7)	0	0	0	I	0	0	0	4 (7)	0
1991–92	4 (5)	0	0	0	I (1)	0	I	0	6 (6)	0
1992–93	24 (5)	I	3	0	0 (I)	0	6	0	33 (6)	I
TOTAL	31 (17)	I	3	0	2 (2)	0	7	0	43 (19)	I

ASHCROFT Lee

Winger
Born: Preston, 7 September 1972.
Career: July 1991 Preston North End 78 (13) 13. August 1993 West Bromwich Albion 66 (24) 17. March 1996 on loan Notts County 4 (2) 0. September 1996 Preston North End 63 (1) 22. August 1998 Grimsby Town 52 (9) 15. July 2001 WIGAN ATHLETIC 37 (9) 8. October 2002 on loan Port Vale 3 (0) 0. December 2002 on loan Huddersfield Town 4 (0) 0. Southport.

A fast and tricky winger who prefers to play on the left but can also figure on the opposite flank, Lee Ashcroft worked his way up through the ranks of his home-town club Preston North End before making his debut as a substitute during a 2–1 defeat at Wigan Athletic in November 1990. After establishing himself as a regular member of the Lilywhites, he went on to win representative honours for England at Under-21 level, but in the summer of 1993 he left Deepdale to join West Bromwich Albion for a fee of £250,000.

In his early days at the Hawthorns, he was unable to hold down a regular place and was loaned out to Notts County. He returned to score some vital goals for the Baggies but in September 1996 he left Albion to rejoin Preston North End.

His speed on the right wing finally restored the balance that the Lilywhites had been missing during Lee Cartwright's long absence through injury. Described as 'a scorer of great goals rather than a great goalscorer' he still ended the 1997–98 season as the club's leading scorer, netting a hat-trick in a 3–1 win over Fulham. Towards the end of that season, Ashcroft rejected a move to the Latics and celebrated by scoring his 50th career goal against Wigan at the end of transfer-deadline week.

On leaving Deepdale for the second time during the close season, Lee became Grimsby Town's record £500,000 signing. Injuries made it difficult for him to establish himself in 1998–99 but the following season he formed an attacking partnership with Jack Lester that caused problems for many First Division defences and he finished the campaign as Grimsby's leading scorer.

In the close season, Ashcroft joined Wigan Athletic for £350,000 and made his debut in a goalless draw at Swansea City on the opening day of the 2000–01 season. Unfortunately, partly due to injuries, he failed to live up to expectations, though he did score both Latics' goals in a 2–2 draw at Brentford. He netted again in the following game, an FA Cup second-round tie against Notts County, but then missed the next game through injury; it was that kind of season. The 2000–01 campaign was no better for him as he suffered a frustrating time with injuries and a change in

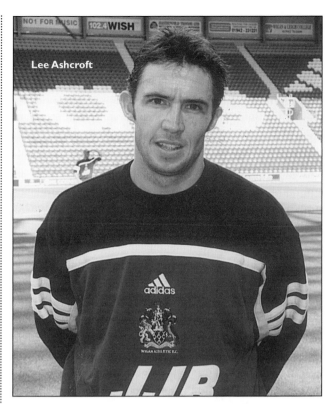
Lee Ashcroft

management. His inconsistency saw him struggle to keep his place and after just one appearance from the bench in the Worthington Cup victory over West Bromwich Albion early the following season, he found himself out of favour.

He acquitted himself well on a loan spell with Port Vale but was not offered a permanent deal and joined Huddersfield Town in a similar capacity. Soon after his return to the JJB Stadium, his contract was paid up and he joined Southport as player-coach.

Wigan Athletic Playing Record

	League		FA Cup		FL Cup		Others		Total	
	App	Gls	App	Gls	App	Gls	App	Gls	App	Gls
2000–01	23 (7)	5	2 (1)	I	I	0	0	0	26 (8)	6
2001–02	14 (2)	3	I	0	0	0	0 (2)	0	15 (4)	3
2002–03	0	0	0	0	0 (I)	0	0	0	0 (I)	0
TOTAL	37 (9)	8	3 (1)	I	I (1)	0	0 (2)	0	41 (13)	9

ASPINALL Warren

Midfield/Forward
Born: Wigan, 13 September 1967.
Career: August 1985 WIGAN ATHLETIC 39 (12) 22. May 1986 Everton 0 (7) 0. February 1987 Aston Villa 40 (4) 14. August 1988 Portsmouth 97 (35) 21. August 1993 on loan Bournemouth 4 (2) 1. October 1993 on loan Swansea City 5 (0) 0. December 1993 Bournemouth 26 (1) 8. March 1995 Carlisle United 99 (8) 12. November 1997 Brentford 41 (2) 5. February 1999 Colchester United 22 (0) 5. September 1999 Brighton and Hove Albion 19 (13) 3.

Wigan-born utility player Warren Aspinall began his career as an apprentice with his home-town club and made his Latics debut in a 1–1 draw with Leyton Orient in March 1985. Forming a formidable strike force with Mike Newell, Aspinall was the club's leading scorer in 1985–86 with 27 League and Cup goals. Included in that total was a hat-trick in a 5–3 win over Wolverhampton Wanderers on the final day of the season.

Eventually his goalscoring exploits – 28 goals in 65 games – attracted the attention of a number of top clubs and in May 1986 Everton paid £150,000 for his services.

On finding first-team opportunities at Goodison Park rather limited, he moved on to Aston Villa for a fee of £300,000 a year later. Having scored 14 goals in 42 games for the Villans, Portsmouth paid a club record £315,000 to take him to Fratton Park.

The former England youth international was a virtual ever-present in his four seasons with Pompey, scoring 28 goals in 159 games, but following loan spells with Bournemouth and Swansea City, he joined the Cherries on a permanent basis in December 1993. After spending the last few games of the 1994–95 season on loan at Carlisle United, he joined the club on a free transfer, scoring the Cumbrian side's first-ever goal on live TV! In 1996–97 he helped Carlisle win the Autowindscreen Shield and was selected for the PFA Third Division select team.

In November 1997, Aspinall was signed by Brentford for £50,000 and in his first full season he helped the Bees win the Third Division Championship. The much-travelled player joined

Warren Aspinall

Colchester United in February 1999 but, after being appointed captain, it all went wrong following the departure of manager Mick Wadsworth. Aspinall joined his 10th club, Brighton and Hove Albion, in September 1999, but during his second season with the Seagulls he suffered an ankle injury that required an operation. Complications set in and he contracted a flesh-eating infection that attacked his ankle ligaments. A lengthy stay in hospital followed and Warren finally announced his retirement on his doctor's advice. The popular Aspinall is aiming to become involved in coaching in the future.

Wigan Athletic Playing Record

	League		FA Cup		FL Cup		Others		Total	
	App	Gls	App	Gls	App	Gls	App	Gls	App	Gls
1984–85	6 (4)	1	1	0	0	0	0 (4)	0	7 (8)	1
1985–86	33 (8)	21	1 (3)	2	1	0	4	4	39 (11)	27
TOTAL	39 (12)	22	2 (3)	2	1	0	4 (4)	4	46 (19)	28

ASPINALL Wayne

Full-Back
Born: Wigan, 10 December 1964.
Career: Atherton Collieries. June 1983 WIGAN ATHLETIC 8 (0) 0. Skelmersdale United.

Elder brother of Warren, Wayne played his early football for Atherton Collieries where his displays at full-back led to him

joining Wigan Athletic in the summer of 1983. With Alex Cribley and Paul Comstive Latics' regular full-backs, Aspinall had to bide his time, but after Comstive suffered a nasty injury in a goalless draw at Orient, he was drafted into the side for his debut against local rivals Preston North End. He barely put a foot wrong in a 1–0 win for the Latics, for whom Tony Kelly scored the vital goal.

He appeared in seven games at the end of the 1983–84 campaign, but the following season dropped down the pecking

Wayne Aspinall

order, appearing in just one game. In the close season, Wayne Aspinall left Springfield Park to play non-League football for Skelmersdale United.

Wigan Athletic Playing Record

	League		FA Cup		FL Cup		Others		Total	
	App	Gls	App	Gls	App	Gls	App	Gls	App	Gls
1983–84	7	0	0	0	0 (1)	0	0	0	7 (1)	0
1984–85	1	0	0	0	0	0	0 (1)	0	1 (1)	0
TOTAL	8	0	0	0	0 (1)	0	0 (1)	0	8 (2)	0

ATHERTON Peter

Central Defender
Born: Orrell, 6 April 1970.
Career: February 1999 WIGAN ATHLETIC 145 (4) 1. August 1991 Coventry City 113 (1) 0. June 1994 Sheffield Wednesday 214 (0) 9. July 2000 Bradford City 51 (0) 1. February 2001 on loan Birmingham City 10 (0) 0.

Peter Atherton first came through Wigan Athletic's junior ranks as an associated schoolboy before signing as a trainee in the summer of 1986. Prior to turning professional, he made his Football League debut in a goalless draw at Blackpool in October 1987. It was the following season before he claimed a regular place in the Wigan side. Twice voted the Latics' 'Player of the Year', Atherton did not miss a match from 26 November 1988 (apart from one appearance as substitute) until he left Springfield Park to sign for Coventry City for £300,000 in August 1991. Atherton's only goal for the club during his time at Wigan came in a 2–1 defeat at Sheffield United in October 1988.

Atherton had obviously impressed Sky Blues' manager Terry Butcher in two FA Cup ties between Wigan and Coventry and it wasn't long before he established himself at the heart of the Highfield Road club's defence. Within a couple of months he had

Peter Atherton

earned an England Under-21 cap. The unsung and unseen hero of the Sky Blues' defence, he was voted the club's 'Player of the Year' in 1992–93 – a campaign in which he accepted a great deal of responsibility, having five different defensive partners!

In June 1994, Atherton left Highfield Road to join Sheffield Wednesday for a fee of £800,000. Midway through his first season with the club, he was appointed the Owls' captain. Over the next six seasons, he led the team by example, always giving 100 percent for the cause whatever the circumstances. Atherton's strengths are his tackling and anticipation and with a little better distribution he would have been classed as a really top-class defender.

Following Wednesday's relegation from the Premiership in 1999–2000, Atherton remained in the top flight when he joined Bradford City. However, after just one season at Valley Parade, he found himself playing First Division football as the Bantams too lost their top-flight status. Despite being a first-team regular at Bradford, he joined Birmingham City on loan and, after making an impressive debut in a 2–1 win over local rivals West Bromwich Albion, he played an important role in the Blues reaching the First Division play-offs.

On his return to Valley Parade he had an horrendous time with knee problems and made just one appearance in 2001–02 – even then he was stretchered off on the hour mark and underwent another operation! Thankfully he made a full recovery, continuing

to be a robust and solid player in the Bantams' midfield, although most of his Football League appearances have been as a central defender.

Wigan Athletic Playing Record

	League		FA Cup		FL Cup		Others		Total	
	App	Gls	App	Gls	App	Gls	App	Gls	App	Gls
1987–88	14 (1)	0	2	0	1	0	2	0	19 (1)	0
1988–89	39 (2)	1	0	0	1	0	3	0	42 (2)	1
1989–90	45 (1)	0	3	0	4	0	4	0	56 (1)	0
1990–91	46	0	4	0	2	0	5	0	57	0
1991–92	1	0	0	0	1	0	0	0	2	0
TOTAL	144 (4)	1	9	0	9	0	14	0	176 (4)	1

BAILEY Neil

Midfield
Born: Billinge, 26 September 1958.
Career: July 1976 Burnley. September 1978 Newport County 129 (5) 7. October 1983 WIGAN ATHLETIC 31 (10) 2. July 1986 Stockport County 50 (1) 0. March 1987 on loan Newport County 8 (1) 1. September 1992 Blackpool 8 (1) 0.

Midfielder Neil Bailey began his career with Burnley, but after failing to make the grade at Turf Moor, he joined Newport County. During his five seasons at Somerton Park, he helped the Ironsides win promotion to the Third Division in 1979–80 – and finish fourth in Division Two in 1982–83.

Early the following season, Bailey left the Welsh club to join Wigan Athletic and made his debut as a substitute for Paul Comstive in a 2–0 home win over Lincoln City. In fact, Bailey's first five appearances for the club were in the No.12 shirt. Bailey stayed at Springfield Park for almost three seasons, during which time he appeared in eight different outfield positions.

On leaving the Latics, Bailey, who was composed and comfortable on the ball, moved to Stockport County. His stay at Edgeley Park was brief and with the Hatters struggling in the lower

Neil Bailey

reaches of the Fourth Division he rejoined Newport County on loan before joining Blackpool as a non-contract player. On hanging up his boots, Bailey remained at Bloomfield Road as the club's physiotherapist.

Wigan Athletic Playing Record

	League		FA Cup		FL Cup		Others		Total	
	App	Gls	App	Gls	App	Gls	App	Gls	App	Gls
1983–84	16 (7)	1	2 (1)	0	0	0	0 (1)	0	18 (9)	1
1984–85	10 (2)	0	2 (1)	0	3	0	1	0	16 (3)	0
1985–86	5 (1)	1	0	0	0	0	2 (2)	0	7 (3)	1
TOTAL	31 (10)	2	4 (2)	0	3	0	3 (3)	0	41 (15)	2

BAINES Leighton John

Left-Back
Born: Liverpool, 11 December 1984.
Career: January 2003 WIGAN ATHLETIC 28 (3) 0.

Leighton Baines was still a trainee when he made his first-team debut for the Latics as a substitute for Neil Roberts in the 3–1 Worthington Cup victory over Premiership side West Bromwich Albion in October 2002.

One of the most promising players to come through the Latics' youth ranks in recent years, the Liverpool-born Baines then made the starting line-up for the FA Cup first-round tie at Hereford United, which the Latics won 1–0. His League debut came in the local derby against Oldham Athletic and again he helped the side keep a clean sheet in a 2–0 win.

Confident on the ball, with accurate distribution and strong in the tackle, his performances – he was given a run of five consecutive League games later in the season – led to him being rewarded with a two-year professional contract. Baines also won the club's 'Young Player of the Year' award.

Last season he was voted the Latics' 'Young Player of the Year' for the second year in succession and as the club's regular left-back he has been offered a new contract

Wigan Athletic Playing Record

	League		FA Cup		FL Cup		Others		Total	
	App	Gls	App	Gls	App	Gls	App	Gls	App	Gls
2002–03	6	0	2	0	1 (1)	0	1 (1)	0	10 (2)	0
2003–04	23 (3)	0	1	0	1	0	0	0	25 (3)	0
TOTAL	29 (3)	0	3	0	2 (1)	0	1 (1)	0	35 (5)	0

BALMER Stuart Murray

Central Defender
Born: Falkirk, 20 September 1969.
Career: May 1987 Glasgow Celtic. August 1990 Charlton Athletic 201 (26) 8. September 1998 WIGAN ATHLETIC 99 (2) 4. July 2001 Oldham Athletic 35 (1) 6. October 2002 on loan Scunthorpe United 6 (0) 0. December 2002 Boston United 21 (0) 0.

Scottish youth international Stuart Balmer began his career with Scottish giants Celtic but, being unable to break into the club's first team, he left Parkhead in the summer of 1990, joining Charlton Athletic for £120,000.

Able to play at right-back or in central defence, he is good in the air and distributes the ball well. Towards the end of the 1994–95 season he was appointed Charlton's captain, but was forced to step down midway through the following campaign after suffering a punctured lung against Grimsby Town. On his return he formed a solid partnership with Richard Rufus at the heart of the Addicks' defence but in 1997–98 he found first-team opportunities limited. Balmer left the Valley early the following season, joining Wigan Athletic for a fee of £200,000.

He made his Latics debut in a 2–0 home win over Macclesfield Town, going on to score in a 3–3 draw at Northampton Town. A member of the side that beat Millwall at Wembley in the Autowindscreen Shield Final, he was once again a virtual ever-present in 1999–2000. As Wigan's acting captain, he led the Latics out at Wembley in the Second Division play-off final against Gillingham. Injuries prevented him from playing in a good

Stuart Balmer

number of matches in 2000–01, and he had trouble recapturing his old form, though he did score the goal that gave the Latics a 1–0 win at Bury and three important points in their quest for the play-offs. Hugely popular with Wigan supporters, he was released during the close season.

Joining Oldham Athletic on a free transfer he quickly established himself in the Boundary Park club's defence. Netting in three consecutive games – he finished the season with six, the most prolific of his career – he found first-team opportunities at a premium in the second half of the season following a number of additions to the Oldham squad.

After finding himself out of favour at the start of the 2002–03 season, he joined Scunthorpe on loan before linking up with Boston United. It was no coincidence that the move sparked off a big improvement in the Lincolnshire club's defensive record that helped them finish the campaign in a mid-table position.

Wigan Athletic Playing Record

	League		FA Cup		FL Cup		Others		Total	
	App	Gls	App	Gls	App	Gls	App	Gls	App	Gls
1998–99	36	1	3	0	1	0	5	1	45	2
1999–2000	41	2	4	0	4	0	1	0	50	2
2000–01	22 (2)	1	1	0	2	0	6	0	31 (2)	1
TOTAL	99 (2)	4	8	0	7	0	12	0	126 (2)	5

BARACLOUGH Ian Robert

Left wing-back
Born: Leicester, 4 December 1970.

Career: December 1988 Leicester City. March 1990 on loan WIGAN ATHLETIC 8 (1) 2. December 1990 on loan Grimsby Town 1 (3) 0.

August 1991 Grimsby Town 1 (0) 0. August 1992 Lincoln City 68 (5) 10. June 1994 Mansfield Town 47 (0) 5. October 1995 Notts County 107 (4) 10. March 1998 Queen's Park Rangers 120 (5) 1. July 2001 Notts County 63 (4) 5.

Ian Baraclough surprisingly failed to maintain his youthful progress at his home-town club Leicester City, having been chosen for a Football League Youth XI game in Moscow in 1989. After maintaining a healthy strike rate in the then Filbert Street club's reserve side, he made his first-team debut in a Zenith Cup game at Crystal Palace before going on loan to Wigan Athletic.

He made his League debut as a substitute for Phil Daley in a 2–1 home defeat at the hands of Huddersfield Town, but then scored in successive defeats against the two Bristol clubs before he rejoined the Foxes.

After another loan spell and then a permanent move to Grimsby Town, Ian struggled to hold down a first-team place and was transferred to Lincoln City. He was a regular in the Sincil Bank club's midfield before leaving to play for Mansfield Town in the summer of 1994. At Field Mill he was switched to playing in defence, his performances attracting the attention of a number of clubs.

In October 1995 he joined Notts County, where his experience in midfield saw him naturally converted to wing-back with great success. He had made 127 first-team appearances for the Magpies when Queen's Park Rangers bought him for £50,000 in March

Ian Barraclough

1998. Despite having the misfortune to suffer a cracked fibula, Baraclough always maintained consistent form and made a positive contribution to the side.

Released in the summer of 2001, he rejoined Notts County, taking over the troublesome left-back slot. In 2002–03 he was given a more varied role, producing his most influential performances in midfield. He ended the campaign with 16 goals in 204 games in his two spells with the Meadow Lane club.

Wigan Athletic Playing Record

	League		FA Cup		FL Cup		Others		Total	
	App	Gls	App	Gls	App	Gls	App	Gls	App	Gls
1989–90	8 (1)	2	0	0	0	0	0	0	8 (1)	2
TOTAL	8 (1)	2	0	0	0	0	0	0	8 (1)	2

BARLOW Stuart

Forward
Born: Liverpool, 16 July 1968.
Career: June 1990 Everton 24 (47) 10. January 1992 on loan Rotherham United. November 1993 Oldham Athletic 78 (15) 31. March 1998 WIGAN ATHLETIC 72 (11) 40. July 2000 Tranmere Rovers 62 (32) 19. August 2003 Stockport County.

Signed from Sherwood Park of the Liverpool Sunday League in the summer of 1990, Stuart Barlow made the gigantic leap from junior club football to the First Division within 12 months when he made his League debut for Everton against Wimbledon in April 1991. He joined Rotherham United on loan at the beginning of the 1991–92 season but his one League appearance as a substitute for the Millers was cancelled out when Aldershot resigned from the Football League. On his return to Goodison, he enjoyed a short run in the first team in place of Mo Johnson but, following the signing of Paul Rideout, he found first-team opportunities limited. The majority of his games for the Toffees were as a substitute and in November 1995 he moved to Oldham Athletic for a fee of £450,000.

He was the Boundary Park club's leading scorer in 1996–97, his total of 12 goals in 35 games including his first League hat-tricks in a 3–0 win at Bradford City and a 5–1 defeat of Swindon Town. He was leading Oldham's scoring charts again the following season when in March 1998 he was sold to Wigan Athletic for a cut price £45,000.

He made his debut in a 1–1 draw at Preston North End before scoring on his first game at Springfield Park as the Latics beat First Division-bound Watford 3–2. In 1998–99, Barlow enjoyed the best goalscoring season of his career, netting 25 goals in all games and helping the club reach the Second Division play-offs and win the Autowindscreen Shield at Wembley. Barlow's goal against Manchester City in the play-off semi-final first leg was the last to be scored at Springfield Park. He was the club's top scorer for a second successive season in 1999–2000 with 21 goals. He created a club record by scoring in six successive matches including a hat-trick in a 4–1 victory at Preston. His terrific form in the first half of the campaign saw him score 21 goals by the turn of the year but after an ankle operation, the goals dried up. He came off the bench in the play-off final against Gillingham at Wembley to score what looked like being the winning goal.

One of Wigan's most popular players of recent years, he left the club in the summer of 2000, joining Tranmere Rovers on a 'Bosman' free transfer. He took some time to settle in at Prenton Park but gradually began to show some much-improved form, culminating in him scoring the winner for Rovers as they turned a three-goal deficit into a famous 4–3 victory over Southampton. He finished the 2001–02 season as Rovers' leading scorer with 14 Second Division goals including hat-tricks against Notts County and Wrexham within the space of four days! Though it was hoped he would renew his strike partnership with former Wigan teammate Simon Haworth, the 2002–03 campaign saw him sidelined by injury and he was allowed to join Stockport County on a free transfer.

Wigan Athletic Playing Record

	League		FA Cup		FL Cup		Others		Total	
	App	Gls	App	Gls	App	Gls	App	Gls	App	Gls
1997–98	9	3	0	0	0	0	0	0	9	3
1998–99	39 (2)	19	2	1	2	1	6 (1)	4	49 (3)	25
1999–2000	24 (9)	18	3	2	4	1	1	0	32 (9)	21
TOTAL	72 (11)	40	5	3	6	2	7 (1)	4	90 (12)	49

Stuart Barlow

BARNWELL-EDINBORO Jamie

Forward
Born: Hull, 26 December 1975.
Career: July 1994 Coventry City 0 (1) 0. December 1995 on loan Swansea City 2 (2) 0. February 1996 on loan WIGAN ATHLETIC 2 (8) 1. March 1996 Cambridge United 53 (10) 12. Rushden and Diamonds. Stevenage Borough.

Jamie Barnwell-Edinboro

A product of Coventry City's youth policy, Jamie Barnwell-Edinboro made his Premier League debut as a substitute at Middlesbrough but after that a shortage of opportunities saw him going out on loan, first with Swansea City and then Wigan Athletic.

During his time at Springfield Park, he impressed as a striker with great pace and aerial strength, scoring one of the Latics' goals in a 3–1 home win over Cambridge United. In fact, it was the U's who signed Barnwell-Edinboro on a permanent basis on transfer deadline day, March 1996, although his start was temporarily delayed through injury.

Though much was expected of him at the Abbey Stadium, he needed an experienced player alongside him to bring him through and after three seasons of struggle, he left to play on loan for then non-League Rushden and Diamonds before joining Stevenage Borough.

Wigan Athletic Playing Record

	League		FA Cup		FL Cup		Others		Total	
	App	Gls	App	Gls	App	Gls	App	Gls	App	Gls
1995–96	2 (8)	1	0	0	0	0	0	0	2 (8)	1
TOTAL	2 (9)	1	0	0	0	0	0	0	2 (8)	1

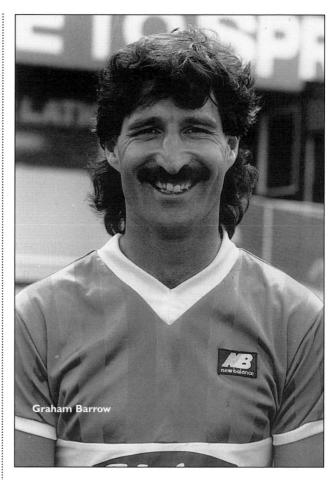

Graham Barrow

BARROW Graham

Midfield
Born: Chorley, 13 June 1954.
Career: Altrincham. July 1981 WIGAN ATHLETIC 173 (6) 36. July 1986 Chester City 244 (4) 17.

Midfielder Graham Barrow joined the Latics from non-League Altrincham in the summer of 1981 and made his Football League debut in a 3–3 draw at Bradford City on the opening day of the 1981–82 season. Barrow's 12 goals that season were instrumental in the club winning promotion to the Third Division and his performances confirmed him as one of the best players in the lower divisions.

Strong in the tackle and good in the air, Barrow missed very few games over the next three seasons and when the Latics won the Freight Rover Trophy Final at Wembley in 1985, Barrow was voted Wigan's 'Man-of-the-Match'. His last game for the Latics came in the same competition in May 1986 when they lost 2–1 to Bolton Wanderers in the Northern Area Final.

Barrow joined Chester City in the close season for a tribunal fixed fee of £6,000. He went on to play in 248 League games for the Cestrians, being employed as player-coach. In 1992 he replaced Harry McNally as Chester's manager before two years later returning to Springfield Park to take charge of the Latics. He later managed Rochdale before taking charge of Chester for a second time.

Wigan Athletic Playing Record

	League		FA Cup		FL Cup		Others		Total	
	App	Gls	App	Gls	App	Gls	App	Gls	App	Gls
1981–82	40 (1)	12	2	0	5	3	0	0	47 (1)	15
1982–83	28	3	0	0	1	0	0	0	29	3
1983–84	42	6	4	0	1	0	1	0	48	6
1984–85	37 (1)	8	3	0	3	0	7	1	50 (1)	9
1985–86	26 (4)	7	4	0	1	0	6	4	37 (4)	11
TOTAL	173 (6)	36	13	0	11	3	14	5	211 (6)	44

BEAGRIE Peter Sidney

Winger
Born: Middlesbrough, 28 November 1965.
Career: September 1983 Middlesbrough 24 (9) 2. August 1986
Sheffield United 81 (3) 11. June 1988 Stoke City 54 (0) 7.
November 1989 Everton 88 (26) 11. September 1991 on loan
Sunderland 5 (0) 1. March 1994 Manchester City 46 (6) 3. July
1997 Bradford City 104 (8) 19. March 1998 on loan Everton 4 (2)
0. January 2001 WIGAN ATHLETIC 7 (3) 1. July 2001
Scunthorpe United 68 (6) 16.

A clever left-sided wingman, Peter Beagrie was an associated schoolboy with Hartlepool United before joining Middlesbrough in the summer of 1983. He made his Football League debut at Oldham Athletic in October 1984 but after two seasons at Ayresome Park in which he failed to hold down a regular first-team spot, he moved to Sheffield United. In his first season at Bramall Lane, he established himself as joint-leading goalscorer and won his first international honour at Under-21 level.

Following the Blades' relegation, he was transferred to Stoke City. His displays for the Potters attracted the attention of several First Division clubs before Everton signed him for £750,000 in November 1989. Unable to perform consistently, he was in and out of the side and though he was loaned to Sunderland, he returned to Goodison where his performances improved.

In March 1994 he joined Manchester City for £1.1 million where he was found to be playing with a hairline fracture of the shin! On returning to first-team action, he then needed surgery to rectify a double hernia after which he failed to recapture his former level of consistency.

Beagrie joined Bradford City for a cut-price £50,000 in July 1997 and at times he thrilled the Valley Parade crowds as he mesmerised the opposition defences. He had a brief loan spell with Everton but then rejoined the Bantams, helping them win promotion to the Premier League. He was a revelation, scoring more goals during the 1998–99 campaign than any other and usually celebrating them with a famous somersault. He had an even better season in 1999–2000 as his vast experience proved invaluable to the Premiership new boys.

After surprisingly finding himself unable to force his way into the Bantams side, he joined the Latics on a short term contract. He made his Wigan debut in a goalless draw against Swindon Town. Despite having lost some of his pace, he proved a talented addition to the Wigan squad and scored a crucial last minute winner in a 2–1 victory over Wycombe Wanderers. Though his great enthusiasm for the game rubbed off on his teammates he was released in the close season and joined Scunthorpe United as their player-coach.

His fitness held up well until February 2002 when a calf injury hampered his progress. He scored 13 goals including five penalties and two direct from corners and won a place in the PFA Division Three team for the season. He remained a key member of the Scunthorpe line-up throughout the 2002–03 campaign, helping them reach the play-offs.

Wigan Athletic Playing Record

	League		FA Cup		FL Cup		Others		Total	
	App	Gls	App	Gls	App	Gls	App	Gls	App	Gls
2000–01	7 (3)	1	0	0	0	0	2	0	9 (3)	1
TOTAL	7 (3)	1	0	0	0	0	2	0	9 (3)	1

BEESLEY Paul

Central Defender
Born: Liverpool, 21 July 1965.
Career: Marine. September 1984 WIGAN ATHLETIC 153 (2) 3.
October 1989 Leyton Orient 32 (0) 1. July 1990 Sheffield United 162
(6) 7. August 1995 Leeds United 19 (3) 0. February 1997 Manchester
City 10 (3) 0. December 1997 on loan Port Vale 3 (0) 0. March 1998
on loan West Bromwich Albion 8 (0) 0. August 1998 Port Vale 33 (2)
3. June 1999 Blackpool 15 (3) 0. Chester City.

Merseysider Paul Beesley began his career with Marine before joining Wigan Athletic in September 1984. He made his League debut in a 2–1 defeat by York City but his only other appearances in the first team that season were in the last two games of the campaign. Learning the centre-half trade from the likes of Colin Methven, Steve Walsh and Andy Holden, Beesley matured into a powerful and clever reader of the game. Firmly established at the heart of the Wigan defence, he left Springfield Park in October 1989 for fellow Third Division club Leyton Orient following a club record £175,000 transfer.

Paul Beesley

After just one season at Brisbane Road in which he was voted Orient's 'Player of the Season', he moved on to Sheffield United in a £365,000 deal, which in turn brought in some extra cash for Wigan. Forming a highly-effective defensive partnership with Brian Gayle, Beesley, who was the Blades' 'Player of the Year' in 1993, appeared in almost 200 games for the Bramall Lane club before joining Leeds United in the summer of 1995 for £250,000. After less than six months at Elland Road, he was on the move again, this time to Manchester City for £500,000.

Knee and ankle injuries restricted his appearances for the then Maine Road club and after loan spells with Port Vale and West Bromwich Albion, he joined the Valiants on a permanent basis. Released in the summer of 1999, he went on to play for Blackpool before joining non-League Chester City.

Wigan Athletic Playing Record

	League		FA Cup		FL Cup		Others		Total	
	App	Gls	App	Gls	App	Gls	App	Gls	App	Gls
1984–85	3	0	0	0	0	0	0	0	3	0
1985–86	17	0	1	0	1	0	2	0	21	0
1986–87	38 (1)	0	2	0	2	0	2	0	44 (1)	0
1987–88	41 (1)	1	2	0	4	0	2	0	49 (1)	1
1988–89	44	2	1	0	2	0	2	0	49	2
1989–90	11	0	0	0	4	0	0	0	15	0
TOTAL	154 (2)	3	6	0	13	0	8	0	181 (2)	3

BENJAMIN Ian Tracey

Forward

Born: Nottingham, 11 December 1961.

Career: May 1979 Sheffield United 4 (1) 3. August 1979 West Bromwich Albion 1 (1) 0. February 1982 Notts County. August 1982 Peterborough United 77 (3) 14. August 1984 Northampton Town 147 (3) 58. October 1987 Cambridge United 20 (5) 2. July 1988 Chester City 18 (4) 2. February 1989 Exeter City 30 (2) 4. March 1990 Southend United 122 (0) 33. November 1992 Luton Town 7 (6) 2. September 1993 Brentford 13 (2) 2. September 1994 WIGAN ATHLETIC 13 (7) 6. Kettering Town.

Much-travelled centre-forward Ian Benjamin began his Football League career with Sheffield United, where after just a handful of games, he was transferred to West Bromwich Albion for £100,000. Unable to win a regular place in the Baggies' first-team line-up, the

Ian Benjamin

former England youth international joined Notts County on a free transfer but was still unable to make much impression and moved on to Peterborough United. He had two good seasons at London Road before signing for Northampton Town in the summer of 1984.

His prolific goalscoring at the County ground helped the Cobblers win the Fourth Division Championship in 1986–87 but early the following season he was on the move again, this time to Cambridge United. There followed brief spells with Chester and Exeter City before he signed for Southend United in March 1990. After rediscovering his shooting boots during his time at Roots Hall, a £50,000 transfer took him to Luton Town. Unable to make much impression at Kenilworth Road, he had a brief spell with Brentford before joining Wigan Athletic in September 1994.

The Latics were his 11th League club and he made his debut in a 1–1 home draw against Scarborough the following month. He scored in each of his next two appearances but injuries restricted his first-team opportunities to just 13 League starts in which he

scored six goals. Towards the end of the following season his contract was paid up and he left to join GM Vauxhall Conference side Kettering Town.

Wigan Athletic Playing Record

	League		FA Cup		FL Cup		Others		Total	
	App	Gls	App	Gls	App	Gls	App	Gls	App	Gls
1994–95	12 (5)	6	0 (1)	0	0	0	0 (1)	0	12 (7)	6
1995–96	1 (3)	0	0	0	0	0	1	1	2 (3)	2
TOTAL	13 (8)	6	0 (1)	0	0	0	1 (1)	1	14 (10)	8

BENNETT Gary Michael

Forward

Born: Liverpool, 20 September 1963.

Career: Kirkby Town. October 1984 WIGAN ATHLETIC 10 (10) 3. August 1985 Chester City 109 (17) 36. November 1988 Southend United 36 (6) 6. March 1990 Chester City 71 (9) 15. August 1992 Wrexham 120 (1) 77. July 1995 Tranmere Rovers 26 (3) 9. March 1996 Preston North End 15 (9) 4. February 1997 Wrexham 15 (0) 5. July 1997 Chester City 37 (4) 11.

Gary Bennett joined Wigan Athletic from Kirkby Town in October 1984, making his Football League debut as a substitute in a 1–1 draw at Cambridge United. Though he couldn't win a regular first-team place, he was a member of the Latics' side that beat Brentford 3–1 at Wembley in the final of the Freight Rover Trophy in 1985. At the end of that season he joined Chester City on a free transfer and in 155 games scored 47 goals before leaving for Southend United. He didn't really settle at Roots Hall and a year later returned to play for Chester.

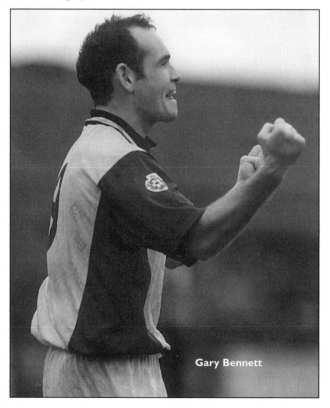

Gary Bennett

In August 1992 Bennett joined Wrexham, and after finishing second in the Division Two scoring charts in 1993–94 with 36 goals including a hat-trick against Hull City, he topped the divisional scoring charts the following season with 39 goals including hat-tricks against Leyton Orient and Wycombe Wanderers. At the end of that season he joined Tranmere Rovers for £300,000 but after a disappointing season at Prenton Park, he became Preston North End's record signing when they paid £200,000 for his services.

During his time at Deepdale he was kept out of first-team action with a series of injuries including a shin fracture. When he did return he netted two goals in a 3–0 derby win over Blackpool before returning to the Racecourse Ground for £100,000. After taking his tally of goals for the Robins to 103 in 170 games, he joined Chester City for a third time.

Wigan Athletic Playing Record

	League		FA Cup		FL Cup		Others		Total	
	App	Gls	App	Gls	App	Gls	App	Gls	App	Gls
1984–85	10 (10)	3	0	0	0	0	3 (1)	1	13 (11)	4
TOTAL	10 (10)	3	0	0	0	0	3 (1)	1	13 (11)	4

BIDSTRUP Stefan

Midfield

Born: Helsingoer, Denmark, 24 February 1975.
Career: Lyngby. November 2000 WIGAN ATHLETIC 10 (5) 2. AaB Aalborg.

Danish midfielder Stefan Bidstrup joined the Latics from Lyngby for a fee of £450,000 in November 2000, the Danish mid-season break.

He made his Latics debut as a substitute for Pat McGibbon in a 2–1 home win over Cambridge United and kept his place in the side for the next match, a first-round FA Cup tie against Dorchester Town. He impressed with his surging runs and pin-point passes and scored in a 3–1 win over the non-League outfit. Despite scoring in wins at Luton Town and Colchester United, he fell out of favour when new boss Steve Bruce took over and at the end of the season his contract was cancelled by mutual agreement.

He subsequently returned to his native Denmark where he signed for AaB Aalborg.

Wigan Athletic Playing Record

	League		FA Cup		FL Cup		Others		Total	
	App	Gls	App	Gls	App	Gls	App	Gls	App	Gls
2000–01	10 (5)	2	2	1	0	0	0	0	12 (5)	3
TOTAL	10 (5)	2	2	1	0	0	0	0	12 (5)	3

BIGGINS Wayne

Forward

Born: Sheffield, 20 November 1961.
Career: November 1979 Lincoln City 8 (0) 1. King's Lynn. Matlock Town. February 1984 Burnley 78 (0) 30. October 1985 Norwich City 66 (13) 16. July 1988 Manchester City 29 (3) 9. August 1989 Stoke City 120 (2) 46. October 1992 Barnsley 44 (3) 16. November 1993 Glasgow Celtic 4 (5) 0. March 1994 Stoke City 18 (9) 6. January 1995 on loan Luton Town 6 (1) 1. July 1995 Oxford United 8 (2) 1. November 1995 WIGAN ATHLETIC 35 (14) 5. Leek Town.

Wayne Biggins began his League career with Lincoln City, scoring for the Imps on his debut in March 1981. However, the following season he was released and drifted into non-League football at King's Lynn and Matlock. He was working as a hod carrier on a building site when Burnley gave him the chance to resurrect his first-class career. He made an immediate impact at Turf Moor, scoring four goals in his first four games including what must have been a very satisfying hat-trick against Lincoln, the club who had

discarded him! His prolific scoring for the Clarets attracted the attention of a number of clubs in the higher divisions and in October 1985, Wayne went to Norwich City for £40,000. He soon became a regular, winning a Second Division Championship medal at the end of his first season at Carrow Road. Not as prolific in the top flight, he left to play for Manchester City, once again delivering the goods, helping the Blues to runners-up spot and promotion to Division One.

In the summer of 1989 he joined Stoke City and though he was the Potters' leading scorer, he couldn't prevent their relegation to the Third Division. He was the club's top scorer for the next two

Wayne Biggins

seasons, helping them beat Stockport County in the Autoglass Trophy Final at Wembley. After a spell with Barnsley, the much-travelled striker joined Celtic, but after failing to settle north of the border, he rejoined Stoke City where he immediately began scoring goals again. After a loan period at Luton Town, he moved to Oxford United in the summer of 1995 before joining Wigan Athletic in January 1996 after an earlier loan spell.

Biggins made his Latics debut in a goalless draw at Northampton Town two months prior to his move becoming permanent. It was the third time in his career that he had been recruited by John Deehan, though sadly injuries restricted his appearances in his first season at Springfield Park. Biggins later relished his new central midfield role and in 1996–97 chipped in with some vital goals as the Latics won the Third Division Championship. However, despite this success, he was still released at the end of the season, joining Leek Town.

Wigan Athletic Playing Record

	League		FA Cup		FL Cup		Others		Total	
	App	Gls	App	Gls	App	Gls	App	Gls	App	Gls
1995–96	15 (1)	2	0	0	0	0	0	0	15 (1)	2
1996–97	20 (13)	3	1	0	1 (1)	0	0 (1)	0	22 (15)	3
TOTAL	35 (14)	5	1	0	1 (1)	0	0 (1)	0	37 (16)	5

BISHOP Charles Darren

Defender
Born: Nottingham, 16 February 1968.
Career: April 1986 Watford. August 1987 Bury 104 (10) 6. July 1991 Barnsley 124 (6) 1. January 1996 on loan Preston North End 4 (0) 0. March 1996 on loan Burnley 9 (0) 0. June 1996 WIGAN ATHLETIC 27 (1) 0. December 1997 Northampton Town 11 (0) 0. Ilkeston Town.

After an apprenticeship at Stoke and a year at Watford without a League appearance, Charlie Bishop joined Third Division Bury in the summer of 1987.

He soon became a regular at Gigg Lane, helping the Shakers to the play-offs in 1990 where they were beaten by Tranmere Rovers in the semi-final. Bishop was transferred to Barnsley for £50,000 in July 1991. He was a regular during much of his time in South Yorkshire but did have a loan spell with Preston North End as the Deepdale club were gearing up for their run-in to the Third Division title. After his return to Barnsley, he joined Burnley on loan but returned to Oakwell before the end of the 1995–96 season amid suggestions that Clarets' manager Adrian Heath was keen to sign him permanently.

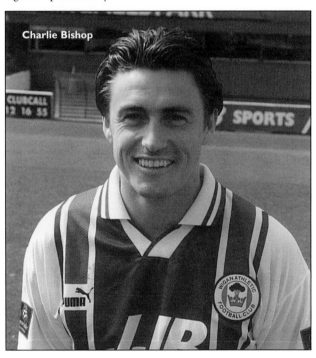
Charlie Bishop

However, Wigan Athletic quickly stepped in, paying £20,000 for Bishop's services. He made his debut in a 5–2 opening day defeat at Wycombe Wanderers in 1996 but then snapped ankle ligaments in the League Cup game against Preston North End. He returned to the first team early in the New Year where he proved to be a valuable member of the club's defensive line-up, winning a Third Division Championship medal. However, after just eight appearances the following season, he was transferred to Northampton Town.

His first season with the Cobblers was blighted both by injury and suspension and midway through the 1998–99 season both player and club decided to part company. He then signed for non-League Ilkeston Town and joined his family business.

Wigan Athletic Playing Record

	League		FA Cup		FL Cup		Others		Total	
	App	Gls	App	Gls	App	Gls	App	Gls	App	Gls
1996–97	20 (1)	0	0	0	1	0	1	0	22 (1)	0
1997–98	7	0	0	0	0	0	1	0	8	0
TOTAL	27 (1)	0	0	0	1	0	2	0	30 (1)	0

BLACK Anthony

Winger
Born: Barrow, 15 July 1969.
Career: Bamber Bridge. March 1995 WIGAN ATHLETIC 17 (14) 2. Accrington Stanley.

As an old-fashioned right-winger, Tony Black arrived at Springfield Park in March 1995 from Unibond League side Bamber Bridge, for whom he scored 16 goals. Displaying lightning speed down the flanks, he made an impressive debut in a 1–1 home draw against Hereford United, winning the 'Man-of-the-Match' award.

The following season he scored his first goals for the club in a second-round FA Cup tie against his home-town club Barrow as the Latics won 4–0. This seemed to give him confidence and he found the net in League games against Bury and Torquay United. He continued to impress, albeit with the majority of his appearances restricted to substitute, until his season came to a tragic end in the 1–0 defeat at Mansfield in March 1996. The speedy winger suffered a broken fibula which kept him out of the Latics side for the whole of the 1996–97 season.

He made just one substitute appearance in the second game of the following season but he wasn't up to the rigours of League football and though he tried a comeback with Accrington Stanley, he announced his retirement from the game on medical advice.

Tony Black

Wigan Athletic Playing Record

	League		FA Cup		FL Cup		Others		Total	
	App	Gls	App	Gls	App	Gls	App	Gls	App	Gls
1994–95	9	0	0	0	0	0	0	0	9	0
1995–96	8 (13)	3	2	2	0	0	0 (1)	0	10 (16)	4
1996–97	0	0	0	0	0	0	0	0	0	0
1997–98	0 (1)	0	0	0	0	0	0 (1)	0	0 (2)	0
TOTAL	17 (14)	2	2	2	0	0	0 (2)	0	19 (18)	4

BOUGHEY Darren John

Forward
Born: Stoke, 16 November 1962.
Career: November 1980 Stoke City 4 (3) 0. January 1991 on loan
WIGAN ATHLETIC 2 (0) 2. March 1991 on loan Exeter City 8 (0) 1.

Darren Boughey began his Football League career with his home-town club Stoke City, but after failing to hold down a regular place, he left the Potteries to join Wigan Athletic on a month's loan in January 1991.

Darren Boughey

He scored on his debut in a 1–1 draw at Mansfield Town but suffered an injury towards the end of he game and was replaced by Jimmy Carberry. However, he had recovered for the following week's game and was on the scoresheet again in a 3–1 defeat at Reading. Despite this, he returned to the Victoria Ground for a few weeks before going out on an extended loan to Exeter City. The Grecians turned down a chance to make the move permanent and in the summer of 1992 he drifted into non-League football.

Wigan Athletic Playing Record

	League		FA Cup		FL Cup		Others		Total	
	App	Gls	App	Gls	App	Gls	App	Gls	App	Gls
1990–91	2	2	0	0	0	0	0	0	2	2
TOTAL	2	2	0	0	0	0	0	0	2	2

BOWEN Mark Rosslyn

Left-Back
Born: Neath, 7 December 1963.
Career: December 1981 Tottenham Hotspur 14 (3) 2. July 1987
Norwich City 315 (5) 24. July 1996 West Ham United 15 (2) 1.
Shimizu, Japan. September 1997 Charlton Athletic 36 (6) 0. August
1999 WIGAN ATHLETIC 7 (0) 0. December 1999 Reading.

Mark Bowen began his Football League career with Tottenham Hotspur, but during his time at White Hart Lane he could never quite lay claim to a regular place in the side due to a surfeit of established stars.

In the summer of 1987 Mark signed for Norwich City and after a short run on the left side of midfield, he made his mark at left-back. It was from here that he made a huge contribution to the side in 1988–89 as the Canaries topped the First Division for most of the campaign, eventually finishing fourth. In 1992–93 when the club finished third in the newly formed Premier League, Bowen was the only ever-present and over the next four seasons he hardly missed a game. Gaining more international caps while at Carrow Road than anyone else, the 1995–96 season ended in controversy for the Neath-born player. He was dropped from the first team and given a free transfer, joining West Ham United after 399 appearances for the East Anglian club.

At Upton Park he had to be content with the role of squad player before being released in March 1997 to take up an offer from Shimizu SP of Japan. He later returned to these shores to play for Charlton Athletic before being recruited by the Latics in the summer of 1999.

Capped 41 times by Wales, Bowen made his Wigan debut in a 3–0 home win over Scunthorpe United on the opening day of the 1999–2000 season, but after appearing in seven league games – four of which were won and three drawn – he was released and joined Reading.

Mark Bowen is now involved in Mark Hughes's backroom staff, taking up a role as coach to the Wales Under-21 side.

Wigan Athletic Playing Record

	League		FA Cup		FL Cup		Others		Total	
	App	Gls	App	Gls	App	Gls	App	Gls	App	Gls
1999–2000	7	0	0	0	3	0	0	0	10	0
TOTAL	7	0	0	0	3	0	0	0	10	0

BRADD Leslie John

Centre-Forward
Born: Buxton, 5 November 1947.
Career: East Sterndale. March 1966 Rotherham United 3 (0) 0.
October 1967 Notts County 379 (16) 125. August 1978 Stockport
County 116 (1) 31. July 1981 WIGAN ATHLETIC 57 (6) 25.
December 1982 on loan Bristol Rovers 1 (0) 1.

When his job as an apprentice mechanic prevented him from playing Saturday football, Les Bradd became an apprentice welder and joined Hope Valley League team East Sterndale. His prolific goalscoring soon attracted the attention of a number of League clubs and in March 1966 he joined Rotherham United. Unable to hold down a regular first-team place at Millmoor, he moved to Notts County in October 1967.

Over the next 11 seasons, Bradd made over 400 League and Cup appearances for the Meadow Lane club, while setting a club League scoring record for the Magpies with 125 goals.

In August 1978 he joined Stockport County, immediately forming a formidable striking partnership with Stuart Lee. In addition to scoring twice on his debut, Bradd netted a seven-minute hat-trick in a 4–4 draw with Barnsley. In his three seasons at Edgeley Park, Bradd played a number of games at centre-half before leaving to join Wigan in the summer of 1981.

He made his League debut on the opening day of the 1981–82 season, scoring in a 3–3 draw at Bradford City. Forming an effective partnership with Peter Houghton, he ended his first

Carl Bradshaw

season at Springfield Park with 20 goals including a devastating hat-trick in a 7–2 win at Scunthorpe United. Not surprisingly the burly striker was voted the club's 'Player of the Year'. The following season, injuries restricted his number of first-team appearances and following the departure of Larry Lloyd as manager, Bradd also left Springfield Park.

He returned to Meadow Lane and after a couple of years running the club's weekly lottery, he became County's Commercial Manager. In 1994 he crossed the River Trent to take up a similar position with Nottingham Forest.

	League		FA Cup		FL Cup		Others		Total	
	App	Gls	App	Gls	App	Gls	App	Gls	App	Gls
1981–82	41	19	2	0	5	1	0	0	48	29
1982–83	16 (6)	6	2	0	4	1	0	0	22 (6)	7
TOTAL	57 (6)	25	4	0	9	2	0	0	70 (6)	36

Wigan Athletic Playing Record

BRADSHAW Carl

Full-Back

Born: Sheffield, 2 October 1968.

Career: July 1986 Sheffield Wednesday 16 (16) 4. August 1986 on loan Barnsley 6 (0) 1. September 1988 Manchester City 1 (4) 0. September 1989 Sheffield United 122 (25) 8. July 1994 Norwich City 55 (10) 2. October 1997 WIGAN ATHLETIC 109 (11) 11. July 2001 Scunthorpe United 18 (3) 1. Alfreton Town.

England youth international Carl Bradshaw, brother of Darren who played for Chesterfield, York City, Newcastle and Peterborough, began his career with his home-town club, Sheffield Wednesday.

After turning professional in August 1986, he made his Football League debut the same month while on loan to Barnsley but despite scoring, the Tykes lost 3–2 to Crystal Palace. He played his first game for Wednesday later that year and scored in a 2–2 draw at Queen's Park Rangers. With his first-team chances at Hillsborough rather limited, he moved to Manchester City in exchange for Imre Varadi. He only played in one full match at Maine Road before returning to Sheffield one year later and signing for United.

He settled in immediately, helping the club gain promotion to the First Division as runners-up in his first season. Sadly he was unable to maintain this form and found himself in and out of the side before moving to Norwich City for £500,000 in the summer of 1994.

Although showing wholehearted commitment, Canaries' manager Martin O'Neill hardly ever included him in the side and he only won a regular spot following the appointment of Gary Megson. An uncomplicated, enthusiastic defender, a ripped thigh muscle forced him to miss a number of matches and, being unable to regain his first-team spot, he joined the Latics on a free transfer in October 1997, following a well-documented off-field offence.

He made his Wigan debut in a 1–1 draw against Luton Town and went on to prove himself a revelation in the Latics' defence. He proved his versatility when called to keep goal in the 2–1 away victory at Wycombe Wanderers and not surprisingly, was voted the club's 'Player of the Year'. Appointed club captain, he was delighted to lift the Autowindscreen Shield at Wembley in 1999 as the Latics beat Millwall 1–0. He then continued to prove his versatility by playing in a number of defensive positions, though the experienced tough-tackling campaigner preferred the right-back position. Injuries again limited his appearances in 2000–01 but he still managed to maintain his 100 percent record from the penalty-spot and score a stunning 30-yarder in the 1–1 draw with

Reading. One of a number of Latics players released at the end of that season, he joined Scunthorpe United, adding vital experience to a young team.

Injuries then set in, with an Achilles problem and a groin operation restricting his appearances. Released at the end of the 2001–02 season, he went to play non-League football for Alfreton Town.

Wigan Athletic Playing Record

	League		FA Cup		FL Cup		Others		Total	
	App	Gls	App	Gls	App	Gls	App	Gls	App	Gls
1997–98	27 (1)	1	1	0	0	0	0	0	28 (1)	1
1998–99	39	6	2	0	3	0	4	0	48	6
1999–2000	21 (5)	1	2	0	2	1	1	1	26 (5)	3
2000–01	22 (5)	3	0	0	1	0	4	0	27 (5)	3
TOTAL	109 (11)	11	5	0	6	1	9	1	129 (11)	13

BRANCH Graham

Winger

Born: Liverpool, 12 February 1972.

Career: Heswall. July 1991 Tranmere Rovers 55 (47) 10. November 1992 on loan Bury 3 (1) 1. December 1997 on loan WIGAN ATHLETIC 2 (1) 0. July 1998 Stockport County 10 (4) 3. December 1998 Burnley 110 (3) 9.

Graham Branch began his Football League career as a jet-paced winger with Tranmere Rovers, having joined the Prenton Park club from Heswall in the summer of 1991. However, his first-team opportunities during his early days with the club were limited due to the form of Pat Nevin and Johnny Morrissey and he had a brief loan spell with Bury.

His career took a distinct upturn in 1995–96 after a proposed £100,000 transfer to Stockport County fell through. The cousin of former Evertonian Michael Branch, he possessed all the attributes to become a leading front man, but over the next couple of seasons, he continued to delight and frustrate Rovers' supporters in equal measure!

Unable to claim a regular place in the Tranmere side, he was loaned out to Wigan Athletic in December 1997, making his debut as a substitute in a 2–2 draw at Wrexham. He had appeared in three games for the Latics when, following a hamstring injury, he was recalled by the Wirral club.

A tall, pacy forward with a venomous shot, he joined Stockport County on a free transfer in the summer of 1998 but within six months had moved on to Burnley. One of the Turf Moor club's most improved players, he helped the Clarets win promotion to the First Division, appearing as a winger or wing-back, though occasionally he was used as an out-and-out striker. He seldom looked out of place in the higher grade of football, though his season finished prematurely when he suffered a knee injury in the East Lancashire derby against Blackburn. Having recovered in readiness for the start of the 2001–02 season, he then suffered damage to an Achilles tendon and was forced to miss the first few months of the new campaign. On his return he looked decidedly short of pace and was switched to left-back. The surprise packet of Burnley's 2002–03 season, he later proved similarly adept in an unfamiliar central defensive role!

Wigan Athletic Playing Record

	League		FA Cup		FL Cup		Others		Total	
	App	Gls	App	Gls	App	Gls	App	Gls	App	Gls
1997–98	2 (1)	0	0	0	0	0	0	0	2 (1)	0
TOTAL	2 (1)	0	0	0	0	0	0	0	2 (1)	0

BRANNAN Gerard Daniel

Midfield/Defender

Born: Prescot, 15 January 1972.

Career: July 1990 Tranmere Rovers 227 (11) 20. March 1997 Manchester City 38 (5) 4. August 1998 on loan Norwich City 10 (1) 1. October 1998 Motherwell 81 (0) 16. February 2001 WIGAN ATHLETIC 49 (3) 0. January 2003 on loan Dunfermline Athletic 8 (0) 0. September 2003 on loan Rochdale. Accrington.

Equally at home in central midfield or in either of the full-back spots, Ged Brannan began his career with Tranmere Rovers. He made his League debut in October 1990 when he came on as a substitute for Johnny Morrissey in a 6–2 home win over Mansfield Town. He remained a regular in the Rovers' team and played left-back in the play-off final win over Bolton Wanderers at Wembley that took Tranmere into the Second Division. Over the next six seasons, Brannan was a virtual ever-present with his best season in terms of goals scored being 1993–94 when he found the net 11 times in 58 games. In March 1997 he joined Manchester City for £750,000.

Ged Brannan

An ever-present in the City side until New Year 1998, he lost his place for tactical reasons. Despite suffering a hairline fracture he took up training just four weeks later and fought his way back into first-team contention. However, he was soon out of favour at Maine Road and started the 1998–99 season on loan at Norwich City before being transferred to Scottish League side Motherwell.

A regular in the Fir Park club's side for over two seasons, helping them finish fourth in the Premier Division in 1999–2000, he joined the Latics in February 2001 for a fee of £170,000.

Brannan made his Latics debut in a goalless home draw against Bristol Rovers, going on to appear in all but one of the club's remaining games. Though he failed to get on the scoresheet, his experience was invaluable in guiding the Latics through to the play-off stages where, sadly, a hamstring injury prevented him from playing. In 2001–02, Brannan was a permanent fixture in the Latics' line-up, scoring his first goal for the club in the Worthington Cup defeat at Blackpool. Towards the end of the campaign, he broke a toe and then suffered a hamstring injury in his reserve-team comeback match. Though he started the following season as the club's first-choice right-back, his failure to produce consistent form saw him go on loan to Dunfermline Athletic for three months before returning to the JJB Stadium towards the end of the season. After a loan spell with Rochdale, he was out of contract and joined Accrington.

Wigan Athletic Playing Record

	League		FA Cup		FL Cup		Others		Total	
	App	Gls	App	Gls	App	Gls	App	Gls	App	Gls
2000–01	12 (1)	0	0	0	0	0	0	0	12 (1)	0
2001–02	31 (2)	0	0	0	1	1	1	0	33 (2)	1
2002–03	6	0	0	0	0	0	1	0	7	0
TOTAL	49 (3)	0	0	0	1	1	2	0	62 (3)	1

BRECKIN Ian

Central Defender

Born: Rotherham, 24 February 1975.

Career: November 1993 Rotherham United 130 (2) 6. July 1997 Chesterfield 208 (4) 8. June 2002 WIGAN ATHLETIC 50 (4) 0.

The Rotherham-born defender began his career with his home-town club, turning professional in November 1993. The nephew of the club's former captain John Breckin (1971–82), he helped the Millers win the Autowindscreen Shield at Wembley in 1996. The following season he was the club's most consistent player and was deservedly appointed Rotherham's skipper. Yet in the close season Breckin, who had appeared in 154 games for the Yorkshire club, was allowed to join Chesterfield for a fee of £100,000.

A tall and commanding central defender, he ended his first season at Saltergate as the club's 'Player of the Year'. Over the next couple of seasons, he developed into a fine perceptive defender, able to play in any of the back four positions, and in 1999–2000 he won the 'Player of the Year' award for a second time. He captained the Spireites for much of the following season and because of the club's financial situation was consistently linked with a move to a bigger club. He had appeared in 249 games for the Saltergate club when, in June 2002, Wigan manager Paul Jewell paid £150,000 for his services.

He made his Latics debut as a substitute for Ged Brannan in the third match of the 2002–03 season, a 2–0 victory over Bristol City, before suspension and a knee operation disrupted his early months with the club. It was only after the Latics had won the Second Division Championship that he got back in the side on a regular basis following an injury to Jason De Vos.

In 2003–04 Breckin, who had understudied both De Vos and Jackson, played on a more regular basis, and though he has yet to find the net for the Latics, has come close on a number of occasions.

Wigan Athletic Playing Record

	League		FA Cup		FL Cup		Others		Total	
	App	Gls	App	Gls	App	Gls	App	Gls	App	Gls
2002–03	7 (2)	0	2	0	0	0	1	0	10 (2)	0
2003–04	43 (2)	0	1	0	3	0	0	0	47 (2)	0
TOTAL	50 (4)	0	3	0	3	0	1	0	57 (4)	0

BROLLY Richard

Winger

Born: York, 5 October 1969.

Career: Illinois University. December 1992 WIGAN ATHLETIC 2 (0) 1.

Though born in York, Richard Brolly was playing football for Illinois University when Wigan Athletic manager Bryan Hamilton brought him to Springfield Park in December 1992.

The pacy winger made his League debut for the Latics in February 1993 in the match against Huddersfield Town. In a game in which Wigan's back four were outstanding, Brolly scored a spectacular winner as the Latics surprisingly took all three points. Though he held on to his place for a visit to Fulham two days later, he then disappeared from the League scene to play non-League football.

Richard Brolly

Wigan Athletic Playing Record

	League		FA Cup		FL Cup		Others		Total	
	App	Gls	App	Gls	App	Gls	App	Gls	App	Gls
1992–93	2	1	0	0	0	0	0	0	2	1
TOTAL	2	1	0	0	0	0	0	0	2	1

BROUGHTON Drewe Oliver

Forward

Born: Hitchin, 25 October 1978.

Career: May 1997 Norwich City 3 (6) 1. August 1997 on loan WIGAN ATHLETIC 1 (3) 0. October 1998 Brentford 1 (0) 0. November 1998 Peterborough United 19 (16) 8. Dagenham and Redbridge. Stevenage. June 2000 Kidderminster Harriers 70 (24) 19.

Drewe Broughton's Football League career began at Norwich City where following prolific scoring performances at youth and reserve level he made his debut. He was unable to hold down a regular place in the Canaries' first team however, and went to Wigan on loan, making his debut in a 1–0 defeat at Bournemouth in the club's first away game of the 1997–98 season. His other three appearances for the Latics during his loan spell were all as a substitute, after which he returned to Carrow Road.

Towards the end of that season, he underwent a hernia operation and, although he had recovered by the start of the 1998–99 campaign, he was allowed to leave for Brentford. Surprisingly he made just one appearance for the Bees, being substituted and was transferred to Peterborough United within three weeks!

Possessing an excellent touch for such a big man, he proved to be a successful purchase during his early days at London Road. However, following the arrival of Jason Lee his first-team opportunities were limited, and though he vowed to fight to win back his place, he enjoyed spells with Dagenham and Redbridge and Stevenage before joining Third Division new boys Kidderminster Harriers.

He scored on his debut at Mansfield and continued to find the net quite regularly in the closing weeks of the campaign. Sadly, much of his contribution to the club's second season of League football came from the substitute's bench, though he still managed to chip in with eight goals, making him the Harriers' record aggregate Football League scorer. He continued to find the net in 2002–03 although he did miss a late penalty against Lincoln on the opening day of the season that would have given the Harriers three points!

Wigan Athletic Playing Record

	League		FA Cup		FL Cup		Others		Total	
	App	Gls	App	Gls	App	Gls	App	Gls	App	Gls
1997–98	1 (3)	0	0	0	0	0	0	0	1 (3)	0
TOTAL	1 (3)	0	0	0	0	0	0	0	1 (3)	0

BROWN John Christopher

Goalkeeper

Born: Bradford, 30 December 1947.

Career: March 1965 Preston North End 67 (0) 0. November 1970 on loan Stockport County 25 (0) 0. July 1975 Stockport County 15 (0) 0. July 1976 WIGAN ATHLETIC 93 (0) 0.

Goalkeeper John Brown attracted the interest of a number of League clubs while playing for Bradford Schoolboys, whom he helped reach the semi-finals of the English Schools' Trophy. After serving 16 months as an apprentice joiner, Brown joined Preston North End and made his League debut as a 17-year-old in a 4–2 defeat against Bolton Wanderers for whom Welsh international centre-forward Wyn Davies netted a hat-trick. He spent most of the 1960s as understudy to Alan Kelly in the Preston goal but took over in 1972 for two first-team seasons.

He was released from Deepdale during Bobby Charlton's brief spell as manager to be replaced by Roy Tunks, later to become a Latics favourite himself. Stockport County snapped him up but after being voted 'Player of the Season' he lost his place in the side through injury and joined the Latics in the summer of 1976 during the club's non-League days.

Though it looked like a backward step, his decision was vindicated two seasons later when the Latics joined the Football League. Brown had made 69 appearances for the club at non-League level before keeping a clean sheet in a goalless draw at Hereford United in the club's first-ever Football League game. The club's first-choice 'keeper for the first two seasons of League football, his experience and bravery served the Latics well. He left Springfield Park at the end of the promotion-winning season of 1981–82, having provided a rock for the team to build on both in the drive to gain admission to the League and the subsequent quest for promotion.

Nowadays the former Latics 'keeper is back working in Preston as a bus driver.

Wigan Athletic Playing Record

	League		FA Cup		FL Cup		Others		Total	
	App	Gls	App	Gls	App	Gls	App	Gls	App	Gls
1978–79	42	0	2	0	3	0	0	0	47	0
1979–80	36	0	6	0	0	0	0	0	42	0
1980–81	9	0	2	0	4	0	0	0	15	0
1981–82	6	0	0	0	2	0	0	0	8	0
TOTAL	93	0	10	0	9	0	0	0	112	0

BROWNBILL Derek Anthony

Forward

Born: Liverpool, 4 February 1954.
Career: February 1972 Liverpool 1 (0) 0. February 1975 Port Vale 84 (8) 13. September 1978 WIGAN ATHLETIC 32 (16) 8. Stafford Rangers. Oswestry Town. Morecambe. Witton Albion. Warrington Town.

Derek Brownbill was a member of Liverpool's FA Youth Cup Final side of 1972, the Reds losing 5–2 on aggregate to Aston Villa, but he did have the consolation of scoring a goal at Anfield in the second leg. Six months later he made his Football League debut for Liverpool in a 1–1 draw at Birmingham City. Later in the season he was substitute for several UEFA Cup games but found it difficult to tie down a first-team place at Anfield and later moved to Port Vale for a fee of £5,000.

In just over three years at Vale Park, Brownbill made over 100 appearances, the highlight of his stay occurring when the Valiants reached the fifth round of the FA Cup only to lose out again to bogey team Aston Villa.

On leaving Port Vale, he joined Cleveland Cobras for a summer of American Football before signing for Wigan Athletic prior to their first season of League football.

A forceful, hardworking and enthusiastic player, Brownbill made his Latics debut as a substitute for Mickey Moore in a 3–0 home win over Rochdale and though a third of his first-team appearances in 1978–79 were in the No.12 shirt, he did manage to score a number of vital goals.

He netted twice in a 4–2 win at Northampton Town and was instrumental in Latics picking up both points in the match against his former club Port Vale. Latics trailed 3–0 when Brownbill replaced Noel Ward. He created Wigan's first goal for hat-trick hero Peter Houghton and smashed in the club's fourth in a 5–3 win.

Injuries limited his first-team appearances the following season and he left to play for Stafford Rangers.

Brownbill later played for a number of other non-League clubs including Oswestry Town, Morecambe and Witton Albion before becoming player-manager of Warrington Town and the manager of Curzon Athletic.

Wigan Athletic Playing Record

	League		FA Cup		FL Cup		Others		Total	
	App	Gls	App	Gls	App	Gls	App	Gls	App	Gls
1978–79	20 (10)	6	0 (2)	0	0	0	0	0	20 (12)	6
1979–80	12 (6)	2	2 (1)	1	2	0	0	0	16 (7)	3
TOTAL	32 (16)	8	2 (3)	1	2	0	0	0	36 (19)	9

BRUCE Alexander Robert

Forward

Born: Dundee, 23 December 1952.
Career: Dundee Juniors. May 1970 Preston North End 55 (7) 22. January 1974 Newcastle United 16 (4) 3. August 1975 Preston North End 288 (13) 135. August 1983 WIGAN ATHLETIC 35 (8) 7.

Dundee-born striker Alex Bruce always wanted to be a professional footballer and after recommendations from scout Jimmy Scott, he joined Preston North End.

His goalscoring exploits for the Deepdale club led to First Division Newcastle United paying out £150,000 for Bruce in the middle of the Magpies' 1974 FA Cup run to Wembley. Being cup-tied with North End, he rarely received an opportunity in Joe Harvey's first team that season and afterwards found it almost impossible to break the Macdonald-Tudor front combination.

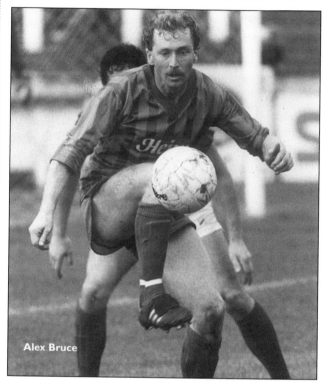

Alex Bruce

He returned to Preston without reaching double figures in any of his three seasons at St James' Park though he did win Under-23 honours for Scotland while on United's books. The North End fans were pleased to have Bruce back and he top-scored for the club in five of the next six seasons. He was the Third Division's leading scorer in 1977–78 and went on to score 157 goals in 363 League matches, not far off Sir Tom Finney's club record.

In August 1983 he moved to Wigan Athletic and made his debut in a goalless draw at Plymouth Argyle on the opening day of the 1983–84 season. Bruce was a virtual ever-present during that campaign until injury forced him to miss a handful of games towards the end of the season. One of his best games for the Latics was the first-round League Cup replay win over Bradford City when he netted twice in a 4–2 defeat of the Bantams. On hanging up his boots, he returned to Preston where he was employed as a leisure centre manager.

Wigan Athletic Playing Record

	League		FA Cup		FL Cup		Others		Total	
	App	Gls	App	Gls	App	Gls	App	Gls	App	Gls
1983–84	32 (5)	7	4	2	1	0	1	0	38 (5)	9
1984–85	3 (3)	0	1 (1)	0	0	0	0	0	4 (4)	0
TOTAL	35 (8)	7	5 (1)	2	1	0	1	0	42 (9)	9

BRUNO Pasquale

Central Defender
Born: Lecce, Italy, 19 June 1962.
Career: Juventus. Fiorentina. November 1995 Heart of Midlothian 33 (2) 1. February 1998 WIGAN ATHLETIC 1 (0) 0. July 1998 Cowdenbeath 4 (0) 0.

Italian centre-half Pasquale Bruno played his early football with Juventus, helping them win Serie 'A' before moving on to play for Fiorentina. In November 1995, the experienced defender moved into Scottish League football with Heart of Midlothian and over the next couple of seasons was a first-team regular at Tynecastle. On losing his place to Paul Ritchie, he joined Wigan Athletic on a short-term contract in February 1998.

Pasquale Bruno

Bruno's only Football League appearance for the Latics came in a 2–0 home defeat at the hands of Grimsby Town when he was replaced by substitute Kevin Sharp. After failing to gain assurances that he would be selected in his preferred sweeper role, he left Springfield Park and after four appearances for Cowdenbeath in 1998–99, he returned to Italy.

Wigan Athletic Playing Record

	League		FA Cup		FL Cup		Others		Total	
	App	Gls	App	Gls	App	Gls	App	Gls	App	Gls
1997–98	1	0	0	0	0	0	0	0	1	0
TOTAL	1	0	0	0	0	0	0	0	1	0

BUCKLEY Glen

Utility player
Born: Standish, 31 August 1960.
Career: Preston North End (non-contract). October 1979 WIGAN ATHLETIC 1 (0) 0.

Standish-born utility player Glen Buckley began his career with Preston North End under Nobby Stiles. Sadly, during his time at

Glen Buckly

Deepdale, he had some problems following a leg operation and left to try and resurrect his career with Wigan Athletic.

Buckley showed his versatility during his early days with the club, playing in every position except goalkeeper for the Latics' reserve side. A hardworking player, he eventually made his League debut for Wigan wearing the No.9 shirt for the match at Newport County in October 1979. Not only did the Latics lose 3–2 but he was replaced by substitute Kevin Smart midway through the second half. It proved to be Buckley's only experience of League football and at the end of the season, he left to try his luck in the United States.

Wigan Athletic Playing Record

	League		FA Cup		FL Cup		Others		Total	
	App	Gls	App	Gls	App	Gls	App	Gls	App	Gls
1979–80	1	0	0	0	0	0	0	0	1	0
TOTAL	1	0	0	0	0	0	0	0	1	0

BUKRAN Gabor

Midfield
Born: Hungary, 16 November 1975.
Career: Honved. Charleroi. Cordoba. Xerex CD. August 1999 Walsall 63 (10) 4. August 2001 WIGAN ATHLETIC 1 (0) 0. SV Salzburg.

The Hungarian international was signed by Walsall from Spanish club Xerex just before the start of the 1999–2000 season, having previously played for Honved, Charleroi and Cordoba.

The skilful midfielder made an immediate impression at the Bescot Stadium, though towards the end of the season, he lost his place during the club's final vain scramble against relegation. He was back in the side at the start of the following season and seemed to be reaching top form again when he netted twice in the match against Cambridge United. However, he then received an uncharacteristic red card at Bury that seemed to affect his performances and at the end of the season, having scored seven goals in 87 games, he was released.

He joined Wigan on a non-contract basis in the summer of 2001 and impressed Latics fans with a spectacular volley in a pre-season friendly against Everton. His only League appearance for the Latics came in the opening game of the season against Brentford but the Hungarian then turned down the offer of a permanent contract and later signed for Austrian club SV Salzburg.

Wigan Athletic Playing Record

	League		FA Cup		FL Cup		Others		Total	
	App	Gls	App	Gls	App	Gls	App	Gls	App	Gls
2001–02	1	0	0	0	0	0	0	0	1	0
TOTAL	1	0	0	0	0	0	0	0	1	0

BULLARD James Richard

Midfield
Born: Newham, 23 October 1978.
Career: Gravesend and Northfleet. February 1998 West Ham United. July 2001 Peterborough United 62 (4) 11. January 2003 WIGAN ATHLETIC 63 (0) 3.

Jimmy Bullard

Central midfielder Jimmy Bullard played non-League football for Gravesend and Northfleet before a £30,000 transfer took him to West Ham United. Unable to break into the Hammers' League side, he was given a free transfer and joined Peterborough United.

He started the 2001–02 season in a wide position but as soon as he was moved into central midfield he blossomed. He delivered some fine defence-splitting passes and waded in with some spectacular goals but was then forced to miss part of the campaign after suffering a broken toe. He continued to be a regular in the 'Posh' midfield for the first half of the 2002–03 season before, having scored 14 goals in 77 games for the London Road club, he was sold to Wigan Athletic for the bargain fee of £275,000.

Making his debut in the goalless draw with Cheltenham, he quickly took over the role of midfield playmaker and opened his

goal account with a superb 25-yard free-kick against Oldham Athletic. An inventive, hardworking performer, having helped the Latics win the Second Division Championship, his fellow professionals rewarded him with a place in the PFA Second Division team for the season.

In 2003–04, Bullard was an ever-present and hasn't missed a game since arriving at the JJB Stadium.

Wigan Athletic Playing Record

	League		FA Cup		FL Cup		Others		Total	
	App	Gls	App	Gls	App	Gls	App	Gls	App	Gls
2002–03	17	1	0	0	0	0	0	0	17	1
2003–04	46	2	1	0	3	1	0	0	50	3
TOTAL	63	3	1	0	3	1	0	0	67	4

BURCHILL Mark James

Striker
Born: Broxburn, 18 August 1980.
Career: Celtic Boys Club. June 1997 Glasgow Celtic 17 (24) 21. September 2000 on loan Birmingham City 4 (9) 4. January 2001 on loan Ipswich Town 2 (5) 1. August 2001 Portsmouth 9 (15) 8. January 2003 on loan Dundee 7 (4) 2. August 2003 on loan WIGAN ATHLETIC 1 (3) 0.

A member of Celtic's Premier League Championship-winning side of 1999–2000, Burchill got off to an explosive start at Parkhead the following term, netting a hat-trick within four minutes in the 7–0 thrashing of Luxembourg's Jeunesse Esch in a UEFA Cup qualifying round tie. However, he failed to win a regular place in Martin O'Neill's team and was soon on his way to Birmingham City in a loan deal.

An effective striker, he was blessed with blinding pace, the ability to kick with either foot and the knack of being in the right place at the right time. He did well at St Andrew's, netting five goals from seven starts in all competitions and becoming a huge crowd favourite, to the extent that the fans raised a petition to pressure the club into signing him permanently. However, that transfer fell

Mark Burchill

through and he joined Ipswich Town on loan for the remainder of the season.

Towards the end of the 2001 close season, he joined Portsmouth for a fee of £600,000 and scored twice on his debut in a 4–2 defeat of Grimsby Town. He netted four goals in five matches when a freak training ground accident resulted in damage to a cruciate ligament and he was sidelined for the remainder of the season. Despite making a full recovery, he was out of favour at Fratton Park and returned north of the border to play for Dundee.

The Scotland international, who has won six full caps for his country, joined Wigan on loan at the start of the 2003–04 season. He made his debut in Latics' first win of the season, a 2–0 defeat of Burnley, but after that made just three more appearances as a substitute.

Wigan Athletic Playing Record

	League		FA Cup		FL Cup		Others		Total	
	App	Gls	App	Gls	App	Gls	App	Gls	App	Gls
2003–04	1 (3)	0	0	0	0	0	0	0	1 (3)	0
TOTAL	1 (3)	0	0	0	0	0	0	0	1 (3)	0

BUTLER John Edward

Full-Back/Midfield
Born: Liverpool, 7 February 1962.
Career: Prescot Cables. January 1982 WIGAN ATHLETIC 238 (7) 15. December 1988 Stoke City 258 (4) 7. June 1995 WIGAN ATHLETIC 52 (4) 1.

John Butler

John Butler played his early football for Prescot Cables before joining the Latics in January 1982. He made his first-team debut in a 1–1 home draw against Rochdale towards the end of the 1981–82 season, though it was the following campaign before he established himself as a regular member of the Wigan side. Over the next six-and-a-half seasons, Butler missed very few games and was a member of the Latics' side that reached the Third Division play-offs in 1986–87.

At Christmas 1988, Butler was surprisingly allowed to leave Springfield Park and joined Stoke City for £75,000. At the Victoria Ground, Butler won a Second Division Championship medal and helped the Potters win the Autoglass Trophy in 1992, beating Stockport County 1–0 in the final. Butler had appeared in 319 League and Cup games for Stoke when in August 1995 he returned to Springfield Park for a second spell with the Latics.

One of the most versatile players ever to have worn the colours of Wigan Athletic, he holds the distinction of having played in every position including goalkeeper. His spell between the posts came against Bury in a Freight Rover Trophy match following an injury to Roy Tunks.

One of the most popular players ever to represent the club, John Butler holds quite a unique record in that he won promotion with the Latics in his first and last season with the club

Wigan Athletic Playing Record

	League		FA Cup		FL Cup		Others		Total	
	App	Gls	App	Gls	App	Gls	App	Gls	App	Gls
1981–82	1	0	0	0	0	0	0	0	1	0
1982–83	37 (3)	4	2	1	1 (1)	0	0	0	40 (4)	5
1983–84	41	3	4	0	2	0	1	0	48	3
1984–85	45	3	4	0	4	0	6	0	59	3
1985–86	37	1	5	0	2	0	4	0	48	1
1986–87	35 (1)	0	2	0	2	0	1	0	40 (1)	0
1987–88	23 (3)	1	2	1	4	0	2	0	31 (3)	2
1988–89	20	3	1	0	2	0	1	0	24	3
1995–96	32	1	3	0	1	0	3	0	39	1
1996–97	20 (4)	0	1	0	0	0	1	0	22 (4)	0
TOTAL	291 (11)	16	24	2	18 (1)	0	19 (0)	0	352 (12)	18

BUTLER Lee Simon

Goalkeeper
Born: Sheffield, 30 May 1966.
Career: Haworth Colliery. June 1986 Lincoln City 30 (0) 0. August 1987 Aston Villa 8 (0) 0. March 1991 on loan Hull City 4 (0) 0. July 1991 Barnsley 118 (2) 0. February 1996 on loan Scunthorpe United 2 (0) 0. July 1996 WIGAN ATHLETIC 63 (0) 0. July 1998 Dunfermline Athletic 35 (0) 0. September 1999 Halifax Town 92 (1) 0. July 2002 Doncaster Rovers.

Goalkeeper Lee Butler played his early football with Haworth Colliery before being given the chance to play League football with Lincoln City. His performances for the Imps led to a £100,000 move to First Division Aston Villa in the summer of 1987. With his first-team opportunities limited because of the fine form of England international Nigel Spink, he went on loan to Hull City before a £165,000 transfer to Barnsley in July 1991. Though he was one of the best 'keepers outside of the top flight, he later found stiff competition for the No.1 jersey at Oakwell from David Watson and, after a loan spell at Scunthorpe United, he left to join Wigan Athletic in the summer of 1996.

Butler made his Latics debut in a 2–1 home win over Northampton Town on the opening day of the 1996–97 season. Though it took him a while to win over the Wigan fans, it all changed when his outstanding displays between the posts

SPRINGFIELD PARK

Lee Butler

midway through the campaign kept the club in the promotion race. An agile shot-stopper, he went on to be ever-present as the Latics won the Third Division Championship, keeping 14 clean sheets. The following season he lost out to Roy Carroll and, finding it hard to regain his first-team place, he left for Dunfermline Athletic.

After just one season at East End Park, he joined Halifax Town where he had an outstanding first season, pulling off a string of superb saves and winning all the 'Player of the Year' trophies. Though injuries hampered his progress in 2000–01 he was the club's first-choice 'keeper come the start of the following season. However, midway through it he was forced to announce his retirement from the game due to a persistent knee injury. He subsequently joined Doncaster Rovers as a replacement for Barry Richardson, who moved to the Shay at around the same time!

Wigan Athletic Playing Record

	League		FA Cup		FL Cup		Others		Total	
	App	Gls	App	Gls	App	Gls	App	Gls	App	Gls
1996–97	46	0	1	0	2	0	1	0	50	0
1997–98	17	0	1	0	1	0	1	0	20	0
TOTAL	63	0	2	0	3	0	2	0	70	0

CAMPBELL David Anthony

Midfield

Born: Derry, Northern Ireland, 2 June 1965.

Career: June 1983 Nottingham Forest 35 (6) 3. February 1987 on loan Notts County 18 (0) 2. October 1987 Charlton Athletic 26 (4) 1. March 1989 on loan Plymouth Argyle 1 (0) 0. March 1989 Bradford City 27 (8) 4. Shamrock Rovers. November 1992 Rotherham United 0 (1) 0. March 1993 Burnley 7 (1) 0. February 1994 on loan Lincoln City 2 (2) 1. Portadown. August 1994 WIGAN ATHLETIC 7 (0) 0. January 1995 Cambridge United 1 (0) 0.

David Campbell

Midfield man David Campbell joined Nottingham Forest as an apprentice after being spotted playing for Oxford Boys' Club, eventually signing professional forms at the City ground in June 1983. Having broken into Forest's first team in 1985, he was still in the process of establishing himself when he won the first of 10 full caps for Northern Ireland against Morocco in April 1986.

After a loan spell with Notts County, Campbell joined Charlton Athletic in October 1987, helping the Addicks avoid relegation from the top flight. Then, after a brief loan period with Plymouth Argyle, he moved to Bradford City in 1989. Following a serious knee injury, he played his way back to full fitness with Shamrock Rovers, later spending a trial period with Rotherham United before joining Burnley in March 1993. He never really established himself with the Clarets and after loan spells with Lincoln City and Portadown, joined Wigan Athletic in the summer of 1994.

He made his debut in a 2–1 defeat at Carlisle United on the opening day of the 1994–95 season, but after appearing in seven games, he joined Cambridge United in January 1995. Unfortunately he suffered a broken leg in his very first game for the U's.

Wigan Athletic Playing Record

	League		FA Cup		FL Cup		Others		Total	
	App	Gls	App	Gls	App	Gls	App	Gls	App	Gls
1994–95	7	0	0	0	4	0	0	0	11	0
TOTAL	7	0	0	0	4	0	0	0	11	0

CAMPBELL Robert McFaul

Forward

Born: Belfast, 13 September 1956.

Career: January 1974 Aston Villa 7 (3) 1. February 1975 on loan Halifax Town 14 (1) 0. April 1975 Huddersfield Town 30 (1) 9. July 1977 Sheffield United 35 (2) 11. Vancouver Canada. September 1978 Huddersfield Town 7 (0) 3. October 1978 Halifax Town 19 (2) 3. Brisbane, Australia. December 1979 Bradford City 147 (1) 76. August 1983 Derby County 11 (0) 4. November 1983 Bradford City 126 (0) 45. October 1986 WIGAN ATHLETIC 61 (8) 27.

Much-travelled striker Bobby Campbell, who was one of Wigan's most popular players, began his Football League career with Aston Villa but was unable to win a regular place and after a loan spell with Halifax Town he joined Huddersfield Town. There followed brief spells with Sheffield United and Halifax Town but during his second period at the Shay, Campbell was sacked for 'persistent misconduct'.

After a spell in Australian football, Campbell returned to play for Bradford City. There was little doubt about Bobby's ability to score goals – he top scored in each of his five full seasons with the club – but doubts remained about his temperament.

In August 1983 he joined Derby County for £70,000 – a record fee received by the Valley Parade club. However, he never settled at the Baseball Ground and, after a horrendous performance against Grimsby Town in November of that year, he returned to Bradford City, first on loan and then on a permanent basis for half the fee City had received!

The City fans adored him and in October 1984 he broke Frank O'Rourke's 69-year-old goalscoring record. While with City he made two appearances for Northern Ireland against Scotland and Wales, the latter as a substitute. In October 1986, having scored 121 goals in 274 League games during his two spells with Bradford City, he joined Wigan Athletic for a fee of £25,000.

Campbell made a goalscoring debut in a 3–1 defeat at Swindon Town and ended his first season at Springfield Park as the club's leading scorer with 20 goals. It was an exciting campaign with

Bobby Campbell

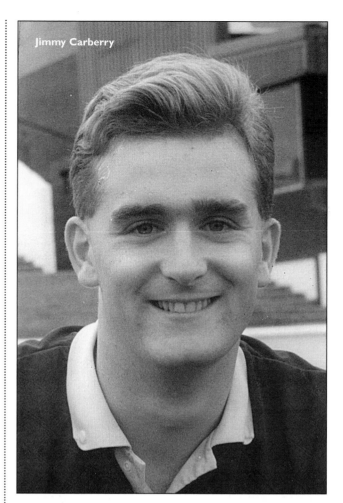
Jimmy Carberry

Wigan finishing fourth in the Third Division and reaching the sixth round of the FA Cup. In 1987–88 Campbell netted a magnificent hat-trick at Burnden Park as Wigan came from behind to beat Bolton Wanderers 5–4 on aggregate in a first round League Cup tie. Despite suffering from a series of niggling injuries, which forced him to miss a number of games, Campbell again topped the club's scoring charts before deciding to retire. He later returned to his beloved Valley Parade as the Yorkshire club's 'Football in the Community' Officer.

Wigan Athletic Playing Record

	League		FA Cup		FL Cup		Others		Total	
	App	Gls	App	Gls	App	Gls	App	Gls	App	Gls
1986–87	33 (2)	16	5	4	0	0	3	0	41 (2)	20
1987–88	28 (6)	11	2	1	4	4	2	0	36 (6)	16
TOTAL	61 (8)	27	7	5	4	4	5	0	77 (8)	36

CARBERRY James

Winger
Born: Liverpool, 13 October 1969.
Career: June 1988 Everton. June 1989 WIGAN ATHLETIC 30 (35) 6.

Able to open up defences with his skill and pace, Jimmy Carberry worked his way up through the ranks at Everton but was unable to break into the club's League side and in the summer of 1989 joined Wigan Athletic on a free transfer. He went straight into the Latics' side for their game at Blackpool on the opening day of the 1989–90 season and though he created a couple of good goalscoring opportunities for Hilditch and Page, the game remained goalless.

Able to play on either flank, Carberry appeared in the majority of games that season but over half of his appearances occurred when he came off the bench. He continued to be a valuable member of the Latics squad the following season but after only a handful of appearances during the early part of the 1991–92 season, he was released.

Wigan Athletic Playing Record

	League		FA Cup		FL Cup		Others		Total	
	App	Gls	App	Gls	App	Gls	App	Gls	App	Gls
1989–90	15 (17)	3	3	0	2 (1)	0	1 (2)	1	21 (20)	4
1990–91	14 (14)	3	0 (1)	0	0	0	1 (1)	0	15 (16)	3
1991–92	1 (4)	0	0	0	0	0	0 (1)	0	1 (5)	0
TOTAL	30 (35)	6	3 (1)	0	2 (1)	0	2 (4)	1	37 (41)	7

CARRAGHER Matthew

Full-Back
Born: Liverpool, 14 January 1976.
Career: November 1993 WIGAN ATHLETIC 102 (17) 0. July 1997 Port Vale 190 (4) 1.

A product of Wigan's youth policy, right-back Matthew Carragher made his League debut as a substitute for Alan Johnson in a 6–3 home win over Chester City in October 1993. He held his place in the side for the rest of the season, at the end of which he was voted the club's 'Young Player of the Year'. In 1994–95, his first full season as a professional, he again won the 'Young Player of the Year' award, his performances attracting the attention of several Premier League clubs. After missing just one game in 1994–95, his first-team appearances became more restricted due to the return to the club of John Butler. However, he still went on to become the youngest-ever player to make a century of league starts for Wigan and picked up a Third Division Championship medal before being given a free transfer in the summer of 1997.

Carragher joined Port Vale, where after sharing the right-back duties with Andy Hill, he began to establish himself in the Valiants side. Sadly, he picked up a cruciate injury at Bolton but fought his way back to full fitness to become one of Vale's most experienced players. In 2001 he captained them to victory against Brentford in the LDV Vans Trophy Final at Cardiff's Millennium Stadium. Now Vale's longest-serving player, his role over the past couple of seasons has varied between full-back, centre-half and sweeper, depending on the chosen formation. When Vale played the Latics at the JJB Stadium in Wigan's Second Division Championship-winning season, Carragher captained the Potteries side to a 1–0 victory. Carragher has now appeared in 220 games for the Valiants.

Roy Carroll

Matthew Carragher

Wigan Athletic Playing Record

	League		FA Cup		FL Cup		Others		Total	
	App	Gls	App	Gls	App	Gls	App	Gls	App	Gls
1993–94	27 (5)	0	4	0	0	0	1 (1)	0	32 (6)	0
1994–95	41	0	2	2	3	1	4	0	50	3
1995–96	23 (5)	0	4	0	1 (1)	0	2	0	30 (6)	0
1996–97	11 (7)	0	0 (1)	0	2	0	0	0	13 (8)	0
TOTAL	102 (17)	0	10 (1)	2	6 (1)	1	7 (1)	0	125 (20)	3

CARROLL Roy Eric

Goalkeeper
Born: Enniskillen, 30 September 1977.
Career: September 1995 Hull City 46 (0) 0. April 1997 WIGAN ATHLETIC 135 (0) 0. August 2001 Manchester United 14 (3) 0.

Northern Ireland international goalkeeper Roy Carroll began his Football League career with Hull City, making a terrific Tigers debut at Swindon Town in January 1996. He retained his place with a series of eye-catching performances, displaying a presence and maturity beyond his years. He attracted many scouts, with Bolton showing a particular interest, but at the end of the season in which he was voted the club's 'Player of the Year', he was still at Boothferry Park. He got his first full international call-up in October 1996 for Northern Ireland's World Cup qualifier against Armenia.

Towards the end of the 1996–97 season, Carroll was surprisingly sold to Wigan Athletic for a fee of £350,000, helping the Tigers out of a financial dilemma. Despite being the Latics' record signing, he had to wait until November 1997 before replacing Lee Butler in the 2–1 defeat at Watford. He went on to become the runner-up in the Latics' 'Player of the Year' award. He was a virtual ever-present in 1998–99, and he maintained a high level of consistency between the posts. Though speculation abounded with stories of a move to a Premiership club, Carroll, who won an Autowindscreen Shield winners' medal, was again voted runner-up in the 'Player of the Year' awards.

Recognised by his fellow professionals with selection for the PFA award-winning Division Two side, he played a large part in the Latics' run of 26 League games without defeat at the start of the 1999–2000 season. An emergency appendix operation saw him miss the last seven games of the season and though speculation continued to link him to one of the top Premiership clubs, he was still at the JJB Stadium for the 2000–01 season. His performances continued to be of the highest class, and he went on to keep 13 clean sheets in 34 first-team outings to help the Latics reach the play-offs for the second successive season.

Firmly established as Northern Ireland's first-choice 'keeper, he eventually left the Latics to join Manchester United for £2.5 million as understudy to Fabian Barthez. He endured something of a baptism of fire when Aston Villa's Darius Vassell beat him after just four minutes of his Premiership debut in September 2001, but his record was impressive throughout the campaign, more than justifying Sir Alex Ferguson's faith in him. Though he was pushed further down the Old Trafford pecking order following the signing of Spanish goalkeeper Ricardo, it all changed again as the season progressed and he bounced back to relegate Ricardo to United's third-choice goalkeeper.

Wigan Athletic Playing Record

	League		FA Cup		FL Cup		Others		Total	
	App	Gls	App	Gls	App	Gls	App	Gls	App	Gls
1997–98	29	0	2	0	1	0	2	0	34	0
1998–99	43	0	3	0	4	0	9	0	59	0
1999–2000	34	0	2	0	3	0	2	0	41	0
2000–01	29	0	1	0	3	0	2	0	35	0
TOTAL	135	0	8	0	11	0	15	0	169	0

CLEGG Michael Jamie

Full-Back

Born: Ashton-under-Lyne, 3 July 1977.

Career: July 1995 Manchester United 4 (5) 0. February 2000 on loan Ipswich Town 3 (0) 0. March 2000 on loan WIGAN ATHLETIC 6 (0) 0. February 2002 Oldham Athletic 12 (2) 0.

England 'B' and Under-21 international Michael Clegg had a tough start to his professional career, having been seen as an average player among the stars of Manchester United's youth team. His perseverance finally paid off when he made his League debut against Middlesbrough in November 1996, a match in which he

Michael Clegg

earned rave reviews. Voted the Pontin's League 'Player of the Year', Clegg appeared for United in both FA Cup and European Cup matches, where his positional play earned plaudits for its maturity.

However, with his first-team opportunities limited owing to the outstanding form of Gary Neville and Dennis Irwin, he went to Ipswich Town on a month's loan as cover for Gary Croft. On transfer deadline day in March 2000, Clegg joined Wigan Athletic on loan, making his debut in a 2–0 home win over Notts County. He was asked to fill a variety of positions during his six-match spell with the Latics, but having found it difficult to adjust to the pace of Second Division football, he returned to Old Trafford.

However, after being confined to reserve-team football – his only senior appearance coming in the Worthington Cup tie against Arsenal – he moved on a free transfer to Oldham Athletic. Immediately installed at right-back, he again struggled to adjust to the requirements of lower division football and after just five starts found himself out of favour. During the early part of the 2002–03 season, it looked as though he was part of manager Iain Dowie's plans, but he soon lost his place and managed just one more start as the season came to a close.

Wigan Athletic Playing Record

	League		FA Cup		FL Cup		Others		Total	
	App	Gls	App	Gls	App	Gls	App	Gls	App	Gls
1999–2000	6	0	0	0	0	0	0	0	6	0
TOTAL	6	0	0	0	0	0	0	0	6	0

COLLINS David Dennis

Midfield/Defender

Born: Dublin, 30 October 1971.

Career: November 1988 Liverpool. January 1992 on loan WIGAN ATHLETIC 9 (0) 0. July 1992 Oxford United 33 (9) 0.

Republic of Ireland Under-21 international David Collins began his career with Liverpool, but despite some impressive performances in the club's reserve side, he couldn't force his way into the Reds' first team.

In January 1992, Latics' manager Bryan Hamilton brought him to Springfield Park on a two-month loan spell and the six-footer made his League debut in a 2–1 home win over Bradford City. Wearing the No.8 shirt, Collins impressed the Wigan faithful but at the end of his stay the Latics board decided not to make an offer for the player.

He returned to Anfield to see out the season with the reserves but in the summer of 1992, he joined Oxford United on a free transfer. Able to play at both centre-half and in midfield, Collins gave the U's three seasons of honest and reliable displays before being released at the end of the 1994–95 campaign.

Wigan Athletic Playing Record

	League		FA Cup		FL Cup		Others		Total	
	App	Gls	App	Gls	App	Gls	App	Gls	App	Gls
1991–92	9	0	0	0	0	0	0	0	9	0
TOTAL	9	0	0	0	0	0	0	0	9	0

COMSTIVE Paul Thomas

Midfield

Born: Southport, 25 November 1961.

Career: October 1979 Blackburn Rovers 3 (3) 0. September 1982 on loan Rochdale 9 (0) 2. August 1983 WIGAN ATHLETIC 35 (0) 2. November 1984 Wrexham 95 (4) 8. July 1987 Burnley 81 (1) 17. September 1989 Bolton Wanderers 42 (7) 3. November 1991 Chester City 55 (2) 6. Southport. Morecambe. Chorley.

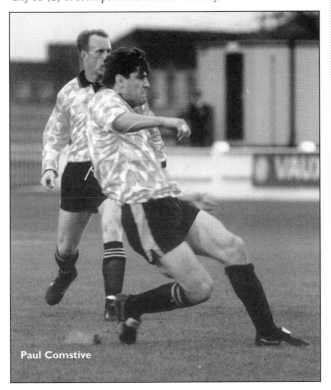

Paul Comstive

Midfielder Paul Comstive played his early football with Blackburn Rovers but struggled to make an impact at Ewood Park and in September 1982 had a loan spell at Rochdale, where he scored on his debut. In August 1983 Wigan Athletic secured him on a free transfer and Paul went straight into their League side at left-back for the opening game of the 1983–84 season at Plymouth Argyle. During his first season with the club, Comstive was sent off in a blaze of controversy at Brentford. Having scored the game's only goal, it appeared that Comstive lost his footing in the treacherous conditions at Griffin Park and although he clattered into the Bees' midfielder Roger Joseph, it wasn't serious enough to warrant a fussy linesman to come racing onto the pitch!

He was transferred to Wrexham in November 1984, again scoring on his debut. He helped them to success in the Welsh Cup in 1985–86 and was in their European Cup Winners' Cup side that lost on away goals to Real Zaragoza the following season. Burnley took him to Turf Moor for £8,000 in July 1987 and it was there that he produced his best goalscoring form, netting 25 goals in 110 games. It was Comstive who twice hit the woodwork with headers in the Sherpa Van Trophy Final at Wembley against Wolves.

In September 1989 Bolton manager Phil Neal paid £37,500 for his services and he was instrumental in the Wanderers coming close to promotion from Division Three in successive seasons. After losing his place, he was transferred to Chester City, ending his League career when he was released from the Deva Stadium in May 1993. He then moved into non-League football with Southport and later joined Morecambe before moving to Chorley.

Wigan Athletic Playing Record

	League		FA Cup		FL Cup		Others		Total	
	App	Gls	App	Gls	App	Gls	App	Gls	App	Gls
1983–84	29	2	4	0	2	0	I	0	36	2
1984–85	6	0	0	0	3	0	0	0	9	0
TOTAL	35 (2)	2	4	0	5	0	I	0	45	2

CONNELLY Dean

Midfield
Born: Jersey, 6 January 1970.
Career: February 1988 Arsenal. June 1990 Barnsley 7 (6) 0. October 1991 on loan WIGAN ATHLETIC 12 (0) 2. August 1992 on loan Carlisle United 0 (3) 0. February 1993 WIGAN ATHLETIC 15 (5) 1. July 1994 Stockport County.

Dean Connelly joined Arsenal as a trainee after being on the books of Celtic as a schoolboy, after having had trials with Dundee and Oldham Athletic. A Scottish schoolboy international, he seemed to have everything going for him when from midfield he gained Scottish youth international caps and helped Arsenal win the Football Combination Championship in 1989–90. However, he was released by the Gunners in the summer of 1990 when he joined Barnsley.

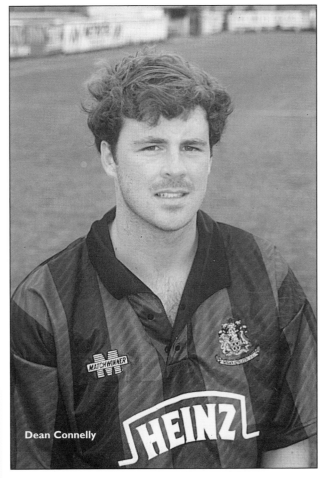

Dean Connelly

His first-team opportunities at Oakwell were limited and in October 1991 he joined Wigan Athletic on loan, making his debut in a 1–1 home draw against Reading. After 12 League starts, in which he scored two goals, he returned to Barnsley before another loan period, this time with Carlisle United. Released by the Yorkshire club in February 1993, he joined the Latics on a permanent basis but was unable to prevent their relegation to the 'new' Third Division. He left Springfield Park at the end of the following season and linked up with Stockport County, but shortly after his arrival at Edgeley Park, his contract was cancelled.

Wigan Athletic Playing Record

	League		FA Cup		FL Cup		Others		Total	
	App	Gls	App	Gls	App	Gls	App	Gls	App	Gls
1991–92	12	2	3	0	0	0	2	0	17	2
1992–93	7	0	0	0	0	0	2	0	9	0
1993–94	8 (5)	I	0	0	0	0	0	0	8 (5)	I
TOTAL	27 (5)	3	3	0	0	0	4	0	34 (5)	3

COOK Paul Anthony

Midfield

Born: Liverpool, 22 June 1967.

Career: Marine. July 1984 WIGAN ATHLETIC 77 (7) 14. May 1988 Norwich City 3 (3) 0. November 1989 Wolverhampton Wanderers 191 (2) 19. August 1994 Coventry City 35 (2) 3. February 1996 Tranmere Rovers 54 (6) 4. October 1997 Stockport County 48 (1) 3. March 1999 Burnley 140 (7) 12. November 2001 on loan WIGAN ATHLETIC 6 (0) 0.

Paul Cook

Paul Cook began his career with non-League Marine before joining Wigan Athletic in the summer of 1984. He was just beginning to get frustrated at the lack of first-team opportunities when in March 1985 he was called into the Latics side for the visit of Walsall. However, it was 1986–87 before he won a regular place in the Wigan team, helping the side finish fourth in Division Three. An important member of the Latics side, he was surprisingly allowed to leave Springfield Park in June 1988, joining Norwich City for a fee of £73,000.

Unable to hold down a regular first-team spot at Carrow Road, he moved to Wolverhampton Wanderers in November 1989 for £250,000. After improving with his probing passes and powerful long-range shooting, he suffered a loss of form and was allowed to join Coventry City for £600,000. However, his patchy form restricted his appearances and he later moved to Tranmere Rovers. He later joined Stockport County for a club record fee of £250,000 and despite fracturing his skull in a fall at home, he made an unexpected comeback with a loan spell at Burnley. The move was made permanent and he was an automatic choice in the Clarets side that won promotion to the First Division in 1999–2000. He continued to be a regular in Stan Ternant's side until December 2001 when he surprisingly let him go on loan to Wigan. Considered by many to be playing the best football of his career, he impressed during his time at the JJB, where he never finished on the losing side.

On his return to Turf Moor he was unable to break into the Clarets side and occasionally even failed to make the bench. The

2002–03 season started badly for him when he was shown a red card against Wolves for a rather innocuous challenge. After that his first-team chances were sporadic and when he did start, he rarely lasted 90 minutes.

Wigan Athletic Playing Record

	League		FA Cup		FL Cup		Others		Total	
	App	Gls	App	Gls	App	Gls	App	Gls	App	Gls
1984–85	2	0	0	0	0	0	0	0	2	0
1985–86	11 (3)	2	1	0	0	0	2 (1)	0	14 (4)	2
1986–87	26 (1)	4	3	0	1	0	2	1	32 (1)	5
1987–88	38 (3)	8	2	0	3	0	1	0	44 (3)	8
2001–02	6	0	0	0	0	0	0	0	6	0
TOTAL	83 (7)	14	6	0	4	0	5 (1)	1	98 (3)	15

COOKE Terence John

Winger

Born: Birmingham, 5 August 1976.

Career: July 1994 Manchester United 1 (3) 0. January 1996 on loan Sunderland 6 (0) 0. November 1996 on loan Birmingham City 1 (3) 0. October 1998 on loan Wrexham 10 (0) 0. January 1999 Manchester City 27 (7) 7. March 2000 on loan WIGAN ATHLETIC 10 (0) 1. September 2000 on loan Sheffield Wednesday 16 (1) 1. March 2002 Grimsby Town 18 (10) 1.

An FA Youth Cup winner with Manchester United, Cooke's introduction on the Old Trafford stage in terms of League football came against Bolton Wanderers in September 1995 when he manufactured a Maradona-style back pass for Paul Scholes to score. Despite his initial success, the talented winger, who possesses an excellent repertoire of skills and lightning pace, was resigned to reserve-team football. He went on loan to Sunderland where he impressed with his tenacious tackling and willingness to cover back in defence. An England Under-21 international, he had further loan spells with his home-town club Birmingham City and Wrexham before a £1 million transfer to Manchester City in January 1999.

His fast and direct wing play and accurate crossing ability stood out in the Second Division. Having made a tremendous contribution to the club's push for automatic promotion, he lost his way a little in 1999–2000. He seemed to become a forgotten man, and after asking to be put on the transfer list, he joined Wigan Athletic on loan.

He made his debut in a 5–1 mauling of Blackpool and while he never recaptured the form that made him a crowd favourite at Maine Road, his displays created a number of goalscoring opportunities for his fellow forwards. His only goal for the Latics came from a free-kick in a 1–1 draw at Chesterfield. There was speculation that he might make a permanent move to the JJB Stadium during the summer, but he returned to Maine Road, later having loan spells at Sheffield Wednesday.

Still finding himself out of favour at Maine Road, Cooke joined Grimsby Town on a short-term contract in March 2002. He created an immediate impression with Mariners' fans, scoring in a 1–1 draw at Norwich City and contributing to the club's struggle to avoid relegation. The move was made permanent in the close season but he was then unable to establish himself and was in and out of the Grimsby side throughout the campaign.

Wigan Athletic Playing Record

	League		FA Cup		FL Cup		Others		Total	
	App	Gls	App	Gls	App	Gls	App	Gls	App	Gls
1999–2000	10	1	0	0	0	0	0	0	10	1
TOTAL	10	1	0	0	0	0	0	0	10	1

COOPER Stephen Brian

Forward

Born: Birmingham, 22 June 1964.
Career: Moor Green. November 1983 Birmingham City. December 1983 on loan Halifax Town 7 (0) 1. September 1994 Newport County 38 (0) 11. August 1985 Plymouth Argyle 58 (15) 15. August 1988 Barnsley 62 (15) 13. December 1990 Tranmere Rovers 16 (16) 3. March 1992 on loan Peterborough United 2 (7) 0. December 1992 on loan WIGAN ATHLETIC 4 (0) 0. August 1993 York City 37 (1) 6. September 1994 Airdrieonians.

Much-travelled striker Stephen Cooper played his early football for Moor Green before joining home-town team Birmingham City in November 1983. Unable to force his way into the Blues side, he went on loan to Halifax Town, where he made his League debut and scored his first goal in the competition. A free transfer took him to Newport County but after just one season at Somerton Park, he was on the move again, this time to Plymouth Argyle. His goalscoring feats for the Pilgrims, whom he helped win promotion to the Second Division in 1985–86, led to a £100,000 move to Barnsley in the summer of 1988. He continued to find the net on a regular basis for the Oakwell club but in December 1990 another £100,000 fee took him to Tranmere Rovers.

Unable to find his goalscoring touch at Prenton Park, he had a brief loan spell at Peterborough United before joining Wigan Athletic in a similar capacity in December 1992. Cooper's first game for the Latics was in the Boxing Day defeat at Bolton Wanderers, and though he appeared in the next three games, he didn't find the net and returned to Tranmere before joining York City at the end of the season. In September 1994 he went north of the border to play for Airdrie, where his goals helped his new club to the Scottish Cup Final.

	League		FA Cup		FL Cup		Others		Total	
	App	Gls	App	Gls	App	Gls	App	Gls	App	Gls
1992–93	4	0	0	0	0	0	2	0	6	0
TOTAL	4	0	0	0	0	0	2	0	6	0

Wigan Athletic Playing Record

CORRIGAN Francis Joseph

Midfield

Born: Liverpool, 13 November 1952.
Career: Ormskirk. August 1972 Blackpool. July 1973 Walsall 1 (0) 0. October 1973 Burton Albion. May 1975 Bangor City. October 1975 Northwich Victoria. March 1978 WIGAN ATHLETIC 113 (3) 12. June 1981 Stafford Rangers.

A former Liverpool Schools' player, Frank Corrigan played in the demanding local leagues for two years before joining Blackpool at the age of 18. After spending a year in the Seasiders' Central League side, he joined Walsall. He spent just three months at Fellows Park, and due to a string of injuries, he only made one League appearance for the Saddlers.

He left League football to spend two seasons playing for Burton Albion in the Southern League, but he wanted to return to his native Liverpool and so moved to Bangor City. Again he failed to settle and moved on to Northwich Victoria, where he proved himself a key player in the Vics' epic FA Cup run of 1976–77 when the Cheshire side reached the fourth round, beating Rochdale, Peterborough United and Watford before losing to Oldham Athletic. The much-travelled midfielder joined Wigan Athletic in March 1978, making his debut in a 2–1 Northern Premier League win over Gainsborough Trinity. Though it took him a little time to produce his best form at Wigan, he eventually silenced his critics by turning in a succession of top-class performances.

After making his Football League debut for the Latics in the goalless draw at Hereford that was the club's inaugural game in the competition, he went on to miss just one game in that 1978–79 season. His first goal for the club came in Latics' first win, a 3–0 defeat of Rochdale, and over the next three seasons, his artistic left-foot and will-to-win attitude were shining examples for his teammates to follow. Corrigan left Springfield Park in the summer of 1981 to play non-League football for Stafford Rangers.

Wigan Athletic Playing Record

	League		FA Cup		FL Cup		Others		Total	
	App	Gls	App	Gls	App	Gls	App	Gls	App	Gls
1978–79	45	4	2	0	3	2	0	0	50	6
1979–80	41 (1)	7	6	1	2	0	0	0	49 (1)	8
1980–81	27 (2)	1	2	0	0	0	0	0	29 (2)	1
TOTAL	113 (3)	12	10	1	5	2	0	0	128 (3)	15

CRIBLEY Alexander

Central Defender

Born: Liverpool, 1 April 1957.
Career: June 1978 Liverpool. October 1980 WIGAN ATHLETIC 268 (3) 16.

Alex Cribley was spotted playing football for his youth club by Liverpool. After a number of appearances for the club's youth side, he was offered professional terms and though he was a regular member of the Anfield club's Central League side, playing in a variety of positions, he couldn't break through into the big time. A tough, skilful player, he decided to accept Ian McNeill's offer of first-team football with Wigan Athletic and joined the Latics in November 1980.

He made his League debut for Wigan at Dean Court against

Alex Cribley

Bournemouth, going on to appear in 30 games that season. In 1981–82 he helped the Latics win promotion to the Third Division and the following season, in which he missed just a handful of games, he scored his first goal for the club in a 3–1 defeat of Wrexham. A virtual ever-present in the Wigan side for the next six seasons, he was a firm favourite with the fans for his enthusiastic approach to the game.

Sadly, in October 1987, Cribley was badly injured in the club's 4–1 defeat at Sunderland. Though he worked hard to recover from his injury, he never returned to full fitness and was forced to retire. Alex Cribley remains with the Latics as the club's physiotherapist.

Wigan Athletic Playing Record

	League		FA Cup		FL Cup		Others		Total	
	App	Gls	App	Gls	App	Gls	App	Gls	App	Gls
1980–81	30	0	2	0	0	0	0	0	32	0
1981–82	29 (2)	0	2	0	4 (1)	0	0	0	35 (3)	0
1982–83	41	1	2	0	4	0	0	0	47	1
1983–84	44	1	4	0	2	0	1	0	51	1
1984–85	30 (1)	1	4	0	4	0	3	0	41 (1)	1
1985–86	38	2	4	0	1	0	6	0	49	2
1986–87	45	8	6	0	2	1	2	1	55	10
1987–88	11	3	0	0	3	0	0	0	14	3
TOTAL	268 (3)	16	24	0	20 (1)	1	12	1	324 (4)	18

CROFT Gary

Left-Back
Born: Burton-on-Trent 17 February 1974
Career: July 1992 Grimsby Town 139 (10) 3. March 1996 Blackburn Rovers 33 (7) 1. September 1999 Ipswich Town 20 (9) 1. January 2002 on loan WIGAN ATHLETIC 7 (0) 0. March 2002 Cardiff City 42 (7) 2.

Beginning his career with Grimsby Town, Gary Croft developed nominally into a defender but with the versatility to play almost anywhere. During his early days with the Mariners, he had the misfortune to miss a League representative game due to suspension but made up for that disappointment when selected by England for the Toulon Under-21 tournament in the summer of 1995. He had played in 169 games for the Blundell Park club when in March 1996 he was sold to Blackburn Rovers for £1.7 million.

Signed predominantly as first-team cover and insurance against injury he eventually replaced Graeme Le Saux during the 1997–98 season before suffering from a spate of niggling injuries including a dislocated shoulder. Unable to win back his place, Croft, who had made just 52 first-team appearances in three-and-a-half years at Ewood Park, joined Ipswich Town in September 1999 for a fee of £800,000.

Shortly after his arrival at Portman Road things started to go wrong for him, when he received a custodial sentence as a result of motoring offences and became the first professional footballer to play in a League game while wearing a 'tag'. Injuries and the competition for places restricted his first-team appearances.

In January 2002 he joined the Latics on loan in order to gain some first-team action. A steady but unspectacular full-back, he appeared in seven League games for Wigan, the last against Cardiff City, whom he later also joined on loan. The move became permanent in March 2002 and the following season he became an integral member of the side that won promotion to the First Division via the play-offs.

Wigan Athletic Playing Record

	League		FA Cup		FL Cup		Others		Total	
	App	Gls	App	Gls	App	Gls	App	Gls	App	Gls
2001–02	7	0	0	0	0	0	0	0	7	0
TOTAL	7	0	0	0	0	0	0	0	7	0

CROMPTON Alan

Midfield
Born: Bolton, 6 March 1958.
Career: March 1975 Sunderland. July 1976 Blackburn Rovers 2 (2) 0. July 1978 WIGAN ATHLETIC 7 (7) 0.

Bolton-born Alan Crompton began life in the engineering trade but spent the bulk of his spare time playing football. At the age of 16 he was playing for Halifax reserves but only part-time, then a year later he was approached by Sunderland. Unable to make the grade at Roker Park, he returned to the north-west with Blackburn Rovers and eventually made his Football League debut.

Unable to command a regular first-team spot with Rovers, Crompton, who was a prolific scorer in the Ewood Park club's Central League team, joined Wigan Athletic in the summer of 1978. After making his debut as a substitute for Geoff Gay in the Latics' 3–0 home defeat at the hands of Grimsby Town in August 1978, Crompton found his first-team opportunities limited as the manager decided to strengthen the midfield section of the team. He was a valuable member of the Latics squad during their first season in the Football League, but after just one further appearance as a substitute midway through the 1979–80 season, he was released.

Wigan Athletic Playing Record

	League		FA Cup		FL Cup		Others		Total	
	App	Gls	App	Gls	App	Gls	App	Gls	App	Gls
1978–79	7 (6)	0	0	0	2	0	0	0	9 (6)	0
1979–80	0 (1)	0	0	0	0	0	0	0	0 (1)	0
TOTAL	7 (7)	0	0	0	2	0	0	0	9 (7)	0

CROMPTON Paul Jonathan

Forward
Born: Orrell, 25 January 1970.
Career: July 1988 WIGAN ATHLETIC 1 (0) 0. June 1990 Altrincham.

A member of the club's Youth Training Scheme, Jonathan Crompton turned professional in July 1988 and the following month made his first-team debut as a substitute for Andy Pilling in a League Cup first-round first leg tie at Preston North End that

Jonathan Crompton

ended goalless. It was his only appearance in the Latics side that season but in the early part of the 1989–90 campaign, following some good displays in the club's reserve side, he made his Football League debut at Brentford. It wasn't the happiest of occasions as Wigan lost 3–1 and Crompton was replaced midway through the second-half by Don Page. Crompton left Springfield Park in the 1990 close season to play non-League football for Altrincham.

Wigan Athletic Playing Record

	League		FA Cup		FL Cup		Others		Total	
	App	Gls	App	Gls	App	Gls	App	Gls	App	Gls
1988–89	0	0	0	0	0 (1)	0	0	0	0 (1)	0
1989–90	1	0	0	0	0	0	0	0	1	0
TOTAL	1	0	0	0	0 (1)	0	0	0	1 (1)	0

CURTIS John

Full-Back

Born: Poulton-le-Fylde, 2 September 1954.
Career: September 1972 Blackpool 96 (6) 0. July 1977 Blackburn Rovers 9 (1) 0. March 1979 WIGAN ATHLETIC 32 (0) 0.

An all-round sportsman, the former English Schools' Hurdles Champion joined his local club Blackpool straight from school, graduating through the ranks before making his League debut at Orient in September 1973. Curtis was a member of the Seasiders' team for four seasons, helping them almost win promotion to the top flight in each of those campaigns. After making 109 League and Cup appearances for the Bloomfield Road club, Curtis joined Blackburn Rovers.

He never really settled at Ewood Park and towards the end of the Latics' first season in the Football League he joined them on loan. He made his debut in a goalless home draw against Hereford United, going on to appear in nine of the last 12 games of that 1978–79 campaign and proving himself a mobile, positive and constructive player.

Once he had discovered how keen everyone was to progress and make the public sit up and take notice, Curtis had no hesitation in joining the Latics on a permanent basis. Sadly, an unfortunate training ground accident resulted in the full-back breaking his leg and forced him to miss the entire 1979–80 season. Though he returned to first-team action the following season, there were games when he struggled and in the close season he was released.

Wigan Athletic Playing Record

	League		FA Cup		FL Cup		Others		Total	
	App	Gls	App	Gls	App	Gls	App	Gls	App	Gls
1978–79	9	0	0	0	0	0	0	0	9	0
1979–80	0	0	0	0	0	0	0	0	0	0
1980–81	23	0	0	0	1	0	0	0	24	0
TOTAL	32	0	0	0	1	0	0	0	33	0

DALEY Philip

Forward

Born: Liverpool, 12 April 1967.
Career: Newtown. October 1989 WIGAN ATHLETIC 152 (9) 40. August 1994 Lincoln City 25 (7) 5.

Liverpool-born striker Phil Daley played his early football for Newtown before joining Wigan Athletic in October 1989. He made his debut in the home match against Shrewsbury Town and though he came close on a couple of occasions to opening his

Latics account, the game was goalless. His first goal for the club came on his next appearance as Wigan beat Walsall 3–1. In 1990–91 he formed a prolific striking partnership with Bryan Griffiths, while the following season he and Gary Worthington netted 29 of Wigan's 59 goals. It was his best season in terms of goals scored – he found the net 14 times in 38 outings. Sadly, injuries hampered his progress over the next two seasons and after losing his place to Pat Gavin, he moved to Lincoln City for a fee of £40,000.

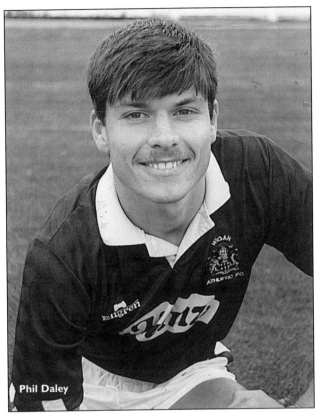

Phil Daley

During his first few weeks at Sincil Bank, Daley suffered a bad knee injury which meant he had to undergo a cartilage operation. Unfortunately the popular striker never fully recovered and after two seasons with the Imps, when he spent most of his time on the bench or in the reserves, he was released.

Wigan Athletic Playing Record

	League		FA Cup		FL Cup		Others		Total	
	App	Gls	App	Gls	App	Gls	App	Gls	App	Gls
1989–90	32 (1)	6	3	0	0	0	4	2	39 (1)	8
1990–91	41	11	1	0	2	0	4	1	48	12
1991–92	37 (1)	14	2 (1)	0	3	0	2	0	44 (2)	14
1992–93	31	6	2	0	4	1	4	3	41	10
1993–94	11 (7)	3	3	0	0	0	2	0	16 (7)	3
TOTAL	152 (9)	40	11 (1)	0	9	1	16	6	188 (10)	47

DALGLISH Paul

Forward

Born: Glasgow, 18 February 1977.
Career: July 1995 Glasgow Celtic. August 1996 Liverpool. November 1997 Newcastle United 6 (5) 1. November 1997 on loan Bury 1 (11) 0. March 1999 Norwich City 25 (18) 2. March 2001 WIGAN ATHLETIC 22 (13) 2. August 2002 Blackpool 20 (7) 1. March 2003 on loan Scunthorpe United 5 (3) 3.

The son of Anfield legend Kenny, Paul Dalglish began his career with Celtic before joining Liverpool. Unable to make the grade at Anfield, he moved to Newcastle United on a free transfer. Still

somewhat lightweight, the striker was loaned out to Bury until the end of the 1997–98 season.

He impressed at Gigg Lane with his speed and ball skills, despite being used mainly as a substitute. Returning to St James' Park for the start of the 1998–99 season, he saw his father leave his job as Newcastle United manager. He remained determined and worked hard enough to earn himself a chance in the Magpies' League side. He also made a scoring debut for Scotland Under-21s against Estonia but, having fallen out of favour, joined Norwich City on loan towards the end of the season. He completed a permanent move to Carrow Road in May 1999 for an initial fee of £300,000, a sum which could have increased to £500,000 depending on future appearances. Unfortunately the front runner displayed only tantalising glimpses of his best form at Carrow Road and joined the Latics on loan.

He was sent-off in Wigan's 3–2 home win over Oxford United and then received his marching orders again two days later as the Latics won 1–0 at Bury. The club's decision not to appeal meant that Dalglish's season was over, though he continued to train with the Latics after they decided to extend his loan spell. At his best when playing down the right, where his strong running causes defenders real problems, he scored a stunning goal in Wigan's 6–1 rout of Stoke City midway through the 2001–02 season but then struggled to hold down a first-team place after the turn of the year following the arrival of Gary Teale.

Released at the end of his contract, he joined Blackpool and scored on his debut in a 5–2 defeat of Luton Town. Though he was in the Seasiders' squad for most of the season, he did have a loan spell with Scunthorpe United. Netting three goals in the final two games of the season, he helped them reach the Third Division play-offs but was then released by Blackpool.

Wigan Athletic Playing Record

	League		FA Cup		FL Cup		Others		Total	
	App	Gls	App	Gls	App	Gls	App	Gls	App	Gls
2000–01	5 (1)	0	0	0	0	0	0	0	5 (1)	0
2001–02	17 (12)	2	1	0	0	0	0	0	18 (12)	2
TOTAL	22 (13)	2	1	0	0	0	0	0	23 (13)	2

DAVIDS Neil Graham

Central Defender
Born: Bingley, 22 September 1955.
Career: August 1973 Leeds United. April 1975 Norwich City 2 (0) 0. September 1975 on loan Northampton Town 9 (0) 0. January 1976 on loan Stockport County 5 (0) 1. July 1977 Swansea City 9 (0) 0. July 1978 WIGAN ATHLETIC 66 (2) 1.

Neil Davids began his career with Leeds United but despite spending five years at Elland Road he was unable to break into the Yorkshire club's first team. One highlight of his career while at Leeds, however, was his selection for the England Youth XI, for whom he netted the winner against Wales at the Hawthorns.

On leaving Elland Road Davids joined Norwich City and made his League debut for the Canaries in the East Anglian derby against Ipswich Town. While at Carrow Road he had loan spells with Northampton Town and Stockport County before joining Swansea City. He never really settled at the Vetch Field and joined Wigan Athletic prior to the club's first game in the Football League.

Nicknamed 'The Beast' he made his debut in the club's inaugural game in League football, a goalless draw at Hereford United, but just as he was establishing himself in the Latics side, he ruptured a tendon in his foot. Even when fully fit, he couldn't force his way back into the side as Fretwell and Ward had formed a solid defensive partnership. However, in 1979–80 Davids missed very few games, helping the Latics to again finish sixth in the Fourth Division. His only goal for the club came in the 3–1 home win over Halifax Town in April 1980. Following the appointment of Larry Lloyd as player-manager, Davids lost his place in the Wigan side and was released. Nowadays he lives in Blackpool, where he has set up his own sales business.

Wigan Athletic Playing Record

	League		FA Cup		FL Cup		Others		Total	
	App	Gls	App	Gls	App	Gls	App	Gls	App	Gls
1978–79	10 (2)	0	0	0	1	0	0	0	11 (2)	0
1979–80	41	1	6	0	0	0	0	0	47	1
1980–81	15	0	0	0	4	0	0	0	19	0
TOTAL	66 (2)	1	6	0	5	0	0	0	77 (2)	1

DE VOS Jason Richard

Central Defender
Born: Ontario, Canada, 2 January 1974.
Career: Montreal Impact. November 1996 Darlington 43 (1) 5. October 1998 Dundee United 91 (2) 2. August 2001 WIGAN ATHLETIC 87 (3) 15.

A Canadian Olympic Games' player, De Vos joined Darlington from Montreal Impact in November 1996, but shortly after establishing himself in the heart of the Quakers' defence, a broken foot curtailed his season. De Vos became the first Darlington player ever to represent his country when he played for Canada against Iran in Toronto in August 1997. He then went on to play in Canada's World Cup qualifying games before another foot injury ended his domestic season. He had appeared in 52 games for Darlington when in October 1998 he joined Dundee United for a club record fee of £400,000. De Vos appeared in 111 games for the Tannadice club before the Latics paid £500,000 for his services in the summer of 2001.

Shortly after making his Wigan debut he broke two bones in his foot in the Worthington Cup tie against Blackpool and it was the turn of the year before he was back in action. The tall centre-back

Jason De Vos

scored his first goal for the club when coming off the bench in the match against Bristol City, but then missed most of January when playing for Canada in the Gold Cup.

In 2002–03 De Vos and Matt Jackson formed an effective partnership at the heart of the Latics' defence, helping the club win the Second Division Championship. An inspirational captain, he netted a number of vital goals – all scored with a broken bone in his foot! Voted 'Player of the Season' by the Wigan fans, De Vos, who has won 39 caps for Canada, also won a place in the PFA Division Two team.

The Canadian international made a disastrous start to the 2003–04 season when, in the 2–0 defeat at Millwall on the opening day of the campaign, he broke his foot. He was out of action until the end of November and though he returned to help the Latics in their fight to make the First Division play-offs, it now looks as though he could be leaving the club.

Wigan Athletic Playing Record

	League		FA Cup		FL Cup		Others		Total	
	App	Gls	App	Gls	App	Gls	App	Gls	App	Gls
2001–02	19 (1)	5	0	0	1	0	0	0	20 (1)	5
2002–03	43	8	1	0	5	0	0	0	49	8
2003–04	25 (2)	2	1	0	0	0	0	0	26 (2)	2
TOTAL	87 (3)	15	2	0	6	0	0	0	95 (3)	15

DE ZEEUW Adrianus (Arjan) Johannes

Central Defender
Born: Castricum, Holland, 16 April 1970.
Career: Telstar, Holland. November 1995 Barnsley 138 (0) 7. July 1999 WIGAN ATHLETIC 126 (0) 6. July 2002 Portsmouth 35 (3) 1.

Arjan De Zeeuw joined Barnsley from Telstar of Holland for £250,000 in November 1995. The central defender made an immediate impact, winning the Oakwell club's 'Player of the Year' award in his first season at the club. A classy and cultured defender, he helped the Tykes win promotion to the Premier League as runners-up to Bolton Wanderers in 1996–97.

A tall, quick player who can pass, tackle and head with equal skill, his ability to read a situation got the Reds out of a number of tight situations as they struggled to come to terms with top-flight football. Towards the end of the 1997–98 season, he played through the pain barrier after suffering a groin injury in the FA Cup tie against Manchester United. Following Barnsley's relegation he looked to be on his way out of Oakwell but a change of manager brought about a change of heart and he spent another season with the club before joining the Latics in the summer of 1999.

He made his Wigan debut in the 3–0 home win over Scunthorpe United on the opening day of the 1999–2000 season. Over the course of the campaign, his height and strength made him extremely dangerous at set pieces. He collected the 'Away Player of the Year' and the Players' 'Player of the Year' awards along with the runners-up spot in the supporters' 'Player of the Year' voting. In 2000–01, De Zeeuw won both the Players' 'Player of the Year' and the supporters' 'Player of the Year' awards and was selected by his fellow professionals for the Second Division PFA Merit Team. Completing a century of games for the club, he skippered the Latics to a place in the play-offs. The following season the composed defender continued to produce some excellent performances for the Latics and was rewarded when he was again named in the PFA Second Division team. A virtual ever-present, he captained a Wigan side, showing total commitment

Arjan De Zeeuw

Tony Diamond

October 1988. In that game he gave a very pleasing display of speed and determination, showing his grit when he returned to the field after having stitches put in a facial wound. He scored on his home debut four days later and again in a 2–2 draw at Preston North End, but after netting twice in six League outings, he was allowed to rejoin Blackburn Rovers.

In August 1989, Diamond was given a free transfer and joined Blackpool, making just a handful of appearances for the Seasiders before entering non-League football.

with his excellent tackling and positional sense. Not surprisingly he again swept the board at the club's end-of-season awards, but during the summer the Dutchman, who had appeared in 146 games for the Latics, joined Portsmouth.

Forming a solid defensive partnership alongside his colleagues at Fratton Park, he helped Pompey win promotion to the Premiership when they won the First Division Championship.

Wigan Athletic Playing Record

	League		FA Cup		FL Cup		Others		Total	
	App	Gls	App	Gls	App	Gls	App	Gls	App	Gls
1999–2000	39	3	3	0	3	0	3	0	48	3
2000–01	45	1	2	0	4	0	2	0	53	1
2001–02	42	2	1	0	1	0	1	0	45	2
TOTAL	126	6	6	0	8	0	6	0	146	6

DIAMOND Anthony John

Forward
Born: Rochdale, 23 August 1968.
Career: June 1986 Blackburn Rovers 9 (17) 3. October 1988 on loan WIGAN ATHLETIC 6 (0) 2. August 1989 Blackpool 2 (1) 1.

Northern Ireland Under-23 international Tony Diamond began his career with Blackburn Rovers, whom he joined as a YTS player. After working his way up through the ranks he was given his League debut with Rovers but found it difficult to hold down a regular first-team place and later joined Wigan Athletic on loan.

He made his Latics debut in a 2–1 win at Southend United in

Wigan Athletic Playing Record

	League		FA Cup		FL Cup		Others		Total	
	App	Gls	App	Gls	App	Gls	App	Gls	App	Gls
1988–89	6	2	0	0	0	0	0	0	6	2
TOTAL	6	2	0	0	0	0	0	0	6	2

DIAZ Isidro

Right-winger
Born: Valencia, Spain, 15 May 1972.
Career: Balanguer, Spain. July 1995 WIGAN ATHLETIC 57 (19) 16. August 1997 Wolverhampton Wanderers 1 (0) 0. December 1997 WIGAN ATHLETIC 1 (1) 0. August 1998 Rochdale 12 (2) 2.

Signed from Balanguer, Izzy Diaz was one of three Spaniards to arrive at Springfield Park in the summer of 1995. He appeared as a substitute in the opening game of the 1995–96 season at Gillingham before his ability to take on defenders at speed won him a regular spot in the Latics side. The pacy right-sided forward ended his first season with the club as Wigan's leading scorer with 10 goals in 31 League starts. A great crowd-pleaser, he continued to find the back of the net the following season and the first of his two

Izzy Diaz

Cup defeat at Notts County. After two starts in LDV Cup games against Oldham Athletic and Walsall, he was given his first taste of League action against the Saddlers as the Latics played out a 1–1 draw against their promotion rivals.

Dickson eventually signed for the club after a compensation package was agreed with Glentoran. The club's chief executive Brenda Spencer, Director of Football John Benson and Hugh himself, made the trip to the Scottish Football Association to meet officials from the Irish side. As Dickson was a non-contract player with the Belfast outfit before joining the Latics, the Scottish FA were used as arbitrators and decided on a one-off payment to Glentoran followed by payment based on appearances and a 15 percent sell-on clause. Sadly things didn't work out for him and in October 2001 he returned to Ireland to play for Linfield.

Wigan Athletic Playing Record

	League		FA Cup		FL Cup		Others		Total	
	App	Gls	App	Gls	App	Gls	App	Gls	App	Gls
2000–01	0 (1)	0	0 (1)	0	0	0	2	0	2 (2)	0
TOTAL	0 (1)	0	0 (1)	0	0	0	2	0	2 (2)	0

DINNING Tony

Midfield
Born: Wallsend, 12 April 1975.
Career: October 1993 Newcastle United. June 1994 Stockport County 159 (32) 25. September 2000 Wolverhampton Wanderers 35 (0) 6. September 2001 WIGAN ATHLETIC 79 (5) 12. November 2003 on loan Walsall. January 2004 on loan Blackpool.

Unable to make the grade with Newcastle United, Dinning joined Stockport County in the summer of 1994 and soon claimed a regular first-team place. After some impressive displays in the County midfield he broke his leg in a match at Sunderland in March 1998, but won his place back after making a full recovery. In 1998–99 he was called upon to fill a number of roles from right-back to centre-half as well as in midfield. He eventually reverted to his more customary central midfield role in 1999–2000, ending the campaign as the Hatters' leading scorer, and was deservedly voted 'Player of the Year' by the Independent Supporters Club.

Early the following season Dinning, who had scored 30 goals in 227 games for Stockport County, was surprisingly sold to Wolverhampton Wanderers for a fee of £600,000. Although he made his Wolves debut at the heart of the defence, he soon switched to his central midfield role, scoring a number of spectacular goals. Yet in September 2001 he was transferred to Wigan Athletic for £750,000. He set up the opening goal for the Latics on his debut at Bury, a match Wigan won 2–0, and then in the home match with Queen's Park Rangers he scored his first goal for the club. Shortly before the transfer deadline, he was loaned to Stoke City and played his part in securing a place for them in the Second Division play-offs. In 2002–03 Dinning was an important factor in the Latics winning the Second Division Championship. A hardworking player with good anticipation, he was always at the heart of the team's endeavours, turning in several outstanding performances.

goals in the 3–0 win at Carlisle United won him the 'Away Goal of the Season' award as Latics ended the campaign as Third Division champions.

However, at the start of the 1997–98 season he left Wigan to spend a trial period with Wolverhampton Wanderers, but after just one appearance for the Molineux club, he re-signed for the Latics on a short-term contract in December 1997. In his 'second debut' game, a 4–0 win against Brentford, he sadly broke a bone in his foot and at the end of the season he was given a free transfer. After a couple of weeks on trial at Tranmere he joined Rochdale, whose manager Graham Barrow was in charge of Wigan when Diaz joined the Latics. Following a bright start at Spotland he faded from the scene and in December 1998 he was allowed to return home to Spain.

Wigan Athletic Playing Record

	League		FA Cup		FL Cup		Others		Total	
	App	Gls	App	Gls	App	Gls	App	Gls	App	Gls
1995–96	31 (6)	10	4	2	2	0	3	0	40 (6)	12
1996–97	26 (13)	6	0 (1)	0	0 (1)	0	0	0	26 (15)	6
1997–98	1 (1)	0	0	0	0	0	0	0	1 (1)	0
TOTAL	58 (20)	16	4 (1)	2	2 (1)	0	3	0	67 (22)	18

DICKSON Hugh Robinson

Defender
Born: Downpatrick, 28 August 1981.
Career: Glentoran. August 2000 WIGAN ATHLETIC 0 (1) 0. Linfield.

The cousin of Preston's David Healy, Hugh Dickson joined the Latics on trial from Glentoran at the start of the 2000–01 season. After impressing, the young central defender made his first-team debut as a substitute for Scott Green in a 2–1 second-round FA

Wigan Athletic Playing Record

	League		FA Cup		FL Cup		Others		Total	
	App	Gls	App	Gls	App	Gls	App	Gls	App	Gls
2001–02	32 (1)	5	1	0	0	0	0	0	33 (1)	5
2002–03	36 (2)	7	2	0	4	0	0	0	42 (2)	7
2003–04	11 (2)	0	0	0	1	0	0	0	12 (2)	0
TOTAL	79 (5)	12	3	0	5	0	0	0	87 (5)	12

DOOLAN John

Right-Back/Midfield
Born: Liverpool, 10 November 1968.
Career: Knowsley United. March 1992 WIGAN ATHLETIC 29 (9) 1.

Versatile performer John Doolan joined the Latics from Knowsley United in March 1992 and made his League debut the following month in a 3–0 home win over Birmingham City. After starting the 1992–93 season as a first-team regular, Doolan, who could play at full-back or in midfield, began to be plagued by injuries and missed most of Wigan's matches over the next two seasons.

He returned to League action in January 1995 and in the match at Colchester United he scored the only goal of the game and, as it transpired, his only goal for the club. After a series of impressive displays in the club's pre 1995–96 season matches, Doolan began the campaign in the No.10 shirt, one of eight different outfield positions he had occupied in his time with Wigan, but sadly he was again troubled by injuries and at the end of the season he was released.

John Doolan

Wigan Athletic Playing Record

	League		FA Cup		FL Cup		Others		Total	
	App	Gls	App	Gls	App	Gls	App	Gls	App	Gls
1991–92	2	0	0	0	0	0	0	0	2	0
1992–93	16 (1)	0	0	0	4	0	1	0	21 (1)	0
1993–94	0	0	0	0	0	0	0	0	0	0
1994–95	9 (7)	1	0	0	0	0	1	0	10 (7)	1
1995–96	2 (1)	0	0	0	1	0	0	0	3 (1)	0
TOTAL	29 (2)	1	0	0	5	0	2	0	36 (9)	1

DUFFY Christopher John

Left-Back/Winger
Born: Eccles, 31 October 1973.
Career: June 1992 Crewe Alexandra. July 1993 WIGAN ATHLETIC 15 (16) 1. February 1995 Northwich Victoria. July 1998 Canvey Island.

A fast, attacking winger, Chris Duffy began his career with Crewe Alexandra but on being unable to break into the Railwaymen's League side, he left Gresty Road in the summer of 1993 to join Wigan Athletic on a free transfer.

Chris Duffy

Latics manager Kenny Swain gave Duffy his League debut at left-back in a 2–0 home defeat at the hands of Scunthorpe United on the opening day of the 1993–94 season. The versatile player appeared in six different numbered shirts that season, scoring his first goal for the club in a 3–2 win at Mansfield Town in January 1994. The following season his first-team appearances were restricted to five as a substitute and after a loan spell with Vauxhall Conference side Northwich Victoria, he joined the Cheshire club on a permanent basis in February 1995. On leaving Northwich he joined Canvey Island and appeared for them in the FA Trophy Final against Forest Green.

Wigan Athletic Playing Record

	League		FA Cup		FL Cup		Others		Total	
	App	Gls	App	Gls	App	Gls	App	Gls	App	Gls
1993–94	15 (12)	1	2	1	1	0	1 (1)	0	19 (13)	2
1994–95	0 (4)	0	0	0	0 (1)	0	0	0	0 (5)	0
TOTAL	15 (16)	1	2	1	1 (1)	0	1 (1)	0	19 (18)	2

EADEN Nicholas Jeremy

Right-Back
Born: Sheffield, 12 December 1972.
Career: June 1991 Barnsley 281 (12) 10. July 2000 Birmingham City 68 (6) 3. September 2002 WIGAN ATHLETIC 83 (0) 0.

Nicky Eaden worked his way up through the ranks at Barnsley before establishing himself as a regular at right-back in the Oakwell club's side. With his assured passing and crossing he was an important member of the Barnsley side that won promotion to the Premiership in 1996–97, his form also earning him selection for the PFA divisional team. He certainly didn't look out of place in the top flight and can look back with some pride at his part in trying to keep the Tykes in the Premiership. He then skippered the side on a number of occasions and took his tally of games, in which he scored 13 goals, to 337 before being out of contract, when he joined Birmingham City in the summer of 2000.

A near ever-present for the Blues in 2000–01, he was very much an unsung hero for the St Andrew's club. He made the starting line-up for the Worthington Cup Final against Liverpool when City lost out so narrowly in a penalty shoot-out. He continued to play for the Blues both at right-back and in midfield but he found his first-team chances limited and in September 2002, after appearing in 90 games, he joined the Latics.

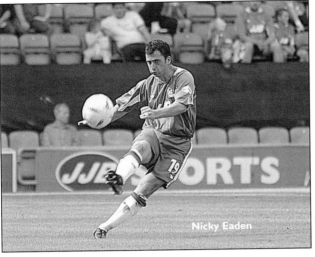
Nicky Eaden

After making his Wigan debut in a 2–2 home draw against Peterborough United, Eaden was an ever-present during the remainder of the season. He worked the flank unselfishly and delivered a string of accurate crosses, very rarely wasting a ball. He was vital in the club's success in winning the Second Division Championship – a campaign in which he made his 400th League appearance against Brentford – and won deserved recognition with selection in the PFA Division Two team. One of the best full-backs in the First Division, the Sheffield-born defender was an ever-present as Latics just missed out on a play-off spot.

Wigan Athletic Playing Record

	League		FA Cup		FL Cup		Others		Total	
	App	Gls	App	Gls	App	Gls	App	Gls	App	Gls
2002–03	37	0	3	0	4	0	1	0	45	0
2003–04	46	0	1	0	3	0	0	0	50	0
TOTAL	83	0	4	0	7	0	1	0	95	0

EDWARDSON Barry John

Midfield
Born: Hindley, 4 November 1972.
Career: July 1991 WIGAN ATHLETIC 0 (1) 0.

Barry Edwardson

Hindley-born midfielder Barry Edwardson joined the Latics on a Youth Training Scheme at the start of the 1991–92 season and after a series of impressive displays in the club's reserve side, he made his Football League debut as a substitute for Bryan Griffiths in an exciting 3–3 draw at Birmingham City. Despite not letting the side down, he didn't appear again and after being released at the end of the season, drifted into non-League football.

Wigan Athletic Playing Record

	League		FA Cup		FL Cup		Others		Total	
	App	Gls	App	Gls	App	Gls	App	Gls	App	Gls
1991–92	0 (1)	0	0	0	0	0	0	0	0 (1)	0
TOTAL	0 (1)	0	0	0	0	0	0	0	0 (1)	0

ELLINGTON Nathan Levi Fontaine

Forward
Born: Bradford, 2 July 1981.
Career: Walton and Hersham. February 1999 Bristol Rovers 76 (40) 35. March 2002 WIGAN ATHLETIC 87 (2) 35.

Nicknamed 'the Duke', Nathan Ellington joined Bristol Rovers from non-League Walton and Hersham in February 1999, despite interest shown by Arsenal and West Ham United. He immediately made an impression with his pace and close control and was given his League debut against Gillingham at the end of that month. Though most of his early appearances for the Pirates were as a substitute, he continued to demonstrate his ability to put the ball

Nathan Ellington

in the net. Following the departure of Jason Roberts to West Bromwich Albion, Ellington became Rovers' main striker and ended the 2000–01 season as the club's leading scorer with 18 goals in all competitions. The following season he netted a superb hat-trick that knocked Derby County out of the FA Cup at Pride Park, and added further trebles against Leyton Orient and Swansea City.

It came as no real surprise when, after scoring 44 goals in 137 games – almost half his appearances being as a substitute – he became Wigan Athletic's first million-pound signing on transfer deadline day in March 2002. He scored on his debut in a 2–1 win at Chesterfield and in his first game at the JJB Stadium as

Northampton Town were beaten 3–0. In 2002–03, he was the Latics' leading scorer in all competitions with 22 goals as the club raced to the Second Division title. One of the highlights of the season was Ellington's memorable hat-trick in the Worthington Cup tie against Premiership West Bromwich Albion. A forward with lightning pace, he was a crucial factor in the Latics' success, despite playing over half a season with a damaged shoulder.

Ellington was Wigan's leading scorer again in 2003–04, his total of 19 goals including braces in the 5–0 rout of Crystal Palace and the 4–2 win over local rivals Preston North End. Having formed a prolific strike partnership with Jason Roberts, Latics fans will be hoping the twin strike force can lead the club into the Premiership next season.

Wigan Athletic Playing Record

	League		FA Cup		FL Cup		Others		Total	
	App	Gls	App	Gls	App	Gls	App	Gls	App	Gls
2001–02	3	2	0	0	0	0	0	0	3	2
2002–03	41 (1)	15	2 (1)	2	5	5	0 (1)	0	48 (3)	22
2003–04	43 (1)	18	1	0	1 (1)	1	0	0	45 (2)	19
TOTAL	87 (2)	35	3 (1)	2	6 (1)	6	0 (1)	0	96 (5)	43

ENTWISTLE Wayne Peter

Forward

Born: Bury, 6 August 1958.

Career: August 1976 Bury 25 (6) 7. November 1977 Sunderland 43 (2) 13. October 1979 Leeds United 7 (4) 2. November 1980 Blackpool 27 (5) 6. March 1982 Crewe Alexandra 11 (0) 0. July 1982 Wimbledon 4 (5) 3. Grays Athletic. August 1983 Bury 80 (3) 32. June 1985 Carlisle United 8 (1) 2. October 1985 Bolton Wanderers 5 (3) 0. August 1986 on loan Burnley 6 (2) 2. October 1986 Stockport County 38 (11) 8. August 1988 Bury 0 (2) 0. October 1988 WIGAN ATHLETIC 24 (5) 6. Altrincham. September 1989 Hartlepool United 2 (0) 0.

An England youth international, Wayne Entwistle began his career with his home-town club Bury before embarking upon a varied

Wayne Entwistle

career with numerous clubs in all divisions of the Football League. He joined Sunderland in November 1977 before Jimmy Adamson signed him for Leeds United. After just a year in the top flight with the Elland Road club, he was released on a free transfer and joined Blackpool. Only a short time later he was at the very bottom of the Fourth Division with Crewe Alexandra.

After his return to Bury in 1983, Entwistle helped the Shakers win promotion to the Third Division in 1984–85 before moving on again, this time to Carlisle United. He then had spells with Bolton Wanderers, Burnley, Stockport County and Bury again before joining Wigan Athletic in October 1988. After making his debut in a 2–1 defeat at Sheffield United, he scored in his first game at Springfield Park as the Latics drew 1–1 against one of his former clubs, Bolton Wanderers. He went on to score seven goals in 33 League and Cup games before moving to his final senior club, Hartlepool United, the 14th stop on his tour around the Football League.

Wigan Athletic Playing Record

	League		FA Cup		FL Cup		Others		Total	
	App	Gls	App	Gls	App	Gls	App	Gls	App	Gls
1988–89	24 (5)	6	1	0	0	0	3	1	28 (5)	7
TOTAL	24 (5)	6	1	0	0	0	3	1	28 (5)	7

EVANS Andrew Clive

Winger/Full-Back

Born: Heswall, 1 May 1957.

Career: May 1975 Tranmere Rovers 175 (3) 27. July 1981 WIGAN ATHLETIC 29 (3) 2. August 1982 Crewe Alexandra 26 (2) 7. August 1983 Stockport County 158 (2) 23. September 1987 Lincoln City 42 (0) 2.

Clive Evans began his League career with Tranmere Rovers after joining the club as an apprentice. He made his debut for the Wirral club in a 2–1 home win over Northampton Town in May 1977, after which he missed very few games over the next four seasons. In fact Evans, who was ever-present in seasons 1977–78 and 1978–79, played in 131 consecutive League games during that period. In 1978–79 he was the club's leading scorer with 11 goals as they were relegated to the Fourth Division. The defensive midfield player had scored 30 goals in 200 games when he was transferred to Wigan Athletic in the summer of 1981.

Evans scored twice on his Latics debut as they drew 3–3 at Bradford City on the opening day of the 1981–82 season, and although he netted in the 4–2 League Cup defeat of Chelsea, they were to be his only League goals for the club. At the end of the season, Evans moved on to Crewe Alexandra but again spent just one season with the Railwaymen before signing for Stockport County.

He spent four full seasons at Edgeley Park, playing on either side of midfield or at full-back, and was outstanding during the club's relegation-haunted season of 1986–87, helping County to safety. In September 1987 he joined Lincoln City, where he played an important role in helping the Imps regain their Football League status. After Lincoln's first season back in Division Four, Evans left League football, having given total commitment to each of his five clubs.

Wigan Athletic Playing Record

	League		FA Cup		FL Cup		Others		Total	
	App	Gls	App	Gls	App	Gls	App	Gls	App	Gls
1981–82	29 (3)	2	1	0	6	1	0	0	36 (3)	3
TOTAL	29 (3)	2	1	0	6	1	0	0	36 (3)	3

FAIRCLOUGH David

Forward

Born: Liverpool, 5 January 1957.

Career: January 1974 Liverpool 64 (34) 34. Toronto Blizzard, Canada. Lucerne, Switzerland. March 1985 Norwich City 1 (1) 0. August 1985 Oldham Athletic 6 (11) 1. Beveren, Belgium. August 1989 Tranmere Rovers 3 (11) 1. August 1990 WIGAN ATHLETIC 4 (3) 1.

Better known as Liverpool's 'Super Sub', David Fairclough played a major role in the Reds' assault on Europe. His greatest moment came against St Etienne in the 1977 quarter-final of the European Cup when he came on as a substitute late in the second-half at Anfield to fire Liverpool into the semi-final. He was used to considerable effect by Liverpool, pulling off his track suit to appear for the last quarter-of-an-hour or so of a game. And on countless occasions it proved successful, as he either scored or laid on a winning goal. Quick and dangerous, he was prepared to run at defences and carry the ball into the penalty area. Yet despite his many attributes, he really only had one season as a Liverpool regular. In most of his seven playing years at Anfield he appeared only occasionally, with half of his games as substitute.

On leaving the Reds, having scored 62 goals in 150 games, he went to Canada to play for Toronto Blizzard before playing for Swiss club Lucerne. On his return to England he turned out for Norwich City and Oldham Athletic before joining Belgian club Beveren SK. In August 1989 he joined Tranmere Rovers but after

David Fairclough

one season at Prenton Park, in which he failed to establish himself as a first-team regular, he joined Wigan Athletic.

He made his debut in a 2–0 home defeat at the hands of Mansfield Town on the opening day of the 1990–91 season. Injuries restricted his appearances but he did get on the scoresheet in the 2–0 win over Grimsby Town midway through the season. He is now a freelance journalist, having successfully completed a course for the National Council for Training Journalists during his playing days.

Wigan Athletic Playing Record

	League		FA Cup		FL Cup		Others		Total	
	App	Gls	App	Gls	App	Gls	App	Gls	App	Gls
1990–91	4 (3)	1	2	0	1	0	0	0	7 (3)	1
TOTAL	4 (3)	1	2	0	1	0	0	0	7 (3)	1

FALLON Shaun

Left-Back

Born: Widnes, 10 September 1970.

Career: July 1989 WIGAN ATHLETIC 2 (1) 0.

Left-back Shaun Fallon joined the Latics as an apprentice and after working his way up through the ranks, made his Football League debut in the No.8 shirt on the final day of the 1988–89 season as Wigan drew 1–1 with Wolverhampton Wanderers. After turning professional during the close season, he appeared in the match against Rotherham United – the club's first home game of 1989–90 – but after just one more appearance as a substitute, he was released.

Wigan Athletic Playing Record

	League		FA Cup		FL Cup		Others		Total	
	App	Gls	App	Gls	App	Gls	App	Gls	App	Gls
1988–89	1	0	0	0	0	0	0	0	1	0
1989–90	1 (1)	0	0	0	0	0	0	0	1 (1)	0
TOTAL	2 (1)	0	0	0	0	0	0	0	2 (1)	0

FARNWORTH Simon

Goalkeeper

Born: Chorley, 28 October 1963.

Career: September 1981 Bolton Wanderers 113 (0) 0. September 1986 on loan Stockport County 10 (0) 0. January 1987 on loan Tranmere Rovers 7 (0) 0. March 1987 Bury 105 (0) 0. June 1990 Preston North End 81 (0) 0. July 1993 WIGAN ATHLETIC 126 (0) 0.

Goalkeeper Simon Farnworth was originally on the books of Manchester United, during which time he was capped by England Schools. When the Reds did not take up their option, Bolton Wanderers stepped in and, under the watchful eye of former Trotters' 'keeper Charlie Wright, he made good progress. After the departure of Jim McDonagh and Bolton's relegation to the Third Division, Farnworth made his League debut in a 2–0 win over Wimbledon on the opening day of the 1983–84 season. The following term he became an ever-present, ousting the more experienced John Platt and later appearing for the Wanderers in the 1986 Freight Rover Trophy Final at Wembley. After losing confidence and his place in the side to Dave Felgate, he enjoyed spells on loan with Stockport County and Tranmere Rovers before joining Bury.

Highly popular with the Shakers' fans, he had appeared in 124 games for the Gigg Lane club when, in the summer of 1990, he moved to Preston North End. He missed few games in three years

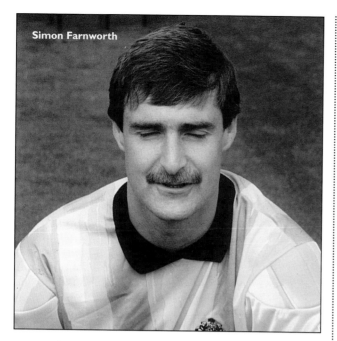

Simon Farnworth

at Deepdale before his move to Wigan in the summer of 1993. Farnworth made his Latics' debut in a 2–0 defeat against Scunthorpe United at the start of the 1993–94 season. A virtual ever-present during his time at Springfield Park, the experienced 'keeper celebrated his 100th consecutive first-team appearance for the club at Walsall in April 1995. His consistent performances were rewarded with the offer of a new contract and, after another good campaign between the posts, he was appointed the club's physiotherapist.

Wigan Athletic Playing Record

	League		FA Cup		FL Cup		Others		Total	
	App	Gls	App	Gls	App	Gls	App	Gls	App	Gls
1993–94	42	0	4	0	2	0	2	0	50	0
1994–95	41	0	2	0	4	0	4	0	51	0
1995–96	43	0	4	0	0	0	3	0	50	0
TOTAL	126	0	10	0	6	0	9	0	151	0

FARRELL Andrew James

Winger/Defender
Born: Colchester, 7 October 1965.
Career: September 1983 Colchester United 98 (7) 6. August 1987 Burnley 237 (20) 19. September 1994 WIGAN ATHLETIC 51 (4) 1. July 1996 Rochdale 113 (5) 6. June 1999 Morecambe.

After trials at Ipswich Town, Andy Farrell joined his home-town club Colchester United, becoming a professional in 1983. He made his League debut in September of that year and in four years at Layer Road, operated in either defence or midfield. After Colchester lost out in the play-offs of 1987 to Wolves, Burnley manager Brian Miller paid just £5,000 to bring the versatile player to Turf Moor.

At the end of his first season with the Clarets, Farrell was in the Burnley team that played at Wembley for the first time in 26 years, losing 2–0 to Wolves in the Sherpa Van Trophy Final. After reaching the play-offs in 1990–91, only to lose to Torquay United, Burnley won the Fourth Division Championship the following season. It was probably Farrell's most impressive campaign in a Burnley shirt, though he did give an immaculate performance as an early substitute for the injured John Francis in the Wembley play-off victory over Stockport County in 1994. He had scored 25 goals in 349 games for Burnley when in September 1994 he joined Wigan Athletic for £10,000.

He made his Latics debut in a 3–1 defeat at Scunthorpe United and over the rest of the campaign, never let the side down whether he was playing in defence or midfield. In his second season at Springfield Park, he found his first-team opportunities restricted by the strength of competition at the club. However, he did manage to score his first League goal for the Latics against Plymouth Argyle, but in July 1996 he left to play for Rochdale, who were then managed by former Wigan favourite Graham Barrow.

Andy Farrell

The veteran utility man was the club's regular centre-half before figuring in various midfield roles, at left-back and even wearing the No.9 shirt for a spell. Released in the summer of 1999, he went to play non-League football for Morecambe before joining Leigh RMI to be in charge of the academy.

Wigan Athletic Playing Record

	League		FA Cup		FL Cup		Others		Total	
	App	Gls	App	Gls	App	Gls	App	Gls	App	Gls
1994–95	30 (1)	0	2	0	1	0	4	1	37 (1)	1
1995–96	21 (3)	1	2 (1)	0	2	0	1	0	26 (4)	1
TOTAL	51 (4)	1	4 (1)	0	3	0	5	1	63 (5)	2

FARRELLY Gareth

Midfield
Born: Dublin, 28 August 1975.
Career: Home Farm. January 1992 Aston Villa 2 (6) 0. March 1995 on loan Rotherham United 9 (1) 2. July 1997 Everton 18 (9) 1. November 1999 Bolton Wanderers 61 (17) 5. March 2003 on loan Rotherham United 6 (0) 0. September 2003 on loan Burnley. November 2003 on loan Bradford City. March 2004 on loan WIGAN ATHLETIC 3 (4) 0.

Republic of Ireland international Gareth Farrelly has had to overcome serious injury to reach the dizzy heights of international football. A former Home Farm player, he was taken to Aston Villa by Ron Atkinson but spent a year and a half on the sidelines with a serious back injury. Farrelly recovered and made his League debut for the Villans against Liverpool in March 1996 and a couple of months later won the first of six caps against Portugal. Unable to win a regular place in the Villa side, Farrelly joined Everton in the summer of 1997 after the Merseyside club had paid £700,000 for his services.

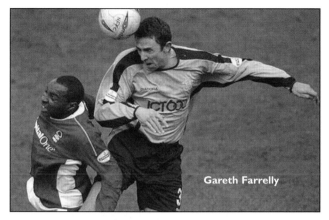

Gareth Farrelly

He scored the goal that secured the Blues' Premiership safety in the last match of the 1997–98 season against Coventry, yet he figured in only 13 minutes of an intensely frustrating 1998–99 campaign as a knee injury, which later required surgery, hampered his progress.

In November 1999, Farrelly was allowed to leave Goodison Park and join Bolton Wanderers on a free transfer, scoring on his debut at Sheffield United with only his second touch of the ball! In 2000–01, Farrelly had an outstanding season, showing the ability and vision to pick out the right pass almost every time. He capped a fine campaign by netting the vital first goal in the play-off final against Preston. Then following a catalogue of injuries and severe competition for midfield places, his first team appearances were restricted and he was loaned out to Rotherham United.

Having spent most of the 2003–04 season on loan at Burnley and Bradford City, he signed a permanent deal in March 2004 that would keep him at the JJB Stadium until the end of the season, this after his contract at the Reebok was cancelled by mutual consent. He made his debut in a goalless draw against Bradford City but then didn't feature in the starting line-up until the club's final two games of the season. Unable to make much of an impression, he has not been offered terms for the forthcoming season.

Wigan Athletic Playing Record

	League		FA Cup		FL Cup		Others		Total	
	App	Gls	App	Gls	App	Gls	App	Gls	App	Gls
2003–04	3 (4)	0	0	0	0	0	0	0	3 (4)	0
TOTAL	3 (4)	0	0	0	0	0	0	0	3 (4)	0

FELGATE David Wynne

Goalkeeper
Born: Blaenau Ffestiniog, 4 March 1960.
Career: August 1978 Bolton Wanderers. October 1978 on loan Rochdale 35 (0) 0. September 1979 on loan Crewe Alexandra 14 (0) 0. March 1980 on loan Rochdale 12 (0) 0. September 1980 Lincoln City 198 (0) 0. November 1984 on loan Cardiff City 4 (0) 0. February 1985 Grimsby Town 36 (0) 0. February 1986 on loan Bolton Wanderers 15 (0) 0. February 1987 Bolton Wanderers 223 (0) 0. October 1993 Chester City 71 (1) 0. July 1995 WIGAN ATHLETIC 3 (0) 0.

A former Welsh schoolboys international goalkeeper, Dave Felgate served his apprenticeship at Burnden Park before turning professional with Bolton Wanderers in August 1978. He was loaned out to gain League experience with both Rochdale and Crewe Alexandra but still couldn't force his way into the Bolton line-up. In September 1980 Lincoln City paid £25,000 for him and it was while at Sincil Bank that he won his only full Welsh cap, coming on as a substitute for Neville Southall in a 5–0 win over Romania in 1984. After a brief loan spell with Cardiff City, he joined Grimsby Town but was unable to settle at Blundell Park and in February 1986 he returned to Bolton on loan.

He helped the Wanderers reach the Freight Rover Trophy Final but had to miss out on a Wembley appearance as his loan period had expired! Eventually he joined Bolton on a permanent basis and was ever-present as the Wanderers won promotion back to the Third Division and also won the club's 'Player of the Year' award. In 1989 he helped Bolton win the final of the Sherpa Van Trophy, but after losing his place to Keith Branagan, he joined Bury. After only a month at Bury he moved to Wolves but his next League appearance came with Chester. He helped them to runners-up spot in the Third Division in 1993–94 but couldn't prevent their relegation a year later.

In August 1995 he joined Wigan Athletic, making his debut in a 2–1 defeat at Gillingham on the opening day of the 1995–96 season. He remained at Springfield Park for the rest of the campaign, understudying another former Bolton 'keeper Simon Farnworth. He later signed for Unibond League side Leigh RMI and, after appearing regularly in their promotion-winning side, continued to feature between the posts as the club entered the Nationwide Conference.

Wigan Athletic Playing Record

	League		FA Cup		FL Cup		Others		Total	
	App	Gls	App	Gls	App	Gls	App	Gls	App	Gls
1995–96	3	0	0	0	2	0	0	0	5	0
TOTAL	3	0	0	0	2	0	0	0	5	0

FILAN John Richard

Goalkeeper
Born: Sydney, Australia, 8 February 1970.
Career: Budapest St George, Australia. March 1993 Cambridge United 68 (0) 0. March 1995 Coventry City 15 (1) 0. July 1997 Blackburn Rovers 61 (1) 0. December 2001 WIGAN ATHLETIC 116 (0) 0.

The Australian international goalkeeper began his Football League career with Cambridge United after joining them from Budapest St George in March 1993. His displays for the U's led to a number of top clubs vying for his signature and two years after making his Cambridge debut, he joined Premiership Coventry City for £300,000. Signed primarily as an understudy to Steve Ogrizovic, he appeared in 18 games in his two-and-a-half years at Highfield Road before Blackburn Rovers paid £700,000 for his services in the summer of 1997.

Replacing the injured Tim Flowers, he was a revelation, going 234 minutes before conceding his first goal, which ranked him third in the club's all-time list of debutant goalkeepers. Unfortunately, two games later he received an horrendous injury in the match against Sheffield United – a broken forearm muscle, ligament damage and a cut down to the bone that was expected to keep him out for the season, but the club were so desperate that he was rushed back into action. With Flowers suspended, Filan started the 1998–99 campaign in Rovers' first team. He was little short of brilliant, with his best display coming against Arsenal at Highbury when he saved two penalties! Following the signing of Alan Kelly, he found himself in and out of the Rovers' side before a shoulder injury kept him out of action for the second half of the 1999–2000 season. Midway through the following season, Souness brought in Brad Friedel and Filan subsequently only featured as cover for injuries before joining Wigan for £450,000 in December 2001.

John Filan

After making his debut against Oldham Athletic, he celebrated his second appearance by saving a penalty against Reading. An outstanding shot stopper with good reflexes, he collected the Latics' 'Player of the Year' award. In 2002–03, the experienced 'keeper was ever-present – well protected by a back four, he went over 750 minutes without conceding a goal and again collected the club's players' 'Player of the Year' award, while also being honoured by his fellow professionals with a place in the PFA Second Division team for the season.

Filan had an outstanding season in 2003–04 and deservedly won the club's 'Player of the Year' award. Having played in 109 consecutive League games from his debut, the sequence was spoiled when, after being sent off in the game against West Bromwich Albion, he was suspended for one game.

Wigan Athletic Playing Record

	League		FA Cup		FL Cup		Others		Total	
	App	Gls	App	Gls	App	Gls	App	Gls	App	Gls
2001–02	25	0	0	0	0	0	0	0	25	0
2002–03	46	0	3	0	5	0	1	0	55	0
2003–04	45	0	1	0	1	0	0	0	47	0
TOTAL	116	0	4	0	6	0	1	0	127	0

FITZHENRY Neil

Central Defender
Born: Wigan, 24 September 1978.
Career: July 1997 WIGAN ATHLETIC 2 (2) 0. May 1999 Chester City. Shamrock Rovers.

Neil Fitzhenry

Old style centre-back Neil Fitzhenry made his Wigan Athletic debut as a substitute for Graham Lancashire in a 1–0 defeat at Bournemouth in the opening away game of the 1997–98 season. After making his first start in a 3–0 home defeat at the hands of Bristol City, a cartilage operation forced him to miss the rest of the campaign.

A former 'Young Player of the Year', his second season at Springfield Park was also dogged by injuries and his only start came in the home derby match against Preston North End which ended all-square at 2–2. Sadly, a recurrence of the knee problem saw him last only 12 minutes, thus forcing him to miss the rest of the Latics' season. Given a free transfer, he joined Chester City but is now playing Irish League football for Shamrock Rovers.

Wigan Athletic Playing Record

	League		FA Cup		FL Cup		Others		Total	
	App	Gls	App	Gls	App	Gls	App	Gls	App	Gls
1997–98	1 (2)	0	0	0	0	0	1	0	2 (2)	0
1998–99	1	0	0	0	0	0	0	0	1	0
TOTAL	2 (2)	0	0	0	0	0	1	0	3 (2)	0

FLYNN Michael John

Midfield
Born: Newport, 17 October 1980.
Career: Newport County. Barry Town. June 2002 WIGAN ATHLETIC 4 (21) 1.

The Newport-born midfielder began his career with his home-town club before joining Welsh League side Barry Town. His performances in the centre of midfield led to a number of clubs showing an interest in him, but it was Latics boss Paul Jewell who secured his signature when he paid £50,000 for his services in the summer of 2002. While with Barry Town, Flynn had won semi-professional honours for Wales.

Used mainly as a substitute during Wigan's Second Division Championship-winning season, he made his first League start in the 2–0 away win at Notts County. Always looking to get forward, he scored his first League goal for the Latics at Bloomfield Road, sealing a 2–0 victory, and then was on target again as Wigan beat Luton Town in a second-round FA Cup match.

Following a foot injury, Flynn only made one League start in 2003–04, but the versatile player remains an important member of the Latics squad and the club have offered him a new contract.

Wigan Athletic Playing Record

	League		FA Cup		FL Cup		Others		Total	
	App	Gls	App	Gls	App	Gls	App	Gls	App	Gls
2002–03	3 (14)	1	0 (2)	1	0 (3)	0	2	0	5 (19)	2
2003–04	1 (7)	0	0	0	0 (1)	0	0	0	1 (8)	0
TOTAL	4 (21)	1	0 (2)	1	0 (4)	0	2	0	6 (27)	2

FRETWELL David

Central Defender
Born: Wakefield, 18 February 1952.
Career: July 1970 Bradford City 247 (6) 5. California Sunshine, United States. October 1978 WIGAN ATHLETIC 111 (1) 0. June 1981 Northwich Victoria.

Though he joined Bradford City as an associate schoolboy, Dave Fretwell decided to stay on at school to take his 'A' levels. While at school he represented Yorkshire and England Senior Schools at the Under-18s level. Although offered the opportunity to sign full-time for Bradford City, he decided to go to Bradford University to study Industrial Management. During his last two years at University, Fretwell was a part-time professional, playing almost 100 games in the Fourth Division before eventually going full-time in 1974. In January of that year he scored one of the quickest-ever own goals when, after 20 seconds of the fourth-round FA Cup tie at Luton, he put the ball past a startled Peter Downsborough.

After appearing in 280 League and Cup games for the Bantams, he played briefly for California Sunshine in the NASL before joining Wigan Athletic in October 1978 for their first season in the Football League. He had provisionally agreed to join Colchester United on his return to these shores but his plans were upset when 'the Sunshine' reached the play-offs and he was four weeks late returning home.

He made his Wigan debut in a 1–1 draw at Huddersfield Town, going on to appear in 33 games as the club finished sixth in the Fourth Division. His value to the club in that first season cannot be underestimated as he brought composure and defensive know-how to a Wigan side finding it hard at that time to adapt to League football. Runner-up in the club's 'Player of the Year' awards, he was ever-present in 1979–80 when the club again finished sixth before leaving to play non-League football for Northwich Victoria, for whom he won both winners' and losers' medals in the FA Trophy.

Wigan Athletic Playing Record

	League		FA Cup		FL Cup		Others		Total	
	App	Gls	App	Gls	App	Gls	App	Gls	App	Gls
1978–79	33	0	2	0	0	0	0	0	35	0
1979–80	46	0	6	0	2	0	0	0	54	0
1980–81	32 (1)	0	2	0	4	0	0	0	38 (1)	0
TOTAL	111 (1)	0	10	0	6	0	0	0	127 (1)	0

FURLONG Carl David

Forward
Born: Liverpool, 18 October 1976.
Career: July 1995 WIGAN ATHLETIC 1 (2) 1. Runcorn.

Trainee Carl Furlong scored on his Football League debut for the Latics in a 4–1 defeat at Scarborough in March 1994. However, despite this impressive start, his progress was hampered by a series of niggling injuries and over the next two seasons, his few

Carl Furlong

appearances were as a substitute. A forward with terrific pace and goalscoring awareness, he looked to have a promising future in the game but at the end of the 1994–95 season, he was surprisingly released and allowed to join Runcorn.

Wigan Athletic Playing Record

	League		FA Cup		FL Cup		Others		Total	
	App	Gls	App	Gls	App	Gls	App	Gls	App	Gls
1993–94	1 (1)	1	0 (1)	0	0	0	0	0	1 (2)	1
1994–95	0 (1)	0	0	0	0	0	0	0	0 (1)	0
TOTAL	1 (2)	1	0 (1)	0	0	0	0	0	1 (3)	1

GARDNER Paul Anthony

Right-Back
Born: Southport, 22 September 1957.
Career: September 1975 Blackpool 149 (3) 1. August 1982 Bury 90 (0) 0. October 1984 Swansea City 4 (0) 0. January 1985 WIGAN ATHLETIC 5 (0) 0.

Full-back Paul Gardner began his Football League career with Blackpool after turning professional with the Bloomfield Road club in the summer of 1975. His impressive displays in the club's Central League side didn't go unnoticed and in September 1976 he made his debut for the Seasiders in a 1–0 home defeat by Chelsea. He went on to play in 22 games that season as Blackpool just missed out on promotion to the top flight. In the following season Gardner was the club's first-choice right-back as they were relegated to the Third Division for the first time in their history. Worse was to follow three seasons later as Blackpool were relegated to the League's basement. Gardner's only League goal came during that relegation season as the Seasiders were beaten 4–2 by Sheffield United.

Gardner joined Bury in the summer of 1982 and was probably the Shakers' most consistent player in the two seasons he spent at Gigg Lane. Brief spells with Swansea City and Preston North End, where he failed to make a first-team appearance, were followed by him joining Wigan Athletic in January 1985. He made his debut the following month as the Latics lost 2–0 at York City. Gardner's five-match spell at Springfield Park came in the middle of a dismal 12–match run without a victory, though in his last game for the club they came close in a 3–3 draw with Cambridge United.

Wigan Athletic Playing Record

	League		FA Cup		FL Cup		Others		Total	
	App	Gls	App	Gls	App	Gls	App	Gls	App	Gls
1984–85	5	0	0	0	0	0	0	0	5	0
TOTAL	5	0	0	0	0	0	0	0	5	0

GARNETT Shaun Maurice

Central Defender
Born: Wallasey, 22 November 1969.
Career: June 1988 Tranmere Rovers 110 (2) 5. October 1992 on loan Chester City 9 (0) 0. December 1992 on loan Preston North End 10 (0) 2. February 1993 on loan WIGAN ATHLETIC 13 (0) 1. March 1996 Swansea City 15 (0) 0. September 1996 Oldham Athletic 165 (8) 9. October 2002 Halifax Town.

Central defender Shaun Garnett worked his way up through Tranmere Rovers' ranks before making his League debut as a substitute in a 3–0 win at Newport County in April 1988. Though he didn't play at all the following season and only made nine appearances in 1989–90, Garnett won a regular place towards the end of the 1990–91 campaign, appearing in the play-off final win over Bolton Wanderers. After loan spells with Chester City and Preston North End, Garnett arrived on loan at Springfield Park in February 1993, making his debut for the Latics in a 2–1 home defeat by Brighton and Hove Albion. Not on the winning side in his first six games for the club, he decided to do something about it and scored the Latics' first goal in a 2–1 win at Leyton Orient. However, after the Latics had suffered two heavy defeats at the hands of Port Vale (home 0–4) and West Bromwich Albion (away 1–5), Garnett returned to Prenton Park.

Shaun Garnett

In March 1996, having appeared in 146 games for the Wirral-based club, he joined Swansea City for a fee of £200,000. He struggled to find his form at the Vetch Field and after just six months he moved to Oldham Athletic for £150,000. A huge favourite at Boundary Park, he was totally committed to Oldham's cause until he fell out of favour with new boss Mick Wadsworth and was transfer listed. He then suffered cruciate ligament damage that ruled him out for the whole of the 2001–02 season. Though the club offered him a contract for the following season, he decided to leave to play non-League football for Halifax Town.

Wigan Athletic Playing Record

	League		FA Cup		FL Cup		Others		Total	
	App	Gls	App	Gls	App	Gls	App	Gls	App	Gls
1992–93	13	1	0	0	0	0	0	0	13	1
TOTAL	13	1	0	0	0	0	0	0	13	1

GAVIN Patrick John

Forward
Born: Hammersmith, 5 June 1967.
Career: Hanwell Town. March 1989 Gillingham 13 (0) 7. June 1989 Leicester City 1 (2) 0. September 1989 on loan Gillingham 18 (16) 1. March 1991 Peterborough United 18 (5) 5. February 1993 Northampton Town 13 (1) 4. July 1993 WIGAN ATHLETIC 37 (5) 8.

After beginning his Football League career with Gillingham, the big, powerful striker was the subject of much argument between the Gills and Leicester City, who wanted to sign him. City averred

Patrick Gavin

that he was a free agent, while the Kent club claimed he was under contract to them. Gavin was initially barred from training with either club until the wrangle over his registration had been sorted out.

The former postman failed to make much of an impact at Filbert Street and in March 1992 he joined Peterborough United. Though his strikes helped Posh to Division Four promotion, success there was short-lived too and he moved to Northampton Town. On the last day of the 1992–93 season, the Cobblers had to win at Shrewsbury to be sure of retaining their Football League status. Though Gavin scored twice as substitute in a 3–2 win, his reward was the cancellation of his contract only a few days later!

Gavin joined Wigan Athletic in the summer of 1993, making his debut in a 2–0 defeat at home to Scunthorpe United. A regular member of the Latics side, his best performance came in a 4–1 home win over Mansfield Town when he scored twice and hit the woodwork. Sadly injuries restricted his appearances the following season and he was given a free transfer.

Wigan Athletic Playing Record

	League		FA Cup		FL Cup		Others		Total	
	App	Gls	App	Gls	App	Gls	App	Gls	App	Gls
1993–94	28 (2)	6	4	1	2	1	1	0	35 (2)	8
1994–95	9 (3)	2	0	0	4	2	0	0	13 (3)	4
TOTAL	37 (5)	8	4	1	6	3	1	0	48 (5)	12

GAY Geoffrey

Midfield
Born: Romford, 4 February 1957.
Career: January 1975 Bolton Wanderers. March 1977 on loan Exeter City 5 (1) 0. August 1977 Southport 40 (0) 5. July 1978 WIGAN ATHLETIC 1 (0) 0.

Romford-born midfielder Geoff Gay began his career with Bolton Wanderers but, being unable to break into their League side, went out on loan to Fourth Division Exeter City. He appeared in six games for the Grecians before returning to Burnden Park, from where, in the summer of 1977, he joined Southport. The Sandgrounders were having a difficult time and though Gay was the club's most consistent performer, he couldn't prevent them from finishing 23rd in the Fourth Division. Following the Haig Avenue club's unsuccessful bid to win re-election to the Football League, Gay joined Wigan Athletic for their first season of League football. His only game for the Latics was against Grimsby Town in the club's first-ever League game at Springfield Park. Not only did the Latics lose 3–0, but Gay was also replaced by substitute Alan Crompton midway through the second half.

Wigan Athletic Playing Record

	League		FA Cup		FL Cup		Others		Total	
	App	Gls	App	Gls	App	Gls	App	Gls	App	Gls
1978–79	1	0	0	0	0	0	0	0	1	0
TOTAL	1	0	0	0	0	0	0	0	1	0

GEMMILL Archibald

Midfield

Born: Paisley, 24 March 1947.
Career: St Mirren. June 1967 Preston North End 93 (5) 13. September 1970 Derby County 261 (0) 17. September 1977 Nottingham Forest 56 (2) 4. August 1979 Birmingham City 97 (0) 12. Jacksonville, United States. September 1982 WIGAN ATHLETIC 11 (0) 0. November 1982 Derby County 63 (0) 8.

Archie Gemmill began his football career with St Mirren before joining Preston North End for £16,000 in June 1967. After three years at Deepdale he moved to Derby County for £60,000 and it was under Brian Clough's management that his career really began to take off. Bringing a competitive edge to every game, he played a significant role in helping the Rams win the League Championship in 1971–72 and again in 1974–75. Gemmill was a non-stop 90-minute competitor, at his best when running with the ball. This industrious side to Gemmill's talent obviously appealed to Clough, because when he was in charge of Nottingham Forest, he went back to Derby to sign him. At the end of his first campaign at the City Ground, Gemmill picked up his third League Championship medal. In 1978–79 he was instrumental in helping Forest to reach the European Cup Final. However, he didn't play on the big day, being on the substitute's bench as Forest beat Malmo 1–0 in Munich.

Archie Gemmill

A valued member of the Scotland squad, he played 43 times at full level and no one who saw his goal against Holland in the 1978 World Cup Finals will forget it, as he threaded his way through the Dutch defence, evading three strong challenges before shooting home past the diving Jongbloed. After leaving Forest, he played for Birmingham City before joining Wigan Athletic on a non-contract basis in September 1982. He made his debut in a 2–0 defeat at Chesterfield before starring on his home debut three days later when he had a hand in all the Latics' goals as they beat Doncaster Rovers 6–3. He was particularly impressive in the two League Cup matches against Manchester City, but left shortly afterwards for a second spell at the Baseball Ground.

He joined Forest's coaching staff in August 1985 and was re-registered as a player early the following year. He later shared the managerial duties at Rotherham United with former Forest colleague John McGovern.

Wigan Athletic Playing Record

	League		FA Cup		FL Cup		Others		Total	
	App	Gls	App	Gls	App	Gls	App	Gls	App	Gls
1982–83	11	0	0	0	2	0	0	0	13	0
TOTAL	11	0	0	0	2	0	0	0	13	0

GILLESPIE Keith Robert

Winger

Born: Bangor, Northern Ireland, 18 February 1975.
Career: February 1993 Manchester United 3 (6) 1. September 1993 on loan WIGAN ATHLETIC 8 (0) 4. January 1995 Newcastle United 94 (19) 11. December 1998 Blackburn Rovers 67 (46) 5. December 2000 on loan WIGAN ATHLETIC 4 (1) 0.

Keith Gillespie

A key member of the successful Manchester United youth side that reached the FA Youth Cup Final two years running, winning it the first time round, Gillespie made an early and astonishing first-team debut in a third-round FA Cup tie against Bury, creating the first goal and scoring the second in a 2–0 win. However, he was unable to win a regular place in the United side and in September 1993 he joined the Latics on loan. He made his debut in a 3–1 defeat at Doncaster Rovers and in an eight-match spell scored four goals, including two brilliant solo efforts from the halfway line in the 6–3 win over Chester City.

On his return to Old Trafford he continued to play mainly reserve-team football and in January 1995 he joined Newcastle United practically unnoticed, being valued at £1 million in the deal that took Andy Cole to Manchester United. The young Northern Ireland international proved that he had the ability to become a huge name in his own right. Gillespie possessed balance and control on the ball and searing pace running at defenders, qualities that could destroy the opposition. However, it was only in 1997–98, following the appointment of Kenny Dalglish, that Gillespie won a regular place in the Magpies side. It was during this campaign that he destroyed the Barcelona defence, enabling Tino Asprilla to score a memorable hat-trick. Unfortunately his season ended on a sad note when a bad ankle injury caused him to miss the FA Cup Final. A move to Middlesbrough was called off for medical reasons as he was still troubled by the injury to his left ankle.

Despite remaining a regular in the Northern Ireland team, he found it difficult to find a starting place in Ruud Gullit's team and in December 1998 he was transferred to Blackburn Rovers for £2.25 million. Still troubled by ankle and hamstring problems, he missed as many games as he played and in December 2000 he rejoined the Latics on loan. In his second spell with the club, he showed that he had lost none of his pace and created a number of goalscoring opportunities for the Latics strikers, but just when it seemed that a permanent deal could be arranged, he returned to Ewood Park, won back his first-team spot and helped Rovers win promotion to the Premiership. He then emerged from being written out of Blackburn's plans to becoming an integral member of the side, though he did remain as enigmatic as ever! Though he regained the confidence to take on his man on the outside, he appeared to have lost half a yard of pace. He remained a regular in the Northern Ireland squad during 2002–03, taking his total of full international caps to 47, but for Rovers he generally found himself on the substitute's bench.

Wigan Athletic Playing Record

	League		FA Cup		FL Cup		Others		Total	
	App	Gls	App	Gls	App	Gls	App	Gls	App	Gls
1993–94	8	4	0	0	0	0	2	0	10	4
2000–01	4 (1)	0	2	0	0	0	0	0	6 (1)	0
TOTAL	12 (1)	4	2	0	0	0	2	0	16 (1)	4

GILLIBRAND Ian Victor

Defender
Born: Blackburn, 24 November 1948. Died: 1989.
Career: December 1965 Arsenal. April 1968 WIGAN ATHLETIC 7 (0) 0.

On leaving school, Ian Gillibrand joined Bertie Mee's Arsenal and in 1966 was a member of their FA Youth Cup winning team. Before joining the Latics, he had trials with Mansfield Town and also his home-town team of Blackburn Rovers, but after being unable to break into either club's League side, Mee recommended him to Alan Saunders, then Wigan's manager. Gillibrand made his Latics debut in a 1–1 draw at Rhyl before making his first appearance at

Springfield Park the following Saturday against Tranmere Rovers reserves in what turned out to be the club's last Cheshire League game.

The following season of 1968–69 saw the start of the newly formed Northern Premier League and at the end of it, Gillibrand was voted the club's first 'Player of the Year'. He was to win the title two seasons later, as well as once being the runner-up. Highlights in his long career with the Latics include the Championship medals under Gordon Milne in 1970–71 and Brian Tiler in 1974–75 while he was also a member of the Wigan side that lost to Scarborough at Wembley in the FA Trophy Final of 1973.

Ian Gillibrand had the great honour of captaining the Latics for their first-ever Football League game at Hereford United in August 1978, having appeared in 651 games for the club in a variety of competitions. On hanging up his boots, he became heavily involved in the coaching side at Springfield Park but sadly one of the greatest defenders and most loyal of players ever to wear the colours of Wigan Athletic died at the tragically young age of 45.

Wigan Athletic Playing Record

	League		FA Cup		FL Cup		Others		Total	
	App	Gls	App	Gls	App	Gls	App	Gls	App	Gls
1978–79	7	0	0	0	3	0	0	0	10	0
TOTAL	7	0	0	0	3	0	0	0	10	0

GLENN David Anthony

Right-back
Born: Wigan, 30 November 1962.
Career: November 1980 WIGAN ATHLETIC 68 (4) 4. August 1983 Blackburn Rovers 23 (1) 0. July 1985 Chester City 70 (3) 1.

David Glenn joined Wigan Athletic as an apprentice professional after starring in local schools' football. He made his Latics debut as a substitute in a 1–0 home win over Port Vale in September 1980 before winning a regular place in the side midway through the club's promotion-winning season of 1981–82. Glenn was one of the Latics most versatile players, appearing in six different outfield positions during his three seasons at the club.

In the summer of 1983, Glenn was transferred to Second Division Blackburn Rovers and in each of his two seasons with the Ewood Park club, came close to winning promotion to the top flight. Glenn ended his League career with Chester City, helping the Cestrians win promotion to the Third Division in his first season with the club. Sadly, after four seasons at Sealand Road, injuries forced his retirement from League football.

Wigan Athletic Playing Record

	League		FA Cup		FL Cup		Others		Total	
	App	Gls	App	Gls	App	Gls	App	Gls	App	Gls
1980–81	8 (3)	2	0	0	0	0	0	0	8 (3)	2
1981–82	35	2	0	0	4	0	0	0	39	2
1982–83	25 (1)	0	0	0	3	0	0	0	28 (1)	0
TOTAL	68 (4)	4	0	0	7	0	0	0	75 (4)	4

GORE Thomas John

Midfield
Born: Liverpool, 26 November 1953.
Career: Tranmere Rovers. January 1974 WIGAN ATHLETIC 102 (0) 14. October 1980 Bury 118 (1) 15. July 1983 Port Vale 33 (3) 2.

Tommy Gore joined Liverpool on schoolboy forms when he was 15 and stayed at Anfield for four years. The highlight of his stay was playing in an FA Youth Cup Final when the Merseysiders were beaten by Aston Villa. When Liverpool and Scotland centre-half Ron Yeats moved to Tranmere Rovers, Gore went with him and spent 18 months on full-time terms. Sadly things didn't work out for him and after joining Wigan on loan he decided to sign just prior to going for a summer break to America. After a wonderful stay in the States, Gore signed as a part-time professional for the Latics on his return. On a later visit to America, he played against the great Pelé for Dallas Tornadoes and he managed to acquire the great man's shirt, which he has kept ever since!

The club's regular penalty-taker, he helped them win the Northern Premier League Championship in 1974–75 and was ever-present in 1977–78 when they were runners-up, as well as being voted the Latics 'Player of the Year'. A busy player who many times brought the crowd to its feet to greet one of his goalscoring right-foot thunderbolts, he had a wonderful first season in League football after making his debut at Hereford United on the opening day of the 1978–79 campaign. An ever-present in the club's first two seasons of League football, he is one of only three players to have appeared in over 100 consecutive League games following his debut.

A very popular player with the Latics fans, he left Springfield Park in October 1980 to join Bury before moving to Port Vale in the summer of 1983. The following year a neck injury forced his retirement from League football. He then had his own central heating firm but now spends his time playing a lot of golf.

Wigan Athletic Playing Record

	League		FA Cup		FL Cup		Others		Total	
	App	Gls	App	Gls	App	Gls	App	Gls	App	Gls
1978–79	46	2	2	1	3	1	0	0	51	4
1979–80	46	9	6	3	2	0	0	0	54	12
1980–81	10	3	0	0	4	3	0	0	14	6
TOTAL	102	14	8	4	9	4	0	0	119	22

GRAY Robert Paul

Forward
Born: Portsmouth, 28 January 1970.
Career: June 1988 Luton Town 2 (5) 1. May 1991 WIGAN ATHLETIC 2 (3) 0.

Paul Gray

Paul Gray worked his way up through the ranks at Kenilworth Road before making his League debut for Luton Town as a substitute for Kingsley Black in a 3–2 defeat at Arsenal in December 1989. He went on to appear in seven games for the Hatters that season, in five of which he came on as substitute, scoring his only goal for the club in a 3–2 home win over Coventry City. He spent the whole of the 1990–91 season in Luton's reserve side before he joined the Latics in the close season. Gray made his Wigan debut on the opening day of the 1991–92 season as a substitute for Bryan Griffiths but couldn't prevent the Latics from losing 1–0 at Shrewsbury Town. He went on to appear in two matches during the early part of the season and although he created a favourable impression, he was unable to find the net.

Wigan Athletic Playing Record

	League		FA Cup		FL Cup		Others		Total	
	App	Gls	App	Gls	App	Gls	App	Gls	App	Gls
1991–92	2 (3)	0	0	0	1 (2)	0	0	0	3 (5)	0
TOTAL	2 (3)	0	0	0	1 (2)	0	0	0	3 (5)	0

GREEN Scott Paul

Right-back/Forward
Born: Walsall, 15 January 1970.
Career: July 1988 Derby County. March 1990 Bolton Wanderers 166 (54) 25. June 1997 WIGAN ATHLETIC 177 (22) 10. February 2003 Wrexham 12 (3) 3.

Scott Green

As a schoolboy, Scott Green played for Stoke City, West Bromwich Albion and Walsall and looked set to join the Saddlers as a YTS trainee until their manager Alan Buckley left the club. Derby County took him on trial, originally as a centre-forward. He failed to get into the Rams team but had done well with Auran Pallo in Finland where he had scored 24 goals in 16 games.

In March 1990, he moved to Bolton Wanderers for £50,000 and made his League debut the following month against Shrewsbury Town. He kept his place for the remainder of the season, helping the Wanderers reach the play-offs. He made a Wembley appearance in the 1991 play-off final against Tranmere Rovers and in 1992 made a memorable substitute appearance against First Division Southampton, scoring a late equaliser in the fifth-round FA Cup tie. In 1994–95 he switched to full-back, helping Wanderers to promotion and playing in the Coca-Cola Cup Final. His 65 substitute appearances in all competitions for the Wanderers stand as a club record, no doubt down to his ability to play in a number of positions.

In June 1997, Green joined Wigan Athletic for £300,000. He scored on his debut in a 5–2 win over Wycombe Wanderers on the opening day of the 1997–98 season, a campaign in which he held down the right-back spot for most of the time. A highly versatile and valuable member of the Wigan squad, he was delighted to be part of the side that won the Autowindscreen Shield at Wembley. After that, Green featured both as an attacking right-back and on the left side of midfield. A tireless worker, he was a virtual ever-present in the first half of the club's Second Division Championship-winning season, at the end of which he was out of contract.

Scott Green played under five managers while with Wigan but no matter who has been in charge, he was always highly thought of. In February 2003 he was allowed to join Wrexham. It proved to be an important signing by Robins' boss Denis Smith as Green provided the extra ingredient that made all the difference during the Welsh club's run-in for promotion.

Wigan Athletic Playing Record

	League		FA Cup		FL Cup		Others		Total	
	App	Gls	App	Gls	App	Gls	App	Gls	App	Gls
1997–98	37 (1)	1	3	0	2	0	2	0	44 (1)	1
1998–99	32 (5)	0	3	0	4	0	4 (1)	0	43 (6)	0
1999–2000	32 (1)	2	4	0	3	0	4	0	43 (1)	2
2000–01	27 (8)	2	3	0	4	0	2	0	36 (8)	2
2001–02	35 (4)	3	1	0	0	0	1	0	37 (4)	3
2002–03	14 (3)	2	3	1	3 (1)	0	2	0	22 (4)	3
TOTAL	177 (22)	10	17	1	16 (1)	0	15 (1)	0	225 (24)	11

GREENALL Colin Anthony

Central Defender

Born: Billinge, 30 December 1963.

Career: January 1981 Blackpool 179 (4) 9. September 1986 Gillingham 62 (0) 5. February 1988 Oxford United 67 (0) 2. January 1990 on loan Bury 3 (0) 0. July 1990 Bury 66 (2) 5. March 1992 Preston North End 29 (0) 1. August 1993 Chester City 42 (0) 1. July 1994 Lincoln City 43 (0) 3. September 1995 WIGAN ATHLETIC 162 (0) 14.

Colin Greenall made his debut for Blackpool on 23 August 1980 in a 1–1 draw at Huddersfield Town aged just 16 years and 237 days, thus becoming the Seasiders' youngest-ever League player. One of a host of players brought to the Bloomfield Road club by Alan Ball, he developed into a dependable defender. While with Blackpool, he won England youth honours and at the age of 20, he was voted the Fourth Division 'Player of the Year' by the PFA. However, following a contractual dispute, he moved to Third Division Gillingham for £40,000. Midway through the 1987–88 season, Oxford United paid £285,000 to take Greenall to the Manor Ground.

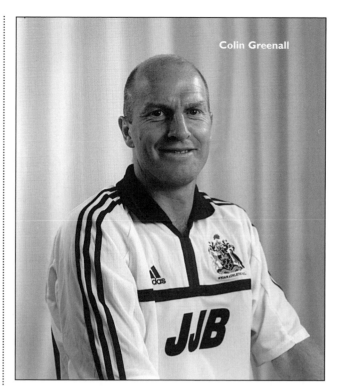
Colin Greenall

After a loan spell with Bury, he joined the Shakers on a permanent basis. Greenall then had spells with Preston North End, Chester City and Lincoln City before joining Wigan Athletic for £45,000 in September 1995. Appointed club captain, Greenall made his Latics debut in a 1–0 home defeat by Plymouth Argyle, later forming an effective central defensive partnership with John Pender. In 1996–97 he was ever-present and instrumental in the club winning the Third Division Championship – he was also voted the Latics supporters' and players' 'Player of the Year'.

Appointed the club's first-team coach, Greenall, who came out of retirement to help the club, won the Man-of-the-Match award in the Latics' Autowindscreen Shield success at Wembley in 1999 as well as having a spell as acting manager following Bruce Rioch's departure. He is now youth team coach at Rochdale.

Wigan Athletic Playing Record

	League		FA Cup		FL Cup		Others		Total	
	App	Gls	App	Gls	App	Gls	App	Gls	App	Gls
1995–96	37	2	3	0	0	0	2 (1)	0	42 (1)	2
1996–97	46	2	1	0	1 (1)	1	1	0	49 (1)	3
1997–98	39	4	3	0	2	0	3	0	47	4
1998–99	40	6	3	1	2	0	9	0	54	7
TOTAL	162	14	10	1	5 (1)	1	15 (1)	0	192 (2)	16

GREW Mark Stuart

Goalkeeper

Born: Bilston, 15 February 1958.

Career: July 1976 West Bromwich Albion 33 (0) 0. December 1978 on loan WIGAN ATHLETIC 4 (0) 0. July 1983 Leicester City 5 (0) 0. October 1983 on loan Oldham Athletic 5 (0) 0. March 1984 Ipswich Town 6 (0) 0. September 1985 on loan Fulham 4 (0) 0. January 1986 on loan West Bromwich Albion 1 (0) 0. June 1986 Port Vale 184 (0) 0. October 1990 on loan Blackburn Rovers 13 (0) 0. August 1992 Cardiff City 21 (0) 0. Stafford Rangers. Hednesford Town.

Goalkeeper Mark Grew began his career with West Bromwich Albion where his debut had in fact been a real oddity for the time: coming on as a substitute goalkeeper in a 1978–79 UEFA Cup tie against Galatasaray. Grew joined the Latics on loan during the club's first season in the Football League. Replacing the injured

John Brown, he made his debut in a 2–1 win at Halifax Town before also being on the winning side in home games against Crewe Alexandra and Aldershot. His final game was at Port Vale, a club he later served for a number of years. The Valiants won 2–1, Mickey Moore having a 'goal' disallowed five minutes from time.

Mark Grew

On leaving the Hawthorns, he joined Leicester City but had an unhappy time at Filbert Street and in March 1984 he moved to Ipswich Town. He fared little better at Portman Road, where he was in the shadow of Paul Cooper. There followed loan spells at Fulham, West Bromwich Albion and Derby County before he joined Port Vale in the summer of 1986. He suffered a serious knee injury early in his Vale career but returned to perform heroically in both their 1988 Cup run and their 1989 promotion campaign. Twice voted the club's 'Player of the Year', he ended his League career with Cardiff City before playing non-League football for Stafford Rangers and Hednesford Town. Grew later returned to Vale Park as the club's Youth Development Officer, before being appointed assistant manager.

Wigan Athletic Playing Record

	League		FA Cup		FL Cup		Others		Total	
	App	Gls	App	Gls	App	Gls	App	Gls	App	Gls
1978–79	4	0	0	0	0	0	0	0	4	0
TOTAL	4	0	0	0	0	0	0	0	4	0

GRIFFITHS Bryan Kenneth

Left winger
Born: St Helens, 26 January 1965.
Career: St Helens Town. November 1988 WIGAN ATHLETIC 176 (13) 44. July 1993 Blackpool 54 (3) 17. October 1993 on loan Scarborough 5 (0) 1. Telford United.

Bryan Griffiths played his early football with his home-town club St Helens Town before signing for Wigan Athletic in November

1988. He went straight into the Latics side for the match against Northampton Town but couldn't prevent the Cobblers winning 3–1. Injury forced him to miss the next four games but he returned to end the season as the club's leading scorer with eight goals in 29 games. Griffiths was joint top-scorer with Don Page in 1990–91 and then headed the charts for a second time in 1992–93, scoring 17 goals in each campaign.

Bryan Griffiths

Without doubt, Griffiths's most spectacular strike for the Latics was the free-kick which left Bruce Grobbelaar standing in the 5–2 League Cup defeat at Anfield in September 1989. A regular in the Wigan side for five seasons, Griffiths had the knack of scoring important goals, but in the summer of 1993, after netting 58 goals in 237 games, he refused terms and left to play for Blackpool.

After a good first season at Bloomfield Road, in which he scored 16 goals, Griffiths suffered from a spate of injuries and after a loan spell at Scarborough, announced his retirement from the game. However, a week later he joined non-League Telford United.

Wigan Athletic Playing Record

	League		FA Cup		FL Cup		Others		Total	
	App	Gls	App	Gls	App	Gls	App	Gls	App	Gls
1988–89	29	8	0	0	0	0	3	1	32	9
1989–90	40 (5)	7	1 (2)	1	3 (1)	1	3 (1)	0	47 (9)	9
1990–91	38 (5)	12	4	3	1 (1)	0	5	2	48 (6)	17
1991–92	26 (2)	4	3	1	4	1	2	0	35 (2)	6
1992–93	43 (1)	13	3	1	4	0	7	3	57 (1)	17
TOTAL	176 (13)	44	11 (2)	6	12 (2)	2	20 (1)	6	219 (18)	58

GRIFFITHS Gareth John

Central Defender
Born: Winsford, 10 April 1970.
Career: Rhyl. December 1993 Port Vale 90 (4) 4. October 1997 on loan Shrewsbury Town 6 (0) 0. July 1998 WIGAN ATHLETIC 44 (9) 2. July 2001 Rochdale 82 (1) 10.

A tall central defender, Gareth Griffiths played his early football for Rhyl before joining Port Vale in February 1993. He made his League debut for the Valiants against Stockport County 12 months later, but after establishing himself at the heart of the Vale defence, he developed a groin injury which required a double hernia

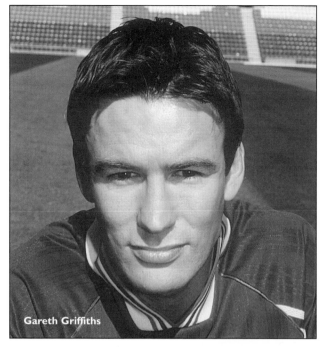

Gareth Griffiths

operation. Following his return to full fitness, he reclaimed his place in the Port Vale side before again struggling with injury. He had a brief loan spell with Shrewsbury Town before leaving the Valiants to join Wigan Athletic in the summer of 1998, having been out of contract.

He made his Wigan debut in the 1–0 home defeat at the hands of Millwall on the opening day of the 1998–99 season and was a first-team regular until suffering a recurrence of a knee injury in the 4–3 FA Cup victory against Blackpool. Robust and hard to pass, he eventually returned to the side towards the end of the campaign to become an invaluable squad member. Though his first-team opportunities in 1999–2000 were limited, he did manage to score his first League goal for the club as the Latics thrashed Blackpool 5–1. Injuries again hampered his progress in 2000–01 but when he did make the side, he never let anyone down. He gained the Latics a point in the promotion battle at Rotherham United with a well-taken goal but was released in the summer when his contract expired.

He joined Rochdale in readiness for the following season where he was a virtual ever-present alongside the experienced Richard Jobson. Tremendous in the air, he dominated most opposing strikers and following Gary Jones's departure, Griffiths was named as the new Dale skipper. Though his form lacked a little consistency in 2002–03, he was again pretty much an automatic choice – his best display coming in the televised FA Cup tie against Wolverhampton Wanderers.

Wigan Athletic Playing Record

	League		FA Cup		FL Cup		Others		Total	
	App	Gls	App	Gls	App	Gls	App	Gls	App	Gls
1998–99	20	0	1	0	4	1	1	0	26	1
1999–2000	16 (6)	1	1	0	0	0	2 (1)	0	19 (7)	1
2000–01	8 (3)	1	3	0	0	0	2	0	13 (3)	1
TOTAL	44 (9)	2	5	0	4	1	5 (1)	0	58 (10)	3

GRIFFITHS Ian James

Left-winger
Born: Birkenhead, 17 April 1960.
Career: February 1979 Tranmere Rovers 110 (6) 5. August 1983 Rochdale 40 (2) 5. September 1984 Port Vale 9 (3) 0. July 1985 WIGAN ATHLETIC 73 (9) 7. Mazda Hiroshima, Japan. August 1990 WIGAN ATHLETIC 6 (5) 0. March 1991 Wrexham 14 (0) 0.

Left-winger Ian Griffiths worked his way up through the ranks Tranmere Rovers before making his League debut at home to Mansfield Town towards the end of the club's relegation season of 1978–79. Following just a handful of appearances over the next two seasons, Griffiths won a regular place in the Rovers' side, but in the summer of 1983, after scoring six goals in 135 games, he left Prenton Park to play for Rochdale. After just one season at Spotland, he was on the move again, this time to Port Vale. Though he played on a fairly regular basis for the Valiants, he had to have a skin graft after trapping a finger in the toilet door of the team coach. A month later he damaged knee ligaments and in July 1985 he left Vale to join Wigan Athletic.

Griffiths made his Latics debut in a 1–0 win at Swansea City on

Ian Griffiths

the opening day of the 1985–86 season, his direct wing play creating a number of goalscoring opportunities for the likes of Warren Aspinall and Mike Newell. The following season, Bobby Campbell benefited from Griffiths's accurate crosses as the Latics finished fourth in Division Three in both campaigns. After a spell playing for Mazda Hiroshima of Japan, Griffiths returned to Springfield Park for the 1990–91 season but, unable to regain the form he had shown in his first spell at the club, he left for Wrexham where he ended his first-class career.

Wigan Athletic Playing Record

	League		FA Cup		FL Cup		Others		Total	
	App	Gls	App	Gls	App	Gls	App	Gls	App	Gls
1985–86	38	3	4	0	2	0	4 (1)	1	48 (1)	4
1986–87	30 (1)	3	4	1	2	0	3	0	39 (1)	4
1987–88	5 (8)	1	0	0	2 (2)	0	0	0	7 (10)	1
1990–91	6 (5)	0	0	0	1 (1)	0	2	0	9 (6)	0
TOTAL	79 (14)	7	8	1	7 (3)	0	9 (1)	1	103 (18)	9

HAMILTON David

Midfield

Born: South Shields, 7 November 1960.

Career: September 1978 Sunderland. January 1981 Blackburn Rovers 104 (10) 7. March 1985 on loan Cardiff City 10 (0) 0. July 1986 WIGAN ATHLETIC 97 (6) 7. August 1989 Chester City 26 (2) 0. August 1990 Burnley 11 (4) 0. Chorley. Barrow. Accrington.

After winning England youth international honours, David Hamilton signed as a professional with Sunderland, serving his apprenticeship on Wearside. In two years at Roker Park, Hamilton failed to break into Sunderland's League side and in January 1981 he joined Blackburn Rovers on a free transfer. Never quite a regular in his time at Ewood Park, where he alternated between full-back and midfield, he joined Wigan Athletic in July 1986 for £16,000.

After making his debut in a 2–0 defeat at Notts County on the opening day of the 1986–87 season, Hamilton was a virtual ever-present, helping the Latics reach the play-offs, where they lost to

David Hamilton

Swindon Town and the sixth round of the FA Cup, the club's best-ever run in the competition before losing to First Division Leeds United. Missing just one game in 1987–88, Hamilton was voted Latics' 'Player of the Year', but after a season on the fringe of first-team action, he moved to Chester City in August 1989.

He later joined Burnley, helping them win the Fourth Division Championship in 1991–92. After his release from Turf Moor, he had spells playing non-League football for Chorley, Barrow and Accrington before spending some time on the coaching staff of Preston North End. He later worked under Graham Barrow at Rochdale.

Wigan Athletic Playing Record

	League		FA Cup		FL Cup		Others		Total	
	App	Gls	App	Gls	App	Gls	App	Gls	App	Gls
1986–87	39 (2)	3	5	0	2	0	0	0	46 (2)	3
1987–88	45	2	2	0	4	1	2	1	53	4
1988–89	13 (4)	2	1	0	0	0	0	0	14 (4)	2
TOTAL	97 (6)	7	8	0	6	1	2	1	113 (6)	9

HARFORD Paul Raymond Thomas

Midfield

Born: Chelmsford, 21 October 1974.

Career: Arsenal. August 1993 Blackburn Rovers. September 1994 on loan WIGAN ATHLETIC 3 (0) 0. December 1994 on loan Shrewsbury Town 3 (3) 0.

The son of Ray Harford, Paul turned professional with Arsenal in the summer of 1993, having been at Highbury as an associated schoolboy and as a trainee. A regular in the club's youth side in 1992–93, he made a couple of appearances in the Arsenal reserve side towards the end of the season. Unable to make the grade, he joined his father at Blackburn Rovers and after a year in the Ewood Park reserve side joined Wigan Athletic on a month's loan in September 1994.

A midfield player with a lovely touch, he made his Latics debut in a 2–1 home defeat by Barnet. He then helped Wigan win by the same scoreline at Hereford United, but after just one more appearance, he returned to Ewood Park. He later had a loan spell with Shrewsbury Town before rejoining Rovers. Still unable to force his way into their first team, he left the club to try his luck in non-League football.

Wigan Athletic Playing Record

	League		FA Cup		FL Cup		Others		Total	
	App	Gls	App	Gls	App	Gls	App	Gls	App	Gls
1994–95	3	0	0	0	0	0	0	0	3	0
TOTAL	3	0	0	0	0	0	0	0	3	0

HART Nigel

Central Defender

Born: Golborne, 1 October 1958.

Career: August 1978 WIGAN ATHLETIC 1 (0) 0. October 1979 Leicester City. August 1981 Blackpool 36 (1) 0. November 1982 Crewe Alexandra 139 (3) 10. February 1987 Bury 33 (12) 2. July 1988 Stockport County 38 (1) 2. August 1989 Chesterfield 45 (1) 2. February 1991 York City 1 (0) 0. Droylsden.

Central defender Nigel Hart, son of ex-Manchester City star Johnny Hart and a brother of current Nottingham Forest manager

Simon Haworth

Paul, he began his League career with Wigan Athletic. His only League game for the Latics was in a 2–1 home win over Hartlepool United in September 1979, after which he joined Leicester City.

But it wasn't until two years later following a move to Blackpool that he extended his senior career. On leaving Bloomfield Road, he joined Crewe Alexandra and in four seasons at Gresty Road he appeared in 142 League and Cup games for the Railwaymen. The much-travelled centre-half then had spells with Bury and Stockport County before joining Chesterfield where his brother was manager. He ended his first-class career with a game for York City before playing non-League football for Droylsden.

Wigan Athletic Playing Record

	League		FA Cup		FL Cup		Others		Total	
	App	Gls	App	Gls	App	Gls	App	Gls	App	Gls
1978–79	1	0	0	0	0	0	0	0	1	0
TOTAL	1	0	0	0	0	0	0	0	1	0

HAWORTH Simon Owen

Forward
Born: Cardiff, 30 March 1977.
Career: August 1995 Cardiff City 27 (10) 9. June 1997 Coventry City 5 (6) 0. October 1998 WIGAN ATHLETIC 99 (18) 44. February 2002 Tranmere Rovers 54 (0) 25.

Simon Haworth began his Football League career with his home-town club Cardiff City, being pitched into the Bluebirds side following an injury crisis at the start of the 1995–96 season. However, it was midway through the following season before he established himself as a first-team regular, scoring some superb goals. A proposed transfer to Norwich City on deadline day fell through but after winning full international honours for Wales, when he played against Scotland, he left Ninian Park to join Coventry City for £500,000. Though he scored on his debut for the Sky Blues in a Coca-Cola Cup game against Everton, his subsequent performances were not as impressive and in October 1998 he joined Wigan Athletic for £600,000 – the club's then record signing.

After making his debut in a 1–0 home win over Northampton Town his progress was hampered by hamstring problems. However, he came back strongly towards the end of the campaign to play at Wembley as part of the side that won the Autowindscreen Shield.

Strong in the air with an excellent first touch, he captained the Wales Under-21 side before scoring the first-ever Football League goal at the JJB Stadium as the Latics beat Scunthorpe United 3–0. He finished the 1999–2000 season as Wigan's second-top scorer with 20 goals, his tremendous strike in the Wembley Second Division play-off final demonstrating his undoubted potential. Haworth topped the club's scoring charts in 2000–01 – his total of 13 goals included the first-ever hat-trick at the JJB Stadium as Latics beat Colchester United 3–1.

Though the Welsh international was sold to Tranmere Rovers in February 2002, he ended the campaign as the Latics' second-highest scorer with 10 goals. Included in this total were superb strikes in the 2–0 wins at Peterborough United and Northampton Town.

At Prenton Park he resumed his old striking partnership with Stuart Barlow, netting five times in the last 12 games of the season. In 2002–03 he was in exceptional form, ending the campaign as the Wirral club's leading scorer with 22 goals in all competitions – the first player to reach the 20-goal mark in a season since John Aldridge. The club's supporters' 'Player of the Year', he was called

up to the Welsh international squad in the close season but was unable to join them as he was still on his honeymoon!

Wigan Athletic Playing Record

	League		FA Cup		FL Cup		Others		Total	
	App	Gls	App	Gls	App	Gls	App	Gls	App	Gls
1998–99	19 (1)	10	1	1	0	0	5	3	25 (1)	14
1999–2000	36 (4)	13	3	3	4	3	5	1	48 (4)	20
2000–01	25 (5)	11	0	0	3	2	1 (1)	0	29 (6)	13
2001–02	19 (8)	10	0	0	1	1	1	0	21 (8)	11
TOTAL	99 (18)	44	4	4	8	6	12 (1)	4	123 (19)	58

HEMMING Christopher Andrew John

Central Defender
Born: Stoke-on-Trent, 13 April 1966.
Career: April 1984 Stoke City 85 (8) 2. January 1989 on loan WIGAN ATHLETIC 4 (0) 0. August 1989 Hereford United 39 (2) 3. Merthyr Tydfil. Macclesfield. Stafford Rangers.

Chris Hemming

Ginger-haired defender Chris Hemming shot to national prominence when it was announced that he had a heart pacemaker fitted. He was almost certainly the first professional sportsman to return to action following such treatment. Hemming began his Football League career with Stoke City and made his debut in a 1–0 defeat against Tottenham Hotspur at White Hart Lane. He made a favourable impression in the Potters side, first at left-back and then in the heart of the defence. A hint of inconsistency restricted his first-team appearances and in January 1989 he joined Wigan Athletic on a month's loan.

He made his Latics debut in a 1–1 home draw against Brentford, but after playing in four games he returned to the Victoria Ground. In August 1989 he joined Hereford United for a fee of £25,000 and, after a couple of seasons, he left to play non-League football for a number of clubs including Merthyr Tydfil, Macclesfield Town and Stafford Rangers.

Wigan Athletic Playing Record

	League		FA Cup		FL Cup		Others		Total	
	App	Gls	App	Gls	App	Gls	App	Gls	App	Gls
1988–89	4	0	0	0	0	0	2	0	6	0
TOTAL	4	0	0	0	0	0	2	0	6	0

HILDERSLEY Ronald

Midfield
Born: Kirkcaldy, 6 April 1965.
Career: April 1983 Manchester City 1 (0) 0. January 1984 on loan Chester City 9 (0) 0. July 1984 Chester City 5 (4) 0. August 1985 Rochdale 12 (4) 0. June 1986 Preston North End 54 (4) 3. February 1988 on loan Cambridge United 9 (0) 3. July 1988 Blackburn Rovers 25 (5) 4. August 1990 WIGAN ATHLETIC 4 (0) 0. November 1991 Halifax Town 21 (10) 2.

Much-travelled midfielder Ronnie Hildersley worked his way up through the junior and reserve sides at Maine Road before making his Football League debut for Manchester City in a 4–1 reversal at Swansea City in March 1983. Midway through the following season he went on loan to Chester City before joining the Cestrians on a permanent basis in the summer of 1984.

Ronnie Hildersley

After an injury-hit season at Sealand Road, Hildersley joined Rochdale on a non-contract basis before signing for Preston North End in June 1986. Hildersley spent two seasons at Deepdale, helping the Lilywhites win promotion to the Third Division as runners-up to Northampton Town. Towards the end of his time at Deepdale he was loaned out to Cambridge United before joining North End's rivals Blackburn Rovers. Hildersley was hampered by a spate of niggling injuries during his time at Ewood Park but when he did play, he continued to play every game to the best of his ability as Rovers challenged for a place in the top flight.

In August 1990 Latics manager Bryan Hamilton brought Ronnie Hildersley to Springfield Park and he made his debut for the club in a 2–0 home defeat by Mansfield Town on the opening day of the 1990–91 season. A bad injury in the next game at Grimsby ruled him out of action until the turn of the year but he couldn't force his way into the side on a regular basis and left to end his first-class career with Halifax Town.

Wigan Athletic Playing Record

	League		FA Cup		FL Cup		Others		Total	
	App	Gls	App	Gls	App	Gls	App	Gls	App	Gls
1990–91	4	0	0	0	1	0	0	0	5	0
TOTAL	4	0	0	0	1	0	0	0	5	0

HILDITCH Mark

Forward
Born: Royton, 20 August 1960.
Career: November 1978 Rochdale 184 (13) 40. August 1983 Tranmere Rovers 47 (2) 12. Altrincham. September 1986 WIGAN ATHLETIC 89 (14) 26. August 1990 Rochdale 12 (4) 2.

Mark Hilditch began his Football League career with Rochdale, signing professional forms for the Spotland club in November 1978. In five seasons with 'The Dale' Hilditch scored 40 goals in 197 games before being transferred to Tranmere Rovers. Injuries hampered his progress at Prenton Park and he moved into non-League football with Altrincham before Wigan Athletic manager Ray Mathias brought him to Springfield Park in September 1986.

He made his debut in a 2–1 home defeat at the hands of Newport County before scoring his first goal for the club four days later in a 5–1 demolition of Walsall. Hilditch helped the Latics reach the play-offs and the sixth round of the FA Cup, beating First Division Norwich City on the way, ending his first season with eight goals in 33 games. Injuries restricted his appearances over the

next couple of seasons but when he did play, he showed his versatility by appearing in midfield, attack and even at right-back.

After playing in nine different outfield positions, Hilditch returned to lead the attack for the start of the 1989–90 season, netting his first hat-trick for the club in a 4–0 win at Mansfield Town. Though he was never a prolific scorer, 'Marco Van' scored a goal in every three games for the Latics before financial restrictions forced the club not to renew his contract. He then returned to Spotland for another season before becoming assistant-manager of Northern Premier League side Mossley.

Wigan Athletic Playing Record

	League		FA Cup		FL Cup		Others		Total	
	App	Gls	App	Gls	App	Gls	App	Gls	App	Gls
1986–87	21 (7)	8	4	0	0	0	1	0	26 (7)	8
1987–88	25 (4)	8	1	1	2 (2)	0	1	0	29 (6)	9
1988–89	23 (2)	3	0	0	2	0	1	0	26 (2)	3
1989–90	20 (1)	7	2	1	3	1	1	0	25 (1)	9
TOTAL	89 (14)	26	7	2	7 (2)	1	3	0	106 (16)	29

HINNIGAN Joseph Peter

Full-back
Born: Liverpool, 3 December 1955.
Career: South Liverpool. May 1975 WIGAN ATHLETIC 66 (0) 10. February 1980 Sunderland 63 (0) 4. December 1982 Preston North End 51 (1) 8. August 1984 Gillingham 99 (4) 7. July 1987 Wrexham 28 (1) 1. August 1988 Chester City 52 (2) 2.

Joe Hinnigan was brought up in the Liverpool area and represented Kirkby Schools at junior under-14 and under-15 levels before signing amateur forms for Everton. After just over a year at Goodison Park, he was released and moved on to Aston Villa. When Villa also released him after six months, a coach of the Kirkby Sunday League side took him to South Liverpool. He was put straight into the South Liverpool Youth XI and helped them

Mark Hilditch

reach three finals, one of which was against Wigan. Within four months he was playing in the Northern Premier League, where more impressive performances led to him joining the Latics in the summer of 1975 for a fee of £1,200.

He played his first game in Wigan colours in a 1–0 win at Worksop Town and over the next three seasons he appeared in 120 Northern Premier League games before making his Football League debut on the opening day of the 1978–79 season at Hereford United. Hinnigan wrote himself into the Latics' history books when he scored the club's first Football League goal in a 3–2 defeat at home to Newport County.

On leaving Springfield Park in February 1980, he joined Sunderland for £135,000 appearing in the last 14 games of the season and helping the north-east club win promotion to the top flight, never playing in a losing side. In December 1982, Hinnigan returned to the north-west with Preston North End, later joining Gillingham whom he helped to finish near the top of the Third Division for three consecutive seasons. After one season with Wrexham, Hinnigan ended his League career with Chester City, later becoming the club's physiotherapist, a position he later held with Wrexham.

Wigan Athletic Playing Record

	League		FA Cup		FL Cup		Others		Total	
	App	Gls	App	Gls	App	Gls	App	Gls	App	Gls
1978–79	39	5	2	0	2	0	0	0	43	5
1979–80	27	5	6	1	2	0	0	0	35	6
TOTAL	66	10	8	1	4	0	0	0	78	11

HOLDEN Andrew Ian

Central Defender
Born: Flint, 14 September 1962.
Career: Rhyl. August 1983 Chester City 100 (0) 17. October 1986 WIGAN ATHLETIC 48 (1) 4. January 1989 Oldham Athletic 22 (0) 4.

Andy Holden was playing non-League football for Rhyl when Chester City paid £3,000 for him in the summer of 1983. His displays for the Cestrians won him Under-21 honours for Wales before, in June 1984, he came on as a substitute for Wales against Israel. After helping Chester win promotion to the Third Division in 1985–86, Holden joined Wigan Athletic early the following season, Ray Mathias paying £45,000 to secure his signature.

Holden made his Latics debut in a 2–0 home win over Carlisle United and in his first season at Springfield Park he was instrumental in the club reaching the sixth round of the FA Cup. Unfortunately he was injured against Rotherham United and forced to sit out the quarter-final meeting with Leeds United. Injuries hampered his progress the following season but, restored to full fitness, he was one of the Latics' better players in 1988–89. However, midway through the season Oldham Athletic paid £130,000 to take the Welsh international to Boundary Park.

The central defender, who was good in the air and strong in the tackle, was forced to give up the game prematurely. After taking up the positions of team coach and reserve-team manager, he was recalled to the Oldham side in 1994–95 during an injury crisis and needless to say, disgraced nobody.

Wigan Athletic Playing Record

	League		FA Cup		FL Cup		Others		Total	
	App	Gls	App	Gls	App	Gls	App	Gls	App	Gls
1986–87	11	1	4	0	0	0	3	0	18	1
1987–88	14 (1)	2	2	0	1	0	2	0	19 (1)	2
1988–89	23	1	1	0	2	0	1	0	27	1
TOTAL	48 (1)	4	7	0	3	0	6	0	64 (1)	4

HOLLIS Stephen John

Full-back

Born: Liverpool, 22 August 1972.

Career: May 1990 Liverpool. Knowsley United. August 1993 WIGAN ATHLETIC 0 (1) 0. Fleetwood.

Full-back Stephen Hollis joined Liverpool as a trainee, but on being unable to make much headway at Anfield, he was released. He drifted into non-League football with Knowsley United where his impressive displays alerted Latics manager Kenny Swain and he joined Wigan in the summer of 1993. Named as substitute for the Latics' opening game of the 1993–94 season against Scunthorpe United, he replaced John Robertson but could do little to change the course of the game, which the visitors won 2–0. It was his only appearance in the Latics side, for in June 1994 he was given a free transfer and joined Fleetwood.

Stephen Hollis

Wigan Athletic Playing Record

	League		FA Cup		FL Cup		Others		Total	
	App	Gls	App	Gls	App	Gls	App	Gls	App	Gls
1993–94	0 (1)	0	0	0	0	0	0	0	0 (1)	0
TOTAL	0 (1)	0	0	0	0	0	0	0	0 (1)	0

HORSFIELD Geoffrey Malcolm

Striker

Born: Barnsley, 1 November 1973.

Career: July 1992 Scarborough 12 (9) 1. March 1994 Halifax Town. August 1996 Witton Albion. May 1997 Halifax Town 10 (0) 7. October 1998 Fulham 54 (5) 22. July 2000 Birmingham City 73 (32) 23. September 2003 WIGAN ATHLETIC 16 (0) 7. January 2004 West Bromwich Albion.

Having started his career with Scarborough, Geoff Horsfield struggled to hold down a first-team place and moved into non-League circles with Halifax Town and later Witton Albion. He rejoined the Shaymen in May 1997, helping the club win promotion to the Football League. Starting the following season with a flurry of goals, his potential was such that Fulham's Kevin Keegan snapped him up for a fee of £325,000.

Looking a typical old-fashioned centre-forward, he held the ball up well, bringing other players into the game and working so hard that he immediately became the idol of the Craven Cottage crowd. Horsfield, who scored 17 goals in 34 League and Cup games, was recognised by his peers with selection to the PFA award-winning Second Division side. He started the following season in a similar vein – six goals in the first five games – but a combination of niggling injuries, the lack of a settled striking partner and poor service restricted his goalscoring opportunities thereafter.

Signed by Birmingham City for a new club record fee of £2 million in the summer of 2000, he had an up-and-down season, but scored twice in the Worthington Cup semi-final second leg win over Ipswich Town. The final against Liverpool, when the Blues came close to causing an upset, was another high point. The bustling striker had another excellent season for Birmingham City in 2001–02, helping the club win promotion to the Premiership via the play-offs.

Developing a taste for scoring in crucial matches – notably the derby games against Aston Villa - he recovered from a double hernia operation to be playing again after just 17 days! Coming into his own as a partner for Christophe Dugarry, it came as a complete surprise when he was allowed to join the Latics for £1 million.

Horsfield scored on his debut in a 4–2 win against Wimbledon in their last-ever match at Selhurst Park and then netted the only goal of the game three days later as Wigan beat West Bromwich Albion at the JJB Stadium. In doing so, he became one of only three players – Peter Houghton and Nathan Ellington being the others – to score on his home and away debuts. Midway through the season, Horsfield left Wigan to join the Baggies, citing the problems travelling from the Midlands each day as his reason for his departure.

Wigan Athletic Playing Record

	League		FA Cup		FL Cup		Others		Total	
	App	Gls	App	Gls	App	Gls	App	Gls	App	Gls
2003–04	16	7	0	0	1	0	0	0	17	7
TOTAL	16	7	0	0	1	0	0	0	17	7

HOUGHTON Peter

Forward

Born: Liverpool, 30 November 1954.

Career: Prescot Town. South Liverpool. January 1978 WIGAN ATHLETIC 169 (16) 62. October 1983 Preston North End 52 (4) 16. November 1984 on loan Wrexham 5 (0) 2. August 1985 Chester City 78 (7) 13. Runcorn.

A member of the Liverpool Schools' FA squad which won the English Schools' Trophy, Peter Houghton played for several local teams after leaving school and took part in several Liverpool area competitions before joining Prescot Town and gaining a Mid-Cheshire League Championship medal. He later moved on to South Liverpool from where he was eventually signed by Wigan Athletic in January 1978. He scored nine goals in 15 games, helping the Latics finish runners-up to Boston in that season's Northern Premier League.

He made his Football League debut at Hereford on the opening day of the 1978–79 season and, although handicapped in the early part of the campaign by a series of injuries, he emerged as the club's leading scorer with 14 goals, including a hat-trick in a 5–3 defeat of Port Vale. He topped the club's scoring charts again the

Geoff Horsfield

Peter Houghton

Graham Houston

through the ranks at Deepdale. He made his debut for the Lilywhites as a substitute against Queen's Park Rangers in February 1980 before establishing himself as a first-team regular towards the end of the following season. He went on to score 11 goals in 128 League games for North End but following their relegation to Division Four in 1984–85 he moved to Burnley as a non-contract player.

following season, while in 1980–81 he netted his second hat-trick for the club in a 3–2 win at Tranmere Rovers. When Wigan were promoted to the Third Division in 1981–82, Houghton, who formed a formidable strike force with Les Bradd, netted 17 goals including another hat-trick in a 6–3 win at Doncaster Rovers.

Houghton endeared himself to the Latics fans with his forceful running and often quite spectacular goals, but was allowed to leave Springfield Park in October 1983 for Preston North End. He later played for Chester City, whose manager was former Latics boss Harry McNally before ending his career playing non-League football for Runcorn. He later worked in the car manufacturing industry.

Wigan Athletic Playing Record

	League		FA Cup		FL Cup		Others		Total	
	App	Gls	App	Gls	App	Gls	App	Gls	App	Gls
1978–79	23 (3)	13	2	1	3	0	0	0	28 (3)	14
1979–80	40 (1)	15	6	0	2	1	0	0	48 (1)	16
1980–81	29 (3)	6	2	2	4	0	0	0	35 (3)	8
1981–82	45 (1)	15	2	0	5 (1)	2	0	0	52 (1)	17
1982–83	27 (7)	12	2	0	3	0	0	0	32 (9)	12
1983–84	5 (1)	1	0	0	2	0	0	0	7 (1)	1
TOTAL	169 (16)	62	14	3	19 (1)	3	0	0	205 (17)	68

HOUSTON Graham Robert

Winger
Born: Gibraltar, 24 February 1960.
Career: March 1978 Preston North End 90 (38) 11. September 1985 Burnley. June 1986 WIGAN ATHLETIC 16 (1) 4. Northwich Victoria. October 1987 Carlisle United 8 (8) 1.

Gilbraltan-born winger Graham Houston began his Football League career with Preston North End after working his way up

Unable to break into the Clarets first team, he spent a season languishing in the club's Central League side before joining Wigan Athletic in the summer of 1986. Houston made his Latics debut in a 2–0 defeat at Notts County but was replaced midway through the second-half by Ian Griffiths. He returned to first-team action seven games into the campaign when an extended run in the side saw him score four goals in a seven-match spell including two in a 4–3 win over Bristol Rovers. At the end of the season, Houston was released and moved into non-League football with Northwich Victoria before returning to League action with Carlisle United where he later ended his first-class career.

Wigan Athletic Playing Record

	League		FA Cup		FL Cup		Others		Total	
	App	Gls	App	Gls	App	Gls	App	Gls	App	Gls
1986–87	16 (1)	4	2	0	2	0	0	0	20 (1)	4
TOTAL	16 (1)	4	2	0	2	0	0	0	20 (1)	4

HUGHES Philip Anthony

Goalkeeper
Born: Belfast 19 November 1964
Career: Manchester United. January 1983 Leeds United 6 (0) 0. July 1985 Bury 80 (0) 0. November 1987 WIGAN ATHLETIC 99 (0) 0. Rochdale. October 1991 Scarborough 17 (0) 0. Guisely.

Goalkeeper Phil Hughes served his apprenticeship with Manchester United but on being released in January 1983, he was snapped up by Leeds United. A Northern Ireland youth international, he was unable to budge Leeds' Scottish international 'keeper David Harvey and in the summer of 1985, he joined Bury on a free transfer.

Phil Hughes

A member of the 1986 Northern Ireland World Cup squad, he was one of a number of young 'keepers earmarked as a possible successor to the brilliant Pat Jennings. He made the first of three full international appearances for Northern Ireland against England at Wembley in April 1987, a match the home side won 2–0. A shoulder injury cost him his place in the Bury side and in November 1987 he joined Wigan Athletic for a fee of £35,000.

He kept a clean sheet on his debut as the Latics won 1–0 at Chesterfield and went on to keep 11 more in the remaining 31 games of the 1987–88 season. Injuries restricted his first-team appearances the following season but early in 1989–90 he replaced Nigel Adkins, after which he tended to share the goalkeeping duties with the former Tranmere 'keeper. Released on a free transfer, he joined Scarborough in October 1991 but left the Yorkshire club at the end of the season. He later played for Guisely for a couple of seasons before moving to Pontefract Colliery.

Wigan Athletic Playing Record

	League		FA Cup		FL Cup		Others		Total	
	App	Gls	App	Gls	App	Gls	App	Gls	App	Gls
1987–88	31	0	2	0	0	0	1	0	34	0
1988–89	16	0	0	0	2	0	0	0	18	0
1989–90	33	0	3	0	0	0	4	0	40	0
1990–91	19	0	0	0	0	0	2	0	21	0
TOTAL	99	0	5	0	2	0	7	0	113	0

HUTCHINSON Robert

Midfield
Born: Glasgow, 19 June 1953.
Career: Montrose. Dundee. Hibernian. July 1980 WIGAN ATHLETIC 34 (1) 3. August 1981 Tranmere Rovers 32 (3) 6. October 1982 Mansfield Town 35 (0) 3. January 1984 Tranmere Rovers 21 (0) 4. July 1984 Bristol City 89 (3) 10. February 1987 Walsall 8 (8) 0. September 1987 on loan Blackpool 3 (3) 0. January 1988 on loan Carlisle United 12 (1) 2.

Bobby Hutchinson began his career as a striker with Montrose before joining Scottish League Cup winners Dundee in the summer of 1974. He was later swapped for Hibernian's Eric

Scheaedler and went on to appear for the Easter Road club in the 1979 Scottish Cup Final. He moved to Wigan Athletic in July 1980 and made his debut in a 2–1 home win over Crewe Alexandra in a Football League Cup first-round first-leg tie. Four days later he scored the Latics' equalising goal in the second leg at Gresty Road which ended 2–2. A versatile player, Hutchinson was a virtual ever-present in the Wigan side during 1980–81, helping them end the campaign in mid-table. However, in the close season, the hardworking midfielder left Springfield Park to play for Tranmere Rovers and later Mansfield Town prior to rejoining the Prenton Park club in January 1984.

Bristol City manager Terry Cooper signed him on a free transfer six months later and he became the Ashton Gate club's captain. He was voted the club's 'Player of the Year' as the Robins won the Freight Rover Trophy at Wembley in 1986. In February 1987 he was sold to Walsall for £10,000, later having loan spells with Blackpool and Carlisle United before returning north of the border.

Wigan Athletic Playing Record

	League		FA Cup		FL Cup		Others		Total	
	App	Gls	App	Gls	App	Gls	App	Gls	App	Gls
1980–81	34 (1)	3	2	0	4	1	0	0	40 (1)	4
TOTAL	34 (1)	3	2	0	4	1	0	0	40 (1)	4

JACKSON Matthew Alan

Defender
Born: Leeds, 19 October 1971.
Career: July 1990 Luton Town 7 (2) 0. March 1991 on loan Preston North End 3 (1) 0. October 1991 Everton 132 (6) 4. March 1996 on loan Charlton Athletic 8 (0) 0. August 1996 on loan Queen's Park Rangers 7 (0) 0. October 1996 on loan Birmingham City 10 (0) 0. December 1996 Norwich City 158 (3) 6. October 2001 WIGAN ATHLETIC 94 (1) 2.

An England Under-21 international, Alan Jackson began his career with Luton Town and had a brief loan spell with Preston North End before Everton paid £600,000 for the young full-back's services in October 1991. Showing great maturity for his age when forcing attackers towards the touchline, then holding the ball up to allow colleagues to recover, he soon won a regular place in the Everton side. A member of the Blues team that won the 1995 FA Cup, beating Manchester United 1–0 in the final, injuries hampered his progress the following season and after the arrival of Marc Hottiger he joined Charlton Athletic on loan. Still unable to hold down a regular place in the Everton side, he had further loan spells with Queen's Park Rangers and Birmingham City before, having played in 165 games for Everton, he joined Norwich City for a fee of £450,000.

His early displays for the Canaries were very impressive and it wasn't long before he was appointed club captain. Taking to the role with great authority, Jackson proved himself a composed, mature defender, able to cope well under pressure and comfortable in possession. Employed both at right-back and as a central defender, Matt Jackson, despite being sidelined for much of the 2000–01 season by injuries, had played in 172 games for the Carrow Road club by the time of his transfer to Wigan Athletic in October 2001.

Initially signed on loan, he continued to show his versatility by appearing at both right-back and in the centre of defence, where he covered for injuries. Though he dislocated his kneecap in the 3–0 home win over Brighton, he had more than demonstrated the danger he posed at set pieces. However, he had to wait until September 2002 before netting his first goal for the club in a 3–1

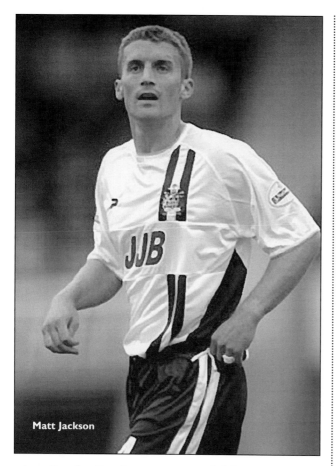

Matt Jackson

promotion to the Third Division in 1984–85 but in November 1986 he joined Dutch First Division club AZ 67 Alkmaar. During his time in Holland, he experienced playing against PSV Eindhoven on the night they clinched the League Championship.

He returned to England in 1988, joining Chester City but his stay at Sealand Road was brief and he soon rejoined Burnley for a second spell. An ever-present in his first two seasons back at Turf Moor, he helped the Clarets win the Fourth Division Championship in 1991–92. In January 1993 he played his 500th League game at Mansfield Town but was sent off for the first time in his career! After taking his total of first-team appearances to 269 he joined Chester for a second time, helping them win promotion from the 'new' Division Three in 1993–94.

Joe Jakub

win at Barnsley. Forming a strong central defensive partnership with Jason De Vos, the pairing was the bedrock of the Latics' success in winning the Second Division Championship.

After some impressive performances at the heart of the Latics defence in 2003–04, Jackson was sent-off in the 4–0 defeat at West Ham United and thereafter found it difficult to win back his place. Though he spent much of the second half of the season on the bench, he was forced to sit out the closing stages of the campaign with an Achilles injury. The popular defender has been offered a new one-year contract for the coming season

Wigan Athletic Playing Record

	League		FA Cup		FL Cup		Others		Total	
	App	Gls	App	Gls	App	Gls	App	Gls	App	Gls
2001–02	26	0	0	0	0	0	0	0	26	0
2002–03	45	1	3	0	5	0	2	0	55	1
2003–04	23 (1)	1	0 (1)	0	3	0	0	0	26 (2)	1
TOTAL	94 (1)	2	3 (1)	0	8	0	2	0	107 (2)	2

JAKUB Yanek (Joe)

Midfield/Full-back

Born: Falkirk, 7 December 1956.

Career: December 1973 Burnley 42 (0) 0. October 1980 Bury 262 (3) 27. AZ 67 Alkmaar, Holland. August 1988 Chester City 42 (0) 1. July 1989 Burnley 161 (2) 8. August 1993 Chester City 35 (1) 0. Colwyn Bay. September 1994 WIGAN ATHLETIC 16 (0) 0.

Joe Jakub began his career with Burnley and though he impressed in the club's Central League side, he found it difficult to break into the Clarets' First Division side. When he did, relegation had been confirmed but Jakub stayed at Turf Moor throughout the club's four-year spell in Division Two, winning a regular spot in 1978–79. Following the club's relegation to the Third Division, Jakub joined Bury where he was appointed club captain.

Ever-present in three consecutive seasons, he led the Shakers to

In the summer of 1994 he joined Wigan Athletic and though he had to wait until the eighth game of the 1994–95 season before making his debut (a 2–0 home defeat at the hands of Carlisle United), his experience in the Latics defence was invaluable. He played his last League game at Exeter in February 1995 at the age of 38 before joining the coaching staff of Preston North End. He was subsequently youth coach at Stockport before following Dave Jones to Southampton in a similar capacity.

Wigan Athletic Playing Record

	League		FA Cup		FL Cup		Others		Total	
	App	Gls	App	Gls	App	Gls	App	Gls	App	Gls
1994–95	16	0	2	0	2	0	3 (1)	0	23 (1)	0
TOTAL	16	0	2	0	2	0	3 (1)	0	23 (1)	0

JARRETT Jason Lee Mee

Midfield

Born: Bury, 14 September 1979.

Career: July 1998 Blackpool 2 (0) 0. October 1999 Wrexham 1 (0) 0. Shelbourne. July 2000 Bury 45 (17) 4. March 2002 WIGAN ATHLETIC 63 (18) 1.

Jason Jarrett

JENKINSON Leigh

Left Winger
Born: Thorne 9 July 1969
Career: June 1987 Hull City 95 (35) 13. September 1990 on loan Rotherham United 5 (2) 0. March 1993 Coventry City 22 (10) 1. November 1993 on loan Birmingham City 2 (1) 0. St Johnstone. June 1998 WIGAN ATHLETIC 3 (4) 0. Heart of Midlothian.

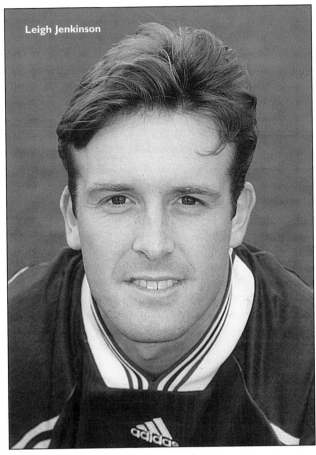

Leigh Jenkinson

Having come through the junior ranks at Blackpool, Jason Jarrett made his first-team debut for the Seasiders when coming off the bench in an FA Cup tie at Wigan in November 1998, a match the Latics won 4–3. Though he showed much promise, Blackpool decided to release him in the close season and he joined Wrexham. Unable to win a regular place in the Robins' starting line-up, he went on loan to League of Ireland club Shelbourne before moving on for a trial period at Bury.

Taken on by his home-town club on a short-term contract, he made such great progress that Shakers boss Andy Preece rewarded him with an 18-month contract in March 2001. An attacking midfield player who excels at linking defence and attack, he was a fixture in the Bury side in 2001–02. But with the club in financial difficulties, he was sold to Wigan for a bargain price of £75,000.

He then featured in a handful of games for the Latics, showing a liking for the hard work and decisive tackling required for a central midfield role. He was a regular in the Wigan side until the turn of the year in the club's Second Division Championship-winning season of 2002–03, netting his first goal for the club in the 1–0 Worthington Cup win at Northampton Town. Later in the season he was used as a valuable squad member, who never let the side down when he was called upon.

Jarrett continued to be an important member of Paul Jewell's squad but found the net only twice during the first month of the season. He is hugely popular with Wigan fans, who will be hoping he can start to find the net on a more regular basis.

Leigh Jenkinson worked his way up through the ranks at Hull City before making his Football League debut in the big Yorkshire clash at home to Sheffield United in February 1988. For the next three seasons he was a useful squad member rather than a regular performer, appearing more often as a substitute than as first-choice. Following a short loan period with Rotherham United, he almost joined the Millers on a permanent basis but the two clubs couldn't agree a fee. After deciding to stay at Boothferry Park, he began to hold down a regular place and in 1991–92 was the Tigers' joint top-scorer. Towards the end of the following season, Coventry City paid £300,000 for his services. One of the fastest men in football, he failed to set the world alight during two years at Highfield Road and after a loan spell with Birmingham City, he went north of the border to play for St Johnstone.

A Wales 'B' international, he spent three seasons at McDiarmid Park before joining the Latics on a free transfer in the summer of 1998. After making his debut in a 1–0 home defeat by Millwall on the opening day of the 1998–99 season, he found his opportunities limited following a change to the wing-back formation and at the end of the year he returned to Scotland to play for Hearts.

Wigan Athletic Playing Record

	League		FA Cup		FL Cup		Others		Total	
	App	Gls	App	Gls	App	Gls	App	Gls	App	Gls
2001–02	5	0	0	0	0	0	0	0	5	0
2002–03	25 (10)	0	3	0	5	1	1 (1)	1	34 (11)	2
2003–04	33 (8)	1	0	0	2	1	0	0	35 (8)	2
TOTAL	63 (18)	1	3	0	7	2	1 (1)	1	74 (19)	4

Wigan Athletic Playing Record

	League		FA Cup		FL Cup		Others		Total	
	App	Gls	App	Gls	App	Gls	App	Gls	App	Gls
1998–99	3 (4)		0 0 (1)		0 3	0	0 (1)	0	6 (6)	0
TOTAL	3 (4)		0 0 (1)		0 3	0	0 (1)	0	6 (6)	0

JEWELL Paul

Forward/Midfield

Born: Liverpool, 28 September 1964.

Career: September 1982 Liverpool. December 1984 WIGAN ATHLETIC 115 (20) 35. July 1988 Bradford City 217 (52) 56. August 1995 on loan Grimsby Town 2 (3) 1.

Paul Jewell was an apprentice with his home-town team Liverpool but, unable to make the grade, he was snapped up by Latics manager Harry McNally for £15,000. He made his League debut for the Latics in a 3–3 draw at Rotherham United in December 1984, while on New Year's Day he scored the winner in a 2–1 defeat of Burnley at Turf Moor. He ended his first season at Springfield Park as the club's second highest scorer with nine goals in 23 starts. It was 1986–87 before he won a regular place in the Latics side, going on to score 15 League and Cup goals including the goal that knocked First Division Norwich City out of the FA Cup. The following season he netted his only hat-trick for the club in a 4–0 win over Aldershot at Springfield Park, a match in which he also missed a penalty. In October 1987, Jewell scored the Latics' quickest-ever goal in the Football League in a 3–0 defeat of Rotherham United.

Paul Jewell

In July 1988 Jewell, having scored 47 goals in 166 games for the Latics, was sold to Bradford City for a fee of £80,000. Initially he was unable to maintain a regular first-team spot at Valley Parade, but the arrival of free-scoring Jimmy Quinn improved his selection chances. A versatile performer who could play in midfield or as a striker, Jewell, who had a brief loan spell at Grimsby Town, went on to score 66 goals in 308 games for the Bantams before hanging up his boots in the summer of 1996.

Appointed manager of Bradford City, he successfully kept the Yorkshire club in the Premier League after they had won promotion to the top flight in 1998–99. Surprisingly, he was later relieved of his duties and joined newly-relegated Sheffield Wednesday. However, with just over half the season gone and the Owls firmly rooted to the foot of the First Division, Jewell lost his job. He is now back with his beloved Wigan Athletic and at the end of his second season in charge, he led the Latics to the First Division as champions of Division Two.

Wigan Athletic Playing Record

	League		FA Cup		FL Cup		Others		Total	
	App	Gls	App	Gls	App	Gls	App	Gls	App	Gls
1984–85	23 (3)	9	2	1	0	0	4 (2)	2	29 (5)	12
1985–86	14 (15)	6	1	0	0	0	3 (2)	1	18 (17)	7
1986–87	38 (1)	9	6	4	1	0	3	2	48 (1)	15
1987–88	40 (1)	11	1	0	4	0	2	2	47 (1)	13
TOTAL	115 (20)	35	10	5	5	0	12 (4)	7	142 (24)	47

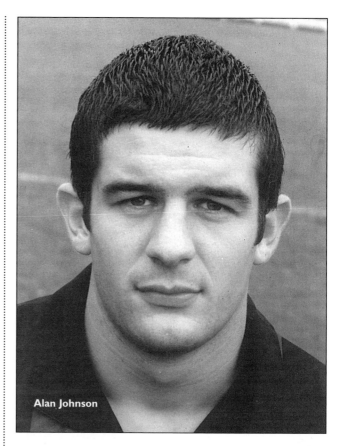

Alan Johnson

JOHNSON Alan Keith

Central Defender

Born: Wigan, 19 February 1971.

Career: March 1989 WIGAN ATHLETIC 163 (17) 13. February 1994 Lincoln City 57 (6) 0. September 1995 on loan Preston North End 2 (0) 0. August 1996 Rochdale 46 (0) 4.

England youth international Alan Johnson impressed in the club's junior and reserve teams before making his Wigan Athletic debut alongside Latics' other debutant Joe Parkinson in a 1–0 win at Mansfield Town in January 1989. Useful at set pieces, he scored his first goal for the club towards the end of that season in a 1–0 defeat of Bury, a result that ensured that the Latics would play Third Division football the following season.

Over the next four seasons, Johnson missed very few matches, but after the club were relegated in 1992–93 he failed to agree a new contract with the Wigan board. He signed a week-to-week contract but in February 1995, this most wholehearted of defenders left to join Lincoln City, the Imps being Wigan's opponents in Johnson's last game for the then Springfield Park club.

A transfer tribunal set the fee at £65,000 but on his arrival at Sincil Bank, his progress was hampered by a series of niggling injuries. Following a loan spell at Preston North End, Johnson left Lincoln and joined Rochdale on a free transfer. An ever-present and 'Player of the Year' in his first season at Spotland, he missed the whole of the 1997–98 campaign through injury and at the end of the following season he was released.

Wigan Athletic Playing Record

	League		FA Cup		FL Cup		Others		Total	
	App	Gls	App	Gls	App	Gls	App	Gls	App	Gls
1988–89	4 (4)	1	0	0	0	0	0 (1)	0	4 (5)	1
1989–90	26 (7)	1	1 (1)	1	0 (1)	0	2 (1)	0	29 (10)	2
1990–91	40 (3)	5	4	0	0 (1)	0	4 (1)	2	48 (5)	7
1991–92	41 (3)	4	2 (1)	0	3	0	2	0	48 (4)	4
1992–93	36	1	3	0	2	1	5	1	46	3
1993–94	16	1	4	0	2	0	1	0	23	1
TOTAL	163 (17)	13	14 (2)	1	7 (2)	1	14 (3)	3	198 (24)	18

JOHNSON Gavin

Left Midfield

Born: Stowmarket, 10 October 1970.

Career: February 1989 Ipswich Town 114 (18) 11. July 1995 Luton Town 4 (1) 0. December 1995 WIGAN ATHLETIC 82 (2) 8. July 1998 Dunfermline Athletic 18 (0) 0. November 1999 Colchester United 84 (8) 3.

Gavin Johnson made his Football League debut for Ipswich Town against Barnsley at Portman Road in February 1989, just a few days after signing professional forms. Though he only played sporadically over the next couple of seasons, he performed well when required. He finally came to the fore in 1991–92, appearing in most of the games during Ipswich's Second Division Championship campaign. Originally a central defender, he was switched to the left side of midfield and it was his goals in the last two games of the season that clinched the title for Ipswich. He missed just two games in 1992–93 but was unfortunate to pick up a knee injury during the final match against Nottingham Forest when his foot got caught in a hole on the Portman Road pitch and necessitated an operation.

Gavin Johnson

Unable to win back his place on a regular basis, he joined Luton Town but his stay at Kenilworth Road was brief and in December 1995 he joined Wigan Athletic for a fee of £15,000. The hardworking midfielder made his Latics debut in a 2–1 home win over Hereford United, going on to play in the last 27 games of the season. Over the next three seasons, Johnson proved that he could play anywhere on the left flank and scored some spectacular goals, especially from dead-ball situations. After helping the Latics win the Third Division Championship in 1996–97, he found his time at Springfield Park dogged by groin problems and in the summer of 1998 he was released.

After a short spell with Dunfermline Athletic he joined Colchester United, where his early performances helped the Layer Road club maintain their Second Division status. A regular until the second half of the 2001–02 season, a succession of injuries to his groin and hip restricted his appearances. Though he returned to the starting line-up at the start of the following campaign, he

broke his leg at Port Vale and then suffered a setback that required a second operation in the spring and he spent this last summer recuperating.

Wigan Athletic Playing Record

	League		FA Cup		FL Cup		Others		Total	
	App	Gls	App	Gls	App	Gls	App	Gls	App	Gls
1995–96	27	3	0	0	0	0	0	0	27	3
1996–97	37	3	1	0	2	0	1	0	41	3
1997–98	18 (2)	2	2	0	2	0	0	0	22 (2)	2
TOTAL	84 (2)	8	3	0	4	0	1	0	92 (2)	8

JOHNSON Stephen Anthony

Forward

Born: Liverpool, 23 June 1957.

Career: Altrincham. November 1977 Bury 139 (15) 52. August 1983 Rochdale 17 (2) 7. February 1984 WIGAN ATHLETIC 50 (1) 18. March 1985 Bristol City 14 (7) 3. December 1985 on loan Rochdale 3 (3) 1. March 1986 on loan Chester City 10 (0) 6. July 1986 Scunthorpe United 59 (13) 20. August 1988 Chester City 35 (3) 10. Huskvarna, Sweden. October 1989 Rochdale 20 (4) 4. Northwich Victoria. Radcliffe Borough. Caernarvon Town.

An outstanding goalscoring record for Altrincham in the Northern Premier League led to Third Division Bury giving Steve Johnson the opportunity to play League football. He didn't disappoint and

Steve Johnson

Graeme Jones

in six seasons at Gigg Lane, he scored 52 goals in 154 League outings. Johnson left the Shakers in the summer of 1983, joining Rochdale for what turned out to be the first of three spells with the Spotland club.

In February 1984 Latics boss Harry McNally paid £20,000 for Johnson. Seldom can there have been a more spectacular debut at Springfield Park, as Johnson destroyed Sheffield United with two goals in a 3–0 win for the Latics. The burly striker put Wigan ahead when he met Tony Kelly's corner with a venomous header and he set the seal on a cracking performance with a 71st minute explosion of a shot. He could have had a hat-trick but shot against the 'keeper's legs after being put clear! In 1984–85 he was joint top-scorer with Mike Newell, both strikers netting 16 League and Cup goal. Sadly for Latics fans, Johnson left the club just before the Freight Rover Trophy Final.

Unable to settle at Ashton Gate, he had loan spells with Rochdale and Chester City before signing for Scunthorpe United. The much-travelled striker later joined the Cestrians on a permanent basis before ending his first-class career with Rochdale, following a spell in Sweden playing for Huskvarna. He later played non-League football for Northwich Victoria, Radcliffe Borough and Caernarvon Town, but is now a financial adviser in Bury.

Wigan Athletic Playing Record

	League		FA Cup		FL Cup		Others		Total	
	App	Gls	App	Gls	App	Gls	App	Gls	App	Gls
1983–84	21	7	0	0	0	0	0	0	21	7
1984–85	29 (1)	11	3	1	4	3	2	1	38 (1)	16
TOTAL	50 (1)	18	3	1	4	3	2	1	59 (1)	23

JONES Graeme Anthony

Forward
Born: Gateshead, 13 March 1970.
Career: Bridlington Town. August 1993 Doncaster Rovers 80 (12) 26. July 1996 WIGAN ATHLETIC 76 (20) 44. November 1999 St Johnstone 31 (10) 7. July 2002 Southend United 18 (3) 2. March 2003 Boston United 2 (1) 1.

Bustling centre-forward Graeme Jones began his career with non-League Bridlington Town before joining Doncaster Rovers for a fee of £10,000 in the summer of 1993. Despite missing a number of games through injury, he was the Belle Vue club's leading scorer in 1993–94 and 1994–95 and had the honour of being the first player in the country to register a goal in the Coca-Cola Cup. He had scored 29 goals in 105 games when he joined the Latics for a then club record fee of £150,000 in July 1996.

He scored on his Wigan debut in a 1–1 draw at Barnet and ended the campaign as the Football League's highest scorer with 33 goals including hat-tricks in the wins over Chester City (home 4–0), Torquay United (home 3–2), Leyton Orient (home 5–1) and Darlington (home 3–2). Not surprisingly he was voted the club's 'Player of the Year', won selection for the Third Division side at the PFA awards night and won a Third Division Championship medal as the Latics pipped Fulham for the title.

Though he was unable to discover his goalscoring form of the previous season in 1997–98 due to a succession of niggling injuries, he was forced to miss the majority of the 1998–99 campaign after damaging cruciate ligaments. He started just one League match the following season before, being frustrated by a lack of first-team chances, he moved to St Johnstone for £100,000, helping them to fifth place in the Scottish Premier Division in his first season at McDiarmid Park.

He remained at the Scottish club for another season but most

of his appearances were when he came off the bench and in the summer of 2002 he joined Southend United. He soon became a popular figure at Roots Hall but halfway through the season he was injured at Carlisle and didn't play for the Shrimps again. Moving to Boston United prior to the transfer deadline, he scored after eight minutes of his debut after coming on as a substitute against Rushden and Diamonds. He started the next two games before hamstring injury ruled him out of the last few games of the season.

Wigan Athletic Playing Record

	League		FA Cup		FL Cup		Others		Total	
	App	Gls	App	Gls	App	Gls	App	Gls	App	Gls
1996–97	39 (1)	31	1	0	1 (1)	1	1	1	42 (2)	33
1997–98	28 (5)	9	3	1	1	0	3	4	35 (5)	14
1998–99	8 (12)	3	0	0	2	0	2 (1)	1	12 (14)	4
1999–2000	1 (2)	1	0	0	0 (2)	0	0	0	1 (4)	1
TOTAL	76 (20)	44	4	1	4 (3)	1	6 (2)	6	90 (25)	52

JONES Philip Andrew

Full-back
Born: Liverpool 1 December 1969
Career: June 1988 Everton 0 (1) 0. March 1990 on loan Blackpool 6 (0) 0. January 1991 WIGAN ATHLETIC 84 (2) 2. August 1993 Bury 4 (0) 0.

Phil Jones began his Football League career at Everton but in almost three years with the Goodison club his only experience of first-team football came in an appearance as a substitute for Neil Adams in a 1–0 home win over Southampton. Jones then had a loan spell with Blackpool, making six appearances for the Seasiders before joining Wigan Athletic in January 1991.

He made his Latics debut as a substitute for Ronnie Hildersley in a 2–0 home win over Fulham the following month before

Phil Jones

appearing in 19 of the remaining 20 games. Jones's first goal in League football came in a 6–1 Latics win at Swansea City in April 1991. During his time with the Latics, the versatile Jones occupied eight different outfield positions, but following the club's relegation to the Third Division in 1992–93 he was released and joined Bury as a non-contract player.

Wigan Athletic Playing Record

	League		FA Cup		FL Cup		Others		Total	
	App	Gls	App	Gls	App	Gls	App	Gls	App	Gls
1990–91	19 (1)	1	0	0	0	0	1	0	20 (1)	1
1991–92	40 (1)	1	2	0	3	1	2	0	47 (1)	2
1992–93	25 (2)	0	1	0	4	0	2	0	32 (2)	0
TOTAL	84 (4)	2	3	0	7	1	5	0	99 (4)	3

KELLY Anthony Gerald

Midfield

Born: Prescot 1 October 1964

Career: Liverpool. Prescot Cables. January 1984 WIGAN ATHLETIC 98 (3) 15. April 1986 Stoke City 33 (3) 4. July 1987 West Bromwich Albion 26 (0) 1. September 1988 on loan Chester City 5 (0) 0. October 1988 on loan Colchester United 13 (0) 2. January 1989 Shrewsbury Town 100 (1) 15. August 1991 Bolton Wanderers 103 (3) 5. September 1994 Port Vale 3 (1) 1. October 1994 Millwall 1 (1) 0. December 1994 Peterborough United 12 (1) 2. July 1995 WIGAN ATHLETIC 2 (0) 0. Altrincham. Halifax Town. Sligo Rovers.

Following his apprenticeship with Liverpool, Tony Kelly had a short spell on trial with Derby County before signing for non-League Prescot Cables. Wigan Athletic manager Harry McNally

Tony Kelly

gave him his chance in League football and he made his debut at right-back in a 1–0 home defeat at the hands of Walsall in November 1983. After moving into midfield, Kelly soon established himself as a first-team regular and was a member of the Latics' successful Wembley Freight Rover Trophy Final team in 1985, scoring one of the goals in a 3–1 win over Brentford.

In April 1986, Stoke City signed him for £80,000 and he spent a year at the Victoria Ground before a £60,000 move to West Bromwich Albion. During 1988–89 he was loaned out to both Chester City and Colchester United before Shrewsbury Town bought him for £30,000 in January 1989. Former Wigan manager Ian McNeill made Kelly captain and he went on to make over a century of League appearances for the Shrews before joining Bolton Wanderers in August 1991 for a £100,000 fee, along with teammate Michael Brown.

Affectionately known as 'Zico', one of Kelly's best goals for the Wanderers came against the Latics in April 1993 as Bolton won 2–0 at Springfield Park. Swapping passes with John McGinlay in a 30-yard run, he went past three Latics defenders before shooting low into the net!

On leaving Burnden Park he joined Port Vale on a free transfer before subsequently spending short periods of time with a number of clubs. After a spell with Peterborough United he returned to Wigan but things didn't work out for him and in February 1996 he joined GM Vauxhall Conference side Altrincham. He later had a spell at Halifax before moving to League of Ireland side Sligo Rovers.

Wigan Athletic Playing Record

	League		FA Cup		FL Cup		Others		Total	
	App	Gls	App	Gls	App	Gls	App	Gls	App	Gls
1983–84	27 (2)	2	1	0	0	0	1	0	29 (2)	2
1984–85	39 (1)	4	4	0	3	0	7	3	53 (1)	7
1985–86	32	9	5	1	2	2	4	1	43	13
1995–96	2	0	0	0	0	0	1	0	3	0
TOTAL	100 (2)	15	10	1	5	2	13	4	128 (3)	22

KELLY Norman

Midfield

Born: Belfast 10 October 1970

Career: July 1989 Oldham Athletic 0 (2) 0. October 1989 on loan WIGAN ATHLETIC 0 (4) 0.

Midfielder Norman Kelly, who represented Northern Ireland at both youth and Under-21 level, began his Football League career with Oldham Athletic, joining the Boundary Park club on a Youth Training Scheme in the summer of 1987. Competition for places in the Oldham side was stiff and after two appearances in the substitute's shirt, he joined Wigan Athletic on loan.

His first game for the Latics was as substitute for Dave Thompson in a 3–0 defeat at Bristol City. Kelly was in fact substitute in each of his four games for the club, with his best performance coming on his home debut in a 3–1 win over Reading. On his return to Boundary Park, Kelly still couldn't force his way into the Oldham side and at the end of the season he left to play non-League football.

Wigan Athletic Playing Record

	League		FA Cup		FL Cup		Others		Total	
	App	Gls	App	Gls	App	Gls	App	Gls	App	Gls
1989–90	0 (4)	0	0	0	0	0	0	0	0 (4)	0
TOTAL	0 (4)	0	0	0	0	0	0	0	0 (4)	0

KENNA Jeffrey Jude

Full-back

Born: Dublin 27 August 1970

Career: April 1989 Southampton 110 (4) 4. March 1995 Blackburn Rovers 153 (2) 1. March 2001 on loan Tranmere Rovers 11 (0) 0. November 2001 on loan WIGAN ATHLETIC 6 (0) 1. December 2001 Birmingham City 57 (1) 1.

Republic of Ireland international full-back Jeff Kenna joined Southampton from Dublin junior club Palmerston Rangers and after a period on loan at Wigan Athletic – where he didn't make the first team – he made his League debut for the Saints against Spurs in January 1992. From then until his £1.5 million transfer to Blackburn Rovers less than three years later, Kenna made the No.2 shirt his own, playing in 133 League and Cup games for the south coast club.

Following his transfer to Rovers in March 1995, he joined Southampton teammates Alan Shearer and Tim Flowers in a Blackburn side that won their first League Championship title since 1914. Initially required to fill in at left-back when Graeme Le Saux was not replaced, he performed well but when switched to right-back he blossomed and became the club's most reliable defender. Injuries then hampered his progress at Ewood Park and though on regaining full fitness he continued to represent the Republic of Ireland, he found himself in and out of the Blackburn side. Two operations on his Achilles tendon during the 1999–2000 season restricted his first-team appearances and midway through the following campaign he went on loan to Tranmere Rovers.

At Prenton Park his experience proved invaluable in what was ultimately an unsuccessful struggle against relegation. In November 2001 he joined Wigan Athletic on a month's loan in an attempt to put himself in the shop window. He was very impressive in his spell with the Latics, firing home a stunning shot in the 6–1 defeat of Stoke City. After returning to Ewood Park he became one of former Wigan boss Steve Bruce's first signings at Birmingham City. Appointed club captain, he helped the Blues consolidate their position in the Premiership following their promotion from Division One. In 2004 he transferred to Derby County.

Wigan Athletic Playing Record

	League		FA Cup		FL Cup		Others		Total	
	App	Gls	App	Gls	App	Gls	App	Gls	App	Gls
2001–02	6	1	1	0	0	0	0	0	7	1
TOTAL	6	1	1	0	0	0	0	0	7	1

KENNEDY Alan Philip

Left-back

Born: Sunderland, 31 August 1954.

Career: August 1972 Newcastle United 155 (3) 9. August 1978 Liverpool 249 (2) 15. September 1985 Sunderland 54 (0) 2. Beerschot, Belgium. October 1987 Hartlepool United 4 (1) 0. Grantham. December 1987 WIGAN ATHLETIC 22 (0) 0. Colne Dynamoes. March 1990 Wrexham 15 (0) 0. Morecambe. Netherfield. Barrow.

Alan Kennedy began his Football League career with Newcastle United where, once he had tasted first-team action as a teenager, he became a terrace favourite. He appeared for the Magpies in the 1974 FA Cup Final after only a handful of senior outings. Also with United, he was capped at Under-23 and 'B' level but had to wait almost a decade before winning full international honours. By that time he had joined Liverpool, Bob Paisley paying £330,000 in August 1978.

Alan Kennedy

Kennedy was in the traditional mould of full-backs, tough and hard-tackling, but he also enjoyed his runs upfield that resulted in many a vital goal. His most memorable goals came in the European Cup Finals of 1981 and 1984. In the latter against AS Roma, he stepped up coolly and fired the most important penalty-kick in the club's history high into the back of the net – the day before he had missed every penalty attempt during practice!

'Barney', as the fans called him, was a great favourite with the Kop and had won five League Championship medals as well as his European honours when in September 1985 he was sold to home-town club Sunderland for £100,000. After a spell playing for Hartlepool United and abroad with Beerschot of Belgium, Kennedy arrived at Springfield Park in December 1987. He made his Latics debut in a 2–0 win at Bury, helping the side record seven wins and a draw in his first eight appearances in Wigan's colours. After helping the Latics to seventh place in the Third Division, he played non-League football for Colne Dynamoes before returning to League action with Wrexham.

He later had a spell playing non-League football for Morecambe before becoming player-manager of Netherfield. After ending his career with Barrow, Alan Kennedy is now a radio personality on Merseyside as well as an accomplished after-dinner speaker.

Wigan Athletic Playing Record

	League		FA Cup		FL Cup		Others		Total	
	App	Gls	App	Gls	App	Gls	App	Gls	App	Gls
1987–88	22	0	0	0	0	0	0	0	22	0
TOTAL	22	0	0	0	0	0	0	0	22	0

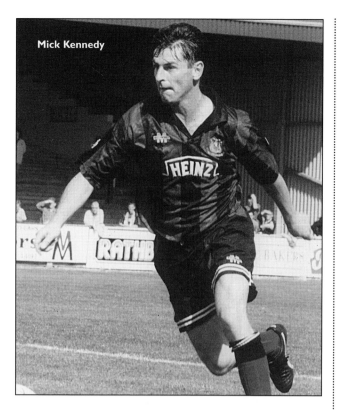

Mick Kennedy

KENNEDY Michael Francis Martin

Midfield

Born: Salford, 9 April 1961.

Career: January 1979 Halifax Town 74 (2) 4. August 1980 Huddersfield Town 80 (1) 9. August 1982 Middlesbrough 68 (0) 5. June 1984 Portsmouth 129 (0) 4. January 1988 Bradford City 45 (0) 2. March 1989 Leicester City 9 (0) 0. August 1989 Luton Town 30 (2) 0. August 1990 Stoke City 51 (1) 3. August 1992 Chesterfield 19 (8) 1. July 1993 WIGAN ATHLETIC 15 (2) 1.

An aggressive, industrious midfielder, Mick Kennedy began his career with Halifax Town where his impressive performances attracted the attention of a number of top-flight clubs. However, when Kennedy refused the offer of a new contract with the Shaymen in August 1980, he moved to Fourth Division Champions Huddersfield Town for a club record £50,000.

He had two years at Leeds Road before joining Middlesbrough for £100,000. In the summer of 1984 he was on the move again, this time to Portsmouth, where he won two full caps for the Republic of Ireland against Iceland and Czechoslovakia. In 1986–87, Kennedy helped Pompey win promotion to the First Division, but following their relegation after just one season in the top flight, he left to play for Bradford City.

There followed spells with Leicester City, Luton Town and Stoke City before he joined Chesterfield in August 1992. It was from the Spireites that the much-travelled player joined Wigan prior to the start of the 1993–94 season. He made his debut in a 1–1 home draw against Wycombe Wanderers, though in almost half of his starts he was substituted. His only goal for the Latics came in the 3–1 home defeat by Torquay United but at the end of a season in which the club finished 19th in the Third Division, he was released.

Wigan Athletic Playing Record

	League		FA Cup		FL Cup		Others		Total	
	App	Gls	App	Gls	App	Gls	App	Gls	App	Gls
1993–94	15 (2)	1	1	0	0	0	0	0	16 (2)	1
TOTAL	15 (2)	1	1	0	0	0	0	0	16 (2)	1

KENNEDY Peter Henry James

Midfield

Born: Lurgan, 10 September 1973.

Career: Portadown. August 1996 Notts County 20 (2) 0. July 1997 Watford 108 (7) 18. July 2001 WIGAN ATHLETIC 60 (5) 2. November 2003 on loan Derby County.

Kennedy began his career as a speedy left-winger with Portadown before a £100,000 transfer took him to Notts County in the summer of 1996. He settled down quickly, his early displays showing him to be comfortable on the ball and a provider of excellent crosses. Then things started to go wrong and he was on the verge of leaving the game after a depressing spell in County's reserves.

Then he was signed unseen by Watford manager Graham Taylor and repaid his faith in him by scoring his first-ever hat-trick in a 3–0 win at Southend United. Despite cracking a bone in his leg, he had done enough to secure selection for the PFA Second Division team and still finished the season as the Hornets' leading scorer with 13 goals and a Second Division Championship medal. The club's only ever-present in their first season back in Division One, his form was such that he won the first of 17 full caps for Northern Ireland.

Following Watford's promotion to the Premiership – he had the distinction of scoring the club's first goal in the top flight – his season was disrupted by a mysterious back injury and a cartilage operation. There followed an Achilles tendon operation before, having scored 22 goals in 134 games, he was placed on the 'open to offers' list in the summer of 2001.

He became Paul Jewell's first signing when the Latics boss paid £300,000 for his services. Though he made a somewhat slow start, he eventually began to provide a more balanced look in the centre of the park. Though favouring a midfield role, he showed his versatility by playing at left-back to cover injuries. His only goal for the club came in Wigan's Second Division Championship winning season of 2002–03 when his superb free-kick helped the Latics to a 1–0 win at Bristol City.

He started the 2003–04 season in fine style, netting in a 2–0 win over Burnley, but then lost form and after spending a spell on loan at Derby County, was released at the end of the season by the Latics.

Wigan Athletic Playing Record

	League		FA Cup		FL Cup		Others		Total	
	App	Gls	App	Gls	App	Gls	App	Gls	App	Gls
2001–02	29 (2)	0	1	0	0	0	1	0	31 (2)	0
2002–03	21 (1)	1	3	0	3	0	2	0	29 (1)	1
2003–04	10 (2)	1	0	0	3	0	0	0	13 (2)	1
TOTAL	60 (5)	2	4	0	6	0	3	0	73 (5)	2

KERR James Stewart

Goalkeeper

Born: Motherwell, 13 November 1974.

Career: May 1993 Glasgow Celtic 33 (1) 0. November 1994 on loan Brighton and Hove Albion 2 (0) 0. August 2001 WIGAN ATHLETIC 8 (0) 0.

Scottish Under-21 international goalkeeper Stewart Kerr joined Celtic in the summer of 1993 and over the next eight seasons was understudy to a number of fine 'keepers. During the early days of his time at Parkhead, he had a brief loan spell with Brighton and Hove Albion but returned north of the border to take his total of first-team appearances to 35 before joining the Latics on a free transfer in August 2001.

An outstanding shot-stopper, who not only commands his area

but organises his defence impressively, he made his debut in the home match against Bristol City – which the Latics lost 2–1, just a day after putting pen to paper. His best performances came in the away matches at Bury (won 2–0) and Bournemouth (lost 0–2) before the Motherwell-born 'keeper suffered a freak spinal injury in training. The injury virtually ended his season, although he did return to the bench for the club's last game of the 2001–02 season against Colchester United.

Wigan Athletic Playing Record

	League		FA Cup		FL Cup		Others		Total	
	App	Gls	App	Gls	App	Gls	App	Gls	App	Gls
2001–02	8	0	0	0	0	0	0	0	8	0
TOTAL	8	0	0	0	0	0	0	0	8	0

KETTLE Brian

Full-back
Born: Prescot, 22 April 1956.
Career: May 1973 Liverpool 3 (0) 0. Houston, United States. August 1980 WIGAN ATHLETIC 14 (0) 1. Formby.

Brian Kettle

Prescot-born defender Brian Kettle began his Football League career with Liverpool but found it difficult to win a regular first-team place at Anfield. He had made just four appearances for the Reds, one of which was in the European Cup, when he decided to try his luck in the United States.

After a couple of seasons playing for Houston, Kettle joined Wigan Athletic in September 1980 and made his debut in a 3–1 defeat at Darlington. After adjusting to the demands of Fourth Division football and having scored his first goal for the club in a 4–1 home defeat of Halifax Town, Kettle was struck down by a severe knee injury in only his 14th game for the club. Though his

recovery was slow, the big-hearted player was looking forward to the 1981–82 season when he was surprisingly allowed to leave Springfield Park and join non-League Formby.

Wigan Athletic Playing Record

	League		FA Cup		FL Cup		Others		Total	
	App	Gls	App	Gls	App	Gls	App	Gls	App	Gls
1980–81	14	1	0	0	0	0	0	0	14	1
TOTAL	14	1	0	0	0	0	0	0	14	1

KILFORD Ian Anthony

Midfield
Born: Bristol, 6 October 1973.
Career: April 1991 Nottingham Forest 0 (1) 0. December 1993 on loan WIGAN ATHLETIC 2 (1) 2. March 1994 WIGAN ATHLETIC 175 (43) 30. August 2002 Bury. November 2002 Scunthorpe United 27 (1) 3.

A central midfielder with a lovely touch and an eye for an opening, Ian Kilford joined Wigan Athletic on a free transfer from Nottingham Forest in March 1994, having made his debut in a goalless home draw with Rochdale while on loan in December 1993. He soon became an established member of the Latics side, enjoying one of his best seasons in 1996–97, a campaign which culminated in him winning a Third Division Championship medal. His versatility and important goals were vital as he was called upon to fill a number of roles from right-back to left-wing!

In 1997–98 he was the club's second-top League scorer, his total of 10 goals including the winners in the home games against Oldham Athletic and Watford. After that, he found it difficult to

Ian Kilford

hold down a regular first-team shirt, but he remained a willing servant. He deservedly won an Autowindscreen Shield winners' medal after the Latics beat Millwall 1–0 in the Wembley Final and started the Second Division Play-off final against Gillingham.

As Wigan's longest-serving player, he was offered a new deal at the start of the 2000–01 season and though he missed very few games in the first half of the campaign, a broken wrist restricted his appearances in the latter stage of the season. In 2001–02 he struggled to force his way into new manager Paul Jewell's plans, finding himself restricted to just a handful of first-team starts. He was used mainly from the bench but whenever called upon, he never let the side down. Out of contract in the summer, he joined Bury but, after finding himself overlooked for the first half of the season, joined Scunthorpe United. He did not miss a match in the second half of the campaign as his experience helped the Irons make the Third Division play-offs.

Wigan Athletic Playing Record

	League		FA Cup		FL Cup		Others		Total	
	App	Gls	App	Gls	App	Gls	App	Gls	App	Gls
1993–94	7 (1)	3	0 (1)	0	0	0	0	0	7 (2)	3
1994–95	35	5	2	1	4	0	3	1	44	7
1995–96	18 (7)	3	1 (1)	0	0	0	2	0	21 (8)	3
1996–97	24 (11)	8	0	0	1	0	1	0	24 (10)	8
1997–98	29 (1)	10	3	0	1 (1)	0	0 (1)	0	33 (3)	10
1998–99	16 (7)	0	3	0	2	0	3 (1)	1	24 (8)	1
1999–2000	18 (3)	1	3	0	3	0	4	0	28 (3)	1
2000–01	23 (1)	2	2	1	3 (1)	1	0	0	28 (2)	4
2001–02	7 (13)	0	0	0	0 (1)	0	1	0	7 (14)	0
TOTAL	177 (44)	32	14 (2)	2	14 (3)	1	14 (2)	2	219 (51)	37

KILNER John Ian

Goalkeeper
Born: Bolton 3 October 1959
Career: October 1977 Preston North End. February 1979 Halifax Town 114 (0) 0. South Africa. July 1983 WIGAN ATHLETIC 4 (0) 0.

Goalkeeper John Kilner began his career with Preston North End, but despite some good performances in the club's Central League side, he failed to make the Lilywhites' first team and in February 1979 moved across the Pennines to play for Halifax Town. Kilner stayed with the Shaymen for four seasons, during which time he was the club's first-choice 'keeper, appearing in 114 League games. Towards the end of his time with the Yorkshire club, his appearances became less frequent and in 1982 he left to play in South Africa.

In the summer of 1983, Kilner joined Wigan Athletic on a non-contract basis and made his debut as a replacement for the injured Roy Tunks at Bradford City. It wasn't the best of debuts as the Latics gave a lacklustre display and were beaten 6–2. He kept his place for the next game and performed heroics in a 2–1 defeat of Rotherham United. He appeared in two more games towards the end of the season, keeping a clean sheet in a 1–0 win over Newport County in his final game for the club.

Wigan Athletic Playing Record

	League		FA Cup		FL Cup		Others		Total	
	App	Gls	App	Gls	App	Gls	App	Gls	App	Gls
1983–84	4	0	1	0	0	0	0	0	5	0
TOTAL	4	0	1	0	0	0	0	0	5	0

KIRBY Ryan Mark

Right-back
Born: Chingford 6 September 1974
Career: July 1993 Arsenal. July 1994 Doncaster Rovers 73 (5) 0. August 1996 WIGAN ATHLETIC 5 (1) 0. September 1996 Northampton Town 0 (1) 0. Stevenage.

Ryan Kirby

Full-back Ryan Kirby began his Football League career with Doncaster Rovers having been released by Arsenal during the summer of 1994. After making his debut as a substitute at Hereford on the opening day of the 1994–95 season he held his place for the remainder of the campaign.

Despite a move to midfield, where he was clearly unsuitable, Kirby was a regular in the Belle Vue club's side, but in the summer of 1996 he was given a free transfer. Following brief spells at Preston North End and Crewe Alexandra he joined the Latics. He made his debut in the second game of the 1996–97 season, a 1–1 draw at Barnet, going on to appear in six games of the club's Third Division Championship-winning season. On leaving Springfield Park he joined Northampton Town on a non-contract basis as defensive cover for first-team players. However, after a few months he opted to join Vauxhall Conference side Stevenage to help in their push for League status. While with the Cobblers he created an unwanted record, having the shortest first-team career of just three minutes, following his only appearance a substitute for the club!

Wigan Athletic Playing Record

	League		FA Cup		FL Cup		Others		Total	
	App	Gls	App	Gls	App	Gls	App	Gls	App	Gls
1996–97	5 (1)	0	0	0	0	0	0	0	5 (1)	0
TOTAL	5 (1)	0	0	0	0	0	0	0	5 (1)	0

KNOWLES James Barry

Left-back
Born: Wigan 25 April 1959
Career: Barrow. October 1984 WIGAN ATHLETIC 124 (3) 3.

Barry Knowles began his career with non-League Barrow before signing for his home-town club Wigan Athletic in the summer of 1984. His first game in Latic's colours came in a 1–1 home draw against Newport County in October of that year. Knowles, who suffered a series of niggling injuries during his first season at Springfield Park, liked nothing better than to get forward and support the attack, scoring his first goal for the club in a 4–2 win over Orient in only his fifth appearance. At the end of his first season he picked up a Freight Rover Trophy winners' medal as Latics beat Brentford 3–1 in the Wembley final.

Knowles, who missed just one game in 1985–86 as Latics finished fourth in Division Three, had an outstanding season, as he did the following campaign when the club repeated its achievements. His only goal that season was the winner on the final day as the Latics won 3–2 at Brentford. His third League goal for the club came on the opening day of the 1987–88 season in a 4–4 draw at Notts County, but at the end of yet another consistent season, the popular defender was released.

Barry Knowles

Wigan Athletic Playing Record

	League		FA Cup		FL Cup		Others		Total	
	App	Gls	App	Gls	App	Gls	App	Gls	App	Gls
1984–85	20	1	0	0	1	0	5	0	26	1
1985–86	45	0	5	1	2	0	6	0	58	1
1986–87	38 (1)	1	6	0	2	0	3	1	49 (1)	2
1987–88	21 (2)	1	2	0	3	0	2	0	28 (2)	1
TOTAL	124 (3)	3	13	1	8	0	16	1	161 (3)	5

LANCASHIRE Graham

Forward
Born: Blackpool 19 October 1972
Career: June 1991 Burnley 11 (20) 8. November 1992 on loan Halifax Town 2 (0) 0. January 1994 on loan Chester City 10 (1) 7. December 1994 Preston North End 11 (12) 2. January 1996 WIGAN ATHLETIC 20 (10) 12. October 1997 Rochdale 54 (29) 23. Hednesford Town.

Graham Lancashire burst onto the Football League scene with a vengeance when in 1991–92 he deputised for Mike Conroy in the Burnley side. In the four games that Conroy missed, Lancashire scored six goals including a hat-trick in a 6–2 victory at Wrexham. However, he was still unable to win a regular place in the Clarets side and after loan spells with Halifax Town and Chester City, he was transferred to Preston North End for £55,000.

Not a regular in the North End side that reached the play-offs in 1994–95 or the side that did even better the following season, he moved to Wigan, initially on loan. Lancashire made his Latics debut in a 3–1 defeat at Scunthorpe United and scored three goals

Graham Lancashire

in four games towards the end of the 1995–96 season before damaged knee ligaments ruled him out of the remaining games. He started the 1996–97 season in tremendous form, scoring 10 goals in the opening 12 games including a hat-trick in a 4–4 League Cup draw at Preston. This led to the 'G Force' partnership with Graeme Jones but tragically for the second time in seven months, his season was wrecked by a serious knee injury. Happily he returned to action towards the end of the season, scoring a goal in the final match against Mansfield Town which saw him win a Third Division Championship medal.

Surprisingly, in October 1997 he was allowed to leave Springfield Park and joined Rochdale for £40,000. He seemed the answer to the Dale's scoring problems after netting twice on his debut, but again injuries hampered his progress, a thigh muscle problem forcing him to miss most of the 1998–99 season. After that, the potent striker who went on to score 25 goals in 94 games found that even more injuries forced him to miss more games than he played in. Out of contract in the summer of 2001, he moved into non-League football with Hednesford Town.

Wigan Athletic Playing Record

	League		FA Cup		FL Cup		Others		Total	
	App	Gls	App	Gls	App	Gls	App	Gls	App	Gls
1995–96	4	3	0	0	0	0	0	0	4	3
1996–97	16 (9)	9	0	0	2	4	0	0	18 (9)	13
1997–98	0 (1)	0	0	0	0 (1)	0	0	0	0 (2)	0
TOTAL	20 (10)	12	0	0	2 (1)	4	0	0	22 (11)	16

LANGLEY Kevin James

Midfield
Born: St Helens, 24 May 1964.
Career: May 1982 WIGAN ATHLETIC 156 (4) 6. July 1986 Everton 16 (0) 2. March 1987 Manchester City 9 (0) 0. January 1988 on loan Chester City 9 (0) 0. March 1988 Birmingham City 74 (2) 2. September 1990 WIGAN ATHLETIC 151 (6) 6.

Kevin Langley was working as a painter and decorator when he wrote to Wigan Athletic asking for a trial. Though Latics manager

Kevin Langley

Ian McNeill offered him an apprenticeship, it was Larry Lloyd who gave Langley his first taste of League football as he made his debut in a 3–1 win over Northampton Town in September 1981. However, it was towards the end of the following season, the club's first in the Third Division, when Langley established himself as a first-team regular. Over the next three seasons he missed few games and helped Latics win the Freight Rover Trophy at Wembley in 1985, but in the summer of 1986 he was sold to First Division Everton for a fee of £120,000.

Unable to make much headway with the Goodison club, he joined Manchester City but could not settle at Maine Road and was loaned out to Chester City. In March 1988 this tall, elegant ball-playing midfielder joined Birmingham City, where he was touted on his arrival as the vital cog in the Blues' engine room and the man to provide the chances that would take the team back into the First Division. In truth, he never looked comfortable with Birmingham's style of play and in September 1990 he rejoined the Latics. He went on to give the then Springfield Park club another four years service, taking his total of first-team appearances to 394, which included at the time, the club's Football League appearance record of 317 in his two spells with the club.

Wigan Athletic Playing Record

	League		FA Cup		FL Cup		Others		Total	
	App	Gls	App	Gls	App	Gls	App	Gls	App	Gls
1981–82	1 (1)	0	0	0	1	0	0	0	2 (1)	0
1982–83	26 (2)	2	2	0	2	0	0	0	30 (2)	2
1983–84	44	1	4	0	2	0	1	0	51	1
1984–85	43		3		4	1	6	0	56	1
1985–86	42 (1)	2	5	0	2	0	6	0	55 (1)	2
1990–91	38 (1)	2	4	0	0	0	5	1	47 (1)	3
1991–92	45	2	3	0	4	0	2	0	54	2
1992–93	40	0	3	0	4	0	7	1	54	1
1993–94	28 (5)	2	3 (1)	0	2	0	1	0	34 (6)	2
TOTAL	307 (10)	12	27 (1)	1	21	1	28	2	383 (11)	16

LAWRENCE James Hubert

Midfield
Born: Balham, 8 March 1970.
Career: Cowes. October 1993 Sunderland 2 (2) 0. March 1994 Doncaster Rovers 16 (9) 3. January 1995 Leicester City 21 (26) 1. June 1997 Bradford City 133 (22) 12. March 2003 Walsall 4 (1) 0. November 2003 on loan WIGAN ATHLETIC 0 (4) 0.

A late starter in the professional game, after serving two years in Parkhurst prison for his part in an armed robbery, Jamie Lawrence was given a rehabilitation break at Roker Park, after starring in Wessex League football on the Isle of Wight.

Jamie Lawrence

After only a handful of outings, a £20,000 fee took him to Belle Vue and his form and flair there prompted Leicester City manager Mark McGhee to splash out £125,000 for his services. He quickly established himself as a member of the Foxes' first-team squad. A pacy, tricky flank player with distinctive piled-up dreadlocks, he spent much of his time at Filbert Street on the bench. He made a memorable appearance as a substitute for Mike Whitlow during the extra-time period of the Coca-Cola Cup Final replay at Hillsborough, the club's 1–0 victory handing him a cup winners' medal. Though it was thought that he would be a major asset to Leicester in the Premiership, he was signed by Bradford City in the summer of 1997 for £50,000.

A great crowd pleaser, he suffered medial knee-ligament damage in his second season at Valley Parade before a double hernia operation restricted his appearances in 1999–2000. Operating both as a full-back and in midfield, his season was disrupted further when he fractured his jaw in a training accident! Though injuries to his hip, toe and wrist continued to blight his Bradford career, he did make his international debut for Jamaica against Trinidad and Tobago and featured regularly for the Reggaeboyz in their World Cup qualifying campaign. In fact, he was voted Jamaica's 'Player of the Year', but his season for Bradford

City did not start until February 2002 after being out with breaks to his arm, wrist and thumb. Midway through the 2002–03 season he was allowed to join Walsall, impressing in his brief period at the Bescot Stadium.

In November 2003 he joined the Latics on a month's loan with Tony Dinning going in the opposite direction. He made four substitute appearances for Wigan but after the Latics had won only one of these matches, he was allowed to rejoin the Saddlers.

Wigan Athletic Playing Record

	League		FA Cup		FL Cup		Others		Total	
	App	Gls	App	Gls	App	Gls	App	Gls	App	Gls
2003–04	0 (4)	0	0	0	0	0	0	0	0 (4)	0
TOTAL	0 (4)	0	0	0	0	0	0	0	0 (4)	0

LEE David Mark

Winger
Born: Whitefield, 5 November 1967.
Career: August 1986 Bury 203 (5) 35. August 1991 Southampton 11 (9) 0. November 1992 Bolton Wanderers 124 (31) 17. July 1997 WIGAN ATHLETIC 61 (22) 11. October 1999 on loan Blackpool 9 (0) 1. August 2000 Carlisle United 1 (12) 0. Halifax Town. Morecambe.

David Lee

Flying winger David Lee represented Lancashire Schoolboys before joining Bury as an apprentice. He turned professional in 1986, making his first-team debut a year later against Carlisle United in the Freight Rover Trophy. He helped the Shakers reach the old Third Division play-offs on two occasions but they lost out to Tranmere Rovers and Bolton Wanderers. He made a total of 249 appearances for Bury, scoring 40 goals, and was the supporters' 'Player of the Year' on three occasions.

In August 1991 he moved to First Division Southampton for £350,000. Things didn't work out on the south coast and he joined Bolton Wanderers on loan. In December 1992 he signed for the Wanderers on a permanent basis for £300,000 and was ever-present for the remainder of that season as Bolton won promotion from Division Three as runners-up to Stoke City. He scored a

memorable Burnden Park goal in the quarter-finals of the League Cup against Premier League Norwich City as Wanderers reached the League Cup Final in 1995. Lee also won a Division One Championship medal and Division One play-off winners' medal before joining Wigan Athletic for £250,000 in the summer of 1997.

Lee made his Latics debut on the opening day of the 1997–98 season, helping Wigan beat Wycombe Wanderers 5–2. After taking time to settle in, the speedy winger, who could run all day and take markers on with ease, proceeded to become a great favourite with the Wigan faithful. The scorer of a number of spectacular goals, Lee had a brief loan spell with Blackpool before joining Carlisle United on a monthly basis at the start of the 2000–01 season. Lee appeared in 13 games for the Cumbrians before seeking his release from Brunton Park. After training with Halifax Town he joined non-League Morecambe, but is now back at the JJB Stadium as the club's youth team coach.

Wigan Athletic Playing Record

	League		FA Cup		FL Cup		Others		Total	
	App	Gls	App	Gls	App	Gls	App	Gls	App	Gls
1997–98	41 (2)	5	3	2	2	1	3	0	49 (2)	8
1998–99	20 (16)	6	1 (2)	0	4	1	2 (4)	1	27 (22)	8
1999–2000	0 (4)	0	0	0	0 (3)	0	0	0	0 (7)	0
TOTAL	61 (22)	11	4 (2)	2	6 (3)	2	5 (4)	1	76 (31)	16

LEONARD Mark Anthony

Forward
Born: St Helens, 27 September 1962.
Career: Witton Albion. February 1982 Everton. March 1983 on loan Tranmere Rovers 6 (1) 0. June 1983 Crewe Alexandra 51 (3) 15. February 1985 Stockport County 73 (0) 23. September 1986 Bradford City 120 (37) 29. March 1992 Rochdale 9 (0) 1. August 1992 Preston North End 19 (3) 1. August 1993 Chester City 28 (4) 8. September 1994 WIGAN ATHLETIC 60 (4) 12. July 1996 Rochdale 72 (0) 6.

After a series of impressive displays for non-League Witton Albion, Everton gave Mark Leonard the chance to turn professional. Unable to make the grade with the Goodison club, he went on loan to nearby Tranmere Rovers, making his League debut in a 1–0

Mark Leonard

Andy Liddell

defeat at Darlington. At the end of the 1982–83 season, he joined Crewe Alexandra, a shining light in the Railwaymen's side as they finished mid-table in Division Four.

In February 1985 he joined Stockport County and in his first full season at Edgeley Park he was the club's leading scorer with 23 League and Cup goals. This prompted Bradford City to pay £40,000 for him in September 1986. Though many of his first-team appearances at Valley Parade were as a substitute, he still continued to find the net on a regular basis before moving to Rochdale for a similar fee in March 1992. His stay at Spotland was brief and five months later he joined Preston North End, again for a fee of £40,000. After just one season at Deepdale, he was on the move again, this time to Chester City before joining Wigan Athletic in September 1994.

At Springfield Park, this enthusiastic, traditional centre-forward, who made his debut in a 2–0 home defeat at the hands of Carlisle United, soon began to show great aerial power, laying on chances for others as well as finding the net himself. After two seasons with the Latics, he rejoined Rochdale for a second spell before injury forced his retirement.

Wigan Athletic Playing Record

	League		FA Cup		FL Cup		Others		Total	
	App	Gls	App	Gls	App	Gls	App	Gls	App	Gls
1994–95	28 (1)	5	2	1	0	0	4	2	34 (1)	8
1995–96	32 (3)	7	4	1	2	0	2	0	40 (3)	8
TOTAL	60 (4)	12	6	2	2	0	6	2	74 (4)	16

LIDDELL Andrew Mark

Forward
Born: Leeds, 28 June 1973.
Career: July 1991 Barnsley 142 (56) 34. October 1998 WIGAN ATHLETIC 206 (10) 70.

Scottish Under-21 international Andy Liddell began his Football League career with Barnsley where, after working his way up through the ranks, he made his debut as a substitute against Portsmouth on the final day of the 1991–92 season. Though on the small side for a striker, he scored his fair share of goals as well as having the ability to unlock defences and provide chances for his colleagues. A tireless worker, his goalscoring in the early games of the 1996–97 season gave the Yorkshire club just the impetus they needed as they went on to win promotion to the Premiership. However, he found first-team opportunities more and more limited as the 1997–98 season progressed and in the main was consigned to the substitute's bench.

In order to play regular first-team football, Liddell signed for Wigan Athletic in October 1998 for a fee of £350,000. He made his debut in a 1–0 home defeat by Manchester City but showed his quality – netting 10 League goals including a brace in the final Football League game at Springfield Park against Chesterfield. An integral member of the Latics side that won the Autowindscreen Shield at Wembley, his bravery saw him continue to play through the pain barrier with a groin injury during the club's hectic run in to make the play-offs.

In 1999–2000 his efforts received their proper reward when he collected the 'Player of the Year' award. Though he was linked with moves to Dundee United and Huddersfield Town, Liddell, who is as his best playing behind two strikers, was an important member of the Latics side in 2000–01 when he netted 10 goals in League and Cup games including both goals in a 2–0 win over Swansea City – a match in which he came very close to scoring his first hat-trick for the club. Instrumental in the club reaching the play-offs for the second successive season, he was voted runner-up in the club's 'Player of the Season' awards.

He finished the 2001–02 season as the Latics' leading scorer with a career-best tally of 18 League goals. He missed several weeks of the season after twisting an ankle at Brighton and on his return he was played in a more advanced striking position. During the course of the season, Liddell netted the club's 1,500th Football League goal and his first-ever hat-trick in the 3–0 defeat of Brighton at the JJB and then another in the 4–1 win against Cambridge United. Not surprisingly he received a call-up from new Scotland coach Berti Vogts for an end-of-season training camp.

Now the club's longest-serving player, he again topped the Latics' scoring charts in 2002–03, netting 16 goals despite missing a quarter of the season through injuries. His penalty in the 3–1 defeat of Chesterfield was the 100th goal of his playing career.

Liddell, who with 70 goals is Wigan's record League scorer, remains an important member of the Latics side and has been offered a one-year deal. However, there is a lot of interest from other clubs, notably Preston North End and Sheffield United, and it looks as though he could be leaving the JJB Stadium.

Wigan Athletic Playing Record

	League		FA Cup		FL Cup		Others		Total	
	App	Gls	App	Gls	App	Gls	App	Gls	App	Gls
1998–99	28	10	0	0	0	0	7	0	35	10
1999–2000	41	8	3	1	3	0	4	0	51	9
2000–01	37	9	2	0	3	1	2	0	44	10
2001–02	33 (1)	18	1	0	0	0	0 (1)	0	34 (2)	18
2002–03	32 (5)	16	1	0	2	0	1	0	36 (5)	16
2003–04	35 (4)	9	0	0	3	0	0	0	38 (4)	9
TOTAL	206 (10)	70	7	1	11	1	14 (1)	0	238 (11)	72

LIGHTFOOT Christopher Ian

Midfield/Defence
Born: Warrington, 1 April 1970.
Career: July 1988 Chester City 263 (14) 32. July 1995 WIGAN ATHLETIC 11 (3) 1. March 1996 Crewe Alexandra 63 (24) 4. September 2000 on loan Oldham Athletic 3 (0) 0. Morecambe.

Chris Lightfoot began his Football League career with Chester City, turning professional with the Cestrians in the summer of 1988 and making his debut in a 1–1 draw against Blackpool on the opening day of the 1988–89 season. Although originally a central defender, he made a number of appearances in midfield. A strong tackling player with good passing ability, he had scored 39 goals in

Chris Lightfoot

328 League and Cup games for Chester, when in July 1995 he became Wigan Athletic's record signing as Latics manager Graham Barrow went back to his old club to pay £87,500 for Lightfoot's services.

He made his Wigan debut in the 2–1 defeat at Gillingham on the first day of the 1995–96 season, scoring his only goal for the club on his first appearance at Springfield Park as Scunthorpe United were beaten 2–1. He missed part of the campaign through an ankle injury, but even when he had recovered, he was unable to win a regular place in the Latics side and in March 1996 he joined Crewe Alexandra for £50,000.

At Gresty Road he quickly settled into the Railwaymen's style, providing both aggression and vision as in 1996–97 he helped them win promotion to the First Division via the play-offs. His early days at the club were marred by injury, although the whole-hearted performer did return to occupy a variety of defensive roles and though he was subsequently released, he had repaid his transfer fee many times over. On leaving Crewe he entered non-League football with Morecambe.

Wigan Athletic Playing Record

	League		FA Cup		FL Cup		Others		Total	
	App	Gls	App	Gls	App	Gls	App	Gls	App	Gls
1995–96	11 (3)	1	2	0	2	0	3	0	18 (3)	1
TOTAL	11 (3)	1	2	0	2	0	3	0	18 (3)	1

LLOYD Laurence Valentine

Central Defender
Born: Bristol, 6 October 1948.
Career: July 1967 Bristol Rovers 43 (0) 1. April 1969 Liverpool 150 (0) 4. August 1974 Coventry City 50 (0) 5. October 1976 Nottingham Forest 148 (0) 6. March 1981 WIGAN ATHLETIC 52 (0) 2.

The towering West Country man began his Football League career at Bristol Rovers before Liverpool manager Bill Shankly stepped in with a £50,000 offer in April 1969. A dominant stopper in the Ron Yeats mould, Shankly saw him as the eventual successor to his vaunted colossus and so it proved. He showed there was more to his game than the obvious asset of aerial power and while lacking pace, he was capable of using the ball well. He won a League Championship medal and UEFA Cup winners' medal in 1973 but after being left out of Liverpool's 1974 FA Cup Final side, he was sold to Coventry City for £225,000.

He failed to settle at Highfield Road and two years later Brian Clough got a bargain when he paid £60,000 to take Lloyd to the City Ground. Within a season of his arrival, Nottingham Forest were League Champions. Lloyd went on to claim two European Cup medals and two League Cup medals with his new club. In March 1981 Lloyd left Forest to become player-manager of Wigan Athletic – making his debut in a 1–0 home defeat by Rochdale. The following season he appeared in 36 League games, leading the Latics to third position in Division Four and promotion for the first time in their history. The former England international, who won four caps for his country, was sacked in April 1983 following the club's disappointing showing. He later managed Notts County but following relegation to Division Two in 1983–84 he was sacked with the club again bottom of the table.

Wigan Athletic Playing Record

	League		FA Cup		FL Cup		Others		Total	
	App	Gls	App	Gls	App	Gls	App	Gls	App	Gls
1980–81	9	0	0	0	0	0	0	0	9	0
1981–82	36	2	0	0	4	2	0	0	40	4
1982–83	7	0	0	0	1	0	0	0	8	0
TOTAL	52	2	0	0	5	2	0	0	57	4

LODGE Paul

Midfield

Born: Liverpool, 13 February 1961.
Career: February 1979 Everton 20 (0) 4. August 1982 on loan WIGAN ATHLETIC 5 (0) 1. January 1983 on loan Rotherham United 4 (0) 0. February 1983 Preston North End 36 (2) 0. July 1984 Bolton Wanderers 4 (0) 0. November 1984 on loan Port Vale 3 (0) 0. March 1985 Stockport County 10 (3) 2. Southport.

England schoolboy international Paul Lodge played his early football with Everton, making his League debut for the Toffees as a substitute for Eamonn O'Keefe in a 3–1 home defeat against Aston Villa. His first full appearance for the Blues was in the Merseyside derby against Liverpool, a match Everton lost 1–0. The midfield playmaker was unable to hold down a regular place at Goodison due to the fine form of Asa Hartford, Steve McMahon and Howard Kendall and in the summer of 1982 he joined Wigan Athletic on loan.

He made his Latics debut in a 2–1 defeat at Lincoln City on the opening day of the 1982–83 season before scoring the winner from the penalty spot on his first appearance at Springfield Park the following week as Brentford were beaten 3–2. Despite some impressive displays, Wigan decided not to pursue their interest in him and after a loan spell with Rotherham United he joined Preston North End. Lodge later played for Bolton Wanderers and had a loan spell with Port Vale before moving to Stockport County. On leaving Edgeley Park, he moved into non-League football with Southport.

Wigan Athletic Playing Record

	League		FA Cup		FL Cup		Others		Total	
	App	Gls	App	Gls	App	Gls	App	Gls	App	Gls
1982–83	5	1	0	0	0	0	0	0	5	1
TOTAL	5	1	0	0	0	0	0	0	5	1

LOVE Michael John

Midfield

Born: Stockport, 27 November 1973.
Career: Hinckley Athletic. January 1996 WIGAN ATHLETIC 0 (3) 0. Sligo Rovers. Wycombe Wanderers. Northampton Town. Stevenage Borough. Nuneaton Borough.

Left-sided midfielder Michael Love played his early football for non-League Hinckley Athletic where, after a series of impressive displays, he joined Wigan Athletic on a free transfer in January 1996. His performances for the club's reserve side led to him making his League debut for the Latics in October 1996 when he came off the bench to replace the injured Graeme Jones in a 3–1 defeat at Colchester United. He made two more appearances as a substitute over the next few weeks before leaving Springfield Park to play for Sligo Rovers in the Irish League. He returned to these shores on transfer deadline day as a non-contract player on trial at Wycombe Wanderers, but failed to make the Adams Park club's first team prior to departing. He had a similar spell with Northampton Town before joining Stevenage Borough. Love later played for Nuneaton Borough, featuring strongly in their FA Cup runs of the late nineties.

Wigan Athletic Playing Record

	League		FA Cup		FL Cup		Others		Total	
	App	Gls	App	Gls	App	Gls	App	Gls	App	Gls
1996–97	0 (3)	0	0	0	0	0	0	0	0 (3)	0
TOTAL	0 (3)	0	0	0	0	0	0	0	0 (3)	0

David Lowe

LOWE David Anthony

Right-winger

Born: Liverpool, 30 August 1965.
Career: June 1983 WIGAN ATHLETIC 179 (9) 40. June 1987 Ipswich Town 121 (13) 37. March 1992 on loan Port Vale 8(1) 2. July 1992 Leicester City 68 (26) 22. February 1994 on loan Port Vale 18 (1) 5. March 1996 WIGAN ATHLETIC 85 (23) 26. July 1999 Wrexham 4 (6) 1. January 2000 on loan Rushden and Diamonds.

Despite his early football being restricted to school and local league level, David Lowe's teacher recommended him to Harry McNally and after a week's training with the Latics first team he was offered an apprenticeship. After injuries had decimated the first-team squad, Lowe made his Wigan debut against Reading in October 1982 and though he appeared out of his depth, the club stuck with him. He won a Freight Rover Trophy medal in 1985, scoring one of the goals in a 3–1 win over Brentford.

In June 1987, Lowe signed for Ipswich Town for a fee of £80,000 and made his debut for the Portman Road club against Aston Villa on the opening day of the 1987–88 season. He ended the campaign as the club's top scorer with 17 goals in 41 games. The hardworking midfielder won England Under-21 honours and continued to find the net for Town. He was the leading scorer again in 1989–90 but two seasons later found himself on loan at Port Vale. He left Ipswich, for whom he had scored 45 goals in 159 games, in the summer of 1992, Leicester City paying £250,000 for him. He shattered his cheekbone in a pre-season friendly against Borussia Moenchengladbach but settled well after his delayed debut for the Foxes, though missing out on the 1993 play-offs. After another loan spell at Port Vale, Lowe rejoined the Latics for a second spell in March 1996 for a fee of £125,000.

In 1996–97 he celebrated his 300th League game for the club and his goal in the final match of the season against Mansfield Town ensured the Latics of the Championship and him of a medal. The following season he was the club's top scorer with 18 goals, setting up a new club aggregate scoring record, his goal in the 5–1

John Lowey

home victory over Burnley being his 60th for the Latics. He ended the season by collecting both the supporters' and the club's 'Player of the Year' trophies. After that he was hampered by injuries but declined an offer to combine playing and coaching at the club and joined Wrexham.

After a good start he dropped out of the first-team set-up and had a loan spell with then non-League Rushden and Diamonds before deciding to hang up his boots.

Wigan Athletic Playing Record

	League		FA Cup		FL Cup		Others		Total	
	App	Gls	App	Gls	App	Gls	App	Gls	App	Gls
1982–83	25 (3)	6	0 (1)	0	1	0	0	0	26 (4)	6
1983–84	37 (3)	8	3 (1)	0	2	0	0	0	42 (4)	8
1984–85	26 (3)	5	3	0	1	0	7	4	37 (3)	9
1985–86	46	5	5	2	2	0	6	3	59	10
1986–87	45	16	5	2	2	0	3	1	55	19
1995–96	7	3	0	0	0	0	0	0	7	3
1996–97	31 (11)	6	1	0	2	0	1	0	35 (11)	6
1997–98	42 (1)	16	2 (1)	1	2	0	3	1	49 (2)	18
1998–99	5 (11)	1	1 (1)	2	3	0	1 (1)	0	10 (13)	3
TOTAL	264 (32)	66	20 (4)	7	15	0	21 (1)	9	320 (37)	82

LOWEY John Anthony

Midfield

Born: Manchester, 7 March 1958.

Career: March 1975 Manchester United. Chicago, United States. July 1977 Blackburn Rovers. December 1977 Port Vale. California, United States. October 1978 Sheffield Wednesday 35 (7) 4. November 1980 Blackburn Rovers 136 (5) 14. July 1986 WIGAN ATHLETIC 1 (2) 0. November 1986 on loan Chesterfield 2 (0) 0. March 1987 on loan York City 3 (3) 0. August 1987 Preston North End 4 (0) 1. March 1988 Chester City 9 (0) 0.

Much-travelled midfielder John Lowey signed apprentice forms for Manchester United but despite a series of impressive displays

for the club's youth and Central League side he failed to force his way into the United side. He went to try his luck in the United States with Chicago before returning to the north-west with Blackburn Rovers. Unable to break into Rovers' first team he joined Port Vale, where injuries kept him out of the side. After another stint in America, Lowey signed for Sheffield Wednesday and at last made his Football League debut, going on to help the Owls win promotion to the Second Division.

In November 1980 Blackburn Rovers persuaded Lowey to return to Ewood Park and over the next five seasons he was one of the club's most consistent players as they challenged for a place in the top flight. Rovers finished in the top six in Division Two on three occasions but in the summer of 1986, having scored 14 goals in 141 League games, he left to join Wigan. After starting the opening game of the 1986–87 season, a 2–0 defeat at Notts County, Lowey made just two more appearances for the Latics over the course of the season, both as a substitute. He had loan spells with Chesterfield and York City before leaving Springfield Park to join Preston North End. Unable to win a regular place in the Deepdale club's side, he moved to Chester City where he ended his career.

Wigan Athletic Playing Record

	League		FA Cup		FL Cup		Others		Total	
	App	Gls	App	Gls	App	Gls	App	Gls	App	Gls
1986–87	1 (2)	0	0	0	0	0	0	0	1 (2)	0
TOTAL	1 (2)	0	0	0	0	0	0	0	1 (2)	0

LYONS Andrew

Winger

Born: Blackpool, 19 October 1966.

Career: Fleetwood Town. October 1992 Crewe Alexandra 7 (4) 2. October 1993 WIGAN ATHLETIC 79 (8) 27. Partick Thistle. Morecambe.

Lively left-winger Andy Lyons began his career with Fleetwood Town in the Lancashire Combination, where his performances led to interest from a number of League clubs. A £15,000 move to Crewe Alexandra followed in October 1992 but Lyons was unable

Andy Lyons

to settle at Gresty Road and 12 months later he left the Railwaymen to play for Wigan Athletic.

Lyons made his Latics debut in a 6–3 home win over Chester City and though he failed to get on the scoresheet he ended the season as the club's leading scorer with 11 goals. He repeated the feat the following season when his total of 15 goals included a hat-trick in a 4–1 home win over Darlington. As well as being the club's leading scorer, he created a number of other goals for his fellow strikers but in 1995–96 he was unable to recapture the form of the previous two seasons. He appeared to be short on confidence and, after failing to hold down a regular place, the nippy winger was allowed to join Partick Thistle.

After an impressive first season at Firhill, Lyons had a spell playing at left-back before reverting to his preferred position. He later returned to non-League football with Morecambe, while working as a postman.

Wigan Athletic Playing Record

	League		FA Cup		FL Cup		Others		Total	
	App	Gls	App	Gls	App	Gls	App	Gls	App	Gls
1993–94	33	11	2	0	0	0	0	0	35	11
1994–95	32	15	2	0	3	0	4	0	41	15
1995–96	14 (8)	1	3 (1)	0	2 (1)	0	3	0	22 (10)	1
TOTAL	79 (8)	27	7 (1)	0	5 (1)	0	7	0	98 (10)	27

McADAM Steven

Full-back
Born: Portadown, 2 April 1960.
Career: Portadown. May 1978 Burnley 5 (0) 0. Barnsley. November 1980 WIGAN ATHLETIC 26 (0) 0.

An Irish youth international defender, Steve McAdam began his Football League career with Burnley whom he joined in 1978 after playing part-time with his home-town club Portadown. A natural left-footed player, he finished the 1979–80 season in the Clarets first team, having replaced Ian Brennan at left-back. He failed to

agree terms that summer and, after a brief spell with Barnsley, joined Wigan Athletic in November 1980. He made his debut for the Latics in a 3–0 home win over Northampton Town and held his place for the rest of the season, the fans appreciating his quiet, no-nonsense attitude to the game. After playing just once in 1981–82 he was surprisingly released and after a period in Irish football, he ended his career with a spell in Cyprus.

Wigan Athletic Playing Record

	League		FA Cup		FL Cup		Others		Total	
	App	Gls	App	Gls	App	Gls	App	Gls	App	Gls
1980–81	25	0	2	0	0	0	0	0	27	0
1981–82	1	0	0	0	0	0	0	0	1	0
TOTAL	26	0	2	0	0	0	0	0	28	0

McCULLOCH Lee Henry

Forward
Born: Bellshill, 14 May 1978.
Career: Cumbernauld United. August 1995 Motherwell 75 (47) 28. March 2001 WIGAN ATHLETIC 98 (26) 21.

Lee McCulloch made his debut in Scottish League football as a substitute for Motherwell in a 3–0 win at Raith Rovers in August 1996, going on to appear in 15 games that season, all but one from the substitute's bench. Though he failed to find the net during that spell, he opened his account with two goals in a 6–2 defeat of Hibernian midway through the following season. His performances in attack for Motherwell led to him winning 14 caps at Under-21 level for Scotland, his first against Latvia in 1997.

In 1999–2000, McCulloch scored 12 goals, helping Motherwell to finish fourth in the Scottish Premier League. In March 2001 he was part of a double swoop by Latics manager Bruce Rioch, bringing both McCulloch and Steve McMillan to the JJB Stadium. McCulloch made his Wigan debut in a goalless home draw against Swindon Town and the player, for whom Hearts had bid £750,000, looked impressive. In Wigan's 3–2 win over Oxford United, McCulloch hit a superb clincher, beating goalkeeper Richard Knight with an overhead kick for the Latics third goal.

Great things were expected of him in 2001–02 and he started the campaign well, scoring in the opening two League matches. McCulloch's physical presence enabled him to hold the ball up well, but after his early season impressive displays, he found himself spending much of the season on the substitute's bench. He did return to the starting line-up after the departure of Simon Haworth to Tranmere, but without the reward of goals his displays deserved. In 2002–03 he was converted from striker to midfield – it was one of the success stories of Wigan's season. Contributing six goals during the course of the Latics' Second Division Championship winning season, he later reverted to a striker's role following injuries to Nathan Ellington and Andy Liddell.

Last season, the 6ft 5in player appeared mainly on the left-side of midfield and scored a number of vital goals. However, the Scottish Under-21 international, who harbours hopes of full international football, lost out following the signing of Alan Mahon.

Wigan Athletic Playing Record

	League		FA Cup		FL Cup		Others		Total	
	App	Gls	App	Gls	App	Gls	App	Gls	App	Gls
2000–01	10	3	0	0	0	0	1	0	11	3
2001–02	24 (10)	6	1	0	0	0	0 (1)	0	25 (11)	6
2002–03	33 (5)	6	0 (1)	0	2	0	0	0	35 (6)	6
2003–04	31 (11)	6	1	0	3	1	0	0	35 (11)	7
TOTAL	98 (26)	21	2 (1)	0	5	1	1 (1)	0	106 (28)	22

Lee McCulloch (left)

McEWAN Stanley

Central Defender
Born: Wishaw, 8 June 1957.
Career: July 1974 Blackpool 204 (10) 24. July 1982 Exeter City 65 (0) 15. March 1984 Hull City 113 (0) 25. December 1987 WIGAN ATHLETIC 26 (3) 4. August 1989 Hartlepool United 14 (0) 2.

An accomplished and determined central defender, Stan McEwan began his career with Blackpool, working his way up through the ranks before making his Football League debut for the Seasiders as a substitute in a 2–0 defeat at West Bromwich Albion in December 1974. It was his only appearance that season and it was midway through the 1975–76 season before he won a regular place in the Blackpool side. Though his first couple of seasons in the Seasiders' team saw him hampered by a series of minor injuries, he bounced back and was ever-present in 1978–79. The scorer of a number of spectacular long-range efforts, he had scored 32 goals in 242 games when he left Bloomfield Road to join Exeter City in the summer of 1982.

With the Grecians struggling to avoid relegation to the Fourth Division, McEwan joined Hull City. He helped the Tigers win a second promotion in 1984–85 and was outstanding the following season as the club came close to entering the top flight for the first time in their history.

In December 1987 Latics manager Ray Mathias brought McEwan to Springfield Park and he made his debut in a 2–0 win at Bury on Boxing Day. He went on to play in all but one of the remaining 24 games, helping the club to finish seventh in the Third Division. Injuries kept him out of the side for most of the 1988–89 campaign and in the close season he joined Hartlepool United, where he later ended his first-class career.

Stan McEwan

Wigan Athletic Playing Record

	League		FA Cup		FL Cup		Others		Total	
	App	Gls	App	Gls	App	Gls	App	Gls	App	Gls
1987–88	23	4	0	0	0	0	0	0	23	4
1988–89	3 (3)	0	1	0	0 (1)	0	0	0	4 (4)	0
TOTAL	26 (3)	4	1	0	0 (1)	0	0	0	27 (4)	4

McGARVEY Scott Thomas

Forward
Born: Glasgow, 22 April 1963.
Career: April 1980 Manchester United 13 (12) 3. March 1984 on loan Wolverhampton Wanderers 13 (0) 2. July 1984 Portsmouth 17 (6) 6. January 1986 on loan Carlisle United 10 (0) 3. July 1986 Carlisle United 25 (0) 8. March 1987 Grimsby Town 49 (1) 7. September 1988 Bristol City 20 (6) 9. May 1989 Oldham Athletic 2 (2) 1. September 1989 on loan WIGAN ATHLETIC 3 (0) 0.

Initially rated as a future Scottish international, Scott McGarvey turned professional with Manchester United in April 1980, a year after coming down to Old Trafford from Celtic Boys' Club in Glasgow. Unable to hold down a regular place in the United side, he had a loan spell at Wolverhampton Wanderers before joining Portsmouth for £50,000 in July 1984. While at Old Trafford, McGarvey was capped by Scotland at Under-23 level but he was unable to find his form at Fratton Park and two years later he moved to Carlisle United, initially on loan before the transfer was made permanent. After a spell playing for Grimsby Town, McGarvey moved to Bristol City in exchange for Tony Caldwell. Though he was ineligible to play in the Littlewoods Cup as City reached the semi-finals, he had his most prolific spell with the Robins, scoring 11 goals in 35 games before joining Oldham Athletic in May 1989.

Hampered by injuries at Boundary Park, he had a spell on loan with Wigan Athletic, making his debut in a 3–1 defeat at Brentford in September 1989. He kept his place for the Latics next game at Bolton Wanderers and then laid on two of Wigan's goals in a 3–0 win over Walsall before returning to Boundary Park. On leaving the game at the end of the season, he set up his own company, 'Moneystone', which sells sand to sports clubs and agricultural concerns from a base at Levenseat Quarry near Glasgow.

Wigan Athletic Playing Record

	League		FA Cup		FL Cup		Others		Total	
	App	Gls	App	Gls	App	Gls	App	Gls	App	Gls
1989–90	3	0	0	0	0	0	0	0	3	0
TOTAL	3	0	0	0	0	0	0	0	3	0

McGIBBON Patrick Colm

Central Defender
Born: Lurgan, 6 September 1973.
Career: Portadown. August 1992 Manchester United. September 1996 on loan Swansea City 1 (0) 0. March 1997 WIGAN ATHLETIC 163 (10) 11. February 2002 on loan Scunthorpe United 6 (0) 0. August 2002 Tranmere Rovers 4 (0) 0. Portadown.

Northern Ireland international defender Pat McGibbon began his career with Portadown before Manchester United paid £100,000 to take him to Old Trafford. He made his debut for the Reds in the League Cup at York City but was sent off after giving away a penalty!
Following a loan spell at Swansea, McGibbon joined Wigan on loan in March 1997 and made his debut in a 2–2 home draw against Hartlepool United. It was McGibbon who scored the goal that beat Colchester United 1–0 to ensure promotion to the Second Division. The move was made permanent in the close season, Latics paying £250,000.

Dominant in the air and strong in the tackle, he formed a solid central defensive partnership with Colin Greenall. Since then, he has missed very few matches and was a valuable member of the Wigan side that defeated Millwall 1–0 to win the Autowindscreen

Pat McGibbon

Shield in 1999 and reached successive play-offs. Though he only found the net twice in 2000–01, one of his efforts rescued a point in the crucial game against Bournemouth when he came off the bench to prevent the Cherries from claiming all three points. Following the arrival of Paul Jewell as manager, he found his first-team opportunities limited. When he did get the chance, the tall centre-half showed his versatility by playing at right-back.

Midway through the 2001–02 season, he joined Scunthorpe United on loan. He did well at Glanford Park, never finishing on the losing side in six matches. Arrangements for a permanent deal collapsed and he returned to the JJB Stadium before being released in the summer. He linked up with former Wigan boss Ray Mathias at Tranmere Rovers before subsequently joining his first club, Irish League side Portadown, for the remainder of the campaign.

Wigan Athletic Playing Record

	League		FA Cup		FL Cup		Others		Total	
	App	Gls	App	Gls	App	Gls	App	Gls	App	Gls
1996–97	10	1	0	0	0	0	0	0	10	1
1997–98	32 (3)	0	3	0	2	0	1	0	38 (3)	0
1998–99	35 (1)	5	2	0	3	0	9	0	49 (1)	5
1999–2000	30 (4)	2	3	0	1 (1)	0	5	0	39 (5)	2
2000–01	38 (2)	2	0 (1)	0	4	0	2	0	44 (3)	2
2001–02	18	0	1	0	1	0	1	0	21	0
TOTAL	163 (10)	10	9 (1)	0	11 (1)	0	18	0	201 (12)	10

McIVOR Ronald William

Full-back
Born: Edinburgh, 23 March 1951.
Career: East Fife. October 1979 WIGAN ATHLETIC 3 (0) 1.

From an early age Ron McIvor was a useful boxer and won Scottish Amateur titles in the 14,15 and 16 years age groups before deciding to concentrate on football. He played junior football for Peebles Rovers and Bonnyrigg Rose and in 1972–73 picked up a Scottish Junior Cup Final runners-up medal. Eventually signed by East Fife, he made his debut in a friendly against Sheffield Wednesday before winning a place in the Bayview Park club's League side. Like many

Scottish League players of his day, he played football part-time while qualifying as an Approved Electrician, but when the Latics offered him full-time terms, it was the realisation of a long-cherished ambition. On his arrival at Springfield Park he had to wait before making a goalscoring debut in a 3–1 defeat at Doncaster Rovers. Able to play on either flank, the gritty Scot made only a couple more appearances before being released at the end of the season.

Wigan Athletic Playing Record

	League		FA Cup		FL Cup		Others		Total	
	App	Gls	App	Gls	App	Gls	App	Gls	App	Gls
1979–80	3	1	0	0	0	0	0	0	3	1
TOTAL	3	1	0	0	0	0	0	0	3	1

McKEARNEY David Jonathan

Left-back/Midfield
Born: Crosby, 20 June 1968.
Career: Prescot Cables. November 1987 Bolton Wanderers. Northwich Victoria. Marine. October 1989 Crewe Alexandra 95 (13) 11. July 1993 WIGAN ATHLETIC 45 (4) 9. Chorley.

Dave McKearney was playing non-League football for Prescot Cables when Bolton Wanderers signed him in November 1987. Despite solid displays in the Trotters' Central League side, he was unable to make the grade and returned to the non-League scene with Northwich Victoria and later Marine. In October 1989, Crewe Alexandra manager Dario Gradi gave him another chance to play League football. McKearney made his Football League debut for the Railwaymen as a substitute in a goalless draw at Preston North End. Able to play in midfield or at left-back, he soon won a regular place in the Crewe side and in four seasons at Gresty Road, scored 18 goals in 145 League and Cup games.

In the summer of 1993 former Crewe assistant-manager Kenny Swain brought McKearney to Springfield Park on a free transfer and he made his Latics debut in a 2–1 defeat at Scunthorpe United on the opening day of the 1993–94 campaign. A first-team regular for most of that season, he netted both goals in a 2–2 home draw against Preston North End and was the club's penalty-taker.

Dave McKearney

Injuries restricted his appearances the following season, though he still found the net five times in 17 starts before surprisingly being released during the summer and joining Chorley.

Wigan Athletic Playing Record

	League		FA Cup		FL Cup		Others		Total	
	App	Gls	App	Gls	App	Gls	App	Gls	App	Gls
1993–94	28	4	4	1	2	0	2	1	36	6
1994–95	17 (4)	5	1	0	0 (1	0	2	0	20 (5)	5
TOTAL	45 (4)	9	5	1	2 (1)	0	4	1	56 (5)	11

McLAUGHLIN Brian

Left-winger
Born: Bellshill, 14 May 1974.
Career: Giffnock North. July 1992 Glasgow Celtic 38 (37) 5. March 1999 Dundee United 1 (2) 0. July 1999 WIGAN ATHLETIC 13 (5) 0. Ayr United.

Brian McLaughlin

Scottish Under-21 left-winger Brian McLaughlin was, at 5ft 4in, one of the smallest players ever to turn out for Celtic in the Premier League. A pacy winger, he joined the Bhoys in the summer of 1992 and during his time at Parkhead he helped them win the Scottish Cup in 1995 by beating Airdrieonians 1–0. He had appeared in 92 League and Cup games for the Scottish giants when he left Parkhead to join Dundee United in March 1999.

His stay at Tannadice was brief and in the close season he joined the Latics. Sadly, his first-team involvement in his first season with the club was limited to a substitute appearance against York City in the Autowindscreen Shield. However, McLaughlin was the Latics leading scorer in the reserves team that collected the Pontins League Division two title. Towards the end of the season he had a trial with French club Niort but nothing came of it and he returned to the JJB Stadium. He appeared on a slightly more regular basis in 2000–01 though he couldn't convert his goalscoring exploits at reserve-team level to the seniors. His only goal for the Latics came in the 3–2 LDV Vans win against Oldham Athletic. In the summer of 2001 he returned north of the border to play for Ayr United.

Wigan Athletic Playing Record

	League		FA Cup		FL Cup		Others		Total	
	App	Gls	App	Gls	App	Gls	App	Gls	App	Gls
1999–2000	0	0	0	0	0 (1)	0	0	0	0 (1)	0
2000–01	13 (5)	0	1 (1)	0	4 (1)	0	2	1	20 (7)	1
TOTAL	13 (5)	0	1 (1)	0	4 (2)	0	2	1	20 (8)	1

McLOUGHLIN Alan Francis

Midfield

Born: Manchester, 20 April 1967.

Career: April 1985 Manchester United. August 1986 Swindon Town 101 (5) 19. March 1987 on loan Torquay United 21 (3) 4. December 1990 Southampton 22 (2) 1. September 1991 on loan Aston Villa. February 1992 Portsmouth 297 (12) 54. December 1999 WIGAN ATHLETIC 12 (10) 1. December 2001 Rochdale 15 (3) 1. Forest Green Rovers.

Republic of Ireland international Alan McLoughlin joined Manchester United in April 1985 but when he left Old Trafford for newly promoted Swindon Town in August 1986 he had yet to experience the cut and thrust of League football. After making his League debut for the Robins he had a brief loan spell with Torquay United before returning to the County Ground, where he developed under the watchful eye of Ossie Ardiles. With Swindon, McLoughlin came to be regarded as one of the most talented midfielders in British football. His excellent vision, driving energy and passing ability earned him an international call-up. Swindon finished in fourth place in Division Two and a McLoughlin goal saw off Sunderland in the play-offs at Wembley. The celebrations were short-lived, however. Swindon were denied their place in the top flight due to financial irregularities and started the 1990–91 season once again as a Second Division club.

In December 1990, Ardiles was forced to sell his star midfielder to Southampton for £1 million, but the move wasn't a success and in February 1992 he moved to Portsmouth for £400,000. During his time at Fratton Park, McLoughlin played in two FA Cup semi-finals as well as a couple of play-off semi-finals.

Capped 42 times by the Republic of Ireland, McLoughlin's second-half equaliser against Northern Ireland in Belfast in November 1993 secured his place in the annals of Irish football folklore and sent the Republic to their second successive World Cup finals. McLoughlin joined the Latics in December 1999, costing manager John Benson £250,000. He made his debut in a 1–0 home win over Brentford, while his only goal that season came in the opening minute of the 2–0 defeat of Gillingham. Unfortunately he sustained a slipped disc at Bristol Rovers, though

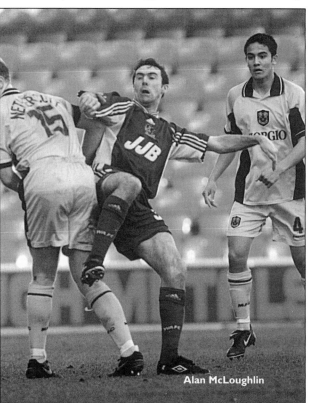

Alan McLoughlin

he returned towards the end of the season to help the club reach the play-offs. In 2000–01 he made just a handful of appearances as a substitute as the Latics preferred to use his experience in the Avon Insurance League. In 2001–02 he struggled even more to find his way into the Wigan side, his only Second Division start coming in the 2–2 draw against Cardiff City at Ninian Park.

McLoughlin was released from his contract and joined Rochdale for the second half of the season. His passing and creativity were vital factors as Dale finished the season in fifth place in Division Three. The play-off semi-finals enabled him to reach a tally of 600 senior games, but he failed to win the offer of a further contract and went to play non-League football for Forest Green Rovers.

Wigan Athletic Playing Record

	League		FA Cup		FL Cup		Others		Total	
	App	Gls	App	Gls	App	Gls	App	Gls	App	Gls
1999–2000	11 (4)	1	0	0	0	0	2	0	13 (4)	1
2000–01	0 (4)	0	0	0	0 (1)	0	1	2	1 (5)	2
2001–02	1 (2)	0	0	0	0	0	1	0	2 (2)	0
TOTAL	12 (10)	1	0	0	0 (1)	0	4	2	16 (11)	3

McMAHON John

Right-back

Born: Manchester, 7 December 1949.

Career: December 1967 Preston North End 256 (1) 7. September 1970 on loan Southend United 4 (0) 0. September 1979 on loan Chesterfield 1 (0) 0. October 1979 Crewe Alexandra 67 (0) 2. August 1981 WIGAN ATHLETIC 71 (0) 5. August 1983 Tranmere Rovers 39 (1) 0. Curzon Athletic. Irlam Town.

While playing for Manchester Boys, John McMahon was on schoolboy forms with Manchester United, but it was Preston North End who secured his services once he left school. However, when he made his Football League debut in September 1970, he happened to be playing for Southend United, because he had been loaned out to gain experience. On his return to Deepdale he made rapid strides and at the end of the following season he was voted North End's 'Player of the Year'. In 1972–73 he scored his first League goal for the Lilywhites when he netted after just 12 seconds in the 3–3 draw with Bristol City. His consistency didn't go unnoticed and in 1976–77 he was chosen by his fellow professionals for the PFA Third Division side. Twelve years after joining North End he led them to promotion from the Third Division and was awarded a testimonial, but shortly afterwards he left to play for Crewe Alexandra.

After two seasons at Gresty Road, McMahon joined the Latics and made his debut in a 3–3 draw at Bradford City on the opening day of the 1981–82 season. McMahon scored four goals from right-back during that campaign and on each occasion he found the net, the Latics won! After helping the club to promotion, he remained one of the Latics' better players in their first season of higher-grade football but in the summer of 1983, he left Springfield Park to end his League career with Tranmere Rovers. He later played non-League football for Curzon Athletic and Irlam Town.

Wigan Athletic Playing Record

	League		FA Cup		FL Cup		Others		Total	
	App	Gls	App	Gls	App	Gls	App	Gls	App	Gls
1981–82	36	4	1	0	6	0	0	0	43	4
1982–83	35	1	2	0	4	0	0	0	41	1
TOTAL	71	5	3	0	10	0	0	0	84	5

McMILLAN Stephen Thomas

Left-back
Born: Edinburgh, 19 January 1976.
Career: Troon Juniors. August 1993 Motherwell 127 (0) 6. March 2001 WIGAN ATHLETIC 76 (5) 0.

Steve McMillan began his career with Motherwell, making his debut for the Fir Park club as a teenage substitute in a 1–0 home defeat at the hands of St Johnstone on the final day of the 1993–94 season. However, it was midway through the 1996–97 campaign before he established himself as a first-team regular. The tough-tackling left-back scored his first goal in Scottish League football the following season in a 4–1 defeat at Celtic, a campaign in which he won the first of four Scottish Under-21 caps, when he played against Austria. Though his form then suffered a little, by the time the Millennium arrived he was back to his best, displaying quite an eye for goal from direct free-kicks.

Steve McMillan

In March 2001 he moved to Wigan Athletic for £550,000 along with Lee McCulloch, who cost £700,000 as Bruce Rioch sought to strengthen his side for the final few weeks of the season. He made an impressive debut in the goalless home draw against Swindon Town and looked good when going forward, but a hamstring injury kept him on the sidelines during the closing stages of the campaign. In 2001–02, McMillan was one of the most reliable of the Latics' squad. After missing the opening matches of the campaign due to a recurrence of his hamstring injury, he had appeared in only a handful of games before breaking a wrist in the match at Cardiff City. On his return he combined surging runs down the left flank with an ability to deliver pin-point crosses.

Injuries again hampered his progress during the club's Second Division Championship winning season of 2002–03, but when he did turn out he never let anyone down, again producing reliable performances at both left-back and in a midfield role. He started last season as the club's first-choice left-back, when his displays showed him to be one of the best in that position in the First Division. However, his season turned sour when he was again plagued by injuries.

Wigan Athletic Playing Record

	League		FA Cup		FL Cup		Others		Total	
	App	Gls	App	Gls	App	Gls	App	Gls	App	Gls
2000–01	6	0	0	0	0	0	0	0	6	0
2001–02	29	0	0	0	0	0	0	0	29	0
2002–03	28 (4)	0	0	0	4	0	0	0	32 (4)	0
2003–04	13 (1)	0	0	0	1	0	0	0	14 (1)	0
TOTAL	76 (5)	0	0	0	5	0	0	0	81 (5)	0

McMULLEN David

Midfield
Born: Denny, 13 June 1960.
Career: Cumbernauld United. February 1980 WIGAN ATHLETIC 20 (7) 1. Northwich Victoria.

On leaving school, David McMullen joined Cumbernauld United, the junior club from which Kenny Dalglish joined Celtic, but continued to play for a local side, Tryst Youth Club. He gained representative honours with Stirlingshire Select Under-18 teams and played for Cumbernauld United for one-and-a-half seasons before joining Wigan Athletic. McMullen's grandfather's brother was the legendary Jimmy McMullen who captained the famous Scottish 'Wembley Wizards' in 1928 when Scotland defeated England 5–1.

McMullen made his Latics debut as a substitute for David Fretwell in a 1–1 draw at Northampton Town towards the end of the 1979–80 season, making his first full appearance in a 2–1 League Cup win over Crewe Alexandra in August 1980. That season he was a regular in the Latics' side, scoring his only goal for the club in a 1–1 home draw against Scunthorpe United. A skilful and industrious midfielder, he was surprisingly allowed to leave Springfield Park in the summer of 1981 and joined Northwich Victoria.

Wigan Athletic Playing Record

	League		FA Cup		FL Cup		Others		Total	
	App	Gls	App	Gls	App	Gls	App	Gls	App	Gls
1979–80	0 (2)	0	0	0	0	0	0	0	0 (2)	0
1980–81	20 (5)	1	0	0	3	0	0	0	23 (5)	1
TOTAL	20 (7)	1	0	0	3	0	0	0	23 (7)	1

MAHON Alan Joseph

Winger
Born: Dublin, 4 April 1978.
Career: April 1995 Tranmere Rovers 84 (36) 13. July 2000 Sporting Lisbon (Portugal). December 2000 Blackburn Rovers 24 (9) 1. January 2003 on loan Cardiff City 13 (2) 2. January 2004 WIGAN ATHLETIC 13 (1) 1.

An attacking midfielder who burst onto the Football League scene with Tranmere Rovers in 1995–96, the Irish youth international also made his debut for the Republic of Ireland's Under-21 side during the course of that campaign. After finding himself in and out of the side, he won a regular place, though towards the end of the 1997–98 season, a combination of a recurring stomach injury, plus the burden of expectancy, conspired to give him a frustrating time.

However, the following season he found a rich seam of form and caused endless problems for his unfortunate markers. Developing a probing and tricky style of play, rumours began to circulate about a big money move to the Premiership but in the summer of 2000, after making his full international debut for the Republic against Greece, he chose to move to Sporting Lisbon.

He found it difficult to break into the side, although one of his rare appearances came in a European Champions' League game against Real Madrid.

In December 2000 he joined Blackburn Rovers, going on to produce some fine performances to assist the club in their bid for promotion. However, during the following season, he was used mainly as cover for Damien Duff on the left or even at left-back. With the exception of UEFA Cup ties, he was never in the frame at Ewood Park and in January 2003 he joined Cardiff City on loan.

Alan Mahon

Chris Makin

Though he provided the width that had been missing all season, he returned to Ewood Park shortly before the end of the season, thus missing out on the Bluebirds' play-off excitement.

In January 2004, Wigan paid £250,000 for Mahon's services and he made his debut in a 3–1 win at Ipswich Town. Though his only goal to date came against Gillingham in a 3–0 win at the Priestfield Stadium, he has given the Latics a little more stability on the left-side of midfield.

Wigan Athletic Playing Record

	League		FA Cup		FL Cup		Others		Total	
	App	Gls	App	Gls	App	Gls	App	Gls	App	Gls
2003–04	13 (1)	1	0	0	0	0	0	0	13 (1)	1
TOTAL	13 (1)	1	0	0	0	0	0	0	13 (1)	1

MAKIN Christopher Gregory

Full-back

Born: Manchester, 8 May 1973.

Career: November 1991 Oldham Athletic 93 (1) 4. August 1992 on loan WIGAN ATHLETIC 14 (1) 2. June 1996 Marseilles, France. August 1997 Sunderland 115 (5) 1. March 2001 Ipswich Town 73 (0) 0.

Spotted by Oldham Athletic playing in Manchester Schools football, Chris Makin worked his way up through the ranks prior to turning professional during the 1991 close season. Unable to break into the Boundary Park club's first team, he joined Wigan Athletic on loan at the start of the 1992–93 season and made his Football League debut in a 3–2 home defeat by Swansea City. After impressing during a 15–match spell and scoring two goals, including the winner against West Bromwich Albion at Springfield Park. Wigan wanted to sign him permanently but were turned down flat!

On his return to Oldham, the young full-back, who could play on either flank or in midfield was capped by England at Under-21

level and represented the Football League Under-21 side against the Italian Serie 'B' at Huddersfield. He had appeared in 114 League and Cup games for Oldham when, with his contract up, he left the English soccer scene to play for Marseilles. After a year playing in France, he returned to these shores, joining Sunderland for a fee of £500,000. In his first season in the north-east he helped the Wearsiders reach the play-off final where they lost to Charlton Athletic. The following season he picked up a deserved First Division Championship medal and had little problem in adapting to life in the Premiership thanks to his all-action style and commitment.

In March 2001 he was rather surprisingly allowed to leave the Stadium of Light and join Ipswich Town for £1.25 million. After a handful of games towards the end of the 2000–01 campaign, he kept his place in the Ipswich side throughout the following season until an ankle ligament injury against Aston Villa ended his season a month early. Following the appointment of his former Oldham boss Joe Royle, he was handed a central defensive role, where his tackling and pace were the main features of his game.

Wigan Athletic Playing Record

	League		FA Cup		FL Cup		Others		Total	
	App	Gls	App	Gls	App	Gls	App	Gls	App	Gls
1992–93	14 (1)	2	0	0	0	0	0	0	14 (1)	2
TOTAL	14 (1)	2	0	0	0	0	0	0	14 (1)	2

MARTINEZ Roberto

Midfield

Born: Balaguer, Lerida, Spain, 13 July 1973.

Career: CFS Vipla Balaguer. July 1995 WIGAN ATHLETIC 148 (39) 17. July 2001 Motherwell 8 (9) 0. August 2002 Walsall 1 (5) 0. January 2003 Swansea City 19 (0) 2.

Signed from the Spanish Second Division side CFS Vipla Balaguer,

Colin Methven

Roberto Martinez was one of a trio of Spanish players to join the Latics in the summer of 1995. He made his Football League debut on the opening day of the 1995–96 season, scoring Wigan's goal in a 2–1 defeat at Gillingham. In a season in which he left opponents spellbound with a string of match-winning performances, he was the club's leading scorer with 13 goals. Voted the Latics' 'Player of the Year', he had earlier been chosen for the PFA Third Division team.

He was still Wigan's most exciting player in 1996–97 when he helped the club win the Third Division Championship. Named in the PFA side for the second season running, Martinez, who had the ability to create something out of nothing, was a tireless worker. Superbly skilful with excellent passing ability Martinez, the last of the 'Three Amigos' still at the club, won an Autowindscreen Shield medal in 1999 though he later found first-team opportunities limited. In 2000–01 he had something of a mixed time being in and out of the Latics side but he did feature in the play-off encounters with Reading where he produced his best performances of the campaign. Also working on Spanish football for Sky TV, this most popular of players was released in the close season.

He went to play for Scottish Premier League side Motherwell but after one season at the Fir Park Stadium, he returned to Football League action with Walsall. After his handful of appearances for the Saddlers, he served manager Colin Lee for a time in assessing games from the stand before moving to Swansea City. He immediately impressed and, after being awarded the captaincy, was instrumental in helping the Swans' retain their League status.

Wigan Athletic Playing Record

	League		FA Cup		FL Cup		Others		Total	
	App	Gls	App	Gls	App	Gls	App	Gls	App	Gls
1995–96	42	9	4	3	2	1	2	0	50	13
1996–97	38 (5)	4	1	0	2	0	0 (1)	0	41 (6)	5
1997–98	26 (7)	1	2	1	1	0	1 (1)	0	30 (8)	2
1998–99	3 (7)	0	0 (1)	0	2	0	2	0	7 (8)	0
1999–2000	14 (11)	3	3 (1)	0	1	0	0 (3)	0	18 (15)	4
2000–01	25 (9)	0	3	0	3 (1)	0	2	0	33 (10)	0
TOTAL	148 (39)	17	13 (2)	4	11 (1)	1	7 (5)	2	179 (47)	24

METHVEN Colin John

Central Defender
Born: India, 10 December 1955.
Career: East Fife. October 1979 WIGAN ATHLETIC 295 (1) 21. July 1986 Blackpool 166 (7) 11. September 1990 on loan Carlisle United 12 (0) 0. November 1990 Walsall 97 (0) 3.

Although born in India, Colin Methven grew up in Scotland, where on leaving school, he joined the National Coal Board as an Apprentice Electrical Engineer. While with the NCB, he represented the Scottish Miners against Nottingham Miners, the Scots winning 7–0. After being watched by East Fife, Methven had a trial and was signed up for the Bayview club. He was then loaned to Leven Juniors for two seasons of non-League football to help him acquire experience. Methven eventually made his East Fife debut against Stranraer at the end of the 1974–75 season, after which he remained an ever-present in all League and Cup games until joining Wigan Athletic in September 1979.

During his last season with East Fife, he represented Scotland in a four-nation competition at semi-professional level. After making his Latics debut as a substitute for Derek Brownbill in a 4–0 defeat at Huddersfield Town, Methven missed few games in seven seasons with the club. His arrival at Springfield Park saw him add power and determination to an already formidable combination at the heart of the defence. Strong and skilful with tremendous leadership qualities, Methven became a firm favourite with the Wigan fans who elected him 'Player of the Year' in 1979–80 and 1984–85. Methven, who helped the Latics win the Freight Rover Trophy in this latter season, received his greatest honour in 1981–82 when his fellow professionals voted him into the Fourth Division Select XI.

In July 1986, Methven left Springfield Park to join Blackpool for a fee of £20,000. A virtual ever-present for the next four years, he was voted the Seasiders' 'Player of the Year' for two consecutive seasons by the fans, who were angry when he was sold to Walsall in November 1990 after an earlier loan spell with Carlisle United.

Wigan Athletic Playing Record

	League		FA Cup		FL Cup		Others		Total	
	App	Gls	App	Gls	App	Gls	App	Gls	App	Gls
1979–80	34 (1)	2	6	1	0	0	0	0	40 (1)	3
1980–81	46	2	2	0	4	0	0	0	52	2
1981–82	46	9	2	1	6	1	0	0	54	11
1982–83	44	1	2	0	4	0	0	0	50	1
1983–84	39	0	3	0	2	1	1	0	45	1
1984–85	43	0	3	0	3	1	7	0	56	1
1985–86	43	7	5	2	2	0	6	0	56	9
TOTAL	295 (1)	21	23	4	21	3	14	0	353 (1)	28

MILLER David Brian

Defender/Midfield
Born: Burnley, 8 January 1964.
Career: January 1982 Burnley 27 (5) 3. March 1983 on loan Crewe Alexandra 3 (0) 0. July 1985 Tranmere Rovers 25 (4) 1. December 1986 Preston North End 50 (8) 2. Colne Dynamoes. February 1989 on loan Burnley 4 (0) 0. September 1989 Carlisle United 108 (1) 7. March 1992 Stockport County 72 (9) 1. October 1994 WIGAN ATHLETIC 35 (3) 3.

The son of Burnley legend Brian Miller, David was a Clarets fanatic as a youngster and set his heart on playing for the Turf

David Miller

Moor club from an early age. In fact, Brian Miller was the Clarets' manager when David first made his breakthrough into League football as a substitute on New Year's Day 1983. Following his brief appearance at Turf Moor, he spent a short loan period with Crewe Alexandra before returning to Burnley and, under new manager John Bond, scored on his full League debut against Southend United. However, competition for places at Turf Moor was fierce and he was released.

After a season at Tranmere, he joined Colne Dyanmoes but then suddenly, he was back in League football, signing for Preston North End in December 1986.

At the end of his first season, he helped North End win promotion to the Third Division, then after a short loan spell back at Turf Moor, he joined Carlisle United. At Brunton Park, he enjoyed regular first-team football for the first time in his career. His consistency attracted Stockport County, who paid £25,000 for his services in March 1992. He helped the Hatters reach the play-offs in two consecutive seasons before joining the Latics in November 1994. He made his debut in a 5–3 defeat at Doncaster Rovers, holding his place at the heart of the club's defence for the remainder of the 1994–95 season. Injuries and a loss of form restricted his appearances the following season and in May 1996 he was released.

Wigan Athletic Playing Record

	League		FA Cup		FL Cup		Others		Total	
	App	Gls	App	Gls	App	Gls	App	Gls	App	Gls
1994–95	31	3	2	0	0	0	3	0	36	3
1995–96	3 (3)	0	0	0	2	0	0 (1)	0	5 (4)	0
TOTAL	34 (3)	3	2	0	2	0	3 (1)	0	41 (4)	3

MILLETT Michael Paul

Midfield
Born: Wigan, 22 September 1977. Died 1995.
Career: October 1994 WIGAN ATHLETIC 1 (2) 0.

Rated as potentially the biggest asset the Latics have ever produced, England youth international midfielder Michael Millett produced

Michael Millett

a series of impressive performances at junior level before being given his League debut as a substitute in a 2–0 defeat at Walsall in April 1995. A good competitor and strong in the tackle, he started the club's next game but was again on the losing side as the Latics lost 1–0 at Rochdale. Back on the bench for the final game of the season, he replaced Tony Black in a 3–2 defeat of Doncaster Rovers. After just one first-team appearance in 1995–96 when he came off the bench in the League Cup tie against Chester City, Michael Millett tragically died in a car crash, a day before his 18th birthday. Not surprisingly, Latics' season was overshadowed by the tragedy.

Wigan Athletic Playing Record

	League		FA Cup		FL Cup		Others		Total	
	App	Gls	App	Gls	App	Gls	App	Gls	App	Gls
1994–95	1 (2)	0	0	0	0	0	0	0	1 (2)	0
1995–96	0	0	0	0	0 (1)	0	0	0	0 (1)	0
TOTAL	1 (2)	0	0	0	0 (1)	0	0	0	1 (3)	0

MITCHELL James Robert

Full-back
Born: Liverpool, 13 June 1967.
Career: June 1985 WIGAN ATHLETIC 2 (0) 0. Southport.

Full-back James Mitchell joined the Latics on leaving school and after some impressive displays in the club's reserve side, made his League debut in a 2–1 defeat at home to York City in September 1984. He had another outing for the Latics first team that season before turning professional in the close season. However, he failed to add to his total of Football League appearances in 1985–86 as the club had a much stronger squad and spent most of the campaign challenging for promotion to the Second Division. Mitchell left Springfield Park in the summer of 1986 to continue his career with non-League Southport.

Wigan Athletic Playing Record

	League		FA Cup		FL Cup		Others		Total	
	App	Gls	App	Gls	App	Gls	App	Gls	App	Gls
1984–85	2	0	0	0	0	0	0	0	2	0
TOTAL	2	0	0	0	0	0	0	0	2	0

MITCHELL Paul Alexander

Defender
Born: Stalybridge, 26 August 1981.
Career: July 2000 WIGAN ATHLETIC 30 (33) 0. March 2001 on loan Halifax Town 11 (0) 0.

Young defender Paul Mitchell worked his way up through the ranks at the JJB Stadium, making his first-team debut in the 1–0 Worthington Cup win over Scunthorpe United. He kept his place in the squad for the League game at Wrexham two days later but had a disastrous debut. After coming on as a substitute for the injured Scott Green, Mitchell received his marching orders in a match the Latics went on to win 3–1. Though he failed to appear in any further League games, he started Worthington and LDV Cup matches, but then joined Halifax Town on loan before returning to the JJB Stadium where he was offered a 12–month contract.

However, after starting the opening matches of the 2001–02 season at right-back, he subsequently found himself relegated to the bench. Later in the season he was pressed into an emergency role in midfield in the away match at Queen's Park Rangers and went on to enjoy an extended period in the side on merit. The gutsy performer was in and out of the Latics side during their Second Division Championship-winning season but whether he was playing in midfield or as an emergency central defender, he never let the side down. Though he spent most of the 2003–04 season on the bench – making just two starts – he is still considered a valuable member of the Latics' squad and has been offered terms for next season.

Wigan Athletic Playing Record

	League		FA Cup		FL Cup		Others		Total	
	App	Gls	App	Gls	App	Gls	App	Gls	App	Gls
2000–01	0 (1)	0	0 (1)	0	2 (1)	0	1 (1)	0	3 (4)	0
2001–02	16 (7)	0	0	0	1	0	0 (1)	0	17 (8)	0
2002–03	13 (14)	0	1 (1)	0	1 (1)	0	2	0	17 (16)	0
2003–04	1 (11)	0	1	0	0 (1)	0	0	0	2 (12)	0
TOTAL	30 (33)	0	2 (2)	0	4 (3)	0	3 (2)	0	39 (40)	0

MOORE Michael

Forward

Born: Chorley, 20 July 1952.

Career: Blackburn Rovers (Amateur). June 1970 Preston North End. July 1971 Southport 62 (21) 11. Great Harwood. Dallas Tornadoes. Altrincham. WIGAN ATHLETIC. March 1978 Port Vale 13 (0) 0. August 1978 WIGAN ATHLETIC 57 (7) 12. Barrow. Leyland Motors. Glossop. Chorley. Horwich RMI.

On leaving school, Chorley-born forward Mickey Moore joined Blackburn Rovers as an amateur but eventually signed as a professional for Preston North End. Unable to make the grade at Deepdale, he moved on to Southport, where he was a member of the side which won the Fourth Division Championship in 1972–73. Following the Sandgrounders' relegation after just one season of Third Division football, Moore then played part-time for Great Harwood, where the manager was Les Rigby. At the end of the season, Moore crossed the Atlantic to play for Dallas Tornadoes along with Tommy Gore. On returning from America he teamed up with Les Rigby again, this time at Altrincham. The high spot of his time with Altrincham was reaching the FA Challenge Trophy semi-final, in which he was unfortunate to miss a vital penalty!

Latics manager Ian McNeill then brought him to Springfield Park. He immediately endeared himself to the Wigan fans with his hardworking style and his eye for the half-chance proved very popular. After playing a major part in the club's glorious FA Cup run which ended at Birmingham City, he left Wigan, joining Port Vale for a fee of £3,000. After 13 appearances for the Valiants, he was transferred back to Wigan and made his League debut in the 3–2 home defeat at the hands of Newport County in September 1978. It took Moore quite a long time to settle down in his second spell with the Latics but eventually he found his shooting boots and helped the club finish sixth in Division Four. Midway through the following season, Moore left Springfield Park, playing non-League football for a number of clubs including Barrow, Leyland Motors, Glossop, Chorley and Horwich RMI.

Wigan Athletic Playing Record

	League		FA Cup		FL Cup		Others		Total	
	App	Gls	App	Gls	App	Gls	App	Gls	App	Gls
1978–79	40 (1)	9	2	1	0	0	0	0	42 (1)	10
1979–80	17 (6)	3	0	0	0	0	0	0	17 (6)	3
TOTAL	57 (7)	12	2	1	0	0	0	0	59 (7)	13

Steve Morgan

MORGAN Stephen Alphonso

Left-back

Born: Oldham, 19 September 1968.

Career: August 1986 Blackpool 135 (9) 10. July 1990 Plymouth Argyle 120 (1) 6. July 1993 Coventry City 65 (3) 2. March 1996 on loan Bristol Rovers 5 (0) 0. July 1996 WIGAN ATHLETIC 31 (5) 2. September 1997 on loan Bury 5 (0) 0. August 1998 Burnley 17 (0) 0. July 1999 Hull City 17 (2) 1. September 2000 Halifax Town 1 (0) 0. Altrincham. TNS.

A product of Blackpool's youth policy, Steve Morgan worked his way up through the ranks before making his League debut for the Seasiders at Bristol Rovers in April 1986, four months before he established himself at left-back in the Blackpool side, playing in every game that season and missing just two in 1988–89. When Blackpool were relegated to the Fourth Division, Morgan elected to join a new club, signing for Second Division Plymouth Argyle. He spent three seasons at Home Park before falling out of favour with manager Peter Shilton and joined Premier League Coventry City for £150,000. An excellent squad player for the Sky Blues, he later had a loan spell with Bristol Rovers before joining the Latics in July 1996.

He made his debut as a substitute for Wayne Biggins in a 2–1 home win over Northampton Town on the opening day of the 1996–97 season. He scored his first goal for the club in a 2–1 home defeat by Hull City but ended the campaign with a Third Division Championship medal as the Latics won promotion to Division Two. Injuries restricted his appearances the following season and after a loan spell with Bury he moved to Burnley on a free transfer. However, after just one season at Turf Moor, he was released and joined Hull City before ending his League career with Halifax Town. Moving into non-League football, he first played for Altrincham before joining League of Wales club TNS Llansantffraid.

Wigan Athletic Playing Record

	League		FA Cup		FL Cup		Others		Total	
	App	Gls	App	Gls	App	Gls	App	Gls	App	Gls
1996–97	18 (5)	1	0	0	2	0	1	0	21 (5)	1
1997–98	13	1	1	0	0	0	3	0	17	1
TOTAL	31 (5)	2	1	0	2	0	4	0	38 (50	2

MORTON Neil

Forward
Born: Congleton, 21 December 1968.
Career: September 1987 Crewe Alexandra 18 (13) 1. Northwich Victoria. October 1990 Chester City 63 (32) 13. July 1993 WIGAN ATHLETIC 41 (7) 5. Altrincham.

Live-wire striker Neil Morton began his career with Crewe Alexandra, making his Football League debut for the Railwaymen as a substitute in a goalless draw at Shrewsbury Town. Morton's only goal for the Cheshire club came against Bolton Wanderers in a 2–1 win, but in 1988 after a series of injuries and a loss of form, he left Crewe to play non-League football for Northwich Victoria. His prolific goalscoring for the Vauxhall Conference side led to a £50,000 move to Chester City in October 1990.

Morton spent three seasons with the Cestrians, scoring 13 goals in 95 League outings before joining Wigan Athletic on a free transfer in the summer of 1993.

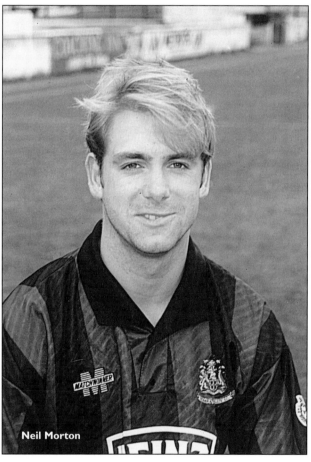

Neil Morton

He made his Latics debut on the opening day of the 1993–94 season as Scunthorpe United took the points with a 2–0 win. He scored the club's first goal of the campaign the following week as Wigan drew 1–1 at Torquay United and played in the majority of the Latics' games. After starting the first nine games of the 1994–95 season, his first-team appearances dwindled following the appointment of Graham Barrow as manager. He left Springfield Park in November 1994 to join Altrincham and played a major part in their shock FA Cup win over the Latics!

Wigan Athletic Playing Record

	League		FA Cup		FL Cup		Others		Total	
	App	Gls	App	Gls	App	Gls	App	Gls	App	Gls
1993–94	32 (7)	4	2	1	2	1	2	0	38 (7)	6
1994–95	9	1	0	0	4	0	1	0	14	1
TOTAL	41 (7)	5	2	1	6	1	3	0	52 (7)	7

MUTCH Andrew Todd

Forward
Born: Liverpool, 28 December 1963.
Career: Southport. February 1986 Wolverhampton Wanderers 277 (12) 96. August 1993 Swindon Town 34 (16) 6. August 1995 on loan WIGAN ATHLETIC 7 (0) 1. March 1996 Stockport County 28 (36) 10. Barrow.

As a youngster, Andy Mutch was an apprentice with both Everton and Liverpool. Unfortunately he was never offered terms by either club and opted for a stint in non-League football with Southport. His goalscoring talent was soon in evidence at Haig Avenue and in February 1986 Wolves manager Sammy Chapman brought him to Molineux.

It was midway through the 1986–87 season that he began to form a deadly scoring partnership with Steve Bull, and though the club were beaten by Aldershot in the play-offs, they won the Fourth Division Championship in 1987–88. That season the two strikers scored 53 of Wolves' 82 goals with Mutch's share being 19. The club also won the Sherpa Van Trophy in 1988 with Mutch scoring the opening goal in the 2–0 win over Burnley in the Wembley final. Even more impressive in 1988–89, they netted 58 of the club's 96 goals to help win the Third Division Championship. At the end of that season, he earned recognition at England 'B' level, appearing in three internationals. He had scored 105 goals in 338 games for Wolves when in the summer of 1993 he was surprisingly allowed to join Swindon Town for £250,000.

Despite being hampered by a series of injuries, he was hugely popular at the County ground but after just five games of the

Andy Mutch

1995–96 season, he was loaned to Wigan Athletic. He scored on his debut in a 1–1 draw at Preston North End but it was his only success in seven consecutive appearances in the No.9 shirt. After the clubs failed to agree terms, he returned to the County Ground before accepting a move to Stockport County. He soon burst into action with a hat-trick over promotion rivals Oxford United and later played an important role in the club winning promotion and reaching the semi-finals of the League Cup. On leaving Edgeley Park he played non-League football for Barrow.

Wigan Athletic Playing Record

	League		FA Cup		FL Cup		Others		Total	
	App	Gls	App	Gls	App	Gls	App	Gls	App	Gls
1995–96	7	1	0	0	0	0	0	0	7	1
TOTAL	7	1	0	0	0	0	0	0	7	1

NEWELL Michael Colin

Forward

Born: Liverpool, 27 January 1965.
Career: Liverpool Juniors. September 1983 Crewe Alexandra 3 (0) 0. October 1983 WIGAN ATHLETIC 64 (8) 25. January 1986 Luton Town 62 (1) 18. September 1987 Leicester City 81 (0) 21. July 1989 Everton 48 (20) 15. November 1991 Blackburn Rovers 113 (17) 28. July 1996 Birmingham City 11 (4) 1. December 1996 on loan West Ham United 6 (1) 0. March 1997 Bradford City 7 (0) 0. July 1997 Aberdeen. March 1999 Crewe Alexandra 1 (3) 0. Doncaster Rovers. February 2000 Blackpool 2 (0) 0.

A former Liverpool junior, Mike Newell was not offered terms at Anfield and made his League debut while on trial with Crewe Alexandra. After failing to impress Dario Gradi he joined Wigan Athletic, playing his first game for the club in a 2–1 home win over Rotherham United in December 1983. After winning a regular place in the Latics side, he scored one of the goals in the club's Freight Rover Trophy Final win over Brentford and in 1985–86 netted 16 goals in 24 games, including a hat-trick in a 5–1 defeat of

Mike Newell

Darlington. Midway through that season, Newell was transferred to First Division Luton Town. In 1986–87 he was ever-present and the Hatters' leading scorer with 12 goals. Shortly afterwards he was signed by Leicester City for a club record £350,000 and in two seasons at Filbert Street hardly missed a match, ending the 1988–89 season as the Foxes' leading scorer.

In the summer of 1989 he joined Everton for £1.1 million but after struggling to score goals, found himself out of the side. In November 1991 he became the first player to cost Blackburn Rovers a million pounds when he accepted an offer from Kenny Dalglish to join the Ewood Park club. He became a great favourite with the Blackburn fans and despite breaking his leg against Newcastle in February 1992, returned for the end of the season. After scoring a vital goal in the first leg of the semi-final play-offs against Derby County he converted the penalty in the final against Leicester City that gave Rovers a 1–0 win and a place in the Premier League. Forming an effective strike partnership with Alan Shearer, he went on to score 42 goals in 157 games before joining Birmingham City for £775,000 in July 1996.

Unable to settle at St Andrew's, he had loan spells with West Ham United and Bradford City before joining Scottish Premier League club Aberdeen in the summer of 1997. He later played for Crewe Alexandra and Doncaster Rovers before ending his League career with Blackpool. After managing Hartlepool United to promotion from the Third Division in 2002–03, Newell left Victoria Park to take charge of Luton Town.

Wigan Athletic Playing Record

	League		FA Cup		FL Cup		Others		Total	
	App	Gls	App	Gls	App	Gls	App	Gls	App	Gls
1983–84	5 (4)	0	0	0	0	0	0	0	5 (4)	0
1984–85	35 (4)	9	4	3	4	1	5 (1)	3	48 (5)	16
1985–86	24	16	4	3	2	0	0	0	30	19
TOTAL	64 (8)	25	8	6	6	1	5 (1)	3	83 (9)	35

NEWMAN Robert Nigel

Central Defender

Born: Bradford-on-Avon, 13 December 1963.
Career: October 1981 Bristol City 382 (12) 52. July 1991 Norwich City 181 (24) 14. December 1997 on loan Motherwell 11 (0) 0. March 1998 on loan WIGAN ATHLETIC 8 (0) 0. July 1998 Southend United 63 (9) 11.

Versatile central defender Rob Newman began his League career with Bristol City, making his debut against Fulham in February 1982, shortly after the 'Ashton Gate Eight' crisis. He was an influential figure as City won promotion in 1983–84, reached two consecutive Freight Rover Trophy Finals at Wembley and the promotion play-offs in 1987–88. Three times ever-present, he skippered the club's 1989–90 promotion success but in July 1991 he moved to Norwich City for a fee of £600,000.

Good in the air and dangerous at set pieces, he scored a number of valuable goals for the Canaries, perhaps none more so than the last minute goal at Barnsley in April 1996 to secure a vital point in a 2–2 draw as the club narrowly avoided consecutive relegations. Having gained UEFA Cup experience with the Carrow Road club, Newman, who appeared in eight different outfield positions during his seven seasons, was reputed to have the hardest shot in English football after winning a Wembley dead-ball competition.

In December 1997 he joined Scottish Premier Division side Motherwell on loan and there were rumours of a permanent move. However, that did not come to fruition and he returned to Carrow Road. Newman joined Wigan Athletic on a loan deal on transfer deadline day, March 1998, making his debut in a 1–1 draw at Preston North End. The veteran central defender endeared himself to the Springfield Park faithful with some fine end of the season displays at the heart of the Wigan defence. The tough tackling defender was only on the losing side once in eight appearances.

Released by Norwich, he joined Southend United on a free transfer and soon became a great favourite with his never-say-die attitude. In a final step towards management he was offered a coaching position at Roots Hall, while the club retained his playing registration. After eventually stepping up to manage the Shrimps, his playing appearances were restricted to a minimum but in May 2003 he parted company with the club, having been replaced by Steve Wignall.

Wigan Athletic Playing Record										
	League		FA Cup		FL Cup		Others		Total	
	App	Gls	App	Gls	App	Gls	App	Gls	App	Gls
1997–98	8	0	0	0	0	0	0	0	8	0
TOTAL	8	0	0	0	0	0	0	0	8	0

NICHOLLS Kevin John Richard

Midfield
Born: Newham, 2 January 1979.
Career: January 1996 Charlton Athletic 4 (8) 1. February 1999 on loan Brighton and Hove Albion 4 (0) 1. June 1999 WIGAN ATHLETIC 19 (9) 0. August 2001 Luton Town 77 (1) 12.

England youth international Kevin Nicholls began his Football League career with Charlton Athletic, making his debut for the Addicks as a substitute against Ipswich Town in September 1996. On his first full League game against Barnsley at the Valley, he scored a spectacular long-range goal in the opening minute. The fierce-tackling midfielder, who could also play in defence, found it difficult to win a place in the Charlton side following their

Kevin Nicholls

promotion to the Premiership and signed for Brighton and Hove Albion on a month's loan. Though he scored on his Seagulls debut, the loan period was cut short because of injury and suspension, after he was booked in all four games he played for the south coast club. Selected in the England squad for the World Under-20 Championships in Nigeria, he joined Wigan in the summer of 1999 for a fee of £250,000.

A knee problem that required surgery had delayed his debut until 23 October when he wore the No.2 shirt in a 2–0 home win over Cardiff City. Unfortunately until the last few games of the campaign, his first season with the club was spoilt by a spate of injuries. He made a disastrous start to the 2001–02 season, being sent off in the Latics' goalless draw at Swansea on the opening day of the campaign. In and out of the Wigan side, he scored the opening goal in the second leg of the play-off match against Reading, only for the Royals to score twice in the final few minutes.

Transferred to Luton Town for just £25,000 prior to the start of the 2001–02 season, he was immediately installed as team captain. Showing incredible spirit and leadership, he was instrumental in the Hatters winning promotion to the Third Division as runners-up to Plymouth Argyle. He continued to lead by example in 2002–03, either urging on his teammates or advocating on behalf of colleagues, although this sometimes got him into trouble with referees!

Wigan Athletic Playing Record										
	League		FA Cup		FL Cup		Others		Total	
	App	Gls	App	Gls	App	Gls	App	Gls	App	Gls
1999–2000	6 (2)	0	0	0	0	0	0	0	6 (2)	0
2000–01	13 (7)	0	0	0	2	0	4	1	19 (7)	1
TOTAL	19 (9)	0	0	0	2	0	4	1	25 (9)	1

NIXON Eric Walter

Goalkeeper
Born: Manchester, 4 October 1962.
Career: Curzon Athletic. December 1983 Manchester City 58 (0) 0. August 1986 on loan Wolverhampton Wanderers 16 (0) 0. November 1986 on loan Bradford City 3 (0) 0. December 1986 on loan Southampton 4 (0) 0. January 1987 on loan Carlisle United 16 (0) 0. March 1988 Tranmere Rovers 341 (0) 0. February 1996 on loan Blackpool 20 (0) 0. September 1996 on loan Bradford City 12 (0) 0. August 1997 Stockport County 43 (0) 0. August 1998 on loan WIGAN ATHLETIC 1 (0) 0. March 1999 WIGAN ATHLETIC 2 (0) 0. July 1999 Tranmere Rovers 1 (4) 0. October 2001 on loan Kidderminster Harriers 2 (0) 0.

Goalkeeper Eric Nixon joined Manchester City from Curzon Athletic in December 1983 but with Alex Williams in such fine form, he had to wait until September 1985 before making his League bow in a 2–2 draw with West Ham United. During his time at Maine Road, Nixon became the first player to appear in all four divisions of the Football League in the same season after loan spells at Southampton, Bradford City, Wolves and Carlisle United.

He joined Tranmere Rovers in March 1988 for £60,000 which was, at the time, a club record fee for the Wirral club. Over the next seven seasons, Nixon missed very few games and was ever-present in seasons 1989–90 and 1991–92. He helped the club win promotion in 1988–89 and 1990–91, when his outstanding display helped Rovers beat Bolton 1–0 after extra-time in the play-off final. After losing his place to Danny Coyne, Nixon had loan spells with Reading and Blackpool. He returned to Prenton Park to share the goalkeeping duties with Coyne in 1996–97, as well as going on loan to Bradford City. At the end of that season Nixon joined Stockport County for £100,000 but after one season at Edgeley

Eric Nixon

Park, he was loaned out to Wigan Athletic, making his debut in a 3–2 win at Oldham Athletic.

In March 1999 he joined the Latics on a free transfer, primarily as cover for Roy Carroll, but he was called into action towards the end of the month, keeping a clean sheet on his last appearance against Bristol Rovers. At the end of the season he returned to Tranmere as goalkeeping coach, but he was registered as a player too and was called on a couple of times as emergency cover. In 2001–02 he came out of retirement to help Kidderminster Harriers when first-choice 'keeper Stuart Brock was suspended. He kept two clean sheets and remarkably also managed an appearance for Tranmere too, when despite his age, he still showed full command of his penalty area. The veteran 'keeper was in his second season as Tranmere's goalkeeping coach in 2002–03 when he was called upon again. Hugely popular at Prenton Park, he continues to be very vocal, whether between the posts or on the bench!

Wigan Athletic Playing Record

	League		FA Cup		FL Cup		Others		Total	
	App	Gls	App	Gls	App	Gls	App	Gls	App	Gls
1998–99	3	0	0	0	0	0	0	0	3	0
TOTAL	3	0	0	0	0	0	0	0	3	0

NOLAN Ian Robert

Full-back
Born: Liverpool, 9 July 1970.
Career: Preston North End. Marine. August 1991 Tranmere Rovers 87 (1) 1. August 1994 Sheffield Wednesday 164 (1) 4. July 2000 Bradford City 17 (4) 0. August 2001 WIGAN ATHLETIC 5 (3) 0. Southport.

Energetic full-back Ian Nolan was on the books of Preston North End but, having failed to make much progress with the Deepdale

club, left to play non-League football with Marine. After a series of impressive performances, Tranmere Rovers paid £10,000 for his services in the summer of 1991. He made his debut for the Wirral club in a 1–1 draw at Wolverhampton Wanderers in October 1991 and went on to play in 40 games, winning the club's 'Player of the Year' award. In 1992–93 he suffered a serious knee injury and missed most of the campaign. Despite regaining full fitness, he faced severe competition from Ged Brannan and Tony Thomas but went on to play in 53 games in 1993–94 as the club reached the play-offs for the second successive season.

In August 1994 Nolan joined Sheffield Wednesday for £1.5 million. Following his arrival at Hillsborough, he missed very few games and was called up to represent Northern Ireland in their World Cup qualifiers, despite his Liverpool upbringing, but in 1997 he suffered a badly broken leg when challenged by Spurs' Justin Edinburgh. The clash broke both tibia and fibia, keeping the immensely spirited and hardworking player out of action for 18 months. He went on to appear in 196 games for the Owls but then in the summer of 2000 he joined Bradford City.

Though he continued to feature for Northern Ireland, he was only a regular for the Bantams in the first half of the season and at the end of the campaign, Nolan, who was out of contract, signed for Wigan Athletic after impressing on a pre-season tour. In only his second appearance in a Wigan shirt, he suffered a stress fracture of the leg in the 2–1 defeat at Brighton. This prevented him from making a real impact and though he did return to first-team action towards the end of the campaign, he left the JJB Stadium the following summer to join Southport.

Wigan Athletic Playing Record

	League		FA Cup		FL Cup		Others		Total	
	App	Gls	App	Gls	App	Gls	App	Gls	App	Gls
2001–02	5 (3)	0	0	0	0	0	0	0	5 (3)	0
TOTAL	5 (3)	0	0	0	0	0	0	0	5 (3)	0

NUGENT Stephen

Forward
Born: Orrell, 7 May 1973.
Career: August 1991 WIGAN ATHLETIC 7 (5) 0. Barrow. Leigh RMI.

Steve Nugent

Steve Nugent became the youngest player to appear in a Latics first team when, at the age of 16 years 132 days, he played in the 1–0 defeat at Leyton Orient on 16 September 1989, coming on as a substitute for Don Page. After that, it was back into the club's reserve side and he didn't appear at all in 1990–91. Nugent made his first start in a Wigan side a month after turning professional, wearing the No.9 shirt in a 3–1 home defeat by Huddersfield Town. He played against Reading three weeks later but was substituted in both games. He was given more of a chance in 1992–93 but he still failed to make much of an impact and in the close season, Nugent was one of 10 players to be released. After a spell with Barrow he moved on to Leigh RMI.

Wigan Athletic Playing Record

	League		FA Cup		FL Cup		Others		Total	
	App	Gls	App	Gls	App	Gls	App	Gls	App	Gls
1989–90	0 (1)	0	0	0	0 (1)	0	0	0	0 (2)	0
1990–91	0	0	0	0	0	0	0	0	0	0
1991–92	2	0	0	0	0	0	0	0	2	0
1992–93	5 (4)	0	0	0	0 (1)	0	1	0	6 (5)	0
TOTAL	7 (5)	0	0	0	0 (2)	0	1	0	8 (7)	0

O'CONNELL Brendan

Midfield/Forward
Born: Lambeth, 12 November 1966.
Career: July 1985 Portsmouth. July 1996 Exeter City 73 (8) 19. June 1988 Burnley 62 (2) 17. November 1989 on loan Huddersfield Town 11 (0) 1. March 1990 Barnsley 212 (28) 35. July 1996 Charlton Athletic 33 (5) 2. August 1997 WIGAN ATHLETIC 17 (0) 5.

After serving his apprenticeship with Portsmouth, Brendan O'Connell had a year as a professional at Fratton Park without breaking into Pompey's League side before joining Exeter City in the summer of 1986. After two years at St James' Park in which he was a consistent scorer, he was surprisingly given a free transfer and joined Burnley. Though not the most elegant of players, he ended his first season at Turf Moor as the Clarets' leading scorer with 18 League and Cup goals. After the Burnley crowd got on his

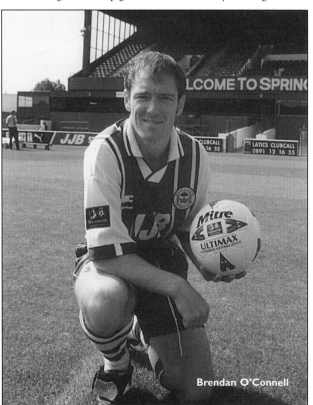

Brendan O'Connell

back, he had a brief loan spell with Huddersfield Town before returning to Turf Moor completely rejuvenated.

Barnsley were obviously impressed and within weeks of his return, he was on his way to Oakwell for a fee of £45,000. Voted the supporters' 'Player of the Year' in his first season with the club, he switched to a midfield role before an Achilles injury kept him out of action. The hardworking player left the Tykes in the summer of 1996, joining Charlton Athletic for £125,000.

He soon won over the Valley faithful with his non-stop running and tenacious tackling and midway through his first season with the club, took over the captaincy. After just one season at the Valley, O'Connell joined Wigan Athletic for a £120,000 fee. He made a dream start for Wigan, scoring a hat-trick on his debut as the Latics beat Wycombe Wanderers 5–2 on the opening day of the 1997–98 season. Having settled in quickly with his new club, his progress was hampered by a serious blood clot on the knee which resulted in the popular player having to give up the game.

Wigan Athletic Playing Record

	League		FA Cup		FL Cup		Others		Total	
	App	Gls	App	Gls	App	Gls	App	Gls	App	Gls
1997–98	17	5	1	0	2	0	0	0	20	5
TOTAL	17	5	1	0	2	0	0	0	20	5

OGDEN Neil

Left-back
Born: Billinge, 29 November 1975.
Career: March 1994 WIGAN ATHLETIC 11 (4) 0. Northwich Victoria.
A local YTS discovery, left-back Neil Ogden made his Wigan Athletic debut as a 17-year-old substitute in a 2–1 defeat of Swansea at the end of the 1992–93 season. With the Latics already relegated, he kept his place for the club's last game of the season

Neil Ogden

and gave a solid display in a goalless draw at Bournemouth. Injuries and a loss of form then restricted his first-team opportunities and over the next couple of seasons he made just a handful of appearances as substitute. He appeared more frequently in 1995–96, playing left-back in 10 consecutive League games. However, on losing his place to Gavin Johnson, he moved to Vauxhall Conference side Northwich Victoria in the closing stages of the campaign, after having his contract cancelled by mutual consent.

Wigan Athletic Playing Record

	League		FA Cup		FL Cup		Others		Total	
	App	Gls	App	Gls	App	Gls	App	Gls	App	Gls
1993–94	0 (2)	0	0 (1)	0	0	0	0	0	0 (3)	0
1994–95	0 (1)	0	0	0	0	0	0	0	0 (1)	0
1995–96	10	0	0 (1)	0	0	0	1	0	11 (1)	0
TOTAL	10 (3)	0	0 (2)	0	0	0	1	0	11 (5)	0

O'KEEFE Eamonn Gerard

Forward

Born: Manchester, 13 October 1953.
Career: Stalybridge Celtic. February 1974 Plymouth Argyle. Hyde United. Saudi Arabia. Mossley. July 1979 Everton 26 (14) 6. January 1982 WIGAN ATHLETIC 56 (2) 25. July 1983 Port Vale 50 (9) 17. March 1985 Blackpool 33 (3) 23. St Patrick's Athletic. March 1989 Chester City 12 (5) 4.

Few young players get the opportunity to fulfil their dream of

Eamonn O'Keefe

becoming professional footballers, but Eamonn O'Keefe got two bites at the cherry! In February 1974, Third Division Plymouth Argyle signed him from non-League Stalybridge Celtic but after failing to impress, he found himself back in the non-League arena without playing a League game. He then had a brief spell with Hyde United, another in Saudi Arabia and was turning out for Mossley when, in July 1979, Everton signed him for £22,500.

Most of his three seasons at Goodison Park were spent in the club's Central League side but he did make his full international debut for the Republic of Ireland in February 1981. Two years earlier he had played for England's semi-pros against Scotland and Holland. This, according to FIFA, made him ineligible to play for Ireland. He fought FIFA's decision and eventually won his case. In January 1982 O'Keefe left Everton and joined Wigan Athletic for a £65,000 fee. He scored on his Latics debut in a 3–2 win over Northampton Town and towards the end of the season in which the club won promotion to the Third Division, he netted hat-tricks in the 3–0 defeat of Crewe Alexandra and a 3–1 victory over Mansfield Town. Revelling in his new striking role, he netted another treble the following season as Latics beat Southend United 4–0, ending the campaign as the club's leading scorer.

In July 1983 he joined Port Vale for £10,000 before moving to Blackpool for a similar fee in March 1985. O'Keefe surpassed himself at Bloomfield Road for in 1985–86, despite a long lay-off due to a knee injury, he was the Seasiders' leading scorer. In September 1986 he announced his retirement from the game because of the recurrence of his knee injury before attempting a comeback, first with St Patrick's Athletic and later Chester City, whom he joined in March 1989. However, after four goals in 17 games for the Cestrians, he was finally forced to retire.

Wigan Athletic Playing Record

	League		FA Cup		FL Cup		Others		Total	
	App	Gls	App	Gls	App	Gls	App	Gls	App	Gls
1981–82	22	9	0	0	0	0	0	0	22	9
1982–83	34 (2)	16	0	0	3	1	0	0	37 (2)	17
TOTAL	56 (2)	25	0	0	3	1	0	0	59 (2)	26

OLIVER James

Midfield

Born: Forfar, 13 January 1958.
Career: Brora Rangers. Dundee United. Ross County. Montrose. July 1980 WIGAN ATHLETIC 1 (1) 0.

After playing his early football for Brora Rangers in his native Scotland, James Oliver joined Dundee United. Unable to make the grade at Tannadice, he had a brief spell in the Highland League with Ross County before joining Montrose. It was from here that Ian McNeill brought him to Springfield Park in the summer of 1980. He had few opportunities to show his true worth during his early days with the Latics, though Fred Eyre's experiment with this strong player in a defensive role was an interesting development. Oliver made his Latics debut at centre-forward at Darlington in September 1980 but he was replaced by David Glenn as Wigan suffered a 3–1 defeat. He came on for Frank Corrigan and set up George Urquhart's winning goal in the match against York City but it was his last appearance in a Wigan shirt before returning to play north of the border.

Wigan Athletic Playing Record

	League		FA Cup		FL Cup		Others		Total	
	App	Gls	App	Gls	App	Gls	App	Gls	App	Gls
1980–81	1 (1)	0	0	0	0	0	0	0	1 (1)	0
TOTAL	1 (1)	0	0	0	0	0	0	0	1 (1)	0

O'NEILL Michael Andrew Martin

Midfield

Born: Portadown, 5 July 1969.
Career: Coleraine. October 1987 Newcastle United 36 (12) 15.
Dundee United. Hibernian. July 1996 Coventry City 3 (2) 0. January
1998 on loan Aberdeen. March 1998 on loan Reading 9 (0) 1.
September 1998 WIGAN ATHLETIC 65 (1) 2. St Johnstone.

Michael O'Neill was playing for Coleraine when he joined Newcastle United as an 18–year-old in October 1987. The transfer created a record £100,000 fee for a Northern Ireland club. Though he was very much a raw talent, he made a big impact on the First Division scene. His intricate style and ball skills knitted with those of Paul Gascoigne and in his first season he netted 13 goals in 21 games to be voted United's 'Player of the Season'. But then the Irishman was struck by illness and injury, losing form dramatically. After being in and out of the side for the following campaign, he was transferred to Dundee United for £350,000.

Michael O'Neill

He later had trials with both Everton and Middlesbrough before moving to Hibernian. He rediscovered much of the talent that had delighted the Tyneside crowd at Easter Road and this prompted a £300,000 transfer to Coventry City in the summer of 1996. The Northern Ireland international failed to settle at Highfield Road and after an extended loan to Aberdeen in January 1998, he was loaned to Reading until the end of the campaign. Playing either on the left-hand side or centre of midfield, O'Neill became the new Wigan manager Ray Mathias's first signing when he arrived at Springfield Park in September 1998.

Still a quality performer, he made his Latics debut in a 2–0 home win over Macclesfield Town and though he failed to score in the League, he netted the winner in the Autowindscreen Shield area final second-leg at Wrexham as the club went on to win the trophy at Wembley. He was enjoying an excellent 1999–2000 season until injuries forced him to miss the final third of the campaign, including the play-offs. The hardworking midfielder

was made available for transfer in the close season and joined St Johnstone, where he became a great favourite with the McDiarmid Park crowd.

Wigan Athletic Playing Record

	League		FA Cup		FL Cup		Others		Total	
	App	Gls	App	Gls	App	Gls	App	Gls	App	Gls
1998–99	35 (1)	0	3	0	1	0	7	3	46 (1)	3
1999–2000	30	2	4	0	4	0	1	0	39	2
TOTAL	65 (1)	2	7	0	5	0	8	3	85 (1)	5

ORMSBY Brendan Thomas Christopher

Central Defender

Born: Birmingham, 1 October 1960.
Career: October 1978 Aston Villa 115 (2) 4. February 1986 Leeds
United 46 (0) 5. January 1990 on loan Shrewsbury Town 1 (0) 0. July
1990 Doncaster Rovers 78 (0) 7. August 1992 Scarborough 15 (1) 1.
Waterford United. August 1994 WIGAN ATHLETIC 2 (0) 0.

Brendan Ormsby

England schoolboy international Brendan Ormsby began his career with Aston Villa, with whom he turned professional in October 1978. The following year he captained the England youth team but just after winning a place in the Villa side, he broke an ankle and missed the whole of the club's League Championship winning season of 1980–81. He played three times in Villa's 1981–82 European Cup winning campaign and had appeared in 117 League games when he joined Leeds United in March 1986.

During the Yorkshire club's play-off match against Charlton Athletic, he severely damaged a cartilage. His injury was so serious that he did not get into the Leeds team for nearly two years. After a loan spell with Shrewsbury Town he resurrected his career with Doncaster Rovers. He then joined Scarborough for a year before working a further year as player-coach of Waterford United. He joined Wigan Athletic in the summer of 1994, but after appearing in two home defeats – Chesterfield (2–3) and Barnet (1–2) he left Springfield Park to become assistant-manager of Northern Counties (East) League side, Farsley Celtic.

Wigan Athletic Playing Record

	League		FA Cup		FL Cup		Others		Total	
	App	Gls	App	Gls	App	Gls	App	Gls	App	Gls
1994–95	2	0	0	0	0	0	0	0	2	0
TOTAL	2	0	0	0	0	0	0	0	2	0

PADULA Diego Gino Mauro

Left-back

Born: Buenos Aires, Argentina, 11 July 1976.
Career: River Plate. Huracan. Xerez, Spain. October 1999 Bristol Rovers. November 1999 Walsall 23 (2) 0. July 2000 WIGAN ATHLETIC 2 (2) 0. July 2002 Queen's Park Rangers 17 (4) 1.

Argentinian-born defender Gino Padula had spells with River Plate, Huracan and Xerez before having trials with Bristol Rovers, Dundee United and Derby County. In November 1999 he linked

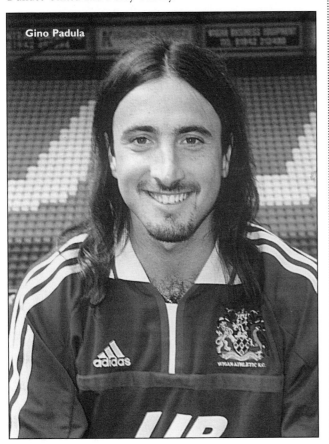
Gino Padula

up with Walsall and after impressing in his first full game, a 2–0 win over Huddersfield Town, he went on to appear in 21 matches before injury ruled him out of the latter stages of the season. A quick, skilful left-back, whose determined tackling, ability in the air and readiness to move forward made him a firm favourite with the Saddlers' fans but in the summer of 2000 he left the Bescot Stadium to join Wigan Athletic.

After coming on as a substitute for Kevin Sharp in a 4–2 League Cup win at Scunthorpe United, Padula spent much of the next three months on the bench before making his first full appearance against Dorchester Town in the FA Cup. His first full League appearance came after the turn of the year as Wigan beat Oldham Athletic 3–1. His first goal for the club came against his old club Walsall in an LDV Trophy match but the Saddlers ran out winners 2–1. Padula was one of several players released by the Latics in the summer as the club sought to trim its squad.

He later joined Queen's Park Rangers but was initially kept out of the side by Tommy Williams. However, once he made his first start he went on to make the left wing-back position his own. A great favourite with the fans, his in-swinging corners resulted in a number of goals in the final weeks of the 2002–03 season.

Wigan Athletic Playing Record

	League		FA Cup		FL Cup		Others		Total	
	App	Gls	App	Gls	App	Gls	App	Gls	App	Gls
2000–01	2 (2)	0	2	0	0 (1)	0	2	1	6 (3)	1
TOTAL	2 (2)	0	2	0	0 (1)	0	2	1	6 (3)	1

PAGE Donald Richard

Forward

Born: Manchester, 18 January 1964.
Career: Runcorn. March 1989 WIGAN ATHLETIC 62 (12) 14. August 1991 Rotherham United 40 (15) 13. February 1993 on loan Rochdale 3 (1) 1. November 1993 Doncaster Rovers 18 (4) 4. July 1994 Chester City 22 (8) 5. July 1995 Scarborough 26 (11) 5.

Don Page

After making his name in non-League football with Runcorn, pacy striker Don Page joined Wigan Athletic in March 1989 and made his debut in a 2–1 reversal at Gillingham. He kept his place in the side for the remaining 15 games of the season, netting his first goal for the club in a 2–1 win at Swansea City. Hopes were high that this prolific scorer at non-League level would find his shooting boots in 1989–90 but though he scored in both major cup competitions, he failed to find the net in 25 League outings!

He certainly made amends the following season when he ended the campaign as joint top-scorer with Bryan Griffiths with 17 goals including a well-taken hat-trick in a 4–0 Leyland DAF Cup win over Chester City. At the end of the season, Page was allowed to leave Springfield Park and join Rotherham United. He continued to find the net on a regular basis for the Millmoor club, but after two seasons fell out with the Millers' manager Phil Henson and, following a loan spell with Rochdale, joined Doncaster Rovers. After less than a season at Belle Vue, he moved to Chester City where he showed his versatility by playing in all of the forward positions. The much-travelled striker ended his League career with Scarborough, where he found it hard to adapt in a struggling team before being released. Page then returned to Millmoor as a member of Rotherham's coaching staff.

Wigan Athletic Playing Record

	League		FA Cup		FL Cup		Others		Total	
	App	Gls	App	Gls	App	Gls	App	Gls	App	Gls
1988–89	13 (2)	2	0	0	0	0	0	0	13 (2)	2
1989–90	18 (7)	0	1	1	4	1	0	0	23 (7)	2
1990–91	31 (3)	12	4	1	1	1	4 (1)	3	40 (4)	17
TOTAL	62 (12)	14	5	2	5	2	4 (1)	3	76 (13)	21

PALADINO Giuseppe (Joe)

Goalkeeper
Born: Whiston, 29 August 1965.
Career: St Helens Town. December 1990 WIGAN ATHLETIC 7 (0) 0. Altrincham.

Joe Paladino

Goalkeeper Joe Paladino joined the Latics from St Helens Town in December 1990 following a series of impressive displays which had a number of lower division clubs after his signature. On his arrival at Springfield Park, Paladino went straight into the Wigan side for the match at Brentford, following injuries to the club's regular 'keeper Nigel Adkins and Northern Ireland international Phil Hughes. Despite making a number of fine saves, Paladino couldn't prevent the Latics from losing 1–0. He held his place for the next few games before relinquishing his position to the now recovered Hughes. Paladino came back for the last two games of the season and kept a clean sheet in a 3–0 defeat of Bradford City on his last appearance at Springfield Park. In the close season, with both goalkeepers fully recovered, Paladino was allowed to leave and returned to non-League football with Altrincham. Paladino later took up boxing but without much success.

Wigan Athletic Playing Record

	League		FA Cup		FL Cup		Others		Total	
	App	Gls	App	Gls	App	Gls	App	Gls	App	Gls
1990–91	7	0	0	0	0	0	1	0	8	0
TOTAL	7	0	0	0	0	0	1	0	8	0

PARKINSON Joseph Simon

Midfield
Born: Eccles, 11 June 1971.
Career: March 1989 WIGAN ATHLETIC 115 (4) 6. July 1993 Bournemouth 30 (0) 1. March 1994 Everton 88 (2) 3.

Lively central midfielder Joe Parkinson joined the Latics on a YTS scheme and after a series of outstanding displays for the club's reserve side, made his League debut as a substitute for Mark

Joe Parkinson

Hilditch in a 2–1 win over Blackpool in September 1988. In his first full game a few months later, Parkinson scored the only goal of the game as Wigan beat Mansfield Town 1–0 at Field Mill. It was 1989–90 when Parkinson established himself as a first-team regular at Springfield Park and over the next four seasons he only missed games when injured. A member of the Latics side relegated to the Third Division, he left the north-west to play for Bournemouth.

Before his first season at Dean Court was over, Parkinson had signed for Premier League side Everton for £250,000. After winning an FA Cup medal with Everton in 1995, Parkinson's progress was monitored by both the English and Welsh international managers, until his impetus was shattered by chronic knee problems. Sadly, one of the Blues' most underrated performers was later forced to give up the game.

Wigan Athletic Playing Record

	League		FA Cup		FL Cup		Others		Total	
	App	Gls	App	Gls	App	Gls	App	Gls	App	Gls
1988–89	8 (4)	1	0	0	0	0	2	0	10 (4)	1
1989–90	33	2	2	0	3	1	3	0	41	3
1990–91	25	0	4	0	2	0	2	0	33	0
1991–92	36	5	3	0	2	0	1	0	42	5
1992–93	13	0	0	0	4	0	0	0	17	0
TOTAL	115 (4)	8	9	0	11	1	8	0	143 (4)	9

PATTERSON Darren James

Central Defender

Born: Belfast, 15 October 1969.

Career: July 1988 West Bromwich Albion. April 1989 WIGAN ATHLETIC 69 (28) 6. July 1992 Crystal Palace 22 (0) 1. August 1995 Luton Town 52 (4) 0. October 1996 on loan Preston North End 2 (0) 0. July 1998 Dundee United 23 (2) 0. December 2000 York City 4 (2) 0. February 2001 Oxford United 20 (0) 1.

Darren Patterson

Northern Ireland international Darren Patterson began his career with West Bromwich Albion but in April 1989, after being unable to make the grade with the Baggies, he left the Hawthorns to join Wigan Athletic on a free transfer. He had to wait until the fifth game of the 1989–90 season before making his League debut, coming on as a substitute to replace Steve Senior in a 1–0 defeat at Leyton Orient, and though he appeared in 29 games that campaign, more than half were in the role of substitute. It was a similar story the following season but in 1991–92 this versatile player established himself as a first-team regular. His form was so impressive that at the end of the season Crystal Palace paid £225,000 for his services.

He spent two seasons in the Eagles' reserve side before being given his chance in the League side. Shortly afterwards he was sold to Luton Town for £100,000, but his debut for the Hatters was delayed due to a tendon injury. The strong-tackling defender was later hampered by injuries and had a brief loan spell at Preston North End before leaving Kenilworth Road to try his luck north of the border with Scottish Premier League side Dundee United.

He spent two seasons at Tannadice but during much of his time there he was plagued by injuries. He then had a brief spell with York City before joining Oxford United. He spent virtually all the 2001–02 season recovering from an Achilles injury and after making 20 appearances decided to retire.

Wigan Athletic Playing Record

	League		FA Cup		FL Cup		Others		Total	
	App	Gls	App	Gls	App	Gls	App	Gls	App	Gls
1989–90	12 (17)	1	2	0	1 (1)	0	2	0	17 (18)	1
1990–91	18 (10)	4	0 (4)	1	2	0	4	0	24 (14)	5
1991–92	39 (1)	1	3	0	4	3	1	0	47 (1)	4
TOTAL	69 (28)	6	5 (4)	1	7 (1)	3	7	0	88 (33)	10

PATTERSON Ian Daniel

Central Defender

Born: Chatham, 4 April 1973.

Career: March 1992 Sunderland. August 1993 Burnley 0 (1) 0. March 1994 WIGAN ATHLETIC 2 (2) 0. Stalybridge Celtic on loan.

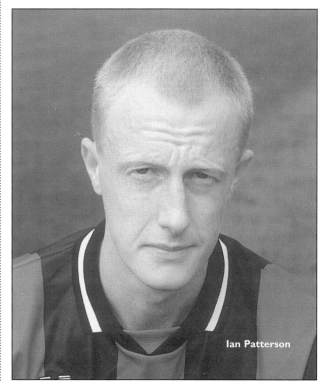
Ian Patterson

Defender Ian Patterson was not offered a professional contract after his apprenticeship at Sunderland and so in August 1993 he joined Burnley. He made his League debut for the Clarets as a substitute for Andy Farrell in a defeat at Bristol Rovers the following month but it was to be his only appearance for the Turf Moor club.

He moved to Wigan Athletic on transfer deadline day in March 1994 and after making his Latics debut as a substitute in a 4–1 defeat at Crewe Alexandra, he appeared in the final few games of the season. But after failing to make a first-team appearance in 1994–95 he had a brief loan spell with Stalybridge Celtic before leaving Springfield Park.

Wigan Athletic Playing Record

	League		FA Cup		FL Cup		Others		Total	
	App	Gls	App	Gls	App	Gls	App	Gls	App	Gls
1993–94	2 (2)	0	0	0	0	0	0	0	2 (2)	0
TOTAL	2 (2)	0	0	0	0	0	0	0	2 (2)	0

PENDER John Patrick

Central Defender
Born: Luton, 19 November 1963.
Career: November 1981 Wolverhampton Wanderers 115 (2) 3. July 1985 Charlton Athletic 41 (0) 0. October 1987 Bristol City 83 (0) 3. September 1990 Burnley 171 (0) 8. August 1995 WIGAN ATHLETIC 67 (3) 1. July 1997 Rochdale 14 (0) 0.

John Pender won Irish youth international honours after joining Wolverhampton Wanderers as an apprentice, becoming professional on his 18th birthday in November 1981. He replaced Joe Gallagher for his First Division debut in March 1982 and became a regular in the Wolves defence that gained promotion back to Division One in 1983 but then suffered two successive relegations in 1984 and 1985. In the summer of 1985 Pender joined Charlton Athletic and was a regular choice in the Addicks side which won promotion from the Second Division in 1985–86 as runners-up to Norwich City. He was sold to Bristol City for £50,000 in October 1987 and although a Third Division club, the Robins reached the League Cup semi-finals. After he lost his place

John Pender

in the City side, Pender joined Burnley for £70,000. Having been appointed the Clarets' captain he led the club to the Fourth Division Championship in 1991–92. After lifting the Endsleigh Trophy at Wembley as Burnley beat Stockport County in the 1994 play-off final, Pender was no longer an automatic choice and in August 1995 he moved to Wigan Athletic for £40,000.

He made his Latics debut in a 2–1 home win over Scunthorpe United and before long was appointed captain. Forming an imposing central defensive partnership with Colin Greenall, he helped Wigan win the Third Division Championship, despite suffering a severe knee injury in the match against Swansea City in January 1997. Pender's only goal for the Latics came in the 3–0 win over Torquay United in February 1996. On leaving Springfield Park, he joined Rochdale, where a recurrence of his knee injury forced him to retire from the first-class game.

Wigan Athletic Playing Record

	League		FA Cup		FL Cup		Others		Total	
	App	Gls	App	Gls	App	Gls	App	Gls	App	Gls
1995–96	40 (1)	1	4	0	0	0	3	0	47 (1)	1
1996–97	27 (2)	0	1	0	2	0	1	0	31 (2)	0
TOTAL	67 (3)	1	5	0	2	0	4	0	78 (3)	1

PENDLEBURY Ian David

Defender
Born: Bolton, 3 September 1983.
Career: July 2001 WIGAN ATHLETIC 4 (0) 0. Leigh RMI.

A promising left-sided defender, Bolton-born Ian Pendlebury played his first game for the Latics against Wrexham at the JJB Stadium in October 2001, a match the visitors won 3–2. Later during the season, he showed his versatility by appearing on the left-side of midfield and was voted the club's 'Young Player of the Year'. Not surprisingly he was also offered a 12-month professional contract during the close season. However, he was unable to get a look in during the 2002–03 season and in March 2003 was allowed to leave the Latics, signing for local Nationwide Conference side, Leigh RMI.

Wigan Athletic Playing Record

	League		FA Cup		FL Cup		Others		Total	
	App	Gls	App	Gls	App	Gls	App	Gls	App	Gls
2001–02	4	0	0	0	0	0	0	0	4	0
TOTAL	4	0	0	0	0	0	0	0	4	0

PENNOCK Anthony

Goalkeeper
Born: Swansea, 10 April 1971.
Career: Clydach United. August 1990 Stockport County. December 1990 on loan WIGAN ATHLETIC 2 (0) 0. June 1991 WIGAN ATHLETIC 8 (0) 0. July 1994 Hereford United 13 (2) 0. Yeovil Town. June 2001 Rushden and Diamonds 3 (2) 0. Farnborough Town.

Goalkeeper Tony Pennock began his career playing Welsh League football for Clydach United, where his consistent displays between the sticks alerted a number of League clubs. In August 1990 he joined Stockport County but was unable to force his way into the Hatters' side. In December of that year following injuries to Nigel Adkins and Phil Hughes, he joined Wigan Athletic on loan. He kept a clean sheet on his debut as the Latics beat Grimsby Town 2–0 with goals from Bryan Griffiths and David Fairclough.

Tony Pennock

Jeff Peron

Though he later returned to Edgeley Park, he joined the Latics on a permanent basis at the end of the season.

Signed as cover for Adkins, the former Tranmere 'keeper's performances in 1991–92 meant that Pennock spent his first full season at Springfield Park in the club's reserve side. When he did get his chance the following season, he made a number of fine saves in a Latics side that was struggling to avoid relegation from the 'new' Second Division. Following the arrival of Simon Farnworth, Pennock again found himself as the club's second-choice 'keeper and in the summer of 1994 he joined Hereford United. Although a competent 'keeper with good all-round ability, he lost his place to Chris McKenzie and after just one season at Edgar Street, he drifted into non-League football with a number of clubs, latterly Yeovil Town before arriving at Rushden and Diamonds in the summer of 2001. Unable to dislodge Billy Turley from the regular custodian's spot, he had a loan spell with Farnborough Town before the move became a permanent one.

Wigan Athletic Playing Record

	League		FA Cup		FL Cup		Others		Total	
	App	Gls	App	Gls	App	Gls	App	Gls	App	Gls
1990–91	2	0	2	0	0	0	0	0	4	0
1991–92	0	0	0	0	0	0	0	0	0	0
1992–93	8	0	1	0	0	0	2	0	11	0
TOTAL	10	0	3	0	0	0	2	0	15	0

PERON Jean (Jeff) Francois

Midfield

Born: St Omer, France, 11 October 1965.

Career: Lens. RC Strasbourg. Caen. August 1997 Walsall 38 (0) 1. September 1998 Portsmouth 46 (2) 3. November 1999 WIGAN ATHLETIC 19 (4) 0.

After joining Walsall from French club Caen during the 1997–98 season, this experienced midfielder, who had earlier played for Lens and RC Strasbourg, gave some outstanding displays in the Saddlers' midfield and ended the campaign being voted 'Player of the Season'. His first goal in League football was a stunning volley to win the game against the Latics and though he sought a transfer in the closing months, he continued to give of his best.

On leaving the Bescot Stadium, Peron joined Portsmouth for £125,000 where his intelligent passing and pace perked up Pompey's season. A player who has great vision, he suffered damage to his calf muscle in October 1999 and this put him out of action for over a month. Once fully fit, he left Fratton Park, joining Wigan Athletic on a free transfer. He made his debut as a substitute for Pat McGibbon in a 2–1 win at Scunthorpe United, going on to appear in almost all the remaining League games. Though he failed to get on the scoresheet, he never let the side down when called into action. The Frenchman was surprisingly released at the end of the season and returned to his homeland.

Wigan Athletic Playing Record

	League		FA Cup		FL Cup		Others		Total	
	App	Gls	App	Gls	App	Gls	App	Gls	App	Gls
1999–2000	19 (4)	0	1	0	0	0	1 (1)	0	21 (5)	0
TOTAL	19 (4)	0	1	0	0	0	1 (1)	0	21 (5)	0

PILLING Andrew James

Midfield

Born: Wigan 30 June 1969.

Career: May 1985 Preston North End 1 (0) 0. July 1987 WIGAN ATHLETIC 131 (25) 20. Leigh RMI.

Though he was born in Wigan, midfielder Andy Pilling began his career with Preston North End, where he joined as a trainee in 1985. However, in a little over two years on the Deepdale staff, his

Andy Pilling

The hard-tackling midfielder played for Manchester City juniors before joining Port Vale's YTS scheme in August 1985. Initially used as a reserve, he was loaned to Hutt Valley United of New Zealand before returning to become a regular in the Vale side. He helped the Valiants win promotion to the Second Division via the play-offs in 1988–89 and was a member of the side which won the Autoglass Trophy in 1993 and gained promotion from the 'new' Second Division in 1993–94. He later captained the side, leading them out at Wembley in the Anglo-Italian Cup Final. He went on to appear in 432 first-team games for Port Vale before joining Wigan Athletic on a free transfer in the summer of 1998.

Andy Porter

only League appearance for the Lilywhites came in a 4–0 defeat at Aldershot on the final day of the 1985–86 season when North End finished one off the bottom of the Fourth Division.

After another season of Central League football, Andy Pilling joined Wigan Athletic in the summer of 1987. He had to wait until November 1987 before making his first appearance in Latics' colours, coming on as a substitute for Bryan Griffiths and scoring Wigan's goal in a 2–1 defeat at Brentford. He kept his place in the Latics side, appearing in the next 19 games before losing his place to Chris Thompson. Pilling, who was an important member of the Wigan side for the next five seasons, scored some vital goals and showed his versatility by appearing in eight different outfield positions. Pilling left Springfield Park in the summer of 1993, following the club's relegation to the Third Division, going on to play non-League football for Leigh RMI.

Wigan Athletic Playing Record

	League		FA Cup		FL Cup		Others		Total	
	App	Gls	App	Gls	App	Gls	App	Gls	App	Gls
1987–88	16 (4)	3	1	0	0	0	1	0	18 (4)	3
1988–89	38 (1)	2	1	0	1	0	3	0	43 (1)	2
1989–90	21 (5)	6	1 (1)	0	1 (1)	0	4	0	27 (7)	6
1990–91	8 (5)	3	1	0	0	0	1 (1)	0	10 (6)	3
1991–92	21 (6)	2	1 (1)	1	0 (1)	0	0 (1)	0	22 (9)	3
1992–93	27 (4)	4	3	0	1	0	5 (1)	1	36 (5)	5
TOTAL	131 (25)	20	8 (2)	1	3 (2)	0	14 (3)	1	156 (32)	22

PORTER Andrew Michael

Midfield

Born: Holmes Chapel, 17 September 1968.

Career: June 1987 Port Vale 313 (44) 22. July 1998 WIGAN ATHLETIC 8 (13) 1. October 1999 on loan Mansfield Town 5 (0) 0. February 2000 on loan Chester City 16 (0) 0.

Porter made his Latics debut as a substitute for Ian Kilford in a 3–0 home win over Blackpool and, while not an automatic choice, he gave everything when called into action. He came back strongly to become part of the Latics side which reached the play-offs and won an Autowindscreen Shield medal despite not being called upon at Wembley. Early the following season, he found his first-team opportunities increasingly limited and went on loan to Mansfield Town. Known as the 'footballing farmer', as he as an interest in the family farming business, the vastly experienced midfielder joined Chester City on loan but was unable to halt City's slide towards relegation.

Wigan Athletic Playing Record

	League		FA Cup		FL Cup		Others		Total	
	App	Gls	App	Gls	App	Gls	App	Gls	App	Gls
1998–99	6 (10)	1	1	0	0 (2)	0	3 (3)	0	10 (15)	1
1999–2000	2 (3)	0	0	0	0 (1)	0	0	0	2 (4)	0
TOTAL	8 (13)	1	1	0	0 (3)	0	3 (3)	0	12 (19)	1

POWELL Gary

Forward

Born: Hoylake, 2 April 1969.

Career: July 1987 Everton. September 1990 on loan Lincoln City 11 (0) 0. November 1990 on loan Scunthorpe United 3 (1) 1. March 1991 on loan WIGAN ATHLETIC 13 (1) 4. August 1991 WIGAN ATHLETIC 44 (26) 13. August 1993 Bury 4 (1) 0.

Gary Powell

Unable to make the grade with Everton, Gary Powell had loan spells with Lincoln City, Scunthorpe United and Wigan Athletic before joining the Latics on a permanent basis in the summer of 1991. Powell made his League debut for Wigan as a substitute for Don Page in a 1–0 home defeat by Tranmere Rovers, but impressed enough to retain his place for the Latics' next game, the local derby against Bolton Wanderers. Though not a prolific scorer, Powell, who played in all five forward positions during his time at Springfield Park, scored some vital goals including the winner at Leyton Orient – Dave Philpott's first game in charge during the club's turbulent 1992–93 season. Surprisingly, at the end of that campaign in which he had been one of the Latics' most consistent players, he was allowed to leave and joined Third Division Bury where he saw out his first-class career.

Wigan Athletic Playing Record

	League		FA Cup		FL Cup		Others		Total	
	App	Gls	App	Gls	App	Gls	App	Gls	App	Gls
1990–91	13 (1)	4	0	0	0	0	0	0	13 (1)	4
1991–92	22 (12)	7	2 (1)	1	3	0	1	0	28 (13)	8
1992–93	22 (14)	6	3	1	3 (1)	0	4 (1)	2	32 (16)	9
TOTAL	57 (27)	17	5 (1)	2	6 (1)	0	5 (1)	2	73 (30)	21

PURDIE Ian

Winger

Born: Bellshill, 7 March 1953.

Career: Aberdeen. Dundee. July 1977 Motherwell 11 (5) 3. July 1978 WIGAN ATHLETIC 54 (1) 12. November 1979 Portsmouth 4 (1) 1. Bangor City.

Scottish Under-23 international winger Ian Purdie began his career with Aberdeen, but after six years at Pittodrie, during which time he helped them to runners-up in the Scottish First Division on two occasions, he left to join Dundee. After two years at Dens Park, Purdie moved to Motherwell but this slight and slender player, with a lethal left foot, struggled to hold down a regular first-team place and ventured south of the border to play for Wigan Athletic.

After making his debut in the club's first-ever Football League game, a goalless draw at Hereford United, Purdie went on to have a good first season with the Latics, ending the campaign as second top scorer to Peter Houghton with 11 goals. Surprisingly, after only a handful of games the following season, Purdie was allowed to leave Springfield Park and join Portsmouth. Sadly, a series of niggling injuries restricted his first-team appearances at Fratton Park and though he scored his first goal for the club in a 2–0 win at Northampton Town on the final day of the 1979–80 campaign, he was released in the close season and went to play non-League football for Bangor City.

Wigan Athletic Playing Record

	League		FA Cup		FL Cup		Others		Total	
	App	Gls	App	Gls	App	Gls	App	Gls	App	Gls
1978–79	46	11	2	0	3	0	0	0	51	11
1979–80	8 (1)	1	0	0	2	0	0	0	10 (1)	1
TOTAL	54 (1)	12	2	0	5	0	0	0	61 (1)	12

QUINN Anthony Michael

Forward

Born: Liverpool, 24 July 1959.

Career: Everton. Formby. Liverpool. January 1979 WIGAN ATHLETIC 36 (7) 14. Witton Albion.

Having joined Everton as an associate schoolboy, Quinn played in the club's junior sides for almost three seasons before leaving to play a handful of games for Formby in the Cheshire County League. He later joined Liverpool, helping the 'A' team to win the Lancashire League Division One Championship. He also played for the Liverpool County FA Youth XI and helped his side win the English FA County Youth Cup competition.

Released by the Anfield side, he joined Wigan Athletic and was soon rattling in the goals for the Latics' second team. In 1978–79 he was not only the reserves' leading scorer with 35 goals, but also the leading scorer in the Lancashire League Division One. After turning full-time professional and patiently waiting in the wings, Quinn made his League debut as a substitute against Lincoln City in October 1979.

Following that game, he was to achieve the distinction of scoring eight goals in his next 12 appearances, including one at Walsall which highlighted his ability to finish off moves in almost clinical fashion. He continued to find the net for the Latics on a regular basis over the next season but on losing his place to his namesake Mick Quinn, he left to play non-League football for Witton Albion.

Wigan Athletic Playing Record

	League		FA Cup		FL Cup		Others		Total	
	App	Gls	App	Gls	App	Gls	App	Gls	App	Gls
1979–80	17 (2)	9	4 (1)	0	0	0	0	0	21 (3)	9
1980–81	19 (5)	5	0	0	1	0	0	0	20 (5)	5
TOTAL	36 (7)	14	4 (1)	0	1	0	0	0	41 (8)	14

QUINN Michael

Forward

Born: Liverpool, 2 May 1962.

Career: Derby County apprentice. September 1979 WIGAN ATHLETIC 56 (13) 19. July 1982 Stockport County 62 (1) 39. January 1984 Oldham Athletic 78 (2) 34. March 1986 Portsmouth 115 (6) 54. July 1989 Newcastle United 106 (4) 57. November 1992 Coventry City 57 (7) 25. November 1994 on loan Plymouth Argyle 3 (0) 0. March 1995 on loan Watford 4 (1) 0.

An old-fashioned striker, he first came into football with Derby County whom he joined as an apprentice in the summer of 1978. After being freed by the Rams, he joined Wigan Athletic and made a goalscoring debut in a 3–1 win over Halifax Town in April 1980. Quinn became a regular selection in his second season at Springfield Park, finishing top scorer with 14 League goals including a hat-trick in a 3–0 defeat of Doncaster Rovers. However, after a disappointing campaign in 1981–82, scoring only four goals in 29 appearances – despite which, the Latics won promotion to Division Three – he was released and joined Stockport County. The stocky striker's career took off at Edgeley Park when he became the first County player for 15 years to top 20 goals in a season, finishing with a final tally of 24 League goals. He maintained his prolific scoring rate with 15 League goals in 24 games the following season before he was snapped up by Second Division Oldham Athletic.

Mick Quinn

At Boundary Park he was leading scorer in 1984–85 with 18 League goals and netted another 11 in 1985–86 before his transfer to Portsmouth for a fee Oldham could not afford to refuse. In 1986–87, Pompey won promotion to the top flight although five defeats in the last nine games cost them the Second Division Championship. Quinn led the way with 22 goals but during his three years at Fratton Park he was rarely out of the news, good and bad, scoring regularly and spending a short period in prison! At the end of his contract he opted to join Newcastle United, the fee being decided by the transfer tribunal. He made a sensational start for his new club, scoring four goals on his debut against Leeds United, and quickly became an idol of the St James' Park faithful.

By the end of the season, he had scored 34 League and Cup goals and though he could not maintain that strike-rate, by the time he left for Coventry City in December 1992, he had scored 71 goals in 131 games for the Magpies.

His start at Highfield Road was even more sensational for after scoring twice on his Sky Blues' debut, he proceeded to amass 10 goals in his first six starts and finished the season as top-scorer with 17 goals. He later had loan spells with Plymouth Argyle and Watford before being released by Coventry in the summer of 1995.

Wigan Athletic Playing Record

	League		FA Cup		FL Cup		Others		Total	
	App	Gls	App	Gls	App	Gls	App	Gls	App	Gls
1979–80	4	1	0	0	0	0	0	0	4	1
1980–81	32 (4)	14	2	0	1	0	0	0	35 (4)	14
1981–82	20 (9)	4	2	1	4	1	0	0	26 (9)	6
TOTAL	56 (13)	19	4	1	5	1	0	0	65 (13)	21

RAMAGE Craig Darren

Midfield/Forward

Born: Derby, 30 March 1970.

Career: July 1988 Derby County 33 (9) 4. February 1989 on loan WIGAN ATHLETIC 10 (0) 2. February 1994 Watford 99 (5) 27. February 1997 on loan Peterborough United 7 (0) 0. June 1997 Bradford City 24 (11) 1. August 1999 Notts County 50 (5) 7.

Craig Ramage

England Under-21 international Craig Ramage began his Football League career with his home-town club Derby County but in February 1989 he joined Wigan Athletic on loan. After making his debut in a 1–1 draw at Northampton Town, Ramage scored on his home debut as the Latics beat Chester City 3–0 and then, on his next appearance at Springfield Park, scored the only goal of the game against Cardiff City. Returning to the Baseball Ground, he spent another four seasons with the Rams before joining Watford for a fee of £90,000 in February 1994.

Playing just behind the front two, he responded by topping the Vicarage Road club's scoring charts in his first two seasons with the Hornets. Then a knee injury which led to a cartilage operation cost him his first-team place and he went on loan to Peterborough United. Eventually released by Watford in the summer of 1997 he joined Bradford City on a two-year contract. After a good start, the 1998–99 season was an horrific one for Craig Ramage as he suffered a series of cartilage injuries and did not start a first-team game. Released in the summer he joined Notts County on a free transfer where his skill and experience helped the Magpies push for promotion. Ramage left Meadow Lane in the summer of 2001 having been forced to retire.

Wigan Athletic Playing Record

	League		FA Cup		FL Cup		Others		Total	
	App	Gls	App	Gls	App	Gls	App	Gls	App	Gls
1988–89	10	2	0	0	0	0	0	0	10	2
TOTAL	10	2	0	0	0	0	0	0	10	2

REDFEARN Neil David

Midfield

Born: Dewsbury 20 June 1965.

Career: Nottingham Forest Juniors. June 1982 Bolton Wanderers 35 (0) 1. March 1984 Lincoln City 96 (4) 13. August 1986 Doncaster Rovers 46 (0) 14. July 1987 Crystal Palace 57 (0) 10. November 1988 Watford 22 (2) 3. January 1990 Oldham Athletic 56 (60) 16. September 1991 Barnsley 289 (3) 71. July 1998 Charlton Athletic 29 (1) 3. August 1999 Bradford City 14 (3) 1. March 2000 WIGAN ATHLETIC 18 (4) 7. March 2001 Halifax Town 39 (3) 6. August 2002 Boston United 27 (4) 6.

Neil Redfearn

Much-travelled midfielder Neil Redfearn began his League career with Bolton Wanderers whom he joined from Nottingham Forest juniors in the summer of 1982. Unable to hold down a regular place in the Wanderers side, he joined Lincoln City for £8,250. After two seasons at Sincil Bank, Redfearn moved to Doncaster Rovers before a £100,000 fee took him to Crystal Palace in July 1987. This strong, tenacious midfielder then moved to Watford where he created a bit of FA Cup history by scoring with his team's first kick of the match, which he did direct from a free-kick against Newcastle United. There followed a spell with Oldham Athletic whom he helped win the Second Division Championship in 1990–91 before he joined Barnsley.

A permanent fixture in the Oakwell club's side for seven seasons, he appeared in 156 consecutive League games from his debut before injury ruled him out of the side. During his time with the Tykes, he scored some very important goals, mostly from long-range drives, but his best season was undoubtedly 1996–97. Redfearn not only captained Barnsley to promotion to the Premiership but, nicknamed 'Mr Perpetual Motion' he also top-scored with 19 goals as well as missing a couple of penalties! During his first-ever season in the top flight, he led by example, never hiding from the action even when things were not going right for him or the team. Surprisingly, in the close season of 1998 he was allowed to join newly-promoted Charlton Athletic in a deal thought to be worth £1 million.

Great things were expected of him at the Valley but despite being a regular for most of 1998–99, he managed only three goals. Allowed to join Bradford City, he started the 1999–2000 season off in great style, but after losing his place following the Bantams' decision to alter their formation, he joined Wigan Athletic, his 10th League club, for £112,500 in March 2000. He made his Latics debut in a 1–0 home win over Bury before taking over as the club's penalty-taker. He scored six goals in 12 games including both goals in a 2–0 win over Notts County, adding a late spot-kick to his opening goal, which came directly from a free-kick. At the start of

the 2000–01 season, Redfearn was placed on the transfer list by Bruce Rioch and eventually moved to Halifax Town as player-coach shortly before the transfer deadline.

His first term at the Shay was frustrating as he took on the role of player-manager towards the end of a campaign that saw the Yorkshire club drop into the Conference for the 2002–03 season. Redfearn then moved to Boston United as assistant-manager and though he took time to settle, he was a key figure in the second half of the season when the Pilgrims began to move up the table.

Wigan Athletic Playing Record

	League		FA Cup		FL Cup		Others		Total	
	App	Gls	App	Gls	App	Gls	App	Gls	App	Gls
1999–2000	12	6	0	0	0	0	3	0	15	6
2000–01	6 (4)	1	1	0	0	0	2	0	9 (4)	1
TOTAL	18 (4)	7	1	0	0	0	5	0	24 (4)	7

REDFERN David

Goalkeeper

Born: Sheffield, 8 November 1962.

Career: June 1981 Sheffield Wednesday. March 1985 Rochdale 87 (0) 0. October 1987 on loan WIGAN ATHLETIC 3 (0) 0. Gainsborough Trinity. July 1989 Stockport County 48 (0) 0.

Goalkeeper Dave Redfern began his career with his home-town club Sheffield Wednesday but on being unable to break into the Owls' first team, he left Hillsborough to play for Rochdale. Throughout his time at Spotland, the 'Dale' were constantly languishing near the foot of the Fourth Division, and after losing his place in the Rochdale side, he joined Wigan Athletic on loan. He made his Latics debut for the injured Roy Tunks for the home match against York City and performed admirably in a 1–1 draw. However, the following week, the Latics were on the receiving end of a 4–1 beating by Sunderland and Redfern was at fault for at least two of the goals. His third appearance for the Latics saw him keep a clean sheet in a 3–0 defeat of Rotherham United but with the club having bought Phil Hughes from Bury, Redfern's chances of joining Wigan on a permanent basis disappeared.

After a spell playing non-League football for Gainsborough Trinity, he returned to League action with Stockport County, helping the Hatters win promotion to the Third Division in 1990–91 and reach the play-offs in the following two seasons. Redfern left the first-class scene after losing his place to the ever-improving Neil Edwards.

Wigan Athletic Playing Record

| | League | | FA Cup | | FL Cup | | Others | | Total | |
	App	Gls	App	Gls	App	Gls	App	Gls	App	Gls
1987–88	3	0	0	0	1	0	0	0	4	0
TOTAL	3	0	0	0	1	0	0	0	4	0

REDSHAW Raymond

Forward
Born: Salford, 23 December 1958.
Career: Horwich RMI. July 1984 WIGAN ATHLETIC 2 (2) 0. Northwich Victoria.

A prolific goalscorer with Horwich RMI, Ray Redshaw joined the Latics during the early part of the 1984–85 season and made his debut as a substitute for Paul Beesley in the match against York City. At the time of his introduction, the Latics were trailing 2–1 and though he came close to an equalising goal on a couple of occasions, the Minstermen held on for victory. After another appearance in the No.12 shirt, he made his first start in League football against Newport County in a game which ended all-square at 1–1. Wigan's goal came courtesy of the Welsh club's left-back who, on being put under pressure by Redshaw, put through his own goal. Redshaw made one more appearance, but having failed to get on the scoresheet, returned to non-League football with Northwich Victoria.

Wigan Athletic Playing Record

| | League | | FA Cup | | FL Cup | | Others | | Total | |
	App	Gls	App	Gls	App	Gls	App	Gls	App	Gls
1984–85	2 (2)	0	0	0	0 (1)	0	0	0	2 (3)	0
TOTAL	2 (2)	0	0	0	0 (1)	0	0	0	2 (3)	0

RENNIE Paul Andrew

Central Defender
Born: Nantwich, 26 October 1971.
Career: May 1989 Crewe Alexandra 1 (1) 0. May 1990 Stoke City 4 (0) 0. August 1993 WIGAN ATHLETIC 36 (4) 3.

Paul Rennie made his Football League debut for Crewe Alexandra against Wigan Athletic, coming on as a late substitute for Paul Fishenden in a 1–0 win for the Latics in November 1989. He kept his place in the side for the game against Mansfield Town six days later, a match the Railwaymen won 2–1. However, that was his last first-team appearance as regular centre-half Paul Dyson returned to action. At the end of the season, Rennie left to play for Stoke City but in three seasons at the Victoria Ground, he made only a handful of first-team appearances.

In August 1993 he jumped at the chance of joining Wigan Athletic and made his debut at right-back in a 2–0 home defeat by Scunthorpe United on the opening day of the 1993–94 season. Rennie missed very few games until the match against Northampton the following March when a knee injury resulted in

Paul Rennie

him sitting out the rest of the campaign. Able to play at full-back or in the centre of defence, he scored a spectacular goal against his former club Crewe in the 1994–95 League Cup competition but at the end of the season he was given a free transfer.

Wigan Athletic Playing Record

| | League | | FA Cup | | FL Cup | | Others | | Total | |
	App	Gls	App	Gls	App	Gls	App	Gls	App	Gls
1993–94	25 (1)	2	3	0	2	0	1	0	31 (1)	2
1994–95	11 (3)	1	1	0	3 (1)	1	2	0	17 (4)	2
TOTAL	36 (4)	3	4	0	5 (1)	1	3	0	48 (5)	4

RIMMER Neill

Midfield
Born: Liverpool, 13 November 1967.
Career: May 1984 Everton 0 (1) 0. August 1985 Ipswich Town 19 (3) 3. July 1988 WIGAN ATHLETIC 185 (6) 10.

A former England schoolboy and youth international, Rimmer began his Football League career with Everton, making his debut as a substitute for Paul Wilkinson in a 2–0 defeat at Luton Town on the final day of the 1984–85 season. However, it was his only appearance in the Goodison club's first team and in the close season he joined Ipswich Town. He spent two seasons with the Tractor Boys, though with stiff competition for places, he never really established himself with the East Anglian club.

In the summer of 1988 he joined Wigan Athletic on a free transfer and made his debut for the club on the opening day of the 1988–89 season as the Latics won 2–0 at Bristol Rovers. Rimmer was an important member of the Wigan side for the next eight seasons. A great midfield competitor, strong in the tackle and a good ball-winner, he unfortunately suffered more than his fair

Neil Rimmer

share of injuries in his time at Springfield Park. A willing worker who was also the club captain, he was, in his last campaign with the club, the Latics' longest-serving player.

Wigan Athletic Playing Record

	League		FA Cup		FL Cup		Others		Total	
	App	Gls	App	Gls	App	Gls	App	Gls	App	Gls
1988–89	24 (1)	3	1	0	2	0	0	0	27 (1)	3
1989–90	38	1	2	0	4	0	3	1	47	2
1990–91	34	2	4	2	2	0	5	0	45	4
1991–92	9	0	0	0	3	1	0	0	12	1
1992–93	0 (1)	0	0	0	0	0	0	0	0 (1)	0
1993–94	19 (1)	0	1	0	0	0	2	0	22 (1)	0
1994–95	33	4	1	0	3	0	3	1	40	5
1995–96	28 (3)	0	0	0	1	0	0	0	29 (3)	0
TOTAL	185 (6)	10	9	2	15	1	13	2	222 (6)	15

ROBERTS Jason Andre Davis

Striker
Born: Park Royal, 25 January 1978.
Career: Hayes. September 1997 Wolverhampton Wanderers. December 1997 on loan Torquay United 13 (1) 6. March 1998 on loan Bristol City 1 (2) 1. August 1998 Bristol Rovers 73 (5) 38. July 2000 West Bromwich Albion 75 (14) 24. September 2003 on loan Portsmouth. January 2004 WIGAN ATHLETIC 14 (0) 8.

The nephew of former West Bromwich Albion and England striker Cyrille Regis, Jason Roberts was plucked from non-League Hayes by Wolves during the early part of the 1997–98 season. He was unable to make his mark at Molineux and so to further his experience he was loaned out to Torquay United. He certainly made his mark with the Third Division side, scoring six times in 14 matches before having another loan spell, this time with Bristol City. At Ashton Gate he looked an ideal replacement for Shaun Goater, but after scoring the winner at Oldham, chose to play for Grenada in an international tournament, where he demonstrated his talents as the country's leading goalscorer.

A powerful, well-built striker, he joined Bristol Rovers for a fee of £250,000 in the summer of 1998. He scored a remarkable hat-trick against Welling in the first round of the FA Cup and his confidence grew. Following his 23rd goal in the penultimate match of the campaign against Manchester City, which secured the club's status in the Second Division, he missed the final game of the season to win another cap for Grenada. Voted the club's 'Young Player of the Year', his contribution to the Bristol Rovers team in 1999–2000 was even more remarkable as he netted 25 goals including the 'goal of the season' at Cambridge, when he went past five defenders before shooting home just inside the area. During the close season he was signed by West Bromwich Albion for a club record fee of £2 million. Establishing a fine understanding with Lee Hughes, his direct approach and aggressive style brought him more than his fair share of goals but in 2001–02 he fractured his foot on two separate occasions, the latter bringing his season to a premature close. With Albion now in the Premiership, Roberts took plenty of buffeting from the top flight's defenders. Apart from two spells of suspension, injuries again disrupted his appearances and he found goalscoring difficult as the Baggies returned to the First Division after just one season of Premiership football.

At the beginning of 2003-04, he went on loan to Portsmouth after changing his mind on a transfer to Wigan but eventually joined the Latics in January 2004 for a club record fee of £1.4 million. Roberts scored after just 34 seconds of his Wigan debut in a 4–2 win at Preston and later became the first Latics player to score an international goal when playing for Grenada. Having played with Nathan Ellington at Bristol Rovers, the two strikers again formed a deadly partnership with Roberts scoring eight goals in 14 League outings. Sadly he blotted his copybook by being sent off twice in matches against Stoke and Crystal Palace and this resulted in him missing Wigan's last two games of the season!

Wigan Athletic Playing Record

	League		FA Cup		FL Cup		Others		Total	
	App	Gls	App	Gls	App	Gls	App	Gls	App	Gls
2003–04	14	8	0	0	0	0	0	0	14	8
TOTAL	14	8	0	0	0	0	0	0	14	8

ROBERTS Neil Wyn

Forward
Born: Wrexham, 7 April 1978.
Career: July 1996 Wrexham 58 (17) 17. February 2000 WIGAN ATHLETIC 64 (61) 19. January 2002 on loan Hull City 3 (3) 0.

A product of the much-respected Wrexham youth system, Neil Roberts set the Racecourse Ground alight with five goals in his first five games after coming into the Robins side in September 1997.

Jason Roberts

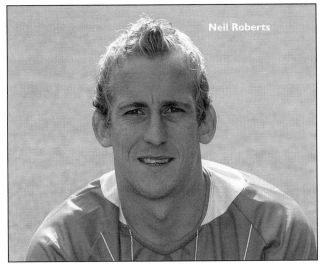
Neil Roberts

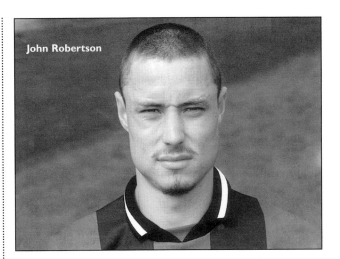
John Robertson

While he was never as prolific after that, he continued to show immense promise for one so young. Though he found his second season of League football much harder, he appeared in two representative games against Italy at Under-21 level and Northern Ireland in a 'B' international. He also suffered an unusual injury – the problem started with a dead leg which turned into a blood clot that calcified, the only cure for this condition being complete rest.

In October 1999, Roberts made his full international debut for Wales when he came on as a substitute for Nathan Blake in the match against Switzerland. Impressing with his high work rate and willingness to probe hard for openings, he moved to Wigan Athletic for £450,000 in February 2000, making his Latics debut in a goalless draw at Burnley. He took time to settle into his new surroundings but his ability to use his body to hold the ball up was soon apparent. After scoring his first goal for the club in a 2–2 draw at Bournemouth, he was forced to miss the play-offs following an operation on his ankle. Though half of his first-team appearances in 2000–01 were made as a substitute, Roberts continued to impress, netting twice in a 3–1 home win over Oldham Athletic. During 2001–02, he drifted in and out of the Wigan side and didn't seem to figure in Paul Jewell's plans. However, he did net twice in a rare outing at Cambridge United as the Latics drew 2–2. Unable to hold down a regular place, he joined Hull City on loan but failed to register a goal in his six appearances for the Boothferry Park club. He returned to the JJB Stadium and ended the season as the reserves' leading scorer, as well as coming off the bench to score twice in the final match of the campaign at Colchester.

The 2002–03 season was Roberts' best season to date. He continued to impress with his high work rate, taking advantage of Andy Liddell's injury to appear regularly in the Latics' forward line. His displays not only brought the best out of Nathan Ellington, but also earned him a recall to the full Welsh squad and a substitute appearance in Azerbaijan.

The hardworking striker signed an extended two-year deal prior to the start of the 2003–04 season but found it difficult to hold down a regular first-team place. Scoring the last goal of the season in the 1–1 home draw against West Ham, it is possible he could leave the JJB in search of first-team football elsewhere.

Wigan Athletic Playing Record

	League		FA Cup		FL Cup		Others		Total	
	App	Gls	App	Gls	App	Gls	App	Gls	App	Gls
1999–2000	8 (1)	1	0	0	0	0	0	0	8 (1)	1
2000–01	17 (17)	6	2	1	0 (1)	1	1 (1)	0	20 (19)	8
2001–02	5 (12)	4	0	0	0	0	1	0	6 (12)	4
2002–03	25 (12)	6	3	0	4 (1)	1	1	0	33 (13)	7
2003–04	9 (19)	2	1	0	2 (1)	0	0	0	12 (20)	2
TOTAL	64 (61)	19	6	1	6 (3)	2	3 (1)	0	79 (65)	22

ROBERTSON John Nicholas

Central Defender
Born: Liverpool, 8 January 1974.
Career: July 1992 WIGAN ATHLETIC 108 (4) 4. December 1995 Lincoln City 38 (2) 1. Northwich Victoria.

Tough-tackling central defender John Robertson joined the Latics as a trainee and after working his way up through the ranks, made his League debut in a 2–1 defeat at Stoke City in August 1992. Dangerous at set pieces, he scored his first goal for the club at Bradford City towards the end of the season but couldn't prevent the Latics from suffering another defeat. Robertson, who was very good in the air, was voted by his teammates as the club's 'Player of the Year' in 1994–95 but early the following season, after the Latics had signed Colin Greenall and John Pender, he was allowed to leave and joined Lincoln City for £15,000.

After an impressive first few games for the Imps, he was kept out of the Lincoln side for most of the club's promotion-winning 1996–97 season by Grant Brown. A wholehearted player, Robertson's never-say-die attitude was very rarely required and in the summer of 1998 after two-and-a-half seasons at Sincil Bank, he was released. He then moved into non-League football with Northwich Victoria.

Wigan Athletic Playing Record

	League		FA Cup		FL Cup		Others		Total	
	App	Gls	App	Gls	App	Gls	App	Gls	App	Gls
1992–93	21 (3)	1	3	0	4	0	3 (1)	0	31 (4)	1
1993–94	34	1	1 (1)	0	2	0	2	0	39 (1)	1
1994–95	39 (1)	1	2	0	4	0	3	0	48 (1)	1
1995–96	14	1	2	0	2	0	0	0	18 1	
TOTAL	108 (4)	4	8 (1)	0	12	0	8 (1)	0	136 (6)	4

RODWELL Anthony

Forward
Born: Southport, 26 August 1962.
Career: Colne Dynamoes. August 1990 Blackpool 137 (5) 17. December 1994 Scarborough 6 (2) 1. January 1995 on loan WIGAN ATHLETIC 5 (0) 1.

Tony Rodwell played his early football for non-League Colne Dynamoes before joining Blackpool on a free transfer in the summer of 1990. He made his debut as a substitute in a 2–0 defeat at Scunthorpe United on the opening day of the 1990–91 season. After that he missed just one game, helping the Seasiders to finish fifth in the Fourth Division and so qualify for that season's play-offs. He scored Blackpool's goal in a 1–1 draw at Scunthorpe in the first leg and was outstanding in the second leg at Bloomfield Road

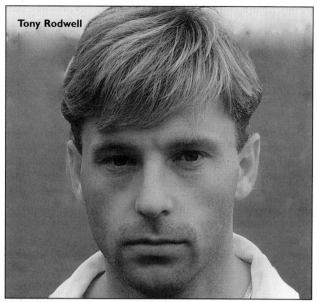
Tony Rodwell

as the Seasiders won 2–1. Blackpool then lost 5–4 on penalties to Torquay United after the game had finished 2–2 after extra-time. In 1991–92 Rodwell had another outstanding season, scoring 11 goals in 42 games including a hat-trick in a 5–2 win at Aldershot. Again the Seasiders qualified for the play-offs and after beating Barnet, won promotion after defeating Scunthorpe United in a penalty shoot-out.

In December 1994 Rodwell was transferred to Scarborough for a fee of £10,000. He started well for the Yorkshire club, but following a change of manager he joined the Latics on loan. He made his debut in the derby game with Preston North End which ended all-square at 1–1, later scoring his only goal for the club in a 3–1 win at Darlington. At the end of his loan spell, he returned to Scarborough before leaving the first-class game at the end of the season.

Wigan Athletic Playing Record

	League		FA Cup		FL Cup		Others		Total	
	App	Gls	App	Gls	App	Gls	App	Gls	App	Gls
1994–95	5	1	0	0	0	0	0	0	5	1
TOTAL	5	1	0	0	0	0	0	0	5	1

ROGERS Alan

Midfield

Born: Liverpool, 3 January 1977.
Career: July 1995 Tranmere Rovers 53 (4) 2. July 1997 Nottingham Forest 135 (2) 17. November 2001 Leicester City 50 (4) 0. February 2004 on loan WIGAN ATHLETIC 5 (0) 0.

The young Tranmere left-back burst on to the League scene in December 1995, earning himself a place in the Wirral club's side on merit. Showing a willingness to support the attack, his tigerish tackling earned him a red card in the first game of the 1996–97 season at Southend. However, during the course of his first full season in the Tranmere side, he was selected for the Football League Under-21 side that played the Italian Serie 'B' equivalent. Not surprisingly, a number of top clubs showed an interest in him and in the summer of 1997, Nottingham Forest paid £2 million for his services.

Signed to replace Stuart Pearce, he was the club's only ever-present and was well worth his First Division Championship medal as both he and Forest headed for Premiership football in 1998–99. At the end of the season he represented the England Under-21 side in the Toulon Tournament. Despite Forest's disastrous Premiership campaign, which ended in relegation back to the First Division, his form led to him being selected for the England 'B' side. He had an excellent 1999–2000 season when he was used both as a left wing-back and a wide left-sided midfield player, finishing the campaign as joint top-scorer. Unfortunately the following season he suffered a serious knee injury at Gillingham, tearing the anterior cruciate ligament. Returning after a long lay-off, he made just a handful of appearances to take his total of games played for Forest to 155 before being sold to Leicester City for £300,000. However, he struggled again with injury and match fitness before becoming an established member of the Leicester City side that won promotion to the Premier League in 2002–03 as runners-up to Portsmouth. In December 2003, Rogers joined the Latics on loan and made his debut in the 1–1 draw at Sunderland. He went on to appear in five games for Wigan but the loan deal was not extended for a further month as the Leicester man was again suffering from injury.

Wigan Athletic Playing Record

	League		FA Cup		FL Cup		Others		Total	
	App	Gls	App	Gls	App	Gls	App	Gls	App	Gls
2003–04	5	0	0	0	0	0	0	0	5	0
TOTAL	5	0	0	0	0	0	0	0	5	0

ROGERS John Charles

Forward

Born: Liverpool, 16 September 1950.
Career: May 1974 WIGAN ATHLETIC. October 1976 Port Vale 25 (10) 6. Altrincham. August 1982 WIGAN ATHLETIC 4 (2) 2. Altrincham. Barrow. Runcorn.

A quick centre-forward who became an England semi-professional international, John Rogers played his early football with Wigan Athletic where he top-scored with 24 goals in the club's Northern Premier League Championship-winning season of 1974–75. Rogers headed the Latics' scoring charts again the following season before in October 1976 he left Springfield Park to play as a part-time professional for Port Vale.

He scored on his debut for the Valiants in a 2–1 home win over Northampton Town, after rewiring council houses in Liverpool during the day! After losing his place in the Vale side he moved to Altrincham before rejoining the Latics for the start of the 1982–83 season. Despite scoring two goals in four starts, things didn't work out for him and he was soon on his way back to Altrincham. He later played for Barrow and Runcorn before hanging up his boots.

Wigan Athletic Playing Record

	League		FA Cup		FL Cup		Others		Total	
	App	Gls	App	Gls	App	Gls	App	Gls	App	Gls
1982–83	4 (2)	2	0	0	2	0	0	0	6 (2)	2
TOTAL	4 (2)	2	0	0	2	0	0	0	6 (2)	2

ROGERS Paul Anthony

Midfield

Born: Portsmouth, 21 March 1965.
Career: Sutton United. January 1992 Sheffield United 120 (5) 10. December 1995 Notts County 21 (1) 2. December 1996 on loan WIGAN ATHLETIC 7 (2) 3. March 1997 WIGAN ATHLETIC 85 (6) 2. July 1999 Brighton and Hove Albion 105 (14) 15.

Hardworking midfielder Paul Rogers was playing non-League football for Sutton United before Sheffield United manager Dave Bassett stepped in with a £35,000 transfer in January 1992. A first-

Paul Rogers

SPORTS
LATICS CLUBCALL
891 12 16 55
JJB
WIGAN ATHLETIC FOOTBALL CLUB
Nationwide
FOOTBALL LEAGUE

team regular at Bramall Lane for four years, a change of management saw him transferred to Notts County. In his first season at Meadow Lane, he helped the Magpies to the Second Division play-off final where they lost to Bradford City. However, midway through the 1996–97 season he lost his place and joined the Latics on loan.

He made his debut as a substitute for Wayne Biggins in a 1–1 draw at Cambridge United, later joining the club on a permanent basis for a fee of £50,000. He appeared in 20 games towards the end of the season, scoring some vital goals in the club's Third Division Championship-winning season. In 1997–98 his involvement and effectiveness grew as the season progressed and the following campaign he was instrumental in the club reaching the play-offs and the Autowindscreen Shield final at Wembley. It was Rogers who scored the Latics' injury-time winner against Millwall but after rejecting a new contract with the club he moved to Brighton and Hove Albion.

Immediately installed as the Seagulls' captain, he led the south coast club to the Third Division Championship in 2000–01. Instrumental in maintaining a high level of team spirit in 2001–02 – an important factor in the Seagulls' second successive promotion – he was rewarded with a new one-year contract in the summer. However, he made just one start in his farewell season before giving his full support to the young players in the reserves and passing on his experience without complaint. After announcing his retirement as a professional, he was rewarded with a position in the club's commercial department.

Wigan Athletic Playing Record

	League		FA Cup		FL Cup		Others		Total	
	App	Gls	App	Gls	App	Gls	App	Gls	App	Gls
1996–97	18 (2)	3	0	0	0	0	0	0	18 (2)	3
1997–98	32 (6)	0	1	0	2	0	2	0	37 (6)	0
1998–99	42	2	2	0	4	0	6	1	54	3
TOTAL	92 (8)	5	3	0	6	0	8	1	109 (8)	6

ROGERSON Lee Antony

Midfield
Born: Darwen, 21 March 1967.
Career: Clitheroe Town. January 1990 WIGAN ATHLETIC 1 (3) 0.

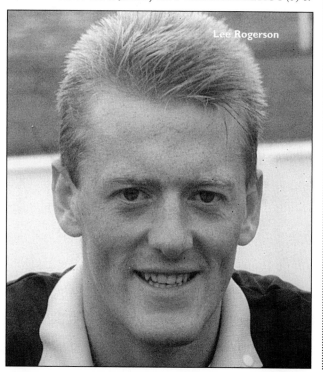
Lee Rogerson

Lee Rogerson began his career with Clitheroe Town, where his displays in midfield and occasionally attack, led to a number of local Football League clubs making inquiries. The Darwen-born player joined Wigan Athletic in January 1990, making his debut towards the end of the season against Blackpool. Coming on as a substitute, he replaced the injured Alan Johnson in a 1–1 draw. There followed another appearance as a substitute before he made his first start at Bristol Rovers. Unfortunately the Latics lost 6–1 and Rogerson was himself replaced by Jimmy Carberry. Early the following season he made another substitute appearance in a 2–1 win over Bolton Wanderers but at the end of the campaign, he was released.

Wigan Athletic Playing Record

	League		FA Cup		FL Cup		Others		Total	
	App	Gls	App	Gls	App	Gls	App	Gls	App	Gls
1989–90	1 (2)	0	0	0	0	0	0 (1)	0	1 (3)	0
1990–91	0 (1)	0	0	0	0 (1)	0	0	0	0 (2)	0
TOTAL	1 (3)	0	0	0	0 (1)	0	0 (1)	0	1 (5)	0

RUSSELL Colin

Forward
Born: Liverpool, 21 January 1961.
Career: April 1978 Liverpool 0 (1) 0. September 1982 Huddersfield Town 64 (2) 23. March 1984 on loan Stoke City 11 (0) 2. August 1984 Bournemouth 65 (3) 14. July 1986 Doncaster Rovers 43 (0) 5. October 1987 Scarborough 12 (1) 2. July 1988 WIGAN ATHLETIC 8 (0) 3. Colne Dynamoes.

Colin Russell began his career with his home-town club Liverpool but with competition for places in the Reds' midfield strong, he made just one appearance as a substitute before moving to Huddersfield Town in September 1982. In his first season at Leeds Road, Russell netted 16 goals in 29 games as the Terriers won promotion to the Second Division. Midway through the following season he suffered a bad knee injury and in an attempt to rediscover his shooting boots, he had a loan spell with Stoke City. In the summer of 1984, Russell moved to Bournemouth but after two seasons at Dean Court in which the Cherries finished in mid-table in the Third Division, he joined Doncaster Rovers. Russell again spent two seasons with the Belle Vue club before moving to Scarborough, his third Yorkshire club, for their first season in the Football League.

In July 1988, Russell joined Wigan Athletic and scored on his debut in a 3–2 defeat at Bristol Rovers on the opening day of the 1988–89 season. He netted twice in the club's first victory of the campaign, a 3–0 defeat of Reading, but after scoring three goals in eight League games, he was allowed to leave Springfield Park for Colne Dynamoes.

Wigan Athletic Playing Record

	League		FA Cup		FL Cup		Others		Total	
	App	Gls	App	Gls	App	Gls	App	Gls	App	Gls
1988–89	8	3	0	0	2	0	0	0	10	3
TOTAL	8	3	0	0	2	0	0	0	10	3

SANTUS Paul Graham

Midfield
Born: Wigan, 8 September 1983.
Career: July 2001 WIGAN ATHLETIC 0 (1) 0.

Paul Santus's Football League career lasted from 4.40pm until

4.45pm on 25 September 2001 (five minutes) as Latics drew 2–2 at Cambridge United. The right-sided midfield player, who was still a trainee, then spent the remainder of the 2001–02 season developing in the Latics reserve and youth teams. Possessing good pace and crossing ability, he was one of three scholars to be awarded a 12–month professional contract in the summer. Unable to force his way into Wigan's Second Division Championship winning squad, he parted company with the club in the summer of 2003.

Wigan Athletic Playing Record

	League		FA Cup		FL Cup		Others		Total	
	App	Gls	App	Gls	App	Gls	App	Gls	App	Gls
2001–02	0 (1)	0	0	0	0	0	0	0	0 (1)	0
TOTAL	0 (1)	0	0	0	0	0	0	0	0 (1)	0

SAVILLE Andrew Victor

Forward

Born: Hull, 12 December 1964.

Career: September 1983 Hull City 74 (27) 18. March 1989 Walsall 28 (10) 5. March 1990 Barnsley 71 (11) 21. March 1992 Hartlepool United 37 (0) 14. March 1993 Birmingham City 51 (8) 17. December 1994 on loan Burnley 3 (1) 1. July 1995 Preston North End 56 (0) 30. October 1996 WIGAN ATHLETIC 17 (8) 4. October 1997 Cardiff City 34 (1) 12. September 1998 on loan Hull City 3 (0) 0. March 1999 Scarborough 0 (9) 0. Gainsborough Trinity.

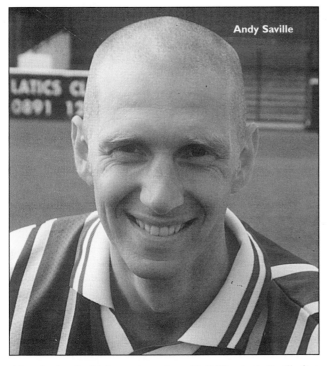

Andy Saville

After signing for his home-town team Hull City, Andy Saville first began to appear regularly in the Tigers' Second Division side during 1986–87 when he was the club's top scorer. He joined Walsall for £100,000 in March 1989, scoring twice on his debut for the Saddlers. After just a year at Fellows Park he moved to Barnsley and in March 1992 was transferred to Hartlepool United for a club record fee of £60,000. Following a £155,000 move to Birmingham City in March 1993, he scored two goals on his debut for the Blues. In 1994–95 he helped the St Andrew's club win the Second Division Championship and triumph in the Autowindscreen Shield against Carlisle United at Wembley. During that season, Saville had a loan spell with Burnley, but it was Preston North End who secured his services in the summer of 1995.

He was an immediate hit at Deepdale, going to score goals for fun, 29 in the League as he guided North End to the Third Division title in his first season with the club. Only Alan Shearer, with 31, scored more goals in English football during that 1995–96 season. Unable to rediscover his goalscoring form the following season, he moved to Wigan Athletic for £125,000 in October 1996. He made his debut in a 2–1 defeat at Swansea City and although he failed to reproduce the kind of scoring form he was noted for, he was hampered by a series of injuries. This meant that the shaven-haired striker never got an extended run in the side, though he did appear in enough games to qualify for another Third Division Championship medal. The following season he found himself faced with heavy competition for forward places and in October 1997 joined Cardiff City for £75.000.

He netted a hat-trick for the Bluebirds in a 3–3 draw at Scunthorpe United but was never going to figure in Frank Burrows' long-term plans. After a loan spell with his first club, Hull, he joined Scarborough but following the club's relegation to the Conference, he was not retained and joined Gainsborough Trinity.

Wigan Athletic Playing Record

	League		FA Cup		FL Cup		Others		Total	
	App	Gls	App	Gls	App	Gls	App	Gls	App	Gls
1996–97	17 (3)	4	1	0	0	0	1	0	19 (3)	4
1997–98	0 (5)	0	0	0	0 (1)	0	0	0	0 (6)	0
TOTAL	17 (8)	4	1	0	0 (1)	0	1	0	19 (9)	4

SCHOFIELD Mark Anthony

Defender

Born: Wigan, 10 October 1966.

Career: July 1985 WIGAN ATHLETIC 1 (1) 0. Leigh RMI.

Tough-tackling defender Mark Schofield joined the Latics straight from school and after some good displays in the club's reserve side, found himself, at the age of 17 years 200 days, named as substitute for the visit to Walsall in April 1984. With the Latics losing 3–0, Schofield replaced Mike Newell for his first taste of League Football. The following season he started just one game, again finishing on the losing side as Latics went down 2–0 at Bristol

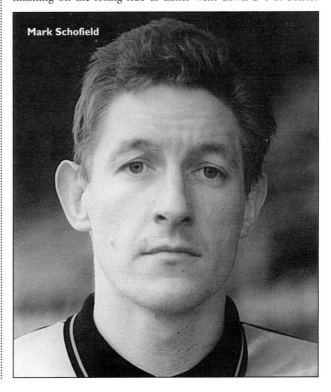

Mark Schofield

Rovers. Unable to hold on to a regular place in the Wigan side, he was released and moved on to play for a number of non-League clubs, his most recent being Leigh RMI.

Wigan Athletic Playing Record

	League		FA Cup		FL Cup		Others		Total	
	App	Gls	App	Gls	App	Gls	App	Gls	App	Gls
1983–84	0 (1)	0	0	0	0	0	0	0	0 (1)	0
1984–85	1	0	0	0	0	0	0	0	1	0
TOTAL	1 (1)	0	0	0	0	0	0	0	1 (1)	0

SEBA Jesus

Winger

Born: Zaragoza, Spain 11 April 1974.
Career: Real Zaragoza. August 1995 WIGAN ATHLETIC 8 (13) 3. Burnley. Bristol Rovers. Real Zaragoza.

Jesus Seba joined the Latics on a free transfer from Real Zaragoza in the summer of 1995 and scored with his first touch in England during a pre-season friendly. He made his League debut in the 2–1 defeat at Gillingham on the opening day of the 1995–96 season before scoring in his first League game at Springfield Park, a 2–1 win over Scunthorpe United. He continued to impress during the first half of the season but then, after losing form, found that his appearances were limited to mainly substitute roles.

A small, compact forward, Seba had good control and the ability to turn defender but still couldn't win a place in the Latics side in 1996–97 and after just two substitute appearances, he had brief trials with Burnley and Bristol Rovers. Sadly, the former Spanish Under-21 international accepted Wigan manager John Deehan's offer to tear up his contract and in October 1996, he returned to Spain to re-sign for Real Zaragoza.

Wigan Athletic Playing Record

	League		FA Cup		FL Cup		Others		Total	
	App	Gls	App	Gls	App	Gls	App	Gls	App	Gls
1995–96	8 (12)	3	0 (2)	0	2	0	1	0	11 (14)	3
1996–97	0 (1)	0	0	0	0 (1)	0	0	0	0 (2)	0
TOTAL	8 (13)	3	0 (2)	0	2 (1)	0	1	0	13 (16)	3

SEDDON Ian Wright

Midfield

Born: Prestbury, 14 October 1950.
Career: June 1969 Bolton Wanderers 51 (13) 4. September 1973 Chester City 62 (11) 7. November 1975 on loan Stockport County 4 (0) 0. January 1976 on loan Chesterfield 2 (0) 0. February 1976 Cambridge United 34 (3) 3. July 1977 Rochdale 30 (1) 3. July 1978 WIGAN ATHLETIC 1 (0) 0.

Much-travelled midfielder Ian Seddon began his Football League career with Bolton Wanderers, making his debut against Cardiff City in August 1969. He was one of a number of youngsters at Burnden Park during this period, who were thrown in at the deep end in an attempt to stave off relegation to the Third Division. He was never a regular in Bolton's midfield as a succession of managers switched between the experienced members of the squad and the youngsters.

In September 1973 Seddon joined Chester City but after two seasons as a virtual ever-present and loan spells with Stockport County and Chesterfield, he left Sealand Road to join Cambridge United. He helped the U's win promotion from Division Four in 1976–77 before moving to Rochdale.

Seddon joined Wigan Athletic, his last League club, in the summer of 1978 and made his only League appearance for the Latics in a 3–2 home defeat at the hands of Newport County. He had previously worn the No.5 shirt in the second-round League Cup defeat at Luton Town. On leaving Springfield Park, Seddon appeared for a number of local non-League clubs.

Wigan Athletic Playing Record

	League		FA Cup		FL Cup		Others		Total	
	App	Gls	App	Gls	App	Gls	App	Gls	App	Gls
1978–79	1	0	0	0	1	0	0	0	2	0
TOTAL	1	0	0	0	1	0	0	0	2	0

SENIOR Stephen

Right-back

Born: Sheffield, 15 May 1963.
Career: May 1981 York City 158 (10) 6. October 1984 on loan Darlington 5 (0) 0. June 1987 Northampton Town 1 (3) 0. October 1987 WIGAN ATHLETIC 107 (2) 3. July 1990 Preston North End 73 (0) 3. Witton Albion. Bamber Bridge.

Steve Senior began his career with York City and during six seasons at Bootham Crescent helped the Minstermen win the Fourth Division Championship in 1983–84. Despite being one of the club's outstanding players during that promotion-winning campaign, he found it difficult to adjust to a higher grade of football and after a loan spell with Darlington, he joined Third Division Northampton Town. Injuries and a loss of form restricted

Steve Senior

his first-team appearances at the County Ground and in October 1987 he joined Wigan Athletic.

Senior made his Latics debut in the No.7 shirt in a 3–0 home win over Rotherham United and over the next few seasons he proved himself to be a solid if unspectacular performer. Senior, who turned out in nine different outfield positions during his stay at Springfield Park, eventually settled into the No.2 shirt. But at the end of the 1989–90 season, his most successful at the club, he was surprisingly allowed to join Preston North End where injury forced his release. He had a brief spell with Witton Albion before helping Bamber Bridge win the Unibond League Championship.

Wigan Athletic Playing Record

	League		FA Cup		FL Cup		Others		Total	
	App	Gls	App	Gls	App	Gls	App	Gls	App	Gls
1987–88	20 (2)	1	2	0	0	0	1	0	23 (2)	1
1988–89	44	2	1	0	2	0	3	0	50	2
1989–90	43	0	3	0	3	1	4	0	53	1
TOTAL	107 (2)	3	6	0	5	1	8	0	126 (2)	4

SHARP Kevin Phillip

Left-back/Midfield

Born: Ontario, Canada, 19 September 1974.

Career: Blackpool Town. Auxerre, France. October 1992 Leeds United 11 (6) 0. November 1995 WIGAN ATHLETIC 156 (22) 10. November 2001 Wrexham 12 (3) 0. August 2002 Huddersfield Town 38 (1) 0.

Although born in Canada, Kevin Sharp was only 18 months old when his family returned to England where his father Frank once had trials with Tranmere Rovers when playing for Flint Town. Kevin Sharp played his early football with Poulton-le-Fylde in the Blackpool League before joining Blackpool Town. He then went on

Kevin Sharp

to the FA National School of Excellence for a couple of years. Together with Jamie Forrester he joined Auxerre in France and the pair cost Leeds United £120,000 in September 1992.

An England youth international, he looked to have a promising future at Elland Road, but slipped down the pecking order and in December 1995 moved to Wigan Athletic for £105,000. A skilful left-sided midfielder, he made his Latics debut in a 3–1 defeat at Plymouth Argyle before scoring in his first game at Springfield Park against Hereford United the following week. In 1996–97 his impressive performances helped the Latics win the Third Division

Championship and though he was often made the scapegoat for some indifferent team performances during the next campaign, he remained a firm favourite with the Wigan fans. He played throughout the 1998–99 season on a week-to-week basis and collected the supporters' 'Away Player of the Season' award. He also picked up a winners' medal following the Latics' 1–0 victory over Millwall in the Autowindscreen Shield final at Wembley. After that injuries and suspensions interrupted his career, though in 2000–01 he made a big contribution in helping the Latics reach the play-offs. Sadly he suffered the agony of conceding a last-minute penalty that led to defeat in the final against Reading.

Having made just one starting appearance in the League for the Latics in 2001–02 he was released and subsequently joined Wrexham on a non-contract basis. However, at the end of the season in which he appeared at both left-back and in midfield, he was not retained.

In the close season he joined Huddersfield Town as cover for the defensive positions but was soon given a regular left-back position due to injuries. Competent and confident on the ball, he soon settled into the pace of Second Division football

Wigan Athletic Playing Record

	League		FA Cup		FL Cup		Others		Total	
	App	Gls	App	Gls	App	Gls	App	Gls	App	Gls
1995–96	20	6	1	0	0	0	0	0	21	6
1996–97	30 (5)	2	1	0	1	0	0 (1)	0	32 (6)	2
1997–98	34 (4)	0	1 (1)	0	1 (1)	0	2	0	38 (6)	0
1998–99	25 (6)	2	1	0	0 (1)	0	8	1	34 (7)	3
1999–2000	16 (4)	0	2 (2)	0	1	0	5	0	24 (6)	0
2000–01	30 (2)	0	1	0	3	1	2	0	36 (2)	1
2001–02	1 (1)	0	0	0	1	0	1	0	3 (1)	0
TOTAL	156 (22)	10	7 (3)	0	7 (2)	1	18 (1)	1	188 (28)	12

SHARRATT Christopher Michael

Winger

Born: West Kirby, 13 August 1970.

Career: Stalybridge Celtic. December 1991 WIGAN ATHLETIC 11 (13) 3. Altrincham.

Winger Chris Sharratt was playing for non-League Stalybridge Celtic when Latics manager Bryan Hamilton persuaded him to join the then Springfield Park club in December 1991. He made his debut as a substitute for Gary Powell in a 1–1 home draw against

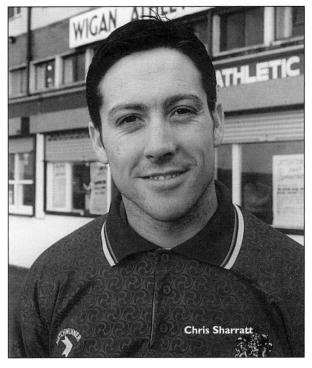

Chris Sharratt

Shrewsbury Town in the last game of the year, going on to make four appearances that season, all as substitute. He had made another five appearances in the No.12 shirt in 1992–93 before making his first start at home to Rotherham United in February 1993. He celebrated by scoring Wigan's goal in a 1–1 draw. He played in the majority of games in the second half of the season but in the summer of 1993, following the club's relegation to Division Three, he left the Latics to play for Altrincham.

Wigan Athletic Playing Record

	League		FA Cup		FL Cup		Others		Total	
	App	Gls	App	Gls	App	Gls	App	Gls	App	Gls
1991–92	0 (4)	0	0	0	0	0	0 (1)	1	0 (5)	1
1992–93	11 (9)	3	1 (1)	0	0 (1)	0	2 (4)	1	14 (15)	4
TOTAL	11 (13)	3	1 (1)	0	0 (1)	0	2 (5)	2	14 (20)	5

SHAW Mark

Midfield
Born: St Helens, 15 October 1964.
Career: November 1982 WIGAN ATHLETIC 3 (0) 0.

Midfielder Mark Shaw worked his way up through the ranks at Springfield Park before Latics manager Larry Lloyd gave him his Football League debut at Gillingham in November 1982. Shaw had a hand in both Wigan goals scored by Kevin Langley and David Lowe in a 2–0 win at the Priestfield Stadium. He kept his place in the side for the visit of Sheffield United the following week and had another good game in a 3–2 win over the Blades. Surprisingly he was replaced for the next match against Oxford United which the Latics lost 1–0 before playing in one more game towards the end of the 1982–83 season. Released in the summer, he spent a number of seasons playing local non-League football.

Wigan Athletic Playing Record

	League		FA Cup		FL Cup		Others		Total	
	App	Gls	App	Gls	App	Gls	App	Gls	App	Gls
1982–83	3	0	0	0	0	0	0	0	3	0
TOTAL	3	0	0	0	0	0	0	0	3	0

SHEARER David John

Forward
Born: Inverness 16 October 1958.
Career: Inverness. January 1978 Middlesbrough 88 (9) 23. March 1980 on loan WIGAN ATHLETIC 11 (0) 9. August 1983 Grimsby Town 1 (3) 0. August 1984 Gillingham 82 (11) 42. October 1987 Bournemouth 8 (3) 3. February 1988 Scunthorpe United 16 (0) 8. December 1988 Darlington 6 (1) 0.

David Shearer played his early football in the Highland League for his home-town club Inverness before joining First Division Middlesbrough in January 1978. Unable to win a regular place in the then Ayresome Park club's starting line-up, he arrived on loan at Springfield Park in March 1980 as the Latics pushed for promotion from the Fourth Division.

The 21-year-old made his debut in a goalless draw at Halifax Town before playing in his first game at Springfield Park three days later against Tranmere Rovers, a match which also ended goalless. However, on his third appearance, Shearer became only the second Latics player to score a hat-trick in the Football League as Port Vale were beaten 3–0. He netted twice in a 3–1 win at Scunthorpe United the following day and signed off his spell with another two-goal display that helped shatter Aldershot. Shearer had scored nine

goals in 11 games, helping the Latics finish in sixth position, five points behind the fourth-placed side Portsmouth.

Shearer rejoined Middlesbrough and scored some vital goals for the north-east club before signing for Grimsby Town. Unable to settle at Blundell Park, he moved to Gillingham where his goalscoring feats kept the Kent club near the top of the Third Division for three consecutive seasons. He later had spells with Bournemouth, Scunthorpe United and Darlington before hanging up his boots.

Wigan Athletic Playing Record

	League		FA Cup		FL Cup		Others		Total	
	App	Gls	App	Gls	App	Gls	App	Gls	App	Gls
1979–80	11	9	0	0	0	0	0	0	11	9
TOTAL	11	9	0	0	0	0	0	0	11	9

SHELDON Kevin John

Winger
Born: Cheddleton, 14 June 1956.
Career: June 1973 Stoke City 12 (3) 0. August 1981 WIGAN ATHLETIC 29 (0) 1. August 1982 on loan Port Vale 5 (0) 0. August 1983 Crewe Alexandra 2 (0) 0. Trowbridge. Burton Albion. Leek Town. Telford United.

Nicknamed 'Bomber', Kevin Sheldon had just established himself in Stoke City's League side when in November 1976 he sustained a double fracture of the right leg in a match at Leeds United. After an operation by a top specialist, he began the long road to recovery – and long it certainly was. He was in plaster for six months, then wore a calliper for two months, spent another month on crutches and then finished off his rehabilitation on sticks! Even then the pain wouldn't go away and he had to have another operation before resuming his career.

He joined Wigan Athletic in August 1981 and made his debut in a 3–3 draw at Bradford City on the opening day of the 1981–82 season. He was a virtual ever-present for the first-half of the campaign, scoring his only goal for the club in a 2–0 defeat of Port Vale. Injuries prevented him from making much of a contribution in the second half of the season as the Latics won promotion to the Third Division. After a brief loan spell with Port Vale he returned to Springfield Park but in the summer of 1983 he joined Crewe Alexandra. Sadly his run of bad luck continued as he suffered an Achilles injury and he was forced to leave the first-class scene, later playing non-League football for Trowbridge Town, Burton Albion, Leek and Telford United.

Wigan Athletic Playing Record

	League		FA Cup		FL Cup		Others		Total	
	App	Gls	App	Gls	App	Gls	App	Gls	App	Gls
1981–82	15	1	2	0	6	0	0	0	23	1
1982–83	14	0	2	0	0	0	0	0	16	0
TOTAL	29	1	4	0	6	0	0	0	39	1

SHERIDAN Darren John

Midfield
Born: Manchester, 8 December 1967.
Career: Winsford United. August 1993 Barnsley 149 (22) 5. July 1999 WIGAN ATHLETIC 50 (8) 3. July 2001 Oldham Athletic 54 (7) 3.

Brother of former Republic of Ireland international John Sheridan, Darren is an accomplished passer of the ball. Released by Leeds United as a youngster, he came into professional football

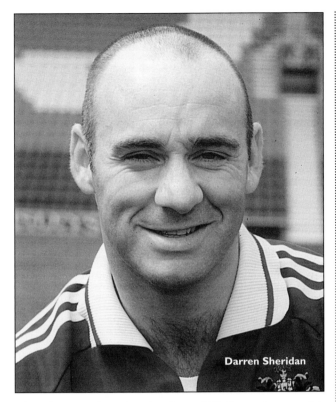

Darren Sheridan

SHYNE Christopher

Goalkeeper
Born: Littleborough, 10 December 1950.
Career: Dyers Arms. January 1977 Rochdale 20 (0) 0. August 1979
WIGAN ATHLETIC 10 (0) 0.

Goalkeeper Chris Shyne was playing amateur football for the Dyers Arms when Rochdale offered him professional terms in January 1977. Though not Dale's first-choice 'keeper, he made 20 appearances over the next two-and-a-half seasons, never letting the side down when he was called upon. He left Spotland in the summer of 1979, joining Wigan Athletic as a replacement for the injured John Brown. Shyne made his debut on the opening day of the 1979–80 season, pulling off a number of good saves in a 2–2 draw at Darlington. He appeared in the club's first 10 games of the season, conceding on average two goals a game and never keeping a clean sheet! Following Brown's return from injury, Shyne never got another look-in and left to play non-League football for a number of clubs.

Wigan Athletic Playing Record

	League		FA Cup		FL Cup		Others		Total	
	App	Gls	App	Gls	App	Gls	App	Gls	App	Gls
1979–80	10	0	0	0	2	0	0	0	12	0
TOTAL	10	0	0	0	2	0	0	0	12	0

SKIPPER Peter Dennis

Central Defender
Born: Hull, 11 April 1958.
Career: Schultz YC. February 1979 Hull City 22 (1) 2. February 1980 on loan Scunthorpe United 0 (1) 0. May 1980 Darlington 91 (0) 4. August 1982 Hull City 264 (1) 17. October 1988 Oldham Athletic 27 (0) 1. July 1989 Walsall 81 (0) 2. September 1991 Wrexham 2 (0) 0. October 1991 WIGAN ATHLETIC 15 (3) 0. Stafford Rangers. November 1992 WIGAN ATHLETIC 73 (0) 4.

Peter Skipper

when he moved to Barnsley from HFS Loans League club Winsford United for just £10,000 in August 1993. He made his League debut for the Tykes in a 1–0 defeat at Sunderland in January 1994 and though he only appeared in a handful of games that season, he became a first-team regular in 1994–95 following an injury crisis at Oakwell. Over the next four seasons he showed his versatility by being equally at home in either the left wing-back or central midfield position and was instrumental in the Yorkshire club winning promotion to the Premier League in 1996–97. An aggressive battler in midfield, he struggled somewhat in the top flight, though he always gave of his best. His progress at Oakwell was hampered by a broken jaw suffered at Crystal Palace in February 1999 and in the close season he moved to Wigan Athletic on a free transfer.

On his arrival at the JJB Stadium, he was reunited with John Benson, the coach who introduced him to League football at Barnsley. After making his Latics debut in a 3–0 win at Scunthorpe United on the opening day of the 1999–2000 season, he appeared in a variety of roles on the left-side for Wigan, scoring the winning goal against Millwall that took the Latics through to the Second Division play-off final. Injuries and a loss of form restricted his appearances during the first-half of the 2000–01 season but he returned to play an important role, helping the Latics qualify for the play-offs. Despite only playing in just over half of the club's games, he was voted third in the 'Player of the Season' awards, yet was still released during the summer.

He joined Oldham Athletic where he teamed up with older brother John. Though he started the season in fine form, enhancing midfield with his combative style, his campaign was disrupted by injuries and a series of suspensions. After serving a seven-match ban at the start of the 2002–03 season, he bounced back and prompted a young Oldham side to the play-offs, while also managing to clean up his disciplinary record!

Wigan Athletic Playing Record

	League		FA Cup		FL Cup		Others		Total	
	App	Gls	App	Gls	App	Gls	App	Gls	App	Gls
1999–2000	25 (6)	3	1 (1)	0	4	0	5	1	35 (7)	4
2000–01	25 (2)	0	0 (1)	0	1	0	0	0	26 (3)	0
TOTAL	50 (8)	3	1 (2)	0	5	0	5	1	61 (10)	4

Hull-born central defender Peter Skipper began his League career with his home-town club, making his debut in a 5–3 defeat at Swansea in March 1979. Unable to hold down a regular place in the Tigers side, he had a brief loan spell with Scunthorpe United before joining Darlington. After two seasons at the Feethams he rejoined Hull City and in his first campaign back at Boothferry Park helped the club win promotion to the Third Division. A couple of seasons later Skipper was instrumental in Hull winning promotion to Division Two but in October 1988, having scored 21 goals in 338 games in his two spells with the club, he signed for Oldham Athletic.

After just one season at Boundary Park he was on the move again, this time to Walsall, but after the Saddlers dropped into the Fourth Division, he moved to Wrexham. Unable to win a regular place in the Robins team he joined the Latics on a non-contract basis, making his debut as a substitute for Darren Patterson in a 1–0 home win over Stoke City. He appeared in 18 of the games that remained in that 1991–92 season before leaving to play non-League football for Stafford Rangers. In November 1992 he rejoined Wigan on a permanent basis and over the next two seasons was a virtual ever-present in a Latics side that suffered relegation to the 'new' Division Three and then struggled to hold on to their League status.

Wigan Athletic Playing Record

	League		FA Cup		FL Cup		Others		Total	
	App	Gls	App	Gls	App	Gls	App	Gls	App	Gls
1991–92	15 (3)	0	0	0	0	0	0	0	15 (3)	0
1992–93	32	1	0	0	0	0	7	1	39	2
1993–94	41	3	4	1	2	0	1	0	48	4
TOTAL	88 (3)	4	4	1	2	0	8	1	102 (3)	6

SMART Kevin Graham

Right-back
Born: Newcastle 17 October 1958.
Career: October 1976 Plymouth Argyle 32 (0) 0. July 1989 WIGAN ATHLETIC 48 (1) 1.

While still at school, Kevin Smart played soccer for Montague and North Fenham Boys' Club and, aged 15, played for his club at Wembley Pool in a five-a-side tournament. As the North of England representatives they beat their South of England counterparts to become English Champions. However, in the Great Britain Championship Final, the Newcastle side lost 8–7 on penalties to a Scottish side. After captaining the Northumberland Boys' Club XI, Smart joined Plymouth Argyle, making his League debut against Luton Town at the age of 18. During his time at Home Park, the Pilgrims were relegated to the Third Division and in the summer of 1978 he left to play for Wigan Athletic.

He made his debut in a 2–0 defeat at Reading and though he did not make an immediate impact, once he had settled in, he turned in a series of outstanding displays. His only goal for the club came in a 2–0 win over Stockport County in March 1979, but early the following season he lost his place to former Bradford City defender David Fretwell and after ending the season in the club's Lancashire League side, he was released.

Wigan Athletic Playing Record

	League		FA Cup		FL Cup		Others		Total	
	App	Gls	App	Gls	App	Gls	App	Gls	App	Gls
1978–79	40	1	2	0	1	0	0	0	43	1
1979–80	8 (1)	0	0	0	2	0	0	0	10 (1)	0
TOTAL	48 (1)	1	2	0	3	0	0	0	53 (1)	1

SMEETS Jorg

Midfield
Born: Amsterdam, Holland, 5 November 1970.
Career: Heracles. October 1997 WIGAN ATHLETIC 10 (14) 3. March 1999 on loan Chester City 1 (2) 0.

Jorg Smeets

Recruited from Dutch club Heracles for a fee of £100,000, Jorg Smeets made his Football League debut in a 2–1 defeat at Grimsby Town in October 1997. Most of his first season at Springfield Park was spent on the bench, though he did score two spectacular goals in a 4–0 home win over Brentford and one in the Boxing Day clash with Wrexham which ended all-square at 2–2. Possessing the smallest feet in the Football League, with a shoe size of 4, Smeets spent a brief loan spell at Chester City midway through the following season after just three appearances as a substitute for the Latics. His last first-team appearance in Wigan colours saw him miss a penalty in the FA Cup second-round penalty shoot-out against Notts County which the Meadow Lane club won 4–2. Unable to make much headway with Wigan his contract was cancelled by mutual consent at the end of the 1998–99 season and he returned to Holland.

Wigan Athletic Playing Record

	League		FA Cup		FL Cup		Others		Total	
	App	Gls	App	Gls	App	Gls	App	Gls	App	Gls
1997–98	10 (13)	3	1	0	0	0	3	0	14 (13)	3
1998–99	0 (1)	0	0 (1)	0	0 (1)	0	0	0	0 (3)	0
TOTAL	10 (14)	3	1 (1)	0	0 (1)	0	3	0	14 (16)	3

SMITH Barry Joseph

Midfield
Born: Wigan, 21 September 1969.
Career: May 1987 WIGAN ATHLETIC 0 (1) 0.

Wigan-born midfielder Barry Smith holds the distinction of making his one and only Football League appearance while still a trainee. Aged 18 years 89 days, he came on as a substitute for Andy Ainscow in a 2–2 home draw against Northampton Town on 19 December 1987. Yet despite continuing to impress in the club's reserve side, he was released at the end of the season.

Wigan Athletic Playing Record

	League		FA Cup		FL Cup		Others		Total	
	App	Gls	App	Gls	App	Gls	App	Gls	App	Gls
1987–88	0 (1)	0	0	0	0	0	0	0	0 (1)	0
TOTAL	0 (1)	0	0	0	0	0	0	0	0 (1)	0

SMITH Jeremy

Forward

Born: Leeds, 20 July 1971.

Career: Goole Town. August 1991 WIGAN ATHLETIC 0 (6) 0. Derry City.

Utility forward Jeremy Smith was playing Northern Premier League football for Goole Town, where his goalscoring achievements made him a target for a number of lower division clubs, when Wigan manager Bryan Hamilton offered him the chance to join the Latics in the summer of 1991. After putting pen to paper, he made his Football League debut as a substitute for Bryan Griffiths in a 3–1 home defeat at the hands of Stockport County. Over the first half of the 1991–92 season, the 20-year-old Smith made six League appearances, all as substitute, but was never on the winning side, nor did he find the net. Though he continued to impress in the club's second string, he was allowed to leave Springfield Park and crossed the sea to play Irish League football for Derry City.

Wigan Athletic Playing Record

	League		FA Cup		FL Cup		Others		Total	
	App	Gls	App	Gls	App	Gls	App	Gls	App	Gls
1991–92	0 (6)	0	0	0	0 (1)	0	0	0	0 (7)	0
TOTAL	0 (6)	0	0	0	0 (1)	0	0	0	0 (7)	0

SMYTH John Michael

Right-back

Born: Dublin, 28 April 1970.

Career: Dundalk. May 1987 Liverpool. August 1990 Burnley. September 1991 WIGAN ATHLETIC 2 (6) 0.

Defender John Smyth began his career with his home-town club Dundalk before joining Liverpool in May 1987. Following three

John Smyth

years at Anfield without a first-team appearance, Smyth signed for Burnley in the summer of 1990. He featured in all three of the Clarets' Lancashire Cup games but was never in contention for a place in the club's League side, particularly after the arrival of John Pender in September 1990, and he was released at the end of the season. He joined Wigan and made his League debut as a substitute in a 2–1 home defeat by Darlington in September 1991 before his first full appearance in the club's next home game, a 1–1 draw with Reading. Released at the end of the campaign, he left Springfield Park to return to play in his native Ireland.

Wigan Athletic Playing Record

	League		FA Cup		FL Cup		Others		Total	
	App	Gls	App	Gls	App	Gls	App	Gls	App	Gls
1991–92	2 (6)	0	0 (1)	0	0 (1)	0	1	0	3 (8)	0
TOTAL	2 (6)	0	0 (1)	0	0 (1)	0	1	0	3 (8)	0

STATHAM Mark Andrew

Goalkeeper

Born: Urmston, 11 November 1975.

Career: March 1993 Nottingham Forest. July 1994 WIGAN ATHLETIC 1 (1) 0.

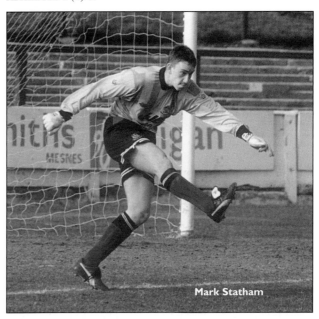

Mark Statham

Goalkeeper Mark Statham was on Nottingham Forest's books as a youngster but due to the fine form of current Welsh international Mark Crossley he couldn't break into the City ground club's first team. In the summer of 1994 Statham joined the Latics as cover for the club's first-choice 'keeper Simon Farnworth. He made his debut at Walsall towards the end of the 1994–95 season after Farnworth had been injured in an aerial challenge. With the former Bolton 'keeper still out injured, Statham started his first League match in Wigan colours the following week, making a number of good saves in a 1–0 defeat at Rochdale. Following the arrival of another former Bolton 'keeper in Dave Felgate in the close season, Statham realised his chances of regular first-team football at Springfield Park were limited and he left to play non-League football.

Wigan Athletic Playing Record

	League		FA Cup		FL Cup		Others		Total	
	App	Gls	App	Gls	App	Gls	App	Gls	App	Gls
1994–95	1 (1)	0	0	0	0	0	0	0	1 (1)	0
TOTAL	1 (1)	0	0	0	0	0	0	0	1 (1)	0

STEEL William James

Forward

Born: Dumfries, 4 December 1959.

Career: June 1978 Oldham Athletic 101 (7) 24. November 1982 on loan WIGAN ATHLETIC 2 (0) 2. January 1983 on loan Wrexham 9 (0) 6. March 1983 Port Vale 27 (1) 6. January 1984 Wrexham 164 (0) 51. On loan Real Coruna. November 1987 Tranmere Rovers 161 (13) 29.

Jim Steel

Dumfries-born striker Jim Steel began his Football League career with Oldham Athletic before joining Wigan on loan in November 1982. Though he only made two appearances for the Springfield Park club, he impressed in home victories over Millwall (3–1) and Sheffield United (3–2) and it was a pity that the club were going through financial difficulties and couldn't afford the £10,000 fee. Steel joined Port Vale and helped the Valiants win promotion to the Third Division but midway through the 1983–84 season he left Vale Park to join Wrexham.

He was the leading scorer at the Racecourse Ground for the next three seasons, netting his first League hat-trick in a 4–3 win over Peterborough United. His performances for the Robins led to FC Porto trying to sign him, but when the deal failed to materialise, he went on loan to Spanish side Real Coruna. Steel later joined Tranmere Rovers, helping the Prenton Park club win promotion from the Fourth Division in 1988–89 and then in 1989–90 after the club had finished fourth in the Third Division, was outstanding in the play-offs where Tranmere lost to Notts County at Wembley. Also that season he scored one of Rovers' goals in a 2–1 win over Bristol Rovers, also at Wembley as the Wirral club won the Leyland DAF Cup. After helping Tranmere win promotion to the Second Division via the play-offs, Steel left the game to join the Merseyside police force.

Wigan Athletic Playing Record

	League		FA Cup		FL Cup		Others		Total	
	App	Gls	App	Gls	App	Gls	App	Gls	App	Gls
1982–83	2	2	0	0	0	0	0	0	2	2
TOTAL	2	2	0	0	0	0	0	0	2	2

STEWART William Ian

Goalkeeper

Born: Liverpool, 1 January 1965.

Career: January 1983 Liverpool. July 1984 WIGAN ATHLETIC 14 (0) 0. August 1986 Chester City 272 (0) 0. July 1994 Northampton Town 26 (1) 0. March 1995 on loan Chesterfield 1 (0) 0. July 1995 Chester City 45 (0) 0.

A former Liverpool apprentice, goalkeeper Billy Stewart joined the Latics on a free transfer in the summer of 1984 and made his Football League debut in a 1–0 home defeat by Millwall after months as understudy to Roy Tunks. He went on to appear in six games that season but was never on the winning side! After appearing in another 1–0 defeat at Bristol City early in 1985–86, he had a run of seven outings towards the end of the campaign to help the Latics finish fourth in Division Three. In the close season he left Springfield Park to join Chester City and in eight seasons with the Cestrians appeared in over 300 League and Cup games.

One of the best 'keepers in the lower divisions, he moved on to Northampton Town in July 1994. He was a regular in the Cobblers side until the arrival of Andy Woodman, when he joined Chesterfield on loan. During his time at Saltergate he helped the Spireites reach the play-offs and was outstanding at Wembley when they clinched promotion to the Second Division by beating Bury 2–0. Released by the Cobblers, he rejoined Chester City and missed just one game on his return to the Deva Stadium. Having taken his total of first-team appearances to 383 he was surprisingly released in the summer of 1996.

Wigan Athletic Playing Record

	League		FA Cup		FL Cup		Others		Total	
	App	Gls	App	Gls	App	Gls	App	Gls	App	Gls
1984–85	6	0	0	0	0	0	1	0	7	0
1985–86	8	0	0	0	0	0	0	0	8	0
TOTAL	14	0	0	0	0	0	1	0	15	0

STILLIE Derek Daniel

Goalkeeper

Born: Irvine, 3 December 1973.

Career: May 1991 Aberdeen 22 (1) 0. August 1999 WIGAN ATHLETIC 42 (2) 0. July 2002 Dunfermline Athletic 21 (0) 0.

Scottish Under-21 international goalkeeper Derek Stillie began his career with Aberdeen and made 28 League and Cup appearances for the Dons when Latics manager John Benson secured his services on a free transfer in the summer of 1999. Signed as understudy to Roy Carroll, he made his League debut for Wigan in a 3–3 draw at Millwall and over the course of the season proved to be a more than capable deputy. He gave a series of impressive displays as a shot-stopper and was only on the losing side once in the League. With Carroll undergoing an emergency appendix operation, Stillie played in the last seven games, collecting the 'Man-of-the-Match' award in the play-off win over Millwall. He retained the goalkeeper's jersey for the Wembley final where the Latics lost 3–2 to Gillingham after extra-time.

He continued to impress in 2000–01, though his first-team appearances were restricted by the fine form of Roy Carroll, but whenever he was called upon, he never let the side down. Following Carroll's departure to Manchester United, Stillie was hoping to make the No.1 jersey his own. After appearing in the first two games of the 2001–02 season, he lost his place to Stewart Kerr. He regained the No.1 shirt in October but then suffered an abductor muscle injury in the 1–1 home draw with Notts County in December which brought his campaign to a premature end. Out

Derek Stillie

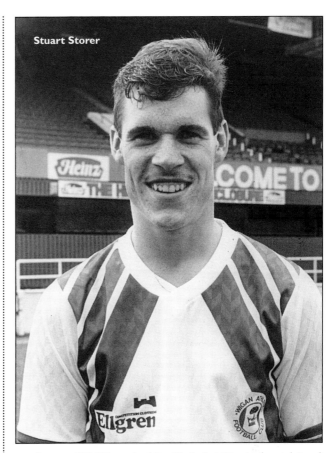

Stuart Storer

of contract at the end of the season, he was allowed to leave the club and returned north of the border to play for Dunfermline Athletic where his displays between the posts helped the Pars finish fifth in the Scottish Premier League.

Wigan Athletic Playing Record

	League		FA Cup		FL Cup		Others		Total	
	App	Gls	App	Gls	App	Gls	App	Gls	App	Gls
1999–2000	12 (1)	0	2	0	1	0	3	0	18 (1)	0
2000–01	17 (1)	0	2	0	1 (1)	0	0	0	20 (2)	0
2001–02	13	0	1	0	1	0	1	0	16	0
TOTAL	42 (2)	0	5	0	3 (1)	0	4	0	54 (3)	0

STORER Stuart John

Winger

Born: Rugby, 16 January 1967.

Career: May 1983 Mansfield Town 0 (1) 0. VS Rugby. January 1985 Birmingham City 5 (3) 0. March 1987 Everton. August 1987 on loan WIGAN ATHLETIC 9 (3) 0. December 1987 Bolton Wanderers 95 (28) 12. March 1993 Exeter City 75 (2) 8. March 1995 Brighton and Hove Albion 114 (28) 11. Atherstone United.

Pacy winger Stuart Storer began his Football League career with Mansfield Town but his one and only appearance for the Stags came when he appeared as a substitute in a 5–0 win over Hartlepool United in October 1983. He drifted into non-League football with his home-town team VS Rugby but was snapped up by Birmingham City in January 1985. He made two top-flight appearances for the St Andrew's club at the end of the 1985–86 season with City already doomed to relegation. He later became embroiled in a transfer row in a move to Everton in March 1987. He signed for the Toffees along with Wayne Clarke for a total of £300,000. Wolves claimed that they were entitled to 50 percent of

any fee over £80,000 received for Clarke but Birmingham claimed he was the makeweight in the deal!

Unable to make the first team at Goodison Park, he started the 1987–88 season by playing 16 games on loan for Wigan Athletic, the first a 4–4 draw at Notts County on the opening day of the season. He later joined Bolton Wanderers on loan before the move was made permanent, Phil Neal paying £25,000 for his services. When Bolton won the Sherpa Van Trophy at Wembley in 1989, Storer came on as a substitute for Jeff Chandler. He made another Wembley appearance in 1991 after helping the Wanderers reach the play-off final. He left Burnden Park in March 1993, joining Exeter City for £25,000.

Two years later he moved to Brighton and Hove Albion and was a regular in the Seagulls side that suffered relegation in 1995–96 and then held on to their League status on the final day of the following season. After that his progress was hampered by a series of niggling injuries and in the summer of 2000, he was released by Brighton manager Mickey Adams and went to play non-League football for Atherstone United.

Wigan Athletic Playing Record

	League		FA Cup		FL Cup		Others		Total	
	App	Gls	App	Gls	App	Gls	App	Gls	App	Gls
1987–88	9 (3)	0	0	0	4	0	0	0	13 (3)	0
TOTAL	9 (3)	0	0	0	4	0	0	0	13 (3)	0

STRONG Gregory

Central Defender

Born: Bolton, 5 September 1975.

Career: October 1992 WIGAN ATHLETIC 28 (7) 3. September 1995 Bolton Wanderers 10 (2) 1. November 1997 on loan Blackpool 11 (0) 1. March 1999 on loan Stoke City 5 (0) 1. March 2000 on loan Motherwell 11 (0) 0. July 2000 Motherwell 62 (2) 3. June 2002 Hull City 3 (0) 0. February 2003 on loan Cheltenham Town 3 (1) 0. March 2003 on loan Scunthorpe United 7 (0) 0.

Bolton-born central defender Greg Strong won England honours at both schoolboy and youth level before turning professional at Springfield Park in October 1992. He made his League debut for the Latics on the opening day of the 1993–94 season in a 2–0 defeat at home by Scunthorpe United. He became a regular in the Wigan side in March 1994, playing a number of games at left-back in a run of just two defeats in the final eight games, lifting the Latics away from the bottom of the League. He had appeared in 45 games for the Latics when he went to Burnden Park on trial before securing a £20,000 move with add-ons dependent upon appearances.

Greg Strong

He made his debut for the Wanderers in the Premier League game against Sheffield Wednesday on New Year's Day 1996. Unable to win a regular place because of the consistency of Chris Fairclough and Gerry Taggert, he was sent out on loan to Blackpool to further his experience and made an immediate impact, scoring the only goal of the game against York City. The following season he had a loan spell at Stoke City where he scored a late winner for the Potters against Wigan Athletic! Due to the absence of Mark Fish, Strong began the 1999–2000 season as the club's first-choice centre-half but, despite a good run of form, he lost out when Fish returned.

He later joined Motherwell on loan, making the move a permanent one in the close season. He gave the Fir Park club good service before joining Hull City in the summer of 2002. Appointed club captain, he was sent off on his second appearance for the Tigers and then faced a two-month lay-off after dislocating an elbow in training. Following the appointment of Peter Taylor as manager, he failed to regain his place in the side and had two spells out on loan, firstly at Cheltenham Town and then at Scunthorpe United.

TAIT Paul

Forward

Born: Newcastle, 24 October 1974.
Career: July 1993 Everton. August 1994 WIGAN ATHLETIC 1 (4) 0. Runcorn. Northwich Victoria. June 1999 Crewe Alexandra 31 (32) 6. November 2001 on loan Hull City 0 (2) 0. July 2002 Bristol Rovers 33 (8) 7.

Paul Tait arrived at Springfield Park from Everton at the beginning of the 1994–95 season with an impressive scoring record with the Toffees' youth side. A strong and direct centre-forward, he made his Football League debut in a 2–1 home defeat by Barnet, when he was replaced late in the game by Chris Duffy. He was on the bench for Latics' next game at Hereford United but came on for Neil Morton as Wigan won their first match of the campaign. Following a spate of niggling injuries, he made a further three appearances in the substitute's shirt that season but failed to get on the scoresheet. He was offered a further three-month contract but in that time failed to add to his first-team appearances.

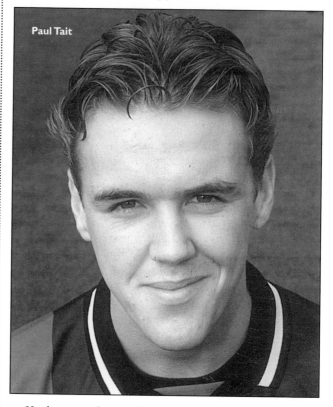

Paul Tait

He then moved on to play non-League football for Runcorn and later Northwich Victoria. He returned to League action with Crewe Alexandra in 1999–2000. Always giving 100 percent whenever he was in the team, more than half of his 63 League appearances were as a substitute. In his third season at Gresty Road he found himself on the fringes of the first-team squad and joined Hull City on loan. Signed primarily as cover for injuries and suspensions, he received few opportunities as the club's regular players came back earlier than expected. In the summer of 2002 he joined Bristol Rovers, soon winning over the supporters after producing some hardworking performances. Though he lost his place towards the end of the campaign, he returned for the final game and scored an equaliser for Rovers in their match against Kidderminster Harriers.

Wigan Athletic Playing Record

	League		FA Cup		FL Cup		Others		Total	
	App	Gls	App	Gls	App	Gls	App	Gls	App	Gls
1993–94	16 (2)	1	0	0	1	0	1	0	18 (2)	1
1994–95	12 (5)	2	1	0	4	0	2 (1)	0	19 (6)	2
TOTAL	28 (7)	3	1	0	5	0	3 (1)	0	37 (8)	3

Wigan Athletic Playing Record

	League		FA Cup		FL Cup		Others		Total	
	App	Gls	App	Gls	App	Gls	App	Gls	App	Gls
1994–95	1 (4)	0	0	0	0	0	0	0	1 (4)	0
TOTAL	1 (4)	0	0	0	0	0	0	0	1 (4)	0

TANKARD Allen John

Left-back
Born: Fleet, 21 May 1969.
Career: May 1987 Southampton 5 (0) 0. July 1988 WIGAN ATHLETIC 205 (4) 4. July 1993 Port Vale 261 (14) 11. August 2001 Mansfield Town 22 (8) 2.

Allen Tankard

An England youth international, Allen Tankard began his Football League career with his local club Southampton when aged just 16, becaming one of the youngest players to represent the Saints. However, after failing to establish himself at the Dell, he joined Wigan Athletic on a free transfer in the summer of 1988. After making his Latics debut in a 3–2 defeat at Bristol Rovers on the opening day of the 1988–89 campaign, Tankard missed very few games in his five seasons with the club, being ever-present in 1990–91 when the Latics finished tenth in the Third Division. Following the club's relegation in 1992–93, Tankard left Springfield Park to join Port Vale, whose manager John Rudge paid £87,500 for his services.

This attacking full-back, who has also had spells in midfield, was a great favourite with Vale fans. Though he suffered a series of hamstring-related injuries during the early part of his Vale Park career, he became a virtual ever-present in the eight years he was with the Valiants. Strong in the tackle and never one to give less than 100 percent, Tankard went on to appear in 324 first-team games for Vale before linking up with Mansfield Town for training during the 2001 close season. Persuaded to stay, his experience was invaluable to a young Mansfield side but at the end of his first season at Field Mill, he decided to hang up his boots.

Wigan Athletic Playing Record

	League		FA Cup		FL Cup		Others		Total	
	App	Gls	App	Gls	App	Gls	App	Gls	App	Gls
1988–89	32 (2)	1	0	0	2	0	2	0	35 (2)	1
1989–90	45	1	3	0	4	0	4	0	56	1
1990–91	46	1	4	0	2	0	5	0	57	1
1991–92	44	0	3	0	3	0	2	0	52	0
1992–93	39 (2)	1	3	0	4	1	7	0	53 (2)	2
TOTAL	205 (4)	4	13	0	15	0	20	0	253 (4)	5

TAYLOR Brian John

Full-back/Winger
Born: Gateshead, 2 July 1949. Died: 1993.
Career: Durham City. February 1968 Coventry City. May 1971 Walsall 204 (12) 25. October 1977 Plymouth Argyle 34 (1) 5. October 1978 Preston North End 93 (6) 1. March 1982 on loan WIGAN ATHLETIC 7 (1) 0.

Brian Taylor began his career with Durham City in his native north-east before joining Coventry City in the summer of 1970. Unable to make the grade with the Sky Blues, he left Highfield Road the following year to sign for Walsall. He stayed at Fellows Park until 1977, scoring 25 goals in 216 League appearances for the Saddlers.

During his stay with Walsall, the West Midlands club came close on a number of occasions to winning promotion to the Second Division. Then came a move to Plymouth, where he scored for Argyle on his debut against Portsmouth. However, the following year he was off to Preston North End where he made 99 League appearances before joining Wigan Athletic on loan in March 1982.

Latics player-manager Larry Lloyd saw Taylor's experience as a vital component in the club's push for promotion to the Third Division. He made his Wigan debut in a 3–0 defeat at Hereford United but thereafter wasn't on the losing side again until the last of his eight appearances on the final day of the season at Aldershot. Despite Latics winning promotion, Taylor returned to Deepdale, leaving the first-class game in the close season.

Wigan Athletic Playing Record

	League		FA Cup		FL Cup		Others		Total	
	App	Gls	App	Gls	App	Gls	App	Gls	App	Gls
1981–82	7 (1)	0	0	0	0	0	0	0	7 (1)	0
TOTAL	7 (1)	0	0	0	0	0	0	0	7 (1)	0

TAYLOR Colin David

Forward
Born: Liverpool, 25 December 1971.
Career: March 1990 Wolverhampton Wanderers 7 (12) 2. January 1992 on loan WIGAN ATHLETIC 7 (0) 2. November 1992 on loan Preston North End 4 (0) 0. February 1993 on loan Doncaster Rovers 2 (0) 0.

England youth international Colin Taylor began his career with Wolverhampton Wanderers and after making his debut as a substitute in a goalless League Cup tie at Hull City, the youngster was given an extended run in the Molineux side. He had scored twice in a 4–1 home win over Millwall when an injury against Watford three games later brought his season to a premature end. In January 1992 Taylor joined the Latics on loan and scored their goal in a 1–1 draw at Fulham on his debut. He netted another one at Leyton Orient as Wigan played four away games on the trot in the space of 23 days. Latics manager Bryan Hamilton decided not to make the move a permanent one and Taylor returned to Molineux before further loan spells with both Preston North End and Doncaster Rovers.

Wigan Athletic Playing Record

	League		FA Cup		FL Cup		Others		Total	
	App	Gls	App	Gls	App	Gls	App	Gls	App	Gls
1991–92	7	2	0	0	0	0	0	0	7	2
TOTAL	7	2	0	0	0	0	0	0	7	2

TAYLOR Robin Graham

Midfield

Born: West Germany, 14 January 1971.
Career: Leicester City. October 1989 WIGAN ATHLETIC 0 (1) 0. Kettering Town.

German-born midfielder Robin Taylor played his early football for Leicester City but despite some impressive performances in the club's reserve side, he was unable to make the grade and was released by Foxes' manager David Pleat. Latics manager Bryan Hamilton gave him the chance to resurrect his career in October 1989 and after playing well in a 1–0 Leyland DAF Cup victory over Bolton Wanderers, he made his League debut as a substitute for Steve Senior in a 1–1 draw at Cardiff City.

However, his contract was terminated and the following year he went up to Loughborough University, where he represented the British Universities in the World Student Games. Taylor subsequently played non-League football for Kettering Town as well as having trials with both West Ham United and Sheffield United.

Wigan Athletic Playing Record

	League		FA Cup		FL Cup		Others		Total	
	App	Gls	App	Gls	App	Gls	App	Gls	App	Gls
1989–90	0 (1)	0	0	0	0	0	1	0	1 (1)	0
TOTAL	0 (1)	0	0	0	0	0	1	0	1 (1)	0

TAYLOR Steven Jeffrey

Forward

Born: Royton, 18 October 1955.
Career: October 1973 Bolton Wanderers 34 (6) 16. October 1975 on loan Port Vale 4 (0) 2. October 1977 Oldham Athletic 45 (2) 25. January 1979 Luton Town 15 (5) 1. July 1979 Mansfield Town 30 (7) 7. July 1980 Burnley 80 (6) 37. August 1983 WIGAN ATHLETIC 29 (1) 7. March 1984 Stockport County 26 (0) 8. November 1984 Rochdale 84 (0) 42. October 1986 Preston North End 5 (0) 2. August 1987 Burnley 38 (7) 6. March 1989 Rochdale 16 (1) 4.

Steve Taylor began his Football League career with Bolton Wanderers, learning his goalscoring trade at Burnden Park before making the first of many career moves. He joined Oldham Athletic in October 1977, netting twice on his debut and top-scoring in his first season at Boundary Park. Two big money transfers, involving Luton and Mansfield in a six-month spell during 1979 didn't work out for him and in the summer of 1980 he joined Burnley for a fee of £35,000. After helping them win the Third Division Championship, Taylor left to join Wigan Athletic in the summer of 1983.

He made his Latics debut in a goalless draw at Plymouth Argyle on the opening day of the 1983–84 season. Taylor, who became the club's penalty-taker, had scored 10 goals in 37 games when in March 1984 he moved on to Stockport County before joining Rochdale eight months later. In 1985–86 he returned the best goalscoring figures of his entire career, hitting 25 of Dale's 57 League goals that season. He later had a spell with Preston North End before rejoining Burnley in 1987. He appeared for the Clarets in the Sherpa Van Trophy Final before ending his League career with another spell at Rochdale. On hanging up his boots, he became manager of non-League Mossley.

Wigan Athletic Playing Record

	League		FA Cup		FL Cup		Others		Total	
	App	Gls	App	Gls	App	Gls	App	Gls	App	Gls
1983–84	29 (1)	7	4	3	2	0	1	0	36 (1)	10
TOTAL	29 (1)	7	4	3	2	0	1	0	36 (1)	10

TEALE Gary

Midfield

Born: Glasgow, 21 July 1978.
Career: June 1996 Clydebank 52 (16) 14. October 1998 Ayr United 94 (7) 13. December 2001 WIGAN ATHLETIC 65 (23) 5.

A right-sided midfield player, Glasgow-born Gary Teale began his career with Clydebank in 1996. In just over two seasons at Burnbrae, he made 77 appearances before joining Ayr United for a fee of £70,000 in October 1998. His impressive displays when he caused defenders all sorts of problems with his blistering pace and mazy runs down both flanks attracted the attention of a number of clubs. He impressed Wigan Athletic manager Paul Jewell in a pre-season friendly but he returned to Somerset Park to take his tally of goals to 18 in 121 matches before eventually joining the Latics for a fee of £200,000 in December 2001.

Gary Teale

Gary Teale is certainly at his best when running at opposition defences and though he came close to scoring on a number of occasions, his only goal of the 2001–02 season came in a 3–1 win at Notts County. During the close season it was hoped he would benefit from a course of body building exercises with Wigan Warriors Rugby League Club but he made an indifferent start to the 2002–03 campaign. Eventually though, he made the right-wing position his own and seemed to get better with each game, scoring a stunning goal in the 3–1 home victory over Chesterfield.

Midway through last season, Teale broke into the Scotland squad but after scoring two stunning goals in the away wins at Preston and Ipswich, he broke his collarbone in the game against Stoke City. On his day, Teale can leave any defence in his wake and Latics supporters hope 2004–05 will prove to be an injury-free season.

Wigan Athletic Playing Record

	League		FA Cup		FL Cup		Others		Total	
	App	Gls	App	Gls	App	Gls	App	Gls	App	Gls
2001–02	22 (1)	1	0	0	0	0	0	0	22 (1)	1
2002–03	28 (10)	2	1 (1)	0	2 (2)	0	2	2	33 (13)	4
2003–04	15 (12)	2	1	0	0 (1)	0	0	0	16 (13)	2
TOTAL	65 (23)	5	2 (1)	0	2 (3)	0	2	2	71 (27)	7

THOMPSON Christopher David

Midfield/Forward
Born: Walsall, 24 January 1960.
Career: July 1977 Bolton Wanderers 66 (7) 18. March 1983 on loan Lincoln City 5 (1) 0. August 1983 Blackburn Rovers 81 (4) 24. July 1986 WIGAN ATHLETIC 67 (7) 14. July 1988 Blackpool 27 (12) 8. March 1990 Cardiff City 1 (1) 0. February 1991 Walsall 3 (0) 0.

Chris Thompson

England youth international Chris Thompson began his Football League career with Bolton Wanderers, making his debut in the Trotters' last season in Division One in 1979–80. The Walsall-born striker switched to midfield, becoming a regular the following season. Although never a prolific scorer, he grabbed some vital goals that helped keep the Wanderers in Division Two but in March 1983 he joined Lincoln City on loan with a view to a permanent transfer. Unfortunately their promotion drive from Division Three failed and in the close season he moved to Blackburn Rovers. At Ewood Park, Thompson reverted to a striking role and in 1984–85 was Blackburn's leading scorer with 15 goals as they just missed out on promotion to Division One.

After suffering a spate of niggling injuries, Thompson joined Wigan Athletic, making his Latics debut in a 2–0 home defeat by Middlesbrough in the second game of the 1986–87 season. In only his fourth game for the club, he netted a hat-trick in a 5–1 win over Walsall, again becoming involved in a near-promotion and helping them reach the sixth round of the FA Cup. Sadly, Thompson's second season at Springfield Park was hampered by injuries and in the summer of 1988 he joined Blackpool. Though he missed very few games for the Seasiders, he left Bloomfield Road after just one season, having a brief spell with Cardiff City before ending his first-class career with his home-town club Walsall.

Wigan Athletic Playing Record

	League		FA Cup		FL Cup		Others		Total	
	App	Gls	App	Gls	App	Gls	App	Gls	App	Gls
1986–87	42 (1)	9	6	3	2	0	3	0	53 (1)	12
1987–88	25 (6)	5	1	0	2	1	1	1	29 (6)	7
TOTAL	67 (7)	14	7	3	4	1	4	1	82 (7)	19

THOMPSON David Stephen

Right-winger
Born: Manchester, 27 May 1962.
Career: North Withington. September 1981 Rochdale 147 (8) 13. August 1986 Notts County 52 (3) 8. October 1987 WIGAN ATHLETIC 107 (1) 14. July 1990 Preston North End 39 (7) 4. August 1992 Chester City 70 (10) 9. August 1994 Rochdale 90 (21) 11.

Winger Dave Thompson started out with North Withington before Rochdale gave him the chance to play in the Football League. He made his debut for the Spotland club in September 1981 and over the next five seasons or so, terrorised full-backs in the lower divisions. He left Rochdale in the summer of 1986, spending just over a season with Notts County before a £35,000 move to Wigan Athletic in October 1987. 'Tommo' made his debut for the Latics in a 3–3 home draw against Brighton and Hove Albion but suffered a knee injury and was forced to sit out the next seven games before returning to play in the final 26 games of the season. Over the next two campaigns, Dave Thompson missed few games and scored some vital goals. In March 1990 he netted his only hat-trick for the club when he scored all the Latics' goals in a 3–1 win at Shrewsbury Town. However, before the start of the following season he had been transferred to Preston North End, the Lilywhites paying £77,500 to take him to Deepdale.

He later had a spell with Chester City before rejoining his first club Rochdale in the summer of 1994. The much-travelled winger took his tally of goals for the Spotland club to 24 in 307 games before deciding to retire.

Dave Thompson

Wigan Athletic Playing Record

	League		FA Cup		FL Cup		Others		Total	
	App	Gls	App	Gls	App	Gls	App	Gls	App	Gls
1987–88	27	2	0	0	0	0	0	0	27	2
1988–89	42	7	1	0	1	0	2	1	46	8
1989–90	38 (1)	5	2 (1)	0	4	2	4	0	48 (2)	7
TOTAL	107 (1)	14	3 (1)	0	5	2	6	1	121 (2)	17

THORNE Peter Lee

Forward

Born: Manchester, 21 June 1973.

Career: June 1991 Blackburn Rovers. March 1994 on loan WIGAN ATHLETIC 10 (1) 0. January 1995 Swindon Town 66 (11) 27. July 1997 Stoke City 147 (11) 65. September 2001 Cardiff City 69 (3) 21.

Peter Thorne first signed for Blackburn Rovers as a trainee before progressing to the club's professional ranks in the summer of 1991. Despite finding the net in the club's Central League side on a regular basis, he was unable to break into the first team and in March 1994 joined the Latics on loan. He made his debut in a 1–1 home draw against Northampton Town and though he appeared in the majority of the club's games towards the end of the 1993–94 season, he failed to find the net.

He returned to Ewood Park but in January 1995 he emerged from the shadows of Alan Shearer and Chris Sutton to become an instant 'hit' at Swindon Town, whom he joined for £225,000. He grabbed two goals on his debut at Burnley and another two a week later in Town's first-leg Coca-Cola Cup semi-final against Bolton Wanderers. Though injuries hampered his progress the following season, he did enough to score 11 goals and help the Robins win the Second Division Championship. Though he continued to find the net, manager Steve McMahon chopped and changed the forward line and after refusing improved terms, Thorne joined Stoke City in the summer of 1997 for a tribunal-fixed fee of £350,000, rising to a maximum of £550,000 linked to appearances.

Back and ankle injuries disrupted his first couple of seasons at the Britannia Stadium but after that his performances were a revelation. In 1999–2000 he became the first City player for some time to net more than 20 goals, a total which included four in the home game against Chesterfield and a hat-trick at Bristol Rovers. His winning goal in the Autowindscreen Shield final typified his sharpness, answering any possible doubts about his goalscoring abilities! In 2000–01 he netted another hat-trick against Bristol Rovers and again finished the season as the Potters' leading scorer. He started the 2001–02 season by netting four goals in six games before being surprisingly sold to Cardiff City.

Injuries kept him out of action for a significant portion of the campaign but he still managed to score eight times for the Bluebirds. In 2002–03 he teamed up well with Welsh international Rob Earnshaw, the two of them scoring 50 goals. Though he didn't have his best season in front of goal, his total of 16 helped the Ninian Park club win promotion to the First Division via the play-offs.

Wigan Athletic Playing Record

	League		FA Cup		FL Cup		Others		Total	
	App	Gls	App	Gls	App	Gls	App	Gls	App	Gls
1993–94	10 (1)	0	0	0	0	0	0	0	10 (1)	0
TOTAL	10 (1)	0	0	0	0	0	0	0	10 (10	0

TIERNEY Lawrence

Midfield

Born: Leith, 4 April 1959.

Career: Heart of Midlothian. Hibernian. July 1980 WIGAN ATHLETIC 4 (3) 0.

After gaining considerable experience in Scottish League football with Heart of Midlothian and Hibernian, Leith-born midfielder Lawrence Tierney came south of the border to play for Wigan Athletic. Tierney made his Latics debut in the Football League Cup Final first round tie against Crewe Alexandra, having a helping hand in Tommy Gore's goals that gave Wigan a 2–1 win. The Scottish midfielder also had a good game in the return at Gresty Road but an unfortunate knee injury towards the end of that second leg forced him to wait before making his League bow in a 3–0 home win over Doncaster Rovers. Unfortunately that was the only time Wigan won when Tierney was in the side and at the end of the season in which the Latics finished 11th in Division Four, he was released and returned to play in Scotland.

Wigan Athletic Playing Record

	League		FA Cup		FL Cup		Others		Total	
	App	Gls	App	Gls	App	Gls	App	Gls	App	Gls
1980–81	4 (3)	0	0	0	2	0	0	0	6 (3)	0
TOTAL	4 (30	0	0	0	2	0	0	0	6 (30	0

TRAYNOR Gregory

Midfield

Born: Salford, 17 October 1984.

Career: June 2001 WIGAN ATHLETIC 0 (1) 0

Greg Traynor is one of the youngest players ever to represent the Latics in a Football League game. The first year trainee was just 16 years 305 days old when he came on as a substitute for Andy Liddell in the match against Brighton and Hove Albion at the Withdean Stadium on 18 August 2001. He went on to make his first start a couple of days later when he gave an accomplished performance in the 3–2 Worthington Cup defeat of Blackpool. A good passer of the ball with bags of potential, Traynor spent the remainder of the season developing in Wigan's reserve and youth sides. It was hoped that he would get a few more run outs in the club's first team in 2002–03 but he missed most of the season through injury.

Wigan Athletic Playing Record

	League		FA Cup		FL Cup		Others		Total	
	App	Gls	App	Gls	App	Gls	App	Gls	App	Gls
2001–02	0 (1)	0	0	0	1	0	0	0	1 (1)	0
TOTAL	0 (1)	0	0	0	1	0	0	0	1 (1)	0

TUNKS Roy William

Goalkeeper

Born: Worthing 21 January 1951.

Career: March 1968 Rotherham United 138 (0) 0. January 1969 on loan York City 4 (0) 0. November 1974 Preston North End 277 (0) 0. November 1981 WIGAN ATHLETIC 245 (0) 0. July 1988 Hartlepool United 5 (0) 0. November 1988 Preston North End 25 (0) 0.

Roy Tunks began his career as a centre-forward, captaining Worthing Boys. He was invited along for a trial for the county team and when the goalkeeper failed to turn up, volunteered to take his place! He began his Football League career with Rotherham United and made the first of 138 appearances for the Millmoor club just a few days after his 17th birthday. During his time with the Yorkshire club, he became dissatisfied and had trials with Newcastle United, Ipswich Town and York City. Eventually, in November 1974, he joined Preston North End for the knock down price of £7,000.

During his time at Deepdale, Tunks helped the Lilywhites win promotion to the Second Division but in November 1981, following the club's relegation the previous season, he left to join Wigan Athletic. Tunks made his Latics debut in a 1–1 home draw against Hereford United and kept 12 clean sheets in 31 games to help the club win promotion to the Third Division. He was ever-

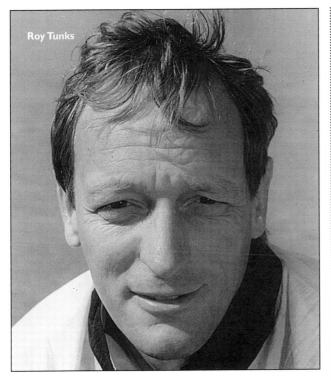
Roy Tunks

present the following season and missed very few games over the next five campaigns before leaving to join Hartlepool United. His stay at the Victoria Ground was brief and he rejoined Preston North End for a second spell towards the end of the 1988–89 season. After a career which lasted for well over 20 years, Roy Tunks now works as a coach for the Lancashire FA.

Wigan Athletic Playing Record

	League		FA Cup		FL Cup		Others		Total	
	App	Gls	App	Gls	App	Gls	App	Gls	App	Gls
1981–82	31	0	2	0	2	0	0	0	35	0
1982–83	46	0	2	0	4	0	0	0	52	0
1983–84	42	0	3	0	2	0	1	0	48	0
1984–85	40	0	4	0	4	0	6	0	54	0
1985–86	38	0	5	0	2	0	6	0	51	0
1986–87	38	0	5	0	2	0	3	0	48	0
1987–88	10	0	0	0	2	0	0	0	12	0
TOTAL	245	0	21	0	18	0	16	0	300	0

URQUHART George Stuart McWilliam

Midfield
Born: Glasgow, 22 April 1950.
Career: St Mirren. Guildford City. Ross County. July 1979 WIGAN ATHLETIC 63 (5) 6.

After playing his early football with Renfrew Juniors, Scottish amateur international midfielder George Urquhart signed for St Mirren in 1968 and eventually made his debut against Celtic's European Cup-winning side. He stayed at Love Street for three seasons but cartilage problems marred his final months with the club. After spending one season playing Southern League football for Guildford City, he returned north of the border to join Ian McNeill at Ross County. During that period, the Highland League club enjoyed its most successful spell and captured a succession of trophies.

After joining Wigan Athletic in the summer of 1979, a series of niggling injuries delayed his entry into the Latics first team. After making his League debut as a substitute for Noel Ward in a 2–1 home defeat at the hands of Portsmouth, Urquhart became a virtual ever-present in the Latics side and was a key figure in the

club's 1979–80 FA Cup run. Urquhart, who brought a cool and thoughtful approach to the game, was released at the end of the 1980–81 season.

Wigan Athletic Playing Record

	League		FA Cup		FL Cup		Others		Total	
	App	Gls	App	Gls	App	Gls	App	Gls	App	Gls
1979–80	37 (4)	4	6	0	0	0	0	0	43 (4)	4
1980–81	26 (1)	2	0	0	0	0	0	0	26 (1)	2
TOTAL	63 (5)	6	6	0	0	0	0	0	69 (5)	6

URQUHART William Murray

Forward
Born: Inverness, 22 November 1956.
Career: Inverness Caledonian. Glasgow Rangers. November 1980 WIGAN ATHLETIC 5 (5) 2. Inverness Caledonian

After impressing for his home-town club Inverness Caledonian, Billy Urquhart joined Rangers. While with the Ibrox club he won a Scottish League Cup-winners' medal against Aberdeen in 1979 and appeared for the Scottish giants in the European Cup quarter-final against Cologne. He joined Wigan Athletic in November 1980 and made his debut for the Latics in a 1–0 home defeat at the hands of Bradford City. In the following game he scored with a powerful header as the Latics beat Northampton Town 3–0. However, he soon lost his place to Peter Houghton who had been out through injury and though Urquhart netted another goal for the Latics when he came on as a substitute for Jeff Wright in a 2–1 defeat at York City, he left Springfield Park at the end of the season, returning north of the border to play for his first club Inverness Caledonian.

Wigan Athletic Playing Record

	League		FA Cup		FL Cup		Others		Total	
	App	Gls	App	Gls	App	Gls	App	Gls	App	Gls
1980–81	5 (5)	2	2	0	0	0	0	0	7 (5)	2
TOTAL	5 (5)	2	2	0	0	0	0	0	7 (5)	2

VAUGHAN John Daniel

Defender
Born: Liverpool, 18 February 1972.
Career: September 1992 Crewe Alexandra 3 (4) 0. July 1993 WIGAN ATHLETIC 2 (2) 0.

John Vaughan

Defender Danny Vaughan began his Football League career with Crewe Alexandra. Strong in the tackle, he made his debut for the Railwaymen in a 3–2 defeat at Barnet in October 1992. Unable to force his way into the Gresty Road club's side on a regular basis, he left to try his luck with the Latics in the summer of 1993. He made his Wigan debut at left-back in the second game of the 1993–94 season in a 1–1 draw against Torquay United at Plainmoor. Replaced near the end of the game by Neil Ogden after suffering a knee injury, it was another couple of weeks before he appeared in the Latics side again. Sadly, he failed to create much of an impression and during the course of he season, his registration was cancelled.

Wigan Athletic Playing Record

	League		FA Cup		FL Cup		Others		Total	
	App	Gls	App	Gls	App	Gls	App	Gls	App	Gls
1993–94	2 (2)	0	0	0	1	0	0	0	3 (2)	0
TOTAL	2 (2)	0	0	0	1	0	0	0	3 (20	0

WALSH Gary

Goalkeeper

Born: Wigan, 21 March 1968.

Career: April 1985 Manchester United 49 (1) 0. August 1988 on loan Airdrieonians 3 (0) 0. November 1993 on loan Oldham Athletic 6 (0) 0. August 1995 Middlesbrough 44 (0) 0. September 1997 Bradford City 131 (1) 0. September 2000 on loan Middlesbrough 3 (0) 0. July 2003 WIGAN ATHLETIC 1 (2) 0.

Wigan-born goalkeeper Gary Walsh came into football through the government's YTS project and signed professional forms for Manchester United in December 1986. Replacing Chris Turner midway through the 1986–87 season, he held his place in the United side for almost a year until he was concussed in a game against Sheffield Wednesday. The arrival of Jim Leighton and then Peter Schmeichel limited his appearances and after almost 10 years at Old Trafford, in which he made 63 appearances and represented England at Under-21 level, he was rescued by former United colleague Bryan Robson to provide Middlesbrough with some competition for the goalkeeping position.

However, after Alan Miller was injured after just three games of the 1995-96 season, Walsh grasped his opportunity and played in 41 consecutive games before being rested for a virus complaint towards the end of the campaign. Known to Boro fans as 'Safehands', injury and illness cost him his place the following season and on recovery he found he couldn't oust Mark Schwarzer.

After a brief loan spell with Bradford City, he joined the Bantams on a permanent basis. Making the art of goalkeeping look easy, he was the club's 'Player of the Year' in 1997–98 and had another outstanding campaign in 1998–99. Then injury – a torn cartilage that required two operations – kept him out of action for six months.

He had a brief loan spell with Middlesbrough but after three games returned to Valley Parade with a muscle tear in his thigh!

On recovery, he won back his place in the side but was unable to prevent the Yorkshire club's relegation. Continuing to be hampered by injuries, Walsh spent much of the next couple of seasons recovering from knee surgery before, having played in 144 games, he was released at the end of the 2002–03 season.

He signed a one-year deal with Wigan to act as cover for John Filan but made his first-team debut in the club's second game of the season, a League Cup game against Hull City. Walsh kept a clean sheet as the Latics ran out 2–0 winners. He also played in the third round tie against his former club Middlesbrough before making his first league start at home to Wimbledon, a match the

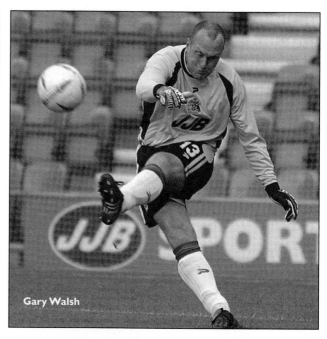

Gary Walsh

Latics lost 1–0. Despite having turned 36, Walsh has been offered a one-year extension to his existing contract.

Wigan Athletic Playing Record

	League		FA Cup		FL Cup		Others		Total	
	App	Gls	App	Gls	App	Gls	App	Gls	App	Gls
2003–04	1 (2)	0	0	0	2	0	0	0	3 (2)	0
TOTAL	1 (2)	0	0	0	2	0	0	0	3 (2)	0

WALSH Steven

Central Defender

Born: Preston, 3 November 1964.

Career: September 1982 WIGAN ATHLETIC 123 (3) 4. June 1986 Leicester City 352 (17) 53. September 2000 Norwich City 1 (3) 0. Tamworth.

After working his way up through the ranks, Steve Walsh made his first-team debut for the Latics in a 2–0 League Cup defeat at Manchester City in October 1982. He went on to appear in 31 League games that season, his first against Newport County in the unfamiliar No.11 shirt! A commanding centre-half who won more than his fair share of headers, he soon established himself at the heart of the Latics defence and in 1984–85 he helped the club win the Freight Rover Trophy beating Brentford 3–1 at Wembley. Injuries ruled him out of the first half of the following season but in the summer of 1986, he left Springfield Park, following Bryan Hamilton to Leicester City for a fee of £100,000.

One of Leicester's longest-serving players, he proved himself one of the most enigmatic during 15 years at Filbert Street. After winning the Foxes' 'Player of the Year' award in 1988, injuries began to hamper his progress but no matter who managed the Filbert Street club, Walsh remained at the heart of the defence. That is until 1993 when he was moved up front, top-scoring with 15 goals, and netted another in the play-offs against Swindon Town. A year later he scored twice against Derby County to lift City into the Premiership. After that injuries and suspensions limited his number of first-team opportunities, the latter causing him to miss the 2000 League Cup Final against Tranmere Rovers. Despite all these setbacks, Walsh stood in fifth place in all-time appearances for the club with a total of 449. However, he finally severed his connections with the Foxes in September 2000, joining former boss Bryan Hamilton at Norwich City.

Steve Walsh

Sadly injuries and other circumstances kept him out of the side and his contract was cancelled by mutual consent shortly before the turn of the year. After leaving Carrow Road, he had a brief spell with Tamworth before setting up a coaching school for local youngsters back in Leicester.

Wigan Athletic Playing Record

	League		FA Cup		FL Cup		Others		Total	
	App	Gls	App	Gls	App	Gls	App	Gls	App	Gls
1982–83	31	0	0	0	1	0	0	0	32	0
1983–84	42	1	3	0	2	0	1	0	48	1
1984–85	40	2	3	0	3	0	7	0	53	2
1985–86	10 (3)	1	0	0	0	0	0 (1)	0	10 (4)	1
TOTAL	123 (3)	4	6	0	6	0	8 (1)	0	143 (4)	4

WARD Anthony

Winger
Born: Warrington, 4 April 1970.
Career: June 1988 Everton. December 1988 on loan Doncaster Rovers 4 (0) 0. June 1989 WIGAN ATHLETIC 8 (3) 2. Chorley.

Anthony Ward joined Everton as a trainee but despite some favourable reviews in the club's Central League side, he couldn't make the breakthrough into the Toffees' first team. In December 1988 he went on loan to Doncaster Rovers, getting his first taste of League football in a 2–2 draw at Tranmere Rovers. He returned to Goodison Park before joining Wigan Athletic in the summer of 1989. He made his debut in a 3–2 defeat at home to Bolton Wanderers and though he didn't figure in the next two games, he had a run of seven games in which he scored two goals later in the season. Unable to force his way into the Wigan side on a more regular basis, he left Springfield Park to play non-League football for Chorley.

Wigan Athletic Playing Record

	League		FA Cup		FL Cup		Others		Total	
	App	Gls	App	Gls	App	Gls	App	Gls	App	Gls
1989–90	8 (3)	2	1	0	0	0	1	0	10 (3)	2
TOTAL	8 (3)	2	1	0	0	0	1	0	10 (3)	2

WARD Mark William

Winger
Born: Huyton, 10 October 1962.
Career: September 1980 Everton. Northwich Victoria. July 1983 Oldham Athletic 84 (0) 12. August 1985 West Ham United 163 (2) 12. December 1989 Manchester City 55 (0) 14. August 1991 Everton 82 (1) 6. March 1994 Birmingham City 63 (0) 7. March 1996
Huddersfield Town 7 (1) 0. September 1996 WIGAN ATHLETIC 5 (0) 0. Leigh RMI.

Mark Ward

After being released by Everton in the summer of 1981 without having played in the club's League side, Mark Ward joined Northwich Victoria and represented the England semi-professional side before signing for Oldham Athletic in August 1983. He made his debut for the Boundary Park club on the opening day of the 1983–84 season, scoring the only goal of the game. An ever-present for two seasons at Oldham, he joined West Ham United for £250,000 in the summer of 1985.

He was an ever-present again in his first season with the Hammers as the club finished third in the First Division. He played in 131 consecutive games from his Football League debut. Creating a number of goals for Tony Cottee and Frank McAvennie, he stayed over four years at Upton Park, hardly missing a game until he was injured in November 1988. Disciplinary problems began to disrupt his appearances and form and following the club's relegation in 1989–90, he moved to Maine Road to play for Manchester City. Ward was only with City for 18 months and in the 1991 close season he was allowed to rejoin Everton, the club that discarded him 10 years earlier.

He later joined Birmingham City as player-coach and after winning Second Division and Autowindscreen Shield medals, he was named by his fellow professionals at the PFA awards night as the division's leading player in his position. Injuries then plagued his career and after a brief spell with Huddersfield Town, he joined Wigan Athletic on a free transfer in September 1996. After making his debut in a 3–1 defeat at Scarborough, he spent a month as a non-contract player at Springfield Park. Unfortunately a hand injury sustained in the 3–2 win over Torquay United ended his spell with the club and after playing a few games for Leigh RMI, he managed Altrincham before being sacked.

Wigan Athletic Playing Record

	League		FA Cup		FL Cup		Others		Total	
	App	Gls	App	Gls	App	Gls	App	Gls	App	Gls
1996–97	5	0	0	0	0	0	0	0	5	0
TOTAL	5	0	0	0	0	0	0	0	5	0

WARD Noel Gerard

Central Defender

Born: Strabane, 8 December 1952.
Career: Derry City. Portadown. Aberdeen. July 1976 WIGAN ATHLETIC 47 (1) 4.

On leaving school in Strabane, Northern Ireland, Noel Ward served an apprenticeship as a fitter and played mostly Gaelic football for two years. After playing in a works' match, Ward went to Derry City on trial and having signed as an amateur, he was selected to play for the Irish youth side against Scotland. He also played in Texaco Cup games and appeared in the Irish Cup Final. Derry City went defunct because of the Troubles and Ward signed for Portadown as a semi-professional. Yet after less than a year, he joined Aberdeen. He made a number of first-team appearances for the Dons, proving his versatility by playing in the back four, up front as a target man and in his last season with the club, as a goalkeeper for the reserves! Following the arrival of Ally MacLeod as manager, Ward was given a free transfer and joined Wigan Athletic.

After two seasons playing for the Latics in the Northern Premier League and helping them finish runners-up in 1977–78, Ward made his Football League debut at centre-half in the club's first match, a goalless draw at Hereford United. Missing just two games in that first season in Division Four, he scored a number of valuable goals including both Wigan's goals in a 2–1 defeat of Huddersfield Town. Appointed club captain and having gained selection for the Northern Ireland squad, he sustained a nasty fracture to his right leg in the game against Portsmouth in September 1979. The big fellow's height, mobility and all-round ability, particularly at set pieces, were sorely missed and at the end of the season he was forced to retire. Nowadays, Noel Ward is a supermarket manager in the town and is a regular visitor to the JJB Stadium.

Wigan Athletic Playing Record

	League		FA Cup		FL Cup		Others		Total	
	App	Gls	App	Gls	App	Gls	App	Gls	App	Gls
1978–79	44	4	2	0	2	0	0	0	48	4
1979–80	3 (1)	0	0	0	2	0	0	0	5 (1)	0
TOTAL	47 (1)	4	2	0	4	0	0	0	53 (1)	4

WARD Robert Andrew

Goalkeeper

Born: West Bromwich, 4 August 1953.
Career: Imperial Star. March 1973 West Bromwich Albion 9 (0) 0. February 1977 on loan Northampton Town 8 (0) 0. September 1977 Blackpool 41 (0) 0. July 1979 WIGAN ATHLETIC 46 (0) 0.

Goalkeeper Bob Ward began his Football League career with his home-town club, West Bromwich Albion, making his debut as a 19-year-old against Sheffield Wednesday. However, much of his time at the Hawthorns was spent in the club's Central League side and after a brief loan spell with Northampton Town, he joined Blackpool for £20,000. No sooner had he arrived at Bloomfield Road than the Seasiders had been drawn away to his former club in the third round of the FA Cup. On a memorable day at the Hawthorns in front of a 21,306 crowd, Ward had an outstanding game, though the joy of the occasion was dampened by the result, a 4–1 defeat for Blackpool. A regular in the Seasiders' team for a couple of seasons, he lost his place to Iain Hesford before moving to Wigan Athletic in the summer of 1980.

He replaced the injured John Brown for the visit of Bury and

had a good game in a 2–1 win. Apart from a three-game spell at the end of November 1980 when he was injured, Ward was a virtual ever-present. He had appeared in nine matches of the club's promotion-winning season of 1981–82 when he lost his place to Roy Tunks. His playing career was ended by a bad back injury. After qualifying as a physiotherapist, he has worked in that capacity for Blackpool and Chelsea and is currently at Middlesbrough.

Wigan Athletic Playing Record

	League		FA Cup		FL Cup		Others		Total	
	App	Gls	App	Gls	App	Gls	App	Gls	App	Gls
1980–81	37	0	0	0	0	0	0	0	37	0
1981–82	9	0	0	0	2	0	0	0	11	0
TOTAL	46	0	0	0	2	0	0	0	48	0

WARNE Paul

Forward

Born: Norwich, 8 May 1973.
Career: Wroxham. July 1997 WIGAN ATHLETIC 11 (25) 3. January 1999 Rotherham United 137 (34) 26

A prolific scorer for one of then Wigan manager John Deehan's former clubs, non-League Wroxham, Paul Warne joined the Latics in the summer of 1997, making his debut as a substitute at Bristol Rovers in the fourth game of the 1997–98 season. His first League start soon followed and he netted the only goal of the game at Blackpool where his strike was later voted the 'Away goal of the season' by Latics supporters. The majority of Warne's appearances that season were from the bench and though he was quick around the penalty box, he still couldn't hold down a regular place in the Latics side. Having scored against Rotherham United in the Autowindscreen Shield, he joined the Millers on loan before the move became permanent in January 1999.

He soon became a big favourite, scoring five goals in his first four games and forming an excellent striking partnership with Leo Fortune-West. He played his part in the Yorkshire club's promotion to Division One in 2000–01 when he was named the Millers' 'Player of the Year'. After being an automatic choice for two seasons, he found himself down the pecking order in 2001–02, though he missed the early part of the campaign through injury. Still with the Millers, he has proved himself a good club man, always willing to tackle any job asked of him with maximum effort.

Wigan Athletic Playing Record

	League		FA Cup		FL Cup		Others		Total	
	App	Gls	App	Gls	App	Gls	App	Gls	App	Gls
1997–98	3 (22)	2	0	0	0	0	0 (2)	0	3 (24)	2
1998–99	8 (3)	1	1	0	0 (1)	0	1	1	10 (4)	2
TOTAL	11 (25)	3	1	0	0 (1)	0	1 (2)	1	13 (28)	4

WEST Paul Darrell

Defender

Born: Stafford, 22 June 1970.
Career: Alcester Town. February 1991 Port Vale. July 1992 Bradford City. August 1993 WIGAN ATHLETIC 2 (1) 0. Morecambe.

Paul West played for Alcester Town before joining Port Vale on trial in January 1991. He was signed permanently for £1,800 the following month but was unable to break into the Valiants' team and was given a free transfer in May 1992. Moving to Bradford

Paul West

City, he spent a season in the Bantams' reserve side before solid displays at the heart of the defence prompted Wigan manager Kenny Swain to bring him to Springfield Park. West made his Football League debut as a substitute for Mick Kennedy in a 2–1 win at Rochdale in the fourth game of the 1993–94 season. He kept his place for the Latics next game at Doncaster Rovers but was substituted later in the proceedings. A series of niggling injuries and the form of Peter Skipper and Alan Johnson prevented him from making further first-team appearances. Able to play at full-back or as a sweeper, he appeared in Wigan's opening game of the 1994–95 season but sadly suffered serious knee ligament damage and he was released at the end of the season and joined Morecambe.

Wigan Athletic Playing Record

	League		FA Cup		FL Cup		Others		Total	
	App	Gls	App	Gls	App	Gls	App	Gls	App	Gls
1993–94	1 (1)	0	0	0	1	0	0	0	2 (1)	0
1994–95	1	0	0	0	0	0	0	0	1	0
TOTAL	2 (1)	0	0	0	1	0	0	0	3 (1)	0

WESTON James John

Midfield
Born: Prescot, 16 September 1955.
Career: Skelmersdale United. January 1974 Blackpool 97 (8) 8. June 1980 Torquay United 38 (0) 1. September 1981 WIGAN ATHLETIC 63 (3) 2.

Always aware that professional football can be a short career, Jimmy Weston opted not to go into it when he left school, opting instead to be an engineer, entering a factory and studying on day release. However, while playing for the factory team, he was spotted by a scout from Coventry City. He was talked into spending a month with the Sky Blues but quickly returned to his native Liverpool because he was homesick. He agreed to play part-time for Skelmersdale United but his talents were spotted again and at the age of 18 he joined Blackpool.

He made his League debut for the Seasiders as a substitute in a 1–0 home win over Notts County in November 1975, going on to play in 115 games for the Bloomfield Road club over the next five seasons. In June 1980, Weston joined Torquay United but after two seasons at Plainmoor, he returned to the north-west to play for Wigan Athletic. Weston made his Latics debut in a goalless draw at Bournemouth in September 1981, going on to appear in 25 games as the club won promotion to the Third Division. Though he only scored one goal, it proved to be the winner as the Latics beat Darlington 2–1. The following season Weston, who appeared in seven different outfield positions, played on a more regular basis but at the end of the campaign, he decided to retire and enter the world of accountancy, for which he had been training part-time throughout his playing career.

Wigan Athletic Playing Record

	League		FA Cup		FL Cup		Others		Total	
	App	Gls	App	Gls	App	Gls	App	Gls	App	Gls
1981–82	22 (3)	1	2	0	0	0	0	0	24 (3)	1
1982–83	41	1	2	0	3	0	0	0	46	1
TOTAL	63 (3)	2	4	0	3	0	0	0	70 (3)	2

WHITE Eric Winston

Winger
Born: Leicester, 26 October 1958.
Career: October 1976 Leicester City 10 (2) 1. March 1979 Hereford United 169 (6) 21. Hong Kong. September 1983 Chesterfield 0 (1) 0. October 1983 Port vale 0 (1) 0. November 1983 Stockport County 4 (0) 0. December 1983 Bury 125 (0) 11. October 1986 on loan Rochdale 4 (0) 0. February 1987 Colchester United 64 (1) 8. October 1988 Burnley 93 (11) 14. March 1991 West Bromwich Albion 13 (3) 1. October 1992 Bury 1 (1) 0. January 1993 Doncaster Rovers 4 (0) 2. February 1993 Carlisle United 6 (0) 0. March 1993 WIGAN ATHLETIC 10 (0) 1.

A speedy, orthodox winger, Winston White's career spanned three decades and more than 500 League games for 13 different clubs! After joining his home-town club Leicester City, he appeared briefly in the First Division for the Foxes, scoring the only goal of his top flight career at Anfield in April 1978. He joined Hereford United for £15,000 in March 1979 and was a virtual ever-present in a four-year stay at Edgar Street. After the club finished bottom of the Fourth Division, White went to play in Hong Kong before returning to England to appear briefly as a non-contract player with Chesterfield, Port Vale and Stockport County before signing for Bury in December 1983. He was ever-present in 1984–85 as the Shakers won promotion to Division Three. However, following a loan spell at Rochdale, White joined Colchester United before signing for Burnley in October 1988. A regular during his time at Turf Moor, he was surprisingly transferred to West Bromwich Albion on deadline day in March 1991 for £35,000. He was released by Albion in October 1992 and later appeared for short spells as a non-contract player with Bury, Doncaster Rovers and Carlisle United.

His final League club was Wigan Athletic whom he joined in March 1993, also as a non-contract player. He made his debut for the Latics in a 2–1 win at Leyton Orient before scoring the game's only goal on his home debut against Hull City. He appeared in the final 10 games of the 1992–93 season but couldn't prevent the

Latics from relegation to the Third Division. Released at the end of the season, he returned to live in Burnley where he has been busy coaching and passing on some of the skills he acquired during his years in the game.

Wigan Athletic Playing Record

	League		FA Cup		FL Cup		Others		Total	
	App	Gls	App	Gls	App	Gls	App	Gls	App	Gls
1992–93	10	1	0	0	0	0	0	0	10	1
TOTAL	10	1	0	0	0	0	0	0	10	1

WHITEHEAD Alan

Central Defender

Born: Bury, 20 November 1956.

Career: Darwen. December 1977 Bury 98 (1) 13. August 1981 Brentford 101 (1) 4. January 1984 Scunthorpe United 106 (2) 8. October 1986 York City 40 (1) 0. March 1987 on loan WIGAN ATHLETIC 2 (0) 0. August 1988 Halifax Town 10 (0) 1.

Alan Whitehead

Alan Whitehead joined his home-town club Bury from non-League Darwen in December 1977 and over the next three-and-a-half seasons, was a virtual ever-present in the Shakers' side. In the summer of 1981 he joined Brentford and in his first two seasons at Griffin Park, his performances at the heart of the Bees' defence almost helped the club win promotion to the Second Division. In January 1984, Whitehead was transferred to Scunthorpe United and though he continued to dominate the majority of opposing forwards, he couldn't prevent the Irons from being relegated in his first season at the Old Show Ground. Whitehead moved to York City in the early part of the 1986–87 season, but before the campaign was over, he joined Wigan Athletic on loan.

After making his debut in a 2–1 win at Newport County, Whitehead struggled with injuries and only managed one more

appearance in a goalless draw at Middlesbrough before returning to Bootham Crescent. The well-travelled central defender later ended his League career with Halifax Town.

Wigan Athletic Playing Record

	League		FA Cup		FL Cup		Others		Total	
	App	Gls	App	Gls	App	Gls	App	Gls	App	Gls
1986–87	2	0	0	0	0	0	0	0	2	0
TOTAL	2	0	0	0	0	0	0	0	2	0

WHITNEY Jonathan David

Left-back

Born: Nantwich, 23 December 1970.

Career: Skelmersdale United. Winsford United. October 1993 Huddersfield Town 17 (1) 0. March 1995 on loan WIGAN ATHLETIC 12 (0) 0. October 1995 Lincoln City 98 (3) 8. February 1998 Hull City 54 (3) 3. King's Lynn.

Jonathan Whitney

Jonathan Whitney began his career with Stalybridge Celtic before joining Cheshire League side Winsford United. In October 1993, Huddersfield Town bought him for £10,000. The hard-tackling left-back's progress at Leeds Road was cut short by a knee ligament injury and in a bid to recover full fitness, he was loaned out to Wigan Athletic in March 1995. His first game in Latics colours came at Chesterfield where he gave a polished performance in a goalless draw. He went on to appear in the final 12 games of the 1994–95 season before rejoining the Terriers. Interestingly, it was Whitney's second spell at Springfield Park, having been there as a trainee.

Finding it difficult to establish himself at Huddersfield, he moved to Lincoln City where in his first season at Sincil Bank, he scored a number of spectacular long-range goals. Unfortunately he damaged a cruciate knee ligament, an injury which put him out of the game for over 12 months. He returned to action in readiness for the start of the 1997–98 season and was instrumental in the club winning promotion to the Second Division. However, in December 1998, he became one of a number of Hull City's pre-Christmas signings and was one of the heroes of the Tigers' 'Great Escape'. He later began studying to qualify as a physiotherapist but left Hull in February 2002 to play non-League football for King's Lynn.

Wigan Athletic Playing Record

	League		FA Cup		FL Cup		Others		Total	
	App	Gls	App	Gls	App	Gls	App	Gls	App	Gls
1994–95	12	0	0	0	0	0	0	0	12	0
TOTAL	12	0	0	0	0	0	0	0	12	0

WHITTAKER Stuart

Winger
Born: Liverpool, 2 January 1975.
Career: Liverpool. May 1993 Bolton Wanderers 2 (1) 0. August 1996 on loan WIGAN ATHLETIC 2 (1) 0. August 1997 Macclesfield Town 29 (2) 4. Altrincham.

Winger Stuart Whittaker started his career with Liverpool, joining the Anfield club as a YTS after representing Sefton Schools in a midfield role. He played regularly in their Lancashire League side and won a Championship medal at that level while at Anfield. He was released in 1993 and joined Bolton Wanderers. The tricky winger became a regular in the club's reserve side before making his Football League debut in an unfamiliar No.9 shirt in a 2–1 win over Luton Town. He kept his place for the final game of the 1993–94 season, a 3–2 defeat at the hands of Burnley. He was a member of the Bolton reserves' Championship-winning side of 1994–95 but after that he struggled to make the Wanderers' first team and in the summer of 1996 he joined Wigan Athletic on loan.

He made his Latics debut in a 4–2 home win over Chester City, a match in which Graeme Jones netted a hat-trick, but he was substituted in the two matches he started. He returned to Burnden Park before, on being released, he joined Macclesfield on a free transfer. In 1997–98 he helped the Silkmen win promotion to the Second Division and continued to impress the following season in the higher grade of football. Unable to regain form and fitness after a groin operation, he was freed by Macclesfield and went on trial with Conference club Altrincham.

Wigan Athletic Playing Record

	League		FA Cup		FL Cup		Others		Total	
	App	Gls	App	Gls	App	Gls	App	Gls	App	Gls
1996–97	2 (1)	0	0	0	0	0	0	0	2 (1)	0
TOTAL	2 (1)	0	0	0	0	0	0	0	2 (1)	0

WHITTLE Maurice

Left-back
Born: Wigan, 15 July 1948.
Career: July 1966 Blackburn Rovers 5 (2) 0. May 1969 Oldham Athletic 307 (5) 39. Fort Lauderdale Strikers. October 1977 WIGAN ATHLETIC. Southport. Barrow. March 1980 WIGAN ATHLETIC 21 (0) 1. Barrow.

After beginning his career with Blackburn Rovers, Maurice Whittle found it difficult to progress at Ewood Park and after making seven League appearances, made the comparatively short trip to Boundary Park, Oldham, where his career really took off. After switching from wing-half to full-back he became a major attraction with his positive attacking runs and powerful left-foot shooting, earning the plaudits of the Oldham fans. He won a Third Division Championship medal in 1973–74 but it wasn't long before he went to play for Fort Lauderdale Strikers in the NASL.

He won an Eastern Division Championship medal with Fort Lauderdale and came face to face on the field of play with the great international stars of the soccer world, among them, Pelé. His contract with Oldham Athletic was cancelled in October 1977 and for a three-month period he played a major part in the transformation of Wigan Athletic from an ambitious non-League club to undisputed challengers for Football League status. It was Maurice Whittle whose strike from a direct free-kick gave the Latics a 1–0 victory over Sheffield Wednesday – a win that meant a third-round FA Cup tie against Birmingham City and national exposure which eventually led to Wigan joining the Football League in 1978.

Whittle eventually left Springfield Park for a second stint at Fort Lauderdale before returning to play non-League football for Southport and Barrow prior to rejoining Wigan in March 1980 to fill the spot left by the departure of Joe Hinnigan to Sunderland. Whittle made his League bow for the Latics in a 2–1 home win over Aldershot, scoring his only goal for the club at this level in a 2–2 draw at Torquay United. On leaving Springfield Park a second time, he rejoined Barrow.

Wigan Athletic Playing Record

	League		FA Cup		FL Cup		Others		Total	
	App	Gls	App	Gls	App	Gls	App	Gls	App	Gls
1979–80	17	1	0	0	0	0	0	0	17	1
1980–81	4	0	0	0	4	0	0	0	8	0
TOTAL	21	1	0	0	4	0	0	0	25	1

WHITWORTH Neil Anthony

Central Defender
Born: Wigan, 12 April 1972.
Career: May 1988 WIGAN ATHLETIC 1 (1) 0. July 1990 Manchester United 1 (0) 0. January 1992 on loan Preston North End 6 (0) 0. February 1992 on loan Barnsley 11 (0) 0. October 1993 on loan Rotherham United 8 (0) 1. December 1993 on loan Blackpool 3 (0) 0. September 1994 Kilmarnock 74 (1) 3. March 1998 on loan WIGAN ATHLETIC 1 (3) 0. July 1998 Hull City 18 (1) 2. August 2000 Exeter City 53 (4) 1.

Signed as a trainee by Wigan Athletic in the summer of 1988, Neil Whitworth made his Football League debut in a 2–0 home defeat at the hands of Leyton Orient in February 1990. After just one more appearance as a substitute he was transferred to Manchester United for £45,000 before he had signed a professional contract for the Latics. After making his United debut at right-back in a match at Southampton in March 1991, Whitworth was loaned out to a number of clubs, namely Preston North End, Barnsley, Rotherham United and Blackpool before a £265,000 transfer took him to Kilmarnock. After four seasons in the Scottish Premier League, Whitworth was released and rejoined the Latics on a short-term contract. He made his second debut for Wigan when he came on as a substitute in a 1–0 home victory over Oldham Athletic but he made just one League start before being released at the end of the 1997–98 season.

Whitworth then joined Hull City, but after just a handful of games, he picked up a troublesome Achilles tendon injury. Following surgery, the ankle joint became infected and this led to another operation and rehabilitation at the National Sports Centre at Lilleshall before being released by the Tigers. He then joined Exeter City for the 2001–02 season but was mainly used as cover for suspensions and injuries. The powerful defender was still unable to hold down a regular place in the Grecians side the following season, but his cause was not helped by the various changes in management at St James' Park during the campaign.

Wigan Athletic Playing Record

	League		FA Cup		FL Cup		Others		Total	
	App	Gls	App	Gls	App	Gls	App	Gls	App	Gls
1989–90	I (I)	0	0	0	0	0	0	0	I (I)	0
1997–98	I (30	0	0	0	0	0	0	0	I (3)	0
TOTAL	2 (4)	0	0	0	0	0	0	0	2 (40	0

WIDDRINGTON Thomas

Midfield

Born: Newcastle, 1 October 1971.
Career: May 1990 Southampton 67 (8) 3. September 1991 on loan WIGAN ATHLETIC 5 (1) 0. July 1996 Grimsby Town 72 (17) 8. March 1999 Port Vale 77 (5) 8. July 2001 Hartlepool United 50 (6) 5. July 2003 Macclesfield Town.

Tommy Widdrington was yet another north-easterner on Southampton's books. While still awaiting a first-team opportunity and in order to gain experience, he had a spell on loan at Wigan Athletic early in 1991–92, making his Football League debut for the Latics at Springfield Park against Hull City. He proved a versatile player, operating at full-back, in central defence and in midfield during his eight games for Wigan. After returning to the Dell, he made his Saints debut, deputising for Alan Shearer in the match at Everton. Moving from midfield, he began to play as a sweeper or just in front of the back four, covering the midfield players making forward runs but in July 1996, after appearing in 90 games for the south-coast club, he became Grimsby Town's £300,000 record signing.

Injuries hampered his progress during his early days at Blundell Park and he struggled to hold down a regular spot in the side. After appearing not to figure in Grimsby manager Alan Buckley's long-term plans, he joined Port Vale on loan before signing on a permanent basis in the summer of 1999. He soon ran into problems at his new club when he was dismissed on his debut against Birmingham City but bounced back to not only establish himself as a first-team regular, but also to win the supporters' 'Player of the Year' award. Surprisingly he was allowed to leave Vale Park in the summer of 2001 and joined Hartlepool United. Hoping to add bite and experience to the side, his campaign was just taking off when he received a hamstring injury which brought his season to a premature end. Having been sidelined for over six months, he recovered to help Hartlepool win promotion in 2002–03 but was then released by manager Mike Newell and joined Macclesfield Town.

Wigan Athletic Playing Record

	League		FA Cup		FL Cup		Others		Total	
	App	Gls	App	Gls	App	Gls	App	Gls	App	Gls
1991–92	5 (I)	0	0	0	2	0	0	0	7 (I)	0
TOTAL	5 (I)	0	0	0	2	0	0	0	7 (I)	0

WIGNALL Mark

Midfield

Born: Preston, 6 December 1962.
Career: December 1980 WIGAN ATHLETIC 34 (0) 0.

Preston-born midfielder Mark Wignall began his career as an associate schoolboy with Blackpool before joining the Latics in December 1980. After a series of impressive displays for the club's reserve side, he made his League debut for Wigan in a 3–1 home win over Darlington in February 1981. He became an overnight favourite of the sometimes critical Latics' crowd, who appreciated his skill, endeavour and courage in getting to grips with more physically endowed opponents.

During the club's promotion-winning season of 1981–82, Wignall played in 25 games and was only on the losing side three times.

An important member of the side that reached the fourth round of the League Cup, he had his best game for the Latics in a 4–2 defeat of Second Division Chelsea. The 18–year-old chipped his first-ever senior goal from over 20 yards over Steve Francis and the Chelsea goalkeeper was again helpless when the same player scored with an arrowing drive from five yards further out. Sadly, injuries then restricted his first-team appearances and he later drifted into non-League football.

Wigan Athletic Playing Record

	League		FA Cup		FL Cup		Others		Total	
	App	Gls	App	Gls	App	Gls	App	Gls	App	Gls
1980–81	9	0	0	0	0	0	0	0	9	0
1981–82	25	0	2	0	4	2	0	0	31	2
TOTAL	34	0	2	0	4	2	0	0	40	2

WILKIE John Carlin

Forward

Born: Dundee, 1 July 1947.
Career: Arbroath. Morton. Ross County. February 1973 Halifax Town 29 (8) 8. Ross County. Elgin City. August 1976 WIGAN ATHLETIC 3 (1) 0.

Dundee-born forward John Wilkie played his early football for Douglas Amateurs, eventually gaining selection for the Scottish Amateur XI. On turning 17, Wilkie joined Arbroath and spent four seasons at Gayfield Park, helping the club win promotion to the Scottish First Division. On leaving Arbroath, Wilkie joined Morton, later playing for Ross County and Ian McNeill. John Wilkie tried his hand in the Football League with Halifax Town but after two years at the Shay he rejoined Ross County and subsequently Elgin City.

After Ian McNeill had moved south of the border to manage Wigan Athletic, Wilkie followed him and for two seasons he was the Latics' leading goalscorer in the Northern Premier League as well as playing a prominent part in the club's FA Cup games against York City, Sheffield Wednesday and Birmingham City. He made his League debut for the Latics in the club's inaugural game at Hereford United but after just four appearances in a Wigan shirt in the Football League, a niggling foot injury kept him side-lined for a lengthy period. Unable to win back his first-team place, he had a spell playing non-League football before working as a chartered accountant. Wilkie is now living in Rhyl, working on holiday parks.

Wigan Athletic Playing Record

	League		FA Cup		FL Cup		Others		Total	
	App	Gls	App	Gls	App	Gls	App	Gls	App	Gls
1978–79	3 (I)	0	0	0	3	0	0	0	6 (I)	0
TOTAL	3 (I)	0	0	0	3	0	0	0	6 (I)	0

WILLIAMS John William

Central Defender

Born: Liverpool, 3 October 1960.

Career: October 1979 Tranmere Rovers 167 (6) 12. July 1985 Port Vale 50 (0) 3. December 1986 Bournemouth 115 (2) 9. October 1991 on loan WIGAN ATHLETIC 4 (0) 0. December 1991 Cardiff City 5 (1) 0.

Tall central defender John Williams began his Football League career with Tranmere Rovers, making his debut in a 4–1 defeat at Swindon Town in March 1979. Over the next two seasons, Williams made just a handful of appearances but in 1980–81 he established himself at the heart of the Tranmere defence and over the next five seasons missed very few games. He went on to score 13 goals in 201 League and Cup games before leaving Prenton Park in July 1985 to join Port Vale for £12,000.

In his first season at Vale Park he helped the club win promotion to the Third Division, but after losing form the following campaign he was allowed to join Bournemouth. An important member of the Dean Court side, he suffered a bad knee injury after which he joined Wigan Athletic on loan. His first game in Latics colours was a 3–3 draw at Birmingham City in October 1991 followed by victories over Exeter City (home 4–1) and Swansea City (home 1–0), but after Wigan were beaten 4–0 at Brentford, he returned to Dean Court before ending his League career with Cardiff City. Williams later returned to Bournemouth as the Community Development Officer before becoming the Cherries' assistant manager.

Wigan Athletic Playing Record

	League		FA Cup		FL Cup		Others		Total	
	App	Gls	App	Gls	App	Gls	App	Gls	App	Gls
1991–92	4	0	0	0	0	0	0	0	4	0
TOTAL	4	0	0	0	0	0	0	0	4	0

WILLIAMS Philip James

Midfield

Born: Swansea, 7 February 1963.

Career: Arsenal. November 1980 Blackpool. Atlanta Chiefs. August 1981 Crewe Alexandra 39 (0) 3. August 1982 WIGAN ATHLETIC 1 (2) 0. September 1983 on loan Chester City 5 (1) 0. December 1983 Crewe Alexandra 14 (6) 3. Northwich Victoria.

The son of Welsh international winger Graham Williams, Phil played his early football for Arsenal, for whom he signed apprentice forms. It was while he was at Highbury that he experienced one of the best moments of his career, representing the Wales Under-18 side in a 2–0 victory over England at Portman Road. He followed Alan Ball from Highbury to Bloomfield Road after the World Cup winner had left to manage the Seasiders. Despite some gutsy performances in Blackpool's Central League side, he was unable to make the grade and left to play for Atlanta Chiefs in the United States.

On his return to these shores he joined Crewe Alexandra, but after one season with the Railwaymen he moved to Wigan Athletic. He made his debut for the Latics as a substitute for Eamonn O'Keefe in a 1–0 home defeat by Portsmouth and when he made his full debut five months later, the Latics again lost 1–0, this time to Orient. His third appearance in Wigan colours at the beginning of the 1983–84 season also resulted in a home defeat as the Latics lost 2–0 to Oxford United.

On leaving Springfield Park, Williams, who had a loan spell with Chester City, ended his League career with his former club, Crewe Alexandra, before playing non-League football with Northwich Victoria.

Wigan Athletic Playing Record

	League		FA Cup		FL Cup		Others		Total	
	App	Gls	App	Gls	App	Gls	App	Gls	App	Gls
1982–83	1 (1)	0	2	0	1	0	0	0	4 (1)	0
1983–84	0 (1)	0	0	0	0	0	0	0	0 (1)	0
TOTAL	1 (2)	0	2	0	1	0	0	0	4 (2)	0

WILSON Andrew William

Midfield

Born: Wigan, 7 January 1965.

Career: Skelmersdale United. August 1987 WIGAN ATHLETIC 1 (1) 0.

Midfielder Andy Wilson was playing for Skelmersdale United when manager Ray Mathias secured his services in the summer of 1987. Though his performances for the club's reserve side were quite impressive, he had to wait until December 1987 before making his Football League debut against Northampton Town. Wearing the No.2 shirt in place of the injured John Butler, he gave a solid display but his only other appearance in the Latics side came the following season when as a substitute he replaced Andy Pilling in a 2–0 home defeat at the hands of Huddersfield Town. Unable to make more of an impression, he was allowed to leave Springfield Park in the close season.

Wigan Athletic Playing Record

	League		FA Cup		FL Cup		Others		Total	
	App	Gls	App	Gls	App	Gls	App	Gls	App	Gls
1987–88	1	0	0	0	0	0	0	0	1	0
1988–89	0 (1)	0	0	0	0	0	0	0	0 (1)	0
TOTAL	1 (1)	0	0	0	0	0	0	0	1 (1)	0

WILSON Ian William

Midfield

Born: Aberdeen, 27 March 1958.

Career: Elgin City. April 1979 Leicester City 276 (9) 17. September 1987 Everton 24 (10) 1. Besikitas, Turkey. February 1991 Derby County 11 (0) 0. August 1991 Bury 21 (3) 1. August 1992 WIGAN ATHLETIC 5 (0) 0. Petershead.

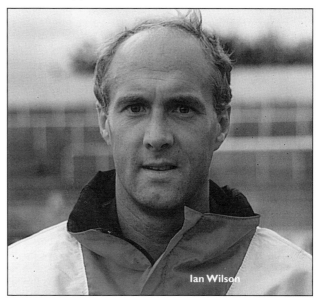

Ian Wilson

A constructive and combative midfielder, Ian Wilson was playing Highland League football for Elgin City before a £30,000 transfer took him to Leicester City. A key member of both Jock Wallace and Gordon Milne's promotion sides, he impressed most in the latter, adopting an advanced role which saw him coming in late behind Lineker and Smith and claiming his fair tally of goals. Belated but deserved international recognition came his way when he followed his call-up at 'B' level in April 1987 with two full Scottish caps a month later.

In August 1989 he left Filbert Street for Everton for a fee of £300,000. He picked up an FA Cup runners-up medal as a Wembley substitute for the Toffees before rejoining Gordon Milne as Besikitas in Turkey. Here he won both League and Cup medals as Besikitas achieved the domestic double for the first time ever in 1990. On his return to England, he had spells with Derby County and Bury, both of whom were relegated! In August 1992 he had a brief non-contract spell under Bryan Hamilton at Wigan, making his debut in a 3–2 home defeat at the hands of Swansea City. He then returned to the Highland League to play for Petershead before becoming assistant-manager to Gordon Milne at Nagoya Grampus Eight in Japan.

Wigan Athletic Playing Record

	League		FA Cup		FL Cup		Others		Total	
	App	Gls	App	Gls	App	Gls	App	Gls	App	Gls
1992–93	5	0	0	0	0 (1)	0	0	0	5 (1)	0
TOTAL	5	0	0	0	0 (1)	0	0	0	5 (1)	0

WOODS Neil Stephen

Forward
Born: York, 30 July 1966.
Career: August 1983 Doncaster Rovers 55 (10) 16. December 1986 Glasgow Rangers 0 (3) 0. August 1987 Ipswich Town 15 (12) 5. March 1990 Bradford City 13 (1) 2. August 1990 Grimsby Town 175 (51) 42. November 1997 on loan WIGAN ATHLETIC 1 (0) 0. January 1998 on loan Scunthorpe United 2 (0) 0. February 1998 Mansfield Town 5 (1) 0. July 1998 York City 5 (3) 0. Southport.

A right-footed playmaker, adept at holding, shielding and laying off the ball, Neil Woods began his career with Doncaster Rovers where his impressive displays led to a £120,000 move to Glasgow Rangers in December 1986. Unable to make much impression at Ibrox, he joined Ipswich Town for a similar fee in the summer of 1987. Injuries prevented him from holding down a regular first-team spot and in March 1990 he left to play for Bradford City. His stay at Valley Parade was brief and in August 1990 he joined Grimsby Town for £82,000. Very fast in the box, with quick reactions in front of goal, Woods scored a number of spectacular goals during his time at Blundell Park.

In November 1997 he was loaned out to the Latics and played his only game for the club in a 1–0 defeat at Southend United when he was substituted. There followed further abortive loan spells with Scunthorpe United and Mansfield Town before the tried and trusted target man, who scored 48 goals in 258 League and Cup games for the Mariners, was released. He then joined his home-town club York City, but after just one season at Bootham Crescent he left to play non-League football for Southport.

Wigan Athletic Playing Record

	League		FA Cup		FL Cup		Others		Total	
	App	Gls	App	Gls	App	Gls	App	Gls	App	Gls
1997–98	1	0	0	0	0	0	0	0	1	0
TOTAL	1	0	0	0	0	0	0	0	1	0

WOODS Raymond Guy

Right-winger
Born: Birkenhead, 7 June 1965.
Career: June 1983 Tranmere Rovers 9 (5) 2. Bangor City. Northwich Victoria. Runcorn. Caernarfon Town. Colne Dynamoes. February 1989 WIGAN ATHLETIC 25 (3) 3. January 1991 Coventry City 21 (0) 1. January 1993 on loan WIGAN ATHLETIC 12 (1) 0. March 1994 Shrewsbury Town 40 (11) 1.

Ray Woods joined Tranmere Rovers as an apprentice in July 1981 having been with the club on associated schoolboy forms since November 1980. He made his Football League debut as a substitute at Bristol Rovers in January 1983 while still an apprentice but found it difficult to hold down a place. After being freed, he signed for Bangor City of the Northern Premier League before having spells with Northwich Victoria and Runcorn of the then Alliance Premier League and Caernarfon Town of the Northern Premier League. In 1988 he joined the all-conquering Colne Dynamoes but he couldn't get a game with them and it was pure chance that his former manager at Tranmere Rovers, Bryan Hamilton, invited him for a trial with Wigan Athletic.

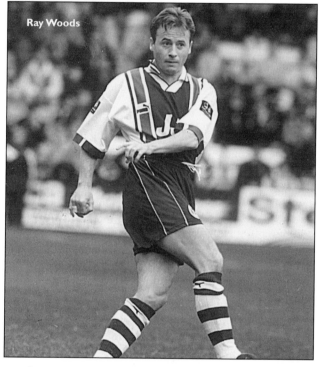

Ray Woods

After eight games at the end of the 1988–89 season, the first of which was against Sheffield United, he was offered a contract but no sooner had he started his Football League comeback than it was ended again by a groin injury which ruled him out for the whole of the 1989–90 season. To his credit, Hamilton kept faith with him and when he shone in two FA Cup games with Coventry City in January 1991, he was immediately signed up by Sky Blues' manager Terry Butcher. Sadly he was plagued by injuries at Highfield Road, where a long standing pelvic injury was diagnosed. He returned to Springfield Park on loan but then signed on a permanent basis for Shrewsbury Town. Again illness and injury restricted his appearances for the Gay Meadow club and in the summer of 1996 he was released.

Wigan Athletic Playing Record

	League		FA Cup		FL Cup		Others		Total	
	App	Gls	App	Gls	App	Gls	App	Gls	App	Gls
1988–89	5 (3)	0	0	0	0	0	0	0	5 (3)	0
1990–91	20	3	4	1	2	0	2	0	28	4
1992–93	12 (1)	0	0	0	0	0	4	3	16 (1)	3
TOTAL	37 (4)	3	4	1	2	0	6	3	49 (4)	7

WORSWICK Michael Anthony

Winger
Born: Preston, 14 March 1945.
Career: Chorley. August 1972 WIGAN ATHLETIC 0 (1) 0. Chorley.

England amateur international winger Micky Worswick joined the Latics from Chorley prior to the start of the 1972–73 Northern Premier League campaign. Worswick, who developed an instant rapport with the Wigan fans, created a bit of history in his first season with the club, for in the 5–0 FA Trophy win over Burton Albion he netted a hat-trick of penalties! Over the next six seasons, Worswick missed very few Northern Premier League matches, being ever-present in 1974–75 when he scored 20 goals as the club won the Championship. During the club's Northern Premier League days, Worswick scored 73 goals in 248 games but in all matches, this speedy winger with an eye for goal scored 102 times. When the Latics entered the Football League, Worswick was coming towards the end of his career and his only appearance was as a substitute for Joe Hinnigan in a 3–2 home defeat at the hands of Newport County. On leaving Springfield Park he returned to Victory Park to end his career with Chorley.

Wigan Athletic Playing Record

	League		FA Cup		FL Cup		Others		Total	
	App	Gls	App	Gls	App	Gls	App	Gls	App	Gls
1978–79	0 (1)	0	0	0	0	0	0	0	0 (1)	0
TOTAL	0 (1)	0	0	0	0	0	0	0	0 (1)	0

WORTHINGTON Gary Lee

Forward
Born: Cleethorpes, 10 November 1966.
Career: November 1984 Manchester United. July 1986 Huddersfield Town. July 1987 Darlington 31 (9) 15. June 1989 Wrexham 64 (4) 18. March 1991 WIGAN ATHLETIC 51 (12) 20. July 1993 Exeter City 8 (7) 1. March 1994 on loan Doncaster Rovers 8 (0) 2.

A member of the famous footballing family that includes his father Dave, formerly of Southend United and Grimsby Town and uncle Frank, Gary Worthington trained with Manchester United from the age of 13 but was released from Old Trafford when his apprenticeship ended. Mick Buxton snapped him up for

Gary Worthington

Huddersfield Town but after only one season he was again released without making a senior appearance. He moved on to Darlington where he made his League debut, but when the Quakers were relegated to the Conference, he signed for Wrexham in June 1988 for £12,000.

Though his two years at the Racecourse Ground was not a happy time, his goals against Colchester United in March 1990 virtually ensured that the Robins' League status was secure. After being made a scapegoat for the club's poor showing the following season, he almost joined Hereford United, but in March 1991 he moved to Wigan Athletic in exchange for Ian Griffiths. Worthington made his Latics debut as a substitute for Andy Pilling in a 1–0 home win over Crewe Alexandra, ending the season with five goals in 10 starts. In 1991–92 Worthington headed the club's goalscoring charts with 18 goals as the Latics finished 15th in the Third Division. However, midway through the following season, he was released and later joined Exeter City. Unable to settle at St James' Park, he had a loan spell with Doncaster Rovers before leaving the first-class game.

Wigan Athletic Playing Record

	League		FA Cup		FL Cup		Others		Total	
	App	Gls	App	Gls	App	Gls	App	Gls	App	Gls
1990–91	10 (2)	5	0	0	0	0	0	0	10 (2)	5
1991–92	34 (7)	15	3	1	3	2	1	0	41 (7)	18
1992–93	7 (3)	0	1	0	2 (2)	1	0 (1)	0	10 (6)	1
TOTAL	51 (12)	20	4	1	5 (2)	3	1 (1)	0	61 (15)	24

WRIGHT Jeffrey Kenneth

Midfield
Born: Alston, 23 June 1952.
Career: Tow Law Town. Netherfield. February 1974 WIGAN ATHLETIC 139 (4) 19. Barrow.

Jeff Wright played his early football for Tow Law Town in the Northern League, but after only 15 games, he signed for Kendal side, Netherfield. Over the next two-and-a-half seasons, he played in over 120 games before being brought to Wigan Athletic by Les Rigby in February 1974. In his first full season with the Latics, he helped the club win the Northern Premier League Championship and was an influential member of the Wigan side which brought memorable FA Cup victories over Shrewsbury Town, York City and Sheffield Wednesday.

He made his Football League debut for the club in their inaugural game in the competition, a goalless draw at Hereford United, and scored his first League goal the following month in a 3–0 home win over Rochdale. Despite being an ever-present in the Latics side in their first two seasons of League football and going on to make 110 consecutive League appearances from his debut, Wright took more stick from the terraces than any other Wigan player at this time! Possessing a range of skills which were not commonplace at this level of football, whenever tested against top-class opponents, Wright's undoubted talent always shone through brightly. On leaving Wigan, he continued his career with Barrow but is now back in the north-east running an insurance business and still playing Sunday football.

Wigan Athletic Playing Record

	League		FA Cup		FL Cup		Others		Total	
	App	Gls	App	Gls	App	Gls	App	Gls	App	Gls
1978–79	46	7	2	0	3	0	0	0	51	7
1979–80	46	5	6	0	2	0	0	0	54	5
1980–81	38	7	2	0	4	1	0	0	44	8
1981–82	9 (4)	0	0	0	1	0	0	0	10 (4)	0
TOTAL	139 (4)	19	10	0	10	1	0	0	159 (4)	20

WRIGHT Mark Andrew

Defender

Born: Manchester, 29 January 1970.
Career: June 1988 Everton 1 (0) 0. August 1990 on loan Blackpool 3 (0) 0. March 1991 Huddersfield Town 25 (7) 1. Accrington Stanley. November 1993 WIGAN ATHLETIC 27 (3) 1. Chorley.

A strong left-footed full-back, Mark Wright made his Football League debut for Everton against Queen's Park Rangers in April 1990 and had an outstanding game in a 1–0 win for the Blues. Unable to force his way into the Everton side, he had a brief loan spell with Blackpool in 1990–91 but towards the end of that season, he left Goodison Park to join Huddersfield Town on a free transfer. After helping the Terriers reach the Third Division play-offs in 1991–92, Wright lost his place in the Huddersfield side and drifted into non-League football with Accrington Stanley before joining the Latics in November 1993.

He made his Wigan debut as a substitute for John Robertson in a 2–0 home defeat at the hands of Carlisle United. He enjoyed playing in an overlapping role and scored his first and only goal for the club in a 1–1 home draw against Northampton Town later in the season. He started the 1994–95 campaign as the club's first-choice left-back but later found his appearances restricted following Graham Barrow's new signings. Released at the end of the season, he went to play non-League football for Chorley.

Wigan Athletic Playing Record

	League		FA Cup		FL Cup		Others		Total	
	App	Gls	App	Gls	App	Gls	App	Gls	App	Gls
1993–94	13 (1)	1	3	0	0	0	0	0	16 (1)	1
1994–95	14 (2)	0	0	0	0	0	0	0	14 (2)	0
TOTAL	27 (3)	1	3	0	0	0	0	0	30 (3)	1

YOUNG David

Midfield

Born: Birkenhead, 27 April 1962.
Career: Mossley. March 1983 WIGAN ATHLETIC 3 (0) 0.

Midfielder David Young was playing non-League football for Mossley when, towards the end of a disappointing 1982–83 season, which saw the departure of manager Larry Lloyd, he was brought to Springfield Park on a non-contract basis. Young, who made his Latics debut in a 2–2 draw at Bournemouth, played in the last three games of the campaign but was never on the winning side as they played out a 1–1 draw at Huddersfield Town before going down 1–0 at home to Preston North End on the last day of the campaign. In the close season, Young left Springfield Park to return to the local non-League scene.

Wigan Athletic Playing Record

	League		FA Cup		FL Cup		Others		Total	
	App	Gls	App	Gls	App	Gls	App	Gls	App	Gls
1982–83	3	0	0	0	0	0	0	0	3	0
TOTAL	3	0	0	0	0	0	0	0	3	0

Managers

Thirteen people have occupied the Wigan Athletic hot seat since the club were admitted to the Football League in 1978, with two of them, obviously gluttons for punishment, taking on the manager's job twice.

Among the managers are players who have performed at the very highest level, winning full international caps, League Championship medals, FA Cup medals and a whole host of achievements of varying degrees. This section charts the managerial sequence since the club's admission to the Fourth Division.

McNEILL Ian McKeand

McNeill began his first-class career with Aberdeen before following his former manager Dave Halliday to Leicester City. He scored 18 goals in the Foxes' Second Division Championship-winning season of 1956–57 but found goals and a regular place in the City side much harder in the top flight. After spells playing for Brighton and Southend United, he entered management with Ross County, leading them to their first-ever Highland League Championship in 1967.

In May 1968 he took charge of Wigan Athletic, having less than three months to prepare a team for the newly formed Northern Premier League. In his first season, the Latics finished runners-up to Macclesfield and were also runners-up to Southport in the Northern Floodlit League Cup. The following season he was surprisingly sacked six weeks after the club's epic FA Cup encounter with Port Vale.

Following spells with Northwich Victoria and Salisbury and also back at Ross County, McNeill rejoined the Latics in April 1976, following the resignation of Brian Tiler. After a disappointing 1976–77 season, the Latics gained admission to the Football League at the end of the following campaign. Appointed full-time manager, he took Wigan to the creditable position of sixth in the first two seasons in the League but in February 1981, following a 3–0 defeat at lowly Port Vale, he was sacked for a second time.

He later managed Shrewsbury Town, where he showed that he still had a good eye for a player and brought in some of the most skilful players to Gay Meadow. Though his transfer dealings were maligned in some quarters, the fact that he steered the Shrews away from relegation was almost fairy-tale. On leaving Shrewsbury, he had spells as assistant-manager at Chelsea and Millwall.

League Record as Wigan Athletic Manager

P	W	D	L	F	A	Success Rate
126	55	33	38	173	151	56%

LLOYD Laurence Valentine

Bill Shankly was looking for a centre-half. The Liverpool boss needed a long-term replacement for his Scottish colossus, Ron Yeats, and was pondering the merits of Larry Lloyd who was still in his first season at the heart of the Bristol Rovers' defence.

In April 1969, the 20-year-old was on his way to Anfield in a £50,000 deal which made him, at the time, Bristol's costliest soccer export. His move to Merseyside brought him medals galore including a League Championship medal in 1973 and a UEFA Cup-winners' medal the same year. When Bob Paisley took over as the Reds' manager, Lloyd was surprisingly sold to Coventry City for £225,000. After a lean period with the Sky Blues, he joined Nottingham Forest and within a season of his arrival at the City Ground, the club were League Champions. He went on to claim two European Cup medals and two League Cup medals with his new club.

In March 1981, Lloyd left Forest to become Wigan Athletic's player-manager. In his first full season in charge, 1981–82, he led the Latics to third place in Division Four and promotion for the first time in the club's history. Having played in 36 games in that Championship-winning season, he played much less the following campaign as the Latics struggled in the higher grade of football. They finished the season in 18th place in Division Three, just two places above the relegated clubs, but Lloyd had parted company on 4 April 1983 with nine games still to play.

He later had a brief spell managing Notts County before leaving soccer to run a pub in Nottingham.

League Record as Wigan Athletic Manager

P	W	D	L	F	A	Success Rate
94	44	21	29	148	121	55%

McNALLY Harry

Harry McNally

Harry McNally never appeared in the Football League, spending the majority of his playing career with Skelmersdale United. Towards the end of his playing days he also coached the side but was then appointed manager of Altrincham and later Southport. After joining Wigan Athletic as their chief scout, he progressed to assistant-manager before taking over the reins in the summer of 1983, following the departure of Larry Lloyd. There then followed two seasons of struggle with the club finishing 15th and 16th respectively in Division Three. In March 1985, McNally decided to resign after being asked to let his assistant Roy Tunks and first-team coach Alex Bruce take charge for a while.

Three months later, McNally was appointed manager of Chester City and took the then Sealand Road club to runners-up spot in Division Four in his first season. In 1988–89 he led the Cestrians to eighth in the Third Division. In 1990, Chester lost their Sealand Road ground – it was sold off to pay massive debts – but though home attendances dropped off alarmingly, McNally kept the club in the Third Division. Despite being rewarded with a four-year contract, McNally's side had a constant struggle to avoid relegation and after a poor start to the 1992–93 season, he was forced to leave the club.

League Record as Wigan Athletic Manager

P	W	D	L	F	A	Success Rate
80	25	25	30	83	102	42%

HAMILTON Bryan

Bryan Hamilton started his playing career with Distillery and earned the first of his 50 Northern Ireland caps while starring for Linfield, before Ipswich Town won the race for his signature in August 1971. Over four years and 153 League games later, Everton paid a substantial fee to take the attacking midfielder to Goodison and he appeared in the 1977 League Cup Final before moving on to Millwall and then Swindon Town, where he entertained thoughts of retirement to concentrate on coaching.

In October 1980, however, he assumed the player-manager's job at Tranmere Rovers and clocked up another 109 League

Bryan Hamilton

appearances before hanging up his boots. Working on the proverbial shoestring, he saw several crises through at Prenton Park before leaving in February 1985 to take up the manager's role at Wigan Athletic. A Freight Rover Trophy win at Wembley in May 1985 was the highlight of his time at Springfield Park and in June 1986, after impressing on a World Cup TV panel with his easy manner and analytical shrewdness, he was appointed manager of Leicester City.

His initial months as team manager saw the Foxes move into the top half of the First Division for the first time in a decade, yet by the end of that 1986–87 campaign, the club were relegated. Unable to halt a slide which threatened to lead to Third Division football, Hamilton was sacked in December 1987.

Shortly afterwards he returned to Wigan as Chief Executive but he later re-assumed control of team matters at Springfield Park until March 1993. Eleven months out of the game followed until Bryan became a surprise choice to succeed Billy Bingham as Northern Ireland's national manager. He later took charge of Norwich City but was at Carrow Road for only a few months.

League Record as Wigan Athletic Manager

P	W	D	L	F	A	Success Rate
229	85	63	81	314	299	46%

MATHIAS Raymond

Ray Mathias, who played all his League football for Tranmere Rovers, started his career in midfield before being converted to full-back. An ever-present in five seasons for the Wirral-based club, he holds the Tranmere record for the most League and Cup appearances – 637 over 18 seasons! Mathias played the last of these matches in September 1984 before turning his hand to coaching. He was later appointed assistant-manager to Bryan Hamilton at Prenton Park.

When the Irishman was dismissed in February 1985, Mathias took over as Tranmere's caretaker manager but was not given the

Ray Mathias

opportunity to do the job on a permanent basis, with Frank Worthington being appointed. Mathias followed Hamilton to Springfield Park, taking over as Latics manager in the summer of 1986. He proceeded to lead the club to one of the most successful seasons with an FA Cup run to the sixth round and fourth place in Division Three and a play-off place. After a poor season with Wigan in 1988–89 when the club finished 17th in the Third Division, Mathias returned to Prenton Park as Tranmere's Training Centre Manager.

In 1998 he returned to manage the Latics for a second time but despite leading the club to success in the Autowindscreen Shield and to the Second Division play-offs, he lost his job in the summer of 1999. He was appointed Tranmere manager in September 2002 and though he led the club to seventh place in Division Two in 2002–03 he was later dismissed and succeeded by Brian Little.

League Record as Wigan Athletic Manager						
P	W	D	L	F	A	Success Rate
184	81	46	57	283	221	52%

PHILPOTTS David Ronald

David Philpott's Football League career consisted of spells playing for Coventry City and Southport – making a total of just 11 appearances before joining Tranmere Rovers. The central defender, who had made his debut for Rovers in a goalless home draw against West Ham United in a League Cup second-round tie became a regular member of the Tranmere side and was ever-present in 1975–76 when the club won promotion to the Third Division. Shortly afterwards he left Prenton Park to spend three-and-a-half years playing in America before returning to these shores for a second spell with Tranmere Rovers. He had taken his career record with the Prenton Park club to 12 goals in 237 games when a back injury forced his retirement in 1984.

In the summer of 1986, he was appointed as the Latics' coach

David Philpotts

and later moved to the role of assistant-manager before replacing Ray Mathias as manager in 1993. He was in charge for just 13 games but 10 of these were lost, with the heaviest defeat a 5–1 reversal at West Bromwich Albion. Following the club's relegation, he was replaced by Kenny Swain.

Dave Philpotts is now back at Prenton Park as the Wirral club's first-team coach and chief scout.

League Record as Wigan Athletic Manager						
P	W	D	L	F	A	Success Rate
13	2	1	10	11	27	18%

SWAIN Kenneth

Kenny Swain began his playing career with Chelsea but had come late to professional football, qualifying as a schoolteacher before moving to Stamford Bridge from Wycombe Wanderers in August

Kenny Swain

1973. He played in a variety of positions for the Blues but his stay in South London was relatively unspectacular and his contribution to the club's promotion in 1977 largely unremarked. Most of the plaudits went to players whose talent was destined to fade after a brief period in the limelight, while the unassuming Merseysider just kept on getting better – especially after his £100,000 transfer to Aston Villa.

Here he discovered that his best position was right-back and went on to win League Championship and European Cup medals with the Villans. He had appeared in 178 games for Villa when he left to continue his career with Nottingham Forest in 1983. He later helped Portsmouth win promotion to the First Division and had a loan spell with West Bromwich Albion before becoming player-coach at Crewe Alexandra. He continued to play League football regularly until he was 39, appearing in 625 games for his six clubs.

He was appointed manager of Wigan Athletic in 1993 but in his only season in charge, the Latics' results were disappointing. They won just 11 of their 42 matches and suffered a number of heavy defeats – losing 5–2 at home to Shrewsbury and 4–1 at both Scarborough and his former club Crewe Alexandra. After the Latics ended the season in 19th place in Division Three, Swain was dismissed. He later managed Grimsby Town.

League Record as Wigan Athletic Manager						
P	W	D	L	F	A	Success Rate
42	11	12	19	51	70	36%

BARROW Graham

After playing his early football for non-League Altrincham, Graham Barrow joined Wigan Athletic in 1981 and went on to score 44 goals in 212 League and Cup games before leaving to play for Chester City in the summer of 1986. Barrow, who appeared in 248 League games for the Cestrians, later became their player-coach before being appointed assistant-manager to Harry

Graham Barrow

McNally. At the start of the 1992–93 season, following the dismissal of Harry McNally, Barrow took over the reins but failed to prevent the then Sealand Road club from being relegated. However, in 1993–94 he led Chester to promotion at the first time of asking as they finished runners-up in Division Three to Shrewsbury Town.

In September 1994, Barrow returned to Springfield Park as Wigan's manager. His appointment certainly sparked a dramatic upturn in the Latics' fortunes. There was even talk of the club reaching the play-offs in 1994–95 but they eventually had to settle for 14th place in Division Three after results fell away towards the end of the campaign. In October 1995, following Wigan's 6–2 home defeat at the hands of Mansfield Town, Barrow was

surprisingly sacked. After eight months out of the game he was appointed manager of Rochdale, a position he held until 1999. He then had a second spell as manager of Chester City before recently returning to Spotland.

League Record as Wigan Athletic Manager						
P	W	D	L	F	A	Success Rate
53	17	14	22	66	77	41%

DEEHAN John Matthew

A striker who did his fair share of creating goals as well as scoring them, John Deehan began his career with Aston Villa, where he formed prolific goalscoring partnerships with both Andy Gray and Brian Little. Deehan helped Villa win the League Cup in 1977 and during his time at the club, won seven caps for England at Under-21 level. During the early part of the 1979–80 season, Deehan left to join West Bromwich Albion but the move didn't work out and in December 1981 he was transferred to Norwich City for £175,000.

While at Carrow Road, Deehan, who scored 70 goals in 197 games for the Canaries, won a League Cup-winners' medal in 1985 and a Second Division Championship medal the following year. On leaving Norwich, Deehan remained in East Anglia with Ipswich Town, whom he helped into the Second Division play-offs. He later had spells playing for Manchester City and Barnsley and, after coaching Norwich City, was appointed the Canaries' manager. As the 1994–95 season unfolded, Norwich, who were eventually relegated, adopted a policy to sell their best players and Deehan resigned in protest.

In October 1995 Deehan was appointed manager of Wigan Athletic and steered the club to 10th in Division Three in his first season at Springfield Park. In 1996–97 he led the Latics to promotion as they finished the campaign as champions of the

Third Division with 87 points. At the end of the following season, in which the club finished in mid-table, Deehan left Wigan to take up a three-year deal at Sheffield United with Steve Bruce, whom he later followed to Huddersfield Town.

League Record as Wigan Athletic Manager						
P	W	D	L	F	A	Success Rate
127	60	26	41	197	156	54%

BENSON John Harvey

Wing-half John Benson began his Football League career with Manchester City, making his debut for the then Maine Road club in 1962. Two years later he joined Torquay United and appeared in 240 League games for the Devon club, helping them win promotion to the Third Division in 1965–66. He later had a spell with Bournemouth before joining Norwich City as player-coach. He returned to Dean Court in 1975 as the Cherries' player-manager, a position he held until 1979. He then rejoined the Canaries as their youth team coach before he was lured back to his first club, Manchester City, as John Bond's assistant. When John Bond resigned in 1983, Benson took over the reins. However, at the end of the season, following City's relegation, he lost his job.

Benson teamed up with Bond again, this time at Burnley, and again he replaced the outspoken Bond following his departure. But like City, the Clarets were relegated and Benson resigned. After a brief spell as Barnsley's chief scout, Benson joined Wigan Athletic as assistant-manager to John Deehan, a position he continued to hold under new manager Ray Mathias. In June 1999 he was appointed as Wigan manager and led the Latics to fourth place in Division Two and a place in the play-offs. After beating Millwall 1–0 over two legs in the semi-final, the Latics lost 3–2 in the Wembley final to Gillingham. Then Benson, as agreed with

John Benson

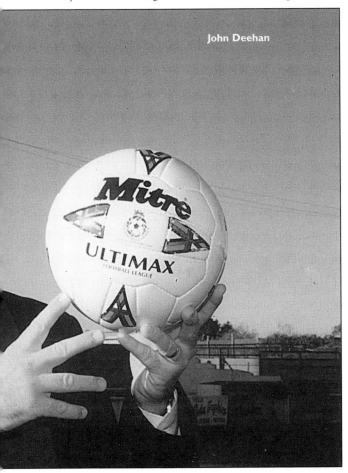

John Deehan

chairman Dave Whelan, stepped down but stayed with the club in an advisory capacity.

He is now with Premiership club Birmingham City as the Blues' General Manager.

League Record as Wigan Athletic Manager						
P	W	D	L	F	A	Success Rate
46	22	17	7	72	38	60%

RIOCH Bruce David

Wing-half Bruce Rioch, who won 24 caps for Scotland, played for Luton Town, Aston Villa, Derby County – where he won a League Championship medal in 1974–75 – Everton, Birmingham City, Sheffield United and Torquay United, where he gained his first experience of League management. However, Rioch's first success in management came following his appointment by Middlesbrough in February 1986. He guided the north-east club from a dire financial position and lifted them from the Third to the First Division within two seasons. In 1986–87 he helped the club win promotion to the Second Division as runners-up to

Bruce Rioch

Bournemouth and in 1987–88 he took the club into the top flight via the play-offs. Boro were relegated in 1988–89 and in March 1990, with the club languishing near the foot of the Second Division, Rioch left Ayresome Park.

In less than a month he was in charge at Millwall and in 1990–91 took the club to the Second Division play-offs, but after their form slumped the following season, he resigned to manage Bolton Wanderers. He achieved promotion in his first season at Burnden Park as the Wanderers finished runners-up in Division Two, while in 1993–94 he led Bolton to the sixth round of the FA Cup. The following season he took the club to the League Cup Final and promotion to the Premiership via the play-offs.

In June 1995, Rioch left Bolton to manage Arsenal but after 15 months he was sacked and joined Queen's Park Rangers as Stewart Houston's assistant. He later managed Norwich City but lost his job midway through the 1999–2000 season. In the summer of 2000, Bruce Rioch replaced John Benson as Latics' manager and though the club only lost one of their first 22 League games and were lying in fourth place in Division Two, Rioch resigned his post after just eight months in charge.

League Record as Wigan Athletic Manager						
P	W	D	L	F	A	Success Rate
34	15	13	6	42	30	57%

BRUCE Stephen Roger

Introduced to League football by Gillingham, Steve Bruce made his debut for the Kent club at Blackpool in August 1979 and after being switched from midfield to a central defensive role, became one of the Third Division's most outstanding players. Norwich City signed him for £125,000 in the summer of 1984 and though the club were relegated at the end of his first season at Carrow Road, he won a League Cup-winners' medal as Sunderland were

Steve Bruce

beaten 1–0. The following season he helped the Canaries win the Second Division Championship, but in December 1987, after what seemed an interminable wrangle with the Norwich board, he joined Manchester United for £800,000.

He won an FA Cup-winners' medal in 1990 and a European Cup Winners-Cup medal in 1991 when he was United's leading scorer with 20 goals – over half of which were penalties. He won a League Cup-winners' medal in 1992 before being appointed captain for the start of the newly formed Premiership. He then led United to three Premier League titles in the space of four years before rejecting a lucrative testimonial at Old Trafford to join Birmingham City. Inspirational at the heart of the Blues' defence, when he left St Andrew's it was to be player-manager of Sheffield United. Bruce left Bramall Lane in the summer of 1999 to manage Huddersfield Town. A little over 12 months later he was sacked before on 4 April 2001 being appointed manager of Wigan Athletic.

On 29 May, Bruce informed the Latics board that he had had an offer to manage elsewhere and two days later, after just 57 days in charge, he was confirmed as Crystal Palace's new manager – their 10th in eight years. His stay at Selhurst Park was also brief as he left to take charge of Birmingham City. After leading the Blues into the Premiership, he has this season managed to keep them in the top half of the table.

League Record as Wigan Athletic Manager						
P	W	D	L	F	A	Success Rate
6	3	1	2	7	8	55%

JEWELL Paul

Latics' current manager Paul Jewell had been an apprentice with Liverpool before joining Wigan Athletic in December 1984. He went on to score 47 goals – including a hat-trick against Aldershot on 1 March 1988 – in 171 games before joining Bradford City. Though he had a loan spell with Grimsby Town, Jewell scored 66 goals in 308 games for the Bantams before hanging up his boots. Appointed Bradford City manager in May 1988, Jewell's side had an outstanding first season under his leadership, finishing the season as runners-up to Sunderland in the First Division and so winning promotion to the Premiership. Though the club struggled in the top flight they avoided a swift return to Division One, ending the campaign in 17th place. But then in the close season, the Bradford board ordered Jewell to stay away from the ground on 'gardening leave' after he had handed in a letter of resignation.

Two days later he joined Sheffield Wednesday on a three-year contract, but after eight months in charge, he was sacked with Peter Shreeve taking over the reins. He was appointed manager of Wigan Athletic in June 2001 – the club's eighth boss in six years. The 2001–02 season saw the club knocked out at the first hurdle in both the League and FA Cups and finish 10th in Division Two. the following season, Jewell led the Latics to the Second Division Championship and in the course of doing so, created a record sequence of 11 League wins between 2 November 2002 and 18 January 2003. In nine of those matches, including the first eight, Latics didn't concede a goal! They ended the season with 100 points – 14 clear of runners-up Crewe Alexandra, winning the title as a result of Bristol City's 1–1 draw at Crewe – that with still four matches to be played.

Wigan had a magnificent 2003–04 season. Virtually ever-present in the play-off places since the campaign began, the club's remarkable rise to football prominence stalled in the most

dramatic fashion on the final day of the season. The Latics were leading West Ham United 1–0 when Brian Deane's header denied them a place in the play-offs with only 49 seconds of the Division One season remaining. Ultimately though, they will rue results such as the 1–0 home defeat to Wimbledon that saw them enter the final day with too much to do. Ending their first season in Division One in seventh place – not a bad effort considering the Latics were labelled relegation certainties at the start of the campaign – Wigan

fans will be hoping Jewell, for whom money will again be made available to strengthen the squad, can lead them to the Premiership next season.

League Record as Wigan Athletic Manager						
P	W	D	L	F	A	Success Rate
138	63	46	29	194	121	57%

Appendices

Honours

Football League
Second Division Champions: 2002–03
Third Division Champions: 1996–97
Fourth Division (Promoted 3rd): 1981–82

FA Cup
Best Season 6th Round: 1986–87

Football League Cup
Best Season 5th Round: 2002–03

Freight Rover Trophy
Winners: 1984–85

Autowindscreen Shield
Winners: 1998–99

Longest League Runs
League Wins: 11, 2 November 2002 – 18 January 2003
League Defeats: 7, 6 April 1993 – 4 May 1993
League Draws: 6, 11 December 2001 – 5 January 2002
Unbeaten League Matches: 25, 8 May 1999 – 3 January 2000
Without a League Win: 14, 9 May 1989 – 17 October 1989
Successive Scoring: 24, 27 April 1996
Successive No-scoring: 4, 15 April 1995

Club Records
Most home wins in a season: 17 – 1981–82, 1985–86, 1996–97
Most home draws in a season: 8 – 1987–88
Most home defeats in a season: 11 – 1992–93
Most home goals in a season: 54 – 1985–86
Most home goals conceded in a season: 34 – 1992–93
Least home wins in a season: 6 – 1992–93, 1993–94
Least home draws in a season: 3 – 1990–91, 1995–96, 1996–97, 1999–2000
Least home defeats in a season: 1 – 1981–82
Least home goals scored in a season: 26 – 1983–84, 1992–93
Least home goals conceded in a season: 16 – 1980–81, 2002–03, 2003–04
Most away wins in a season: 15 – 2002–03
Most away draws in a season: 14 – 1999–2000
Most away goals scored in a season: 36 – 1986–87
Most away goals conceded in a season: 43 – 1991–92
Least away wins in a season: 3 – 1984–85, 1989–90
Least away draws in a season: 4 – 1987–88, 1994–95
Least away defeats in a season: 2 – 1999–2000, 2002–03
Least away goals scored in a season: 17 – 1992–93
Least away goals conceded in a season: 9 – 2002–03
Most wins in a season: 29 – 2002–03
Most draws in a season: 17 – 1999–2000
Most defeats in a season: 25 – 1992–93
Most goals scored in a season: 84 – 1996–97
Most goals conceded in a season: 72 – 1992–93
Least wins in a season: 10 – 1992–93
Least draws in a season: 9 – 1982–83, 1990–91, 1996–97
Least defeats in a season: 4 – 2002–03
Least goals scored in a season 43 – 1992–93
Least goals conceded in a season: 25 – 2002–03

Football League

Final Positions 1978–79 to 2003–04

Season	P	W	D	L	F	A	W	D	L	F	A	Pts	Pos
Division Four													
1978–79	46	14	5	4	40	24	7	8	8	23	24	55	6th
1979–80	46	13	5	5	42	26	8	8	7	34	35	55	6th
1980–81	46	13	4	6	29	16	5	7	11	22	39	47	11th
1981–82	46	17	5	1	47	18	9	8	6	33	28	91	3rd
Division Three													
1982–83	46	10	4	9	35	33	5	5	13	25	39	54	18th
1983–84	46	11	5	7	26	18	5	8	10	20	38	61	15th
1984–85	46	12	6	5	36	22	3	8	12	24	42	59	16th
1985–86	46	17	4	2	54	17	6	10	7	28	31	86	4th
1986–87	46	15	5	3	47	25	10	5	8	36	34	85	4th
1987–88	46	11	8	4	36	23	9	4	10	34	38	72	7th
1988–89	46	9	5	9	28	22	5	9	9	27	31	56	17th
1989–90	46	10	6	7	29	22	3	8	12	19	42	53	18th
1990–91	46	14	3	6	40	20	6	6	11	31	34	69	10th
1991–92	46	11	6	6	33	21	4	8	11	25	43	59	15th
Division Two (Formerly Division Three)													
1992–93	46	6	6	11	26	34	4	5	14	17	38	41	23rd
Division Three													
1993–94	42	6	7	8	33	33	5	5	11	18	37	45	19th
1994–95	42	7	6	8	28	30	7	4	10	25	30	52	14th
1995–96	46	15	3	5	36	21	5	7	11	26	35	70	10th
1996–97	46	17	3	3	53	21	9	6	8	31	30	87	1st
Division Two													
1997–98	46	12	5	6	41	31	5	6	12	23	35	62	11th
1998–99	46	14	5	4	44	17	8	5	10	31	31	76	6th
1999–00	46	15	3	5	37	14	7	14	2	35	24	83	4th
2000–01	46	9	6	8	36	23	7	10	6	30	28	64	10th
2002–03	46	14	7	2	37	16	15	6	2	31	9	100	1st
Division One													
2003–04	46	11	8	4	29	16	7	9	7	31	29	71	7th

Attendances

Average and Highest Football League Attendances

	Average	Highest	
1978–79	6,701	9,427	v Barnsley
1979–80	5,902	8,198	v Portsmouth
1980–81	4,208	6,029	v Rochdale
1981–82	5,839	9,021	v Bournemouth
1982–83	4,439	7,724	v Huddersfield Town
1983–84	3,898	10,045	v Bolton Wanderers
1984–85	3,264	8,871	v Bolton Wanderers
1985–86	4,310	9,485	v Plymouth Argyle
1986–87	3,396	6,857	v Blackpool
1987–88	3,737	6,949	v Sunderland
1988–89	3,134	5,671	v Preston North End
1989–90	2,772	6,850	v Bolton Wanderers
1990–91	2,881	4,728	v Preston North End
1991–92	2,847	5,956	v Birmingham City

1992–93	2,593	5,408	v Bolton Wanderers
1993–94	1,897	3,741	v Preston North End
1994–95	1,748	3,618	v Preston North End
1995–96	2,856	5,567	v Preston North End
1996–97	3,899	7,106	v Mansfield Town
1997–98	3,968	5,649	v Preston North End
1998–99	4,250	6,700	v Manchester City
1999–2000	6,824	15,593	v Preston North End
2000–01	6,774	10,048	v Bristol City
2001–02	5,651	7,783	v Tranmere Rovers
2002–03	7,288	12,783	v Oldham Athletic
2003–04	9,527	20,699	v West Ham United

Appearances

		League	FA Cup	Lg Cup	Total
1	Kevin Langley	307 (10)	27 (1)	21	355 (11)
2	Colin Methven	295 (1)	23	21	339 (1)
3	John Butler	291 (11)	24 (1)	18 (1)	333 (13)
4	Alex Cribley	268 (3)	24	20 (1)	312 (4)
5	David Lowe	264 (32)	20 (3)	15	299 (35)
6	Roy Tunks	245	21	18	284
7	Allan Tankard	205 (4)	13	15	233 (4)
8	Andy Liddell	206 (10)	7	11	224 (10)
9	Scott Green	177 (22)	17	16 (1)	210 (23)
10	Neill Rimmer	184 (6)	10	14	208 (6)
11	Peter Houghton	169 (16)	14	19	204 (17)
12	Ian Kilford	175 (43)	14 (2)	14 (3)	203 (48)
13	Bryan Griffiths	176 (13)	11 (2)	12 (2)	199 (17)
14	Graham Barrow	173 (6)	13	11	197 (6)
15	Alan Johnson	163 (17)	14 (2)	7 (2)	184 (21)
16	Pat McGibbon	163 (10)	9 (1)	11 (1)	183 (12)
17	Nigel Adkins	155	9	15	179
18	Colin Greenall	162	10	5 (1)	177 (1)
19	Paul Beesley	153 (2)	6	13	177 (2)
20	Phil Daley	152 (9)	10 (1)	9	171 (10)

Goals

		League	FA Cup	Lg Cup	Total
1	David Lowe	66	7	0	73
2	Andy Liddell	70	1	1	72
3	Peter Houghton	62	3	3	68
4	Simon Haworth	44	4	6	54
5	Bryan Griffiths	44	6	2	52
6	Stuart Barlow	41	3	3	47
7	Graeme Jones	44	1	1	46
8	Nathan Ellington	35	2	6	43
9	Phil Daley	40	0	1	41
10	Paul Jewell	35	5	0	40
11	Graham Barrow	36	0	3	39
12	Bobby Campbell	27	5	4	36
13	Ian Kilford	32	2	1	35
14	Mike Newell	25	6	1	32
15=	Mark Hilditch	26	2	1	29
	Colin Methven	21	5	3	29
16	Andy Lyons	27	0	1	28
17	Les Bradd	25	0	2	27
18	Eamonn O'Keefe	25	0	1	26
19=	Warren Aspinall	22	2	0	24
	Gary Worthington	20	1	3	24

Roll of Honour

Frank Armstrong

Ian Ball

Gary Bannister

Charlie Barnes

Paul Benbow

Mike Bold

Simon Christopher Box

Stephen Brown

Brandon Bullock

Alan Cain

Dave Callaghan

Chris Carey

Michael Carroll

Linda Clarke

Simon Clegg

Julie Cooke

Stephen Coyle

Granville Crompton

Peter Crook

Andrew Cullen

John Cumberbatch

Mark Cumberbatch

Matthew Darby

Trevor Davies

Scott Denver

Simon Denver

Matthew Edgerton

Gareth J. Edwards

Muriel Edwards

Philip N. Edwards

Stephen Ellison

Jade Erica

John Evans

Gary Fazackerley

Manny Flores

Graham Foster

Mari Foster

Frank France

Michael France

Jon Glover

Lauren Victoria Green

Paul Andrew Green

Richard John Green

Philip Guidice

Stephen J. Halliwell

Michael Harrison

John Heeley

Mark Highton

Martin Holden

Mark Holdsworth

Dale Holford

Craig Darren Hughes

Peter Ingram

Richard Jarrett

Sean Joyce

Jonathan Keddie

Steven Keddie

Dean Kidman

Martin Lewis

Ste Livesey

Matthew Derek Lorton

Kevin MacKenzie

Tommy Madden

Ian Martindale

John Martindale

Olive Martindale

Tony McClure

Anthony McFarlane

Robert Miller

John Oakes

Shaun O'Hara

John Francis Orritt

Liam John Parker

Dr Derek Parkinson

Paul Parkinson

John Pendlebury

Thomas Platt

Irvin Poole

Neil Potter

Wesley Potter

John M. Power

David Prescott

Clifford Pyke

Bernard Ramsdale

Kathryn Richards

Harry Robinson

Darren Ryder

Jon Sanders (Leicester Latics)

Margaret Shaw

Alec Shepherd R.I.P.

Ann Shepherd R.I.P.

Harold Silcock

Martin Silcock

Simon Silcock

Albert Storey

Martin Tarbuck

Sid Thelwell

Peter Thomas

Steven Thorpe

Paul Tymon

Peter Unsworth

Nick Walker

Gerald Ward

Ronald Ward

Stuart Ward

Carl Watson

Stephen P. Weston

David Whalley

Peter White (Matlock)

Mark Whitter

Chris Wilcox

Dave Wilcox

Katie Wilson

Michael H. Winstanley

David S. Woods